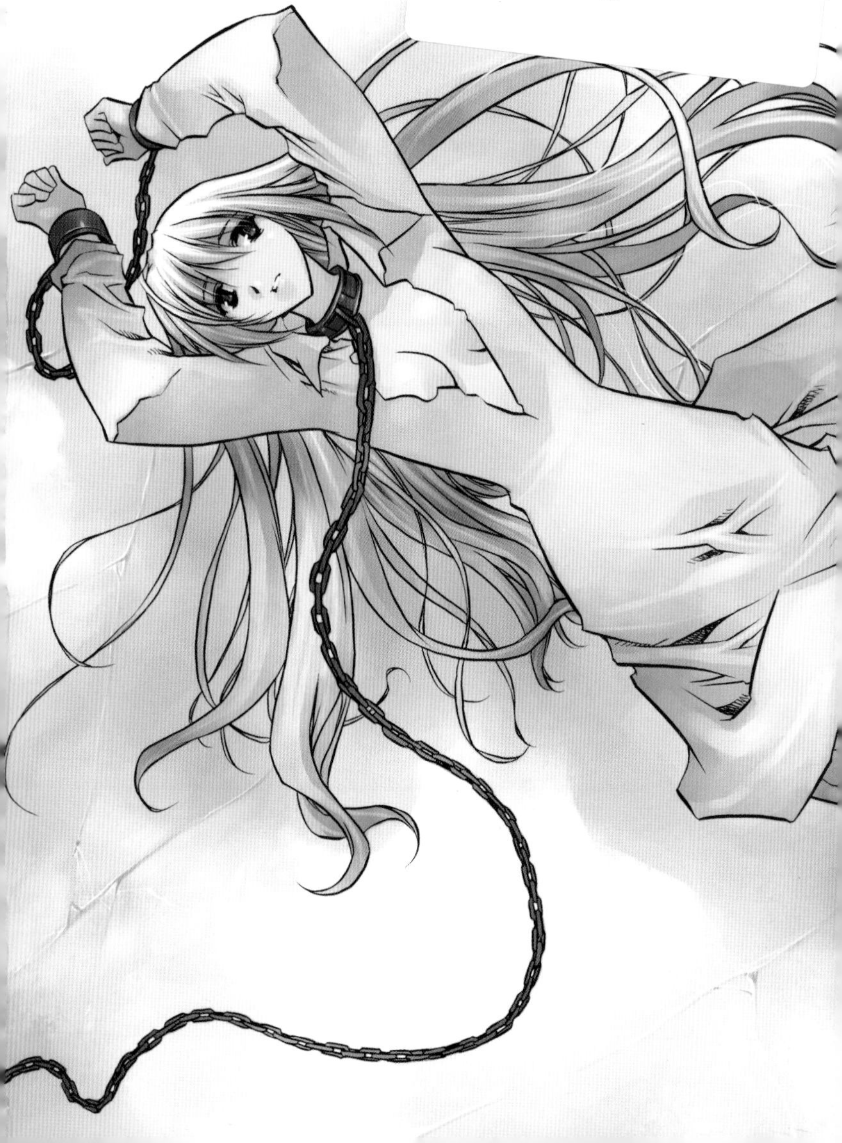

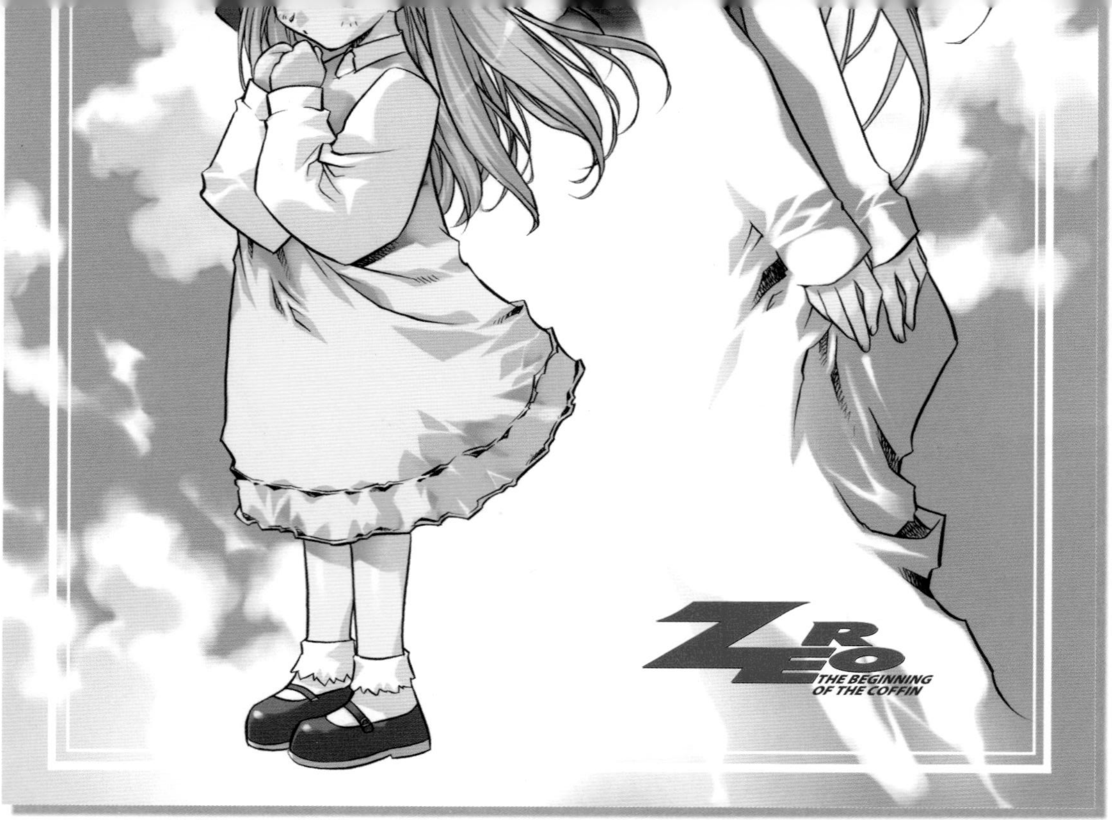
ZERO
THE BEGINNING
OF THE COFFIN

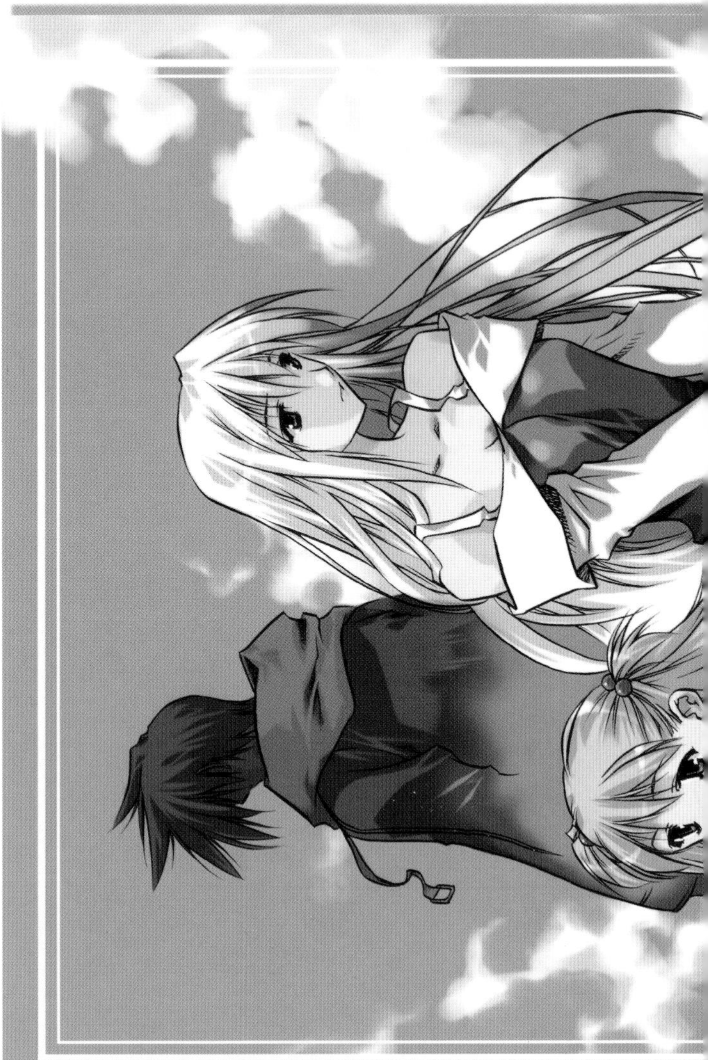

ZERO
THE BEGINNING OF THE COFFIN

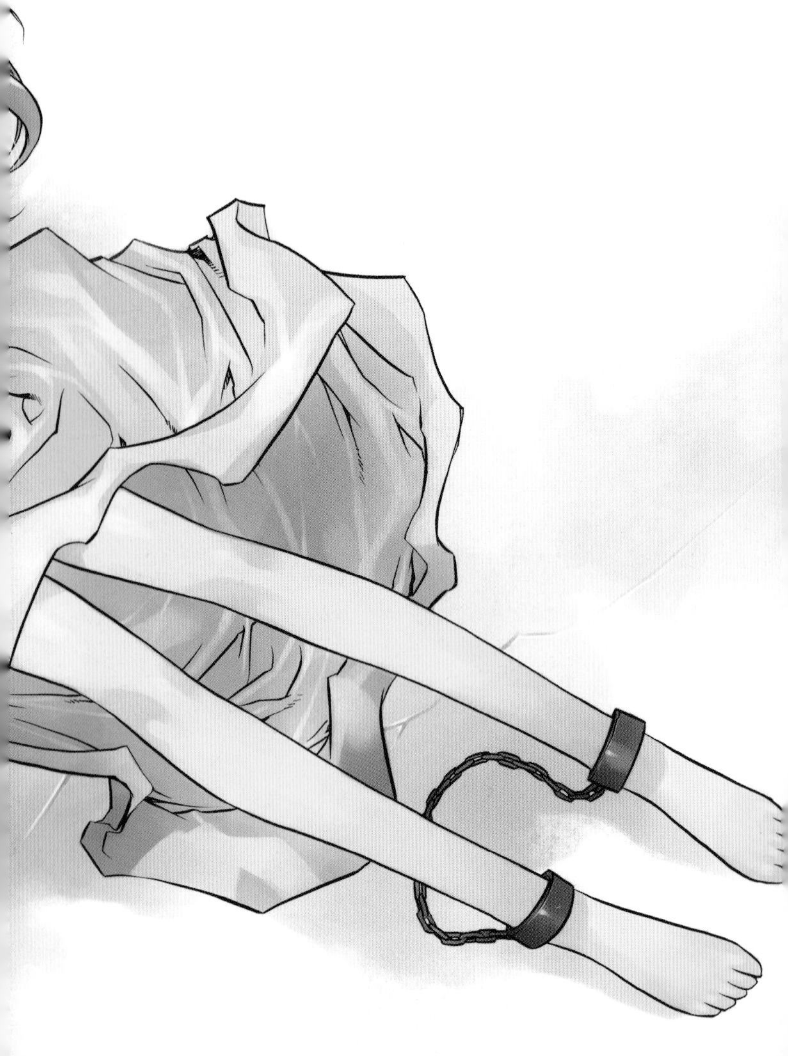

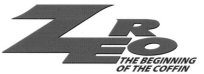

ZERO
THE BEGINNING OF THE COFFIN

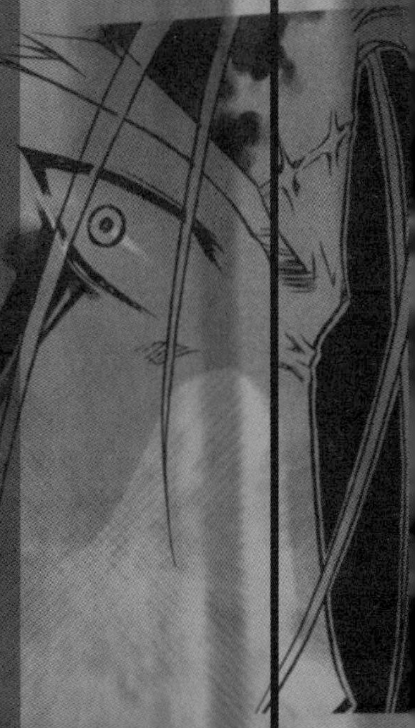

Translator : Je-Wa Jeong

Editor : Je-Wa Jeong / Miho Koto / Soung Lee / Kentaro Abe

Layout : Kentaro Abe

Touch-Up Artist : Miho Koto

Art Director : Soung Lee

Licensing : Masayoshi Kojima

Vice President : Steve Chung

C.E.O. : Jay Chung

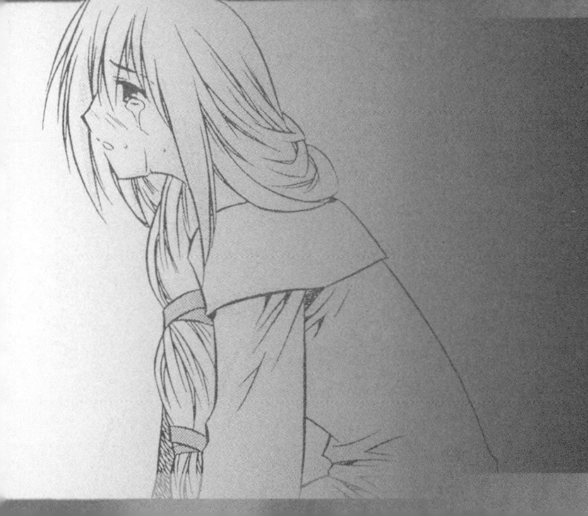

Publisher
Infinity Studios, LLC
525 South 31st St.
Richmond, CA 94804
www.infinitystudios.com

First Edition : January 2006
ISBN : 1-59697-031-6

Printed in China

ZERO

THE BEGINNING OF THE COFFIN

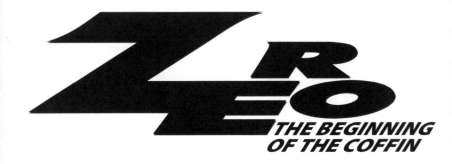

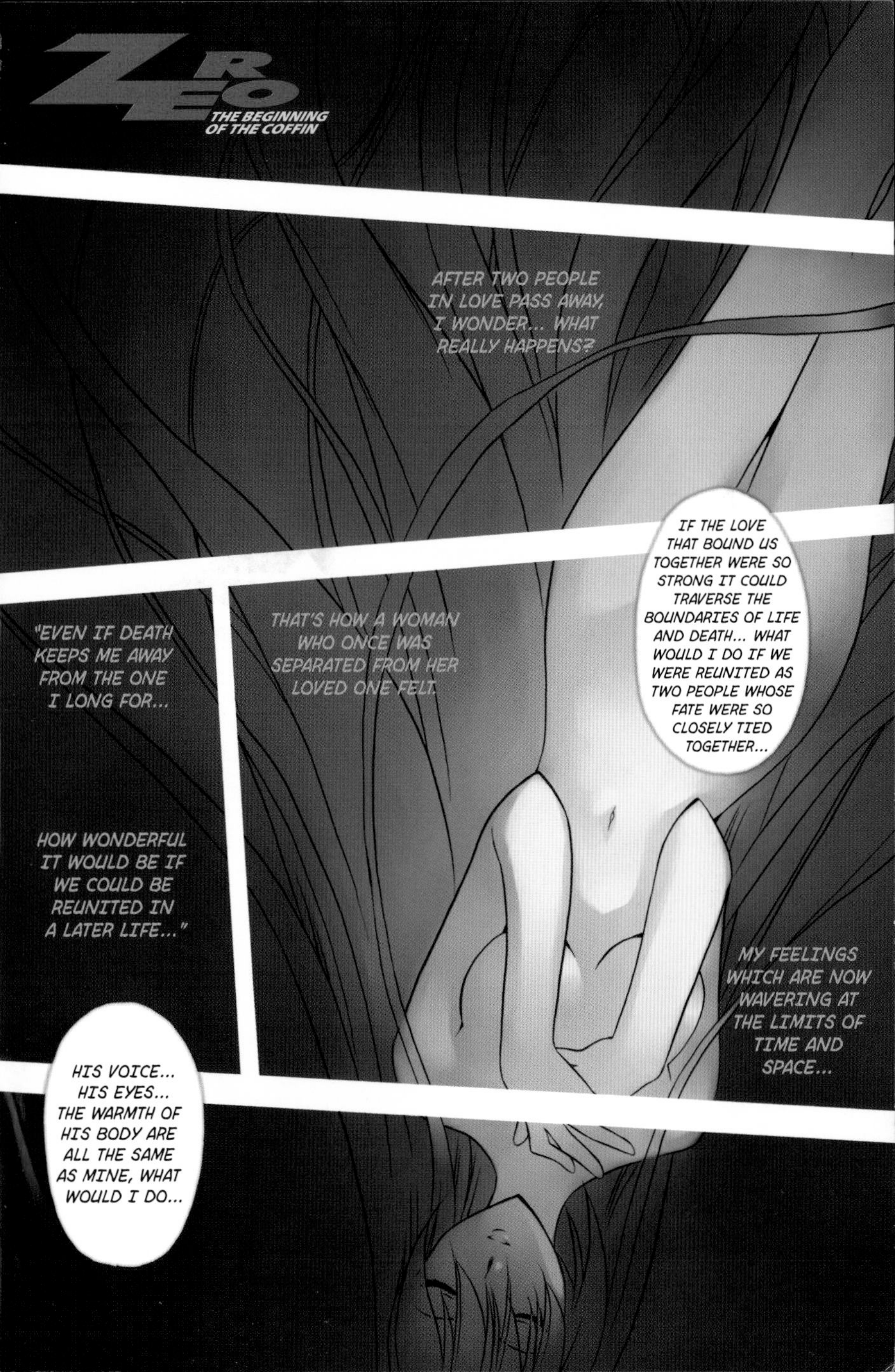
ZERO
THE BEGINNING OF THE COFFIN
AFTER TWO PEOPLE IN LOVE PASS AWAY, I WONDER... WHAT REALLY HAPPENS?
"EVEN IF DEATH KEEPS ME AWAY FROM THE ONE I LONG FOR...
HOW WONDERFUL IT WOULD BE IF WE COULD BE REUNITED IN A LATER LIFE..."
THAT'S HOW A WOMAN WHO ONCE WAS SEPARATED FROM HER LOVED ONE FELT.
IF THE LOVE THAT BOUND US TOGETHER WERE SO STRONG IT COULD TRAVERSE THE BOUNDARIES OF LIFE AND DEATH... WHAT WOULD I DO IF WE WERE REUNITED AS TWO PEOPLE WHOSE FATE WERE SO CLOSELY TIED TOGETHER...
MY FEELINGS WHICH ARE NOW WAVERING AT THE LIMITS OF TIME AND SPACE...
HIS VOICE... HIS EYES... THE WARMTH OF HIS BODY ARE ALL THE SAME AS MINE, WHAT WOULD I DO...

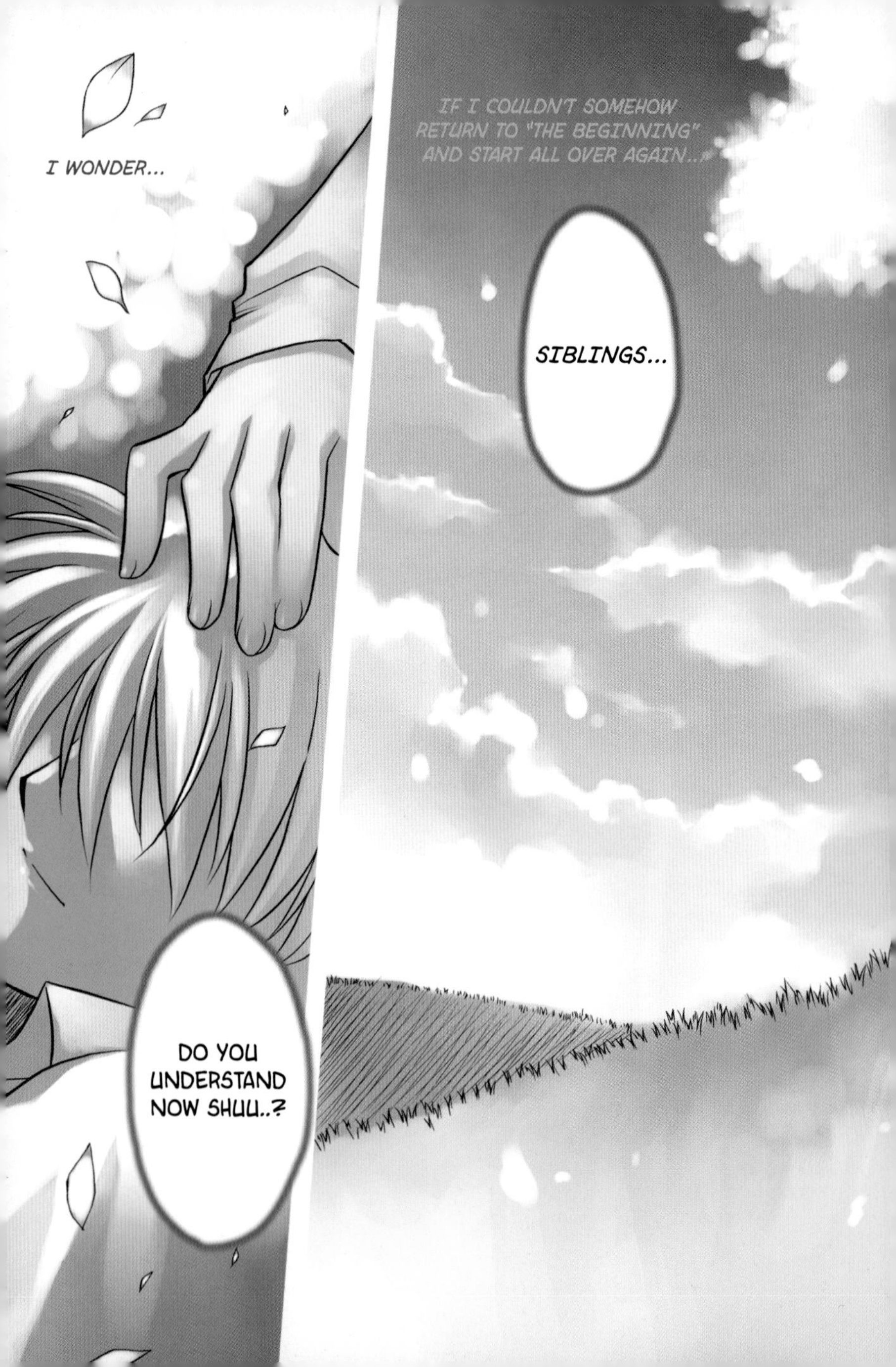
I WONDER...
DO YOU UNDERSTAND NOW SHUU..?
IF I COULDN'T SOMEHOW RETURN TO "THE BEGINNING" AND START ALL OVER AGAIN...
SIBLINGS...

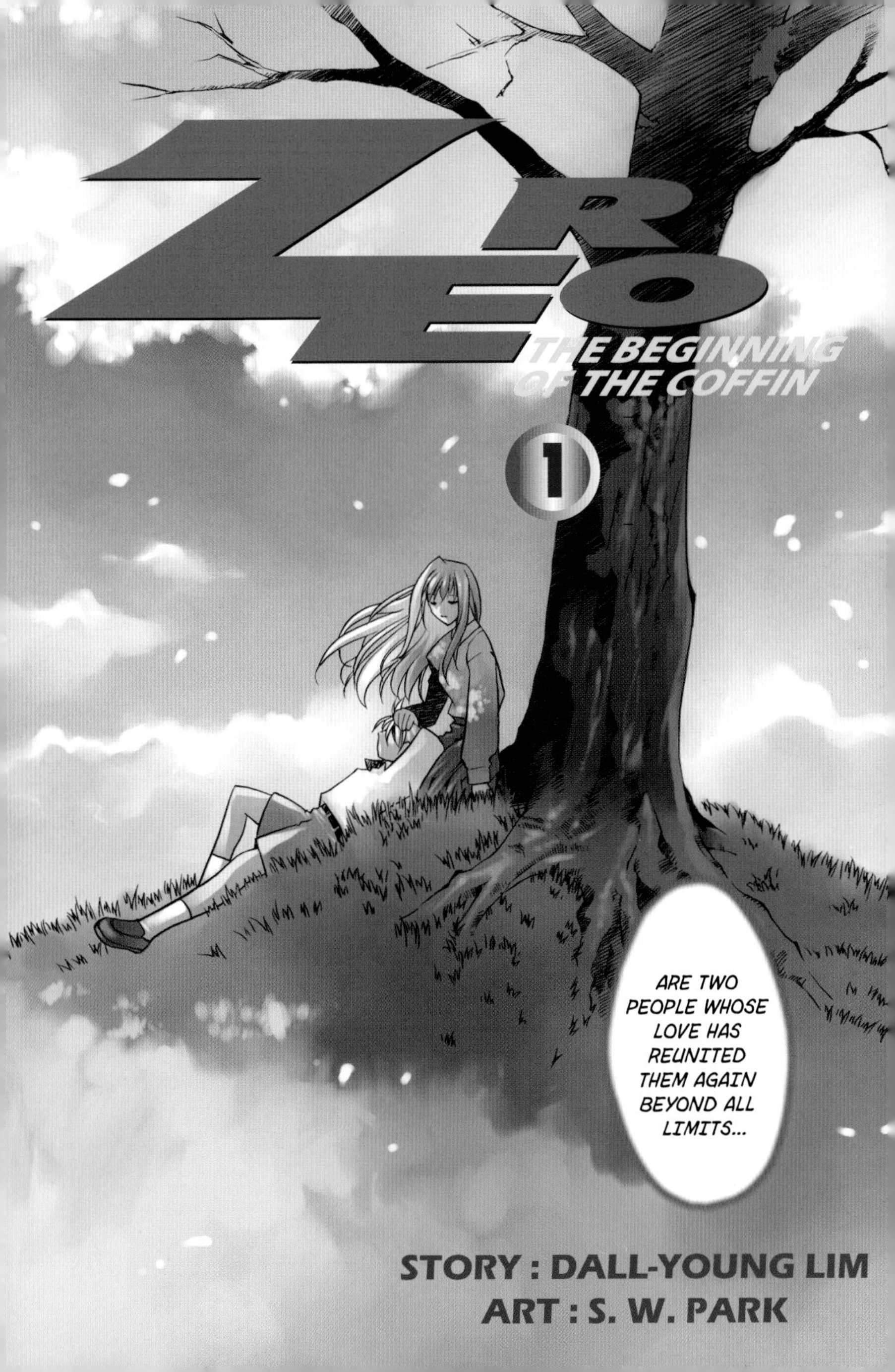

ZERO
THE BEGINNING OF THE COFFIN
1
ARE TWO PEOPLE WHOSE LOVE HAS REUNITED THEM AGAIN BEYOND ALL LIMITS...
STORY : DALL-YOUNG LIM
ART : S. W. PARK

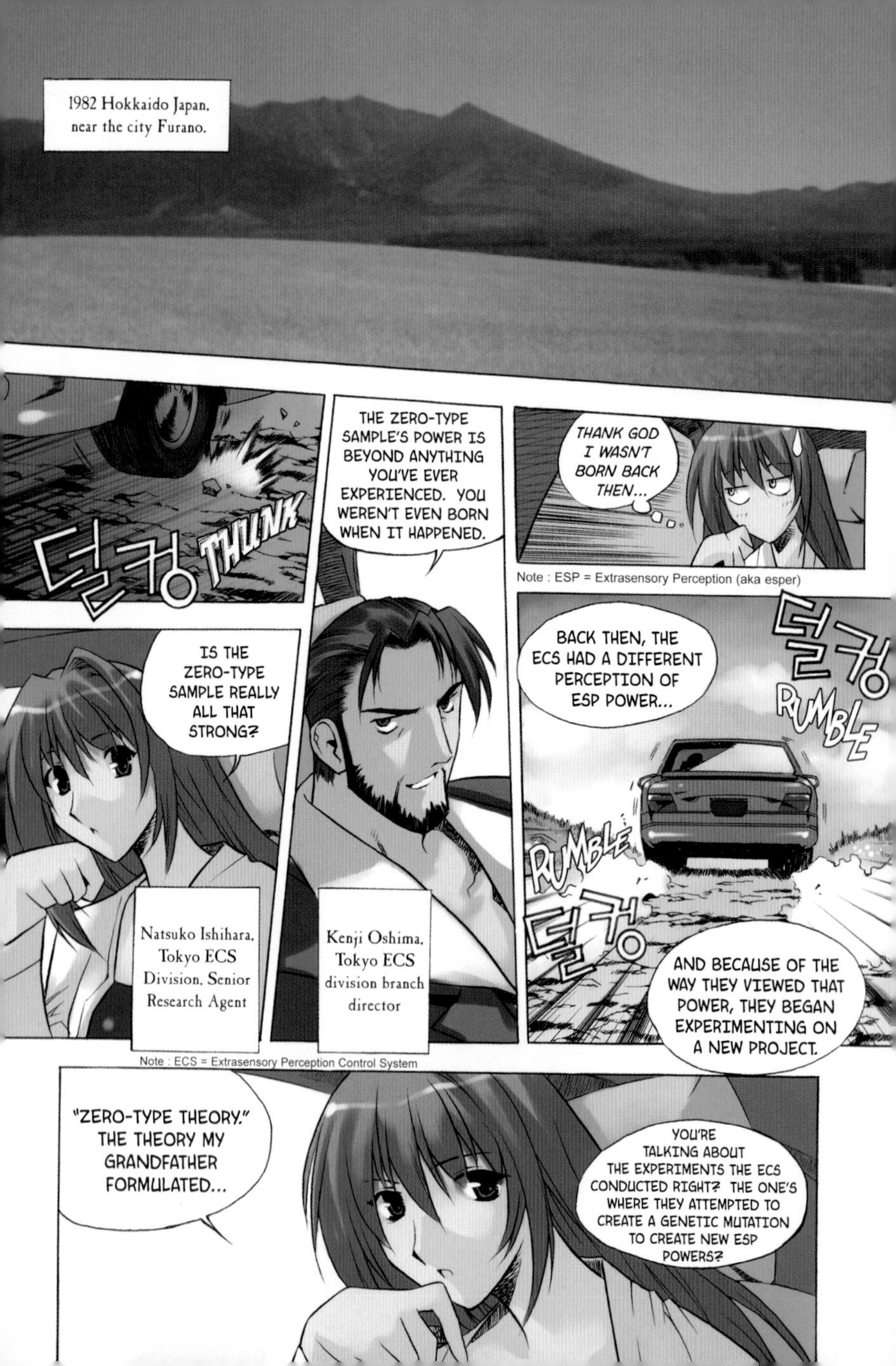

1982 Hokkaido Japan, near the city Furano.
덜컹 THUNK
IS THE ZERO-TYPE SAMPLE REALLY ALL THAT STRONG?
Natsuko Ishihara, Tokyo ECS Division, Senior Research Agent
THE ZERO-TYPE SAMPLE'S POWER IS BEYOND ANYTHING YOU'VE EVER EXPERIENCED. YOU WEREN'T EVEN BORN WHEN IT HAPPENED.
Kenji Oshima, Tokyo ECS division branch director
Note : ECS = Extrasensory Perception Control System
THANK GOD I WASN'T BORN BACK THEN...
Note : ESP = Extrasensory Perception (aka esper)
BACK THEN, THE ECS HAD A DIFFERENT PERCEPTION OF ESP POWER...
덜컹 RUMBLE
RUMBLE 덜컹
AND BECAUSE OF THE WAY THEY VIEWED THAT POWER, THEY BEGAN EXPERIMENTING ON A NEW PROJECT.
"ZERO-TYPE THEORY." THE THEORY MY GRANDFATHER FORMULATED...
YOU'RE TALKING ABOUT THE EXPERIMENTS THE ECS CONDUCTED RIGHT? THE ONE'S WHERE THEY ATTEMPTED TO CREATE A GENETIC MUTATION TO CREATE NEW ESP POWERS?

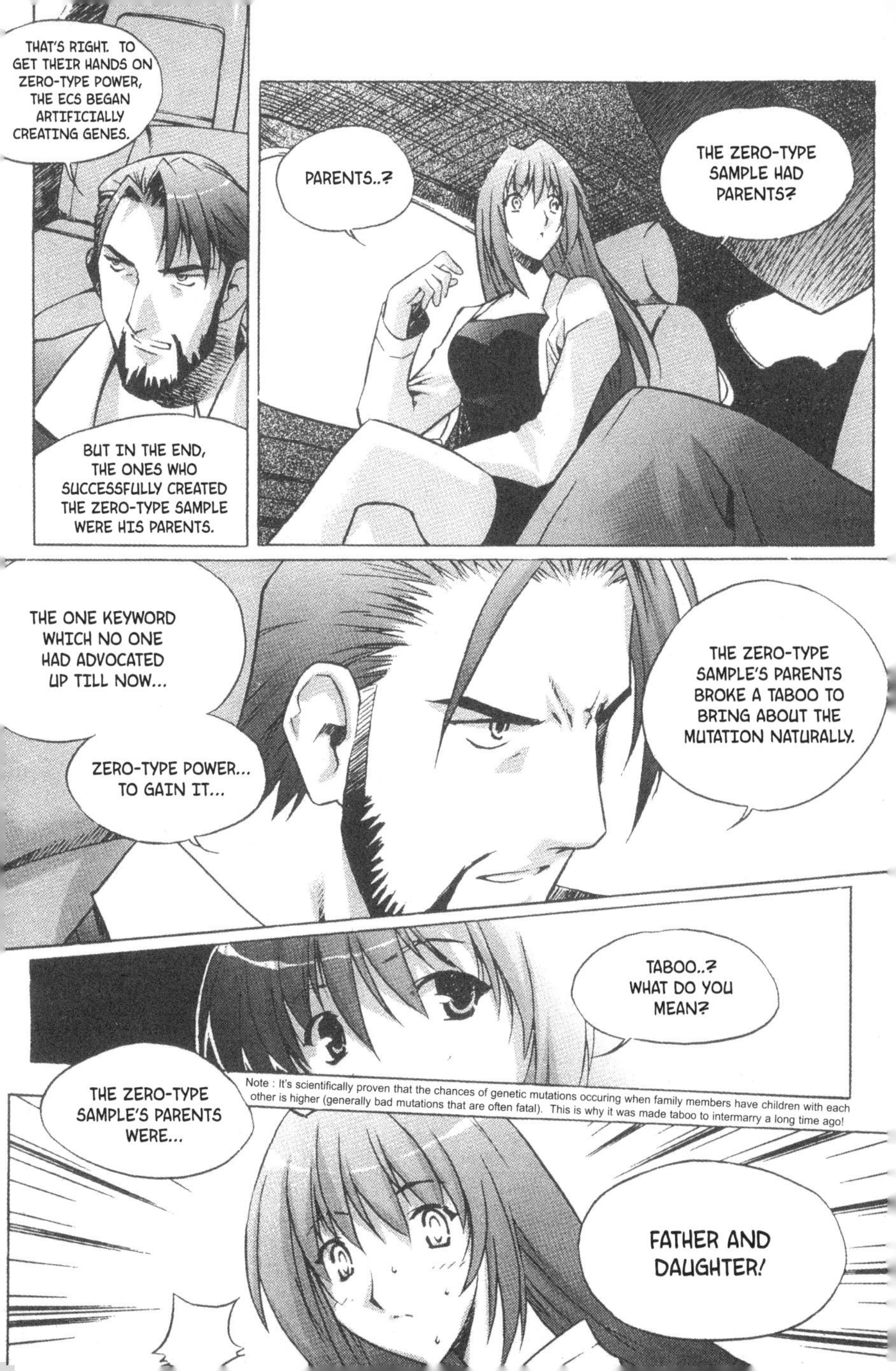
THAT'S RIGHT. TO GET THEIR HANDS ON ZERO-TYPE POWER, THE ECS BEGAN ARTIFICIALLY CREATING GENES.
BUT IN THE END, THE ONES WHO SUCCESSFULLY CREATED THE ZERO-TYPE SAMPLE WERE HIS PARENTS.
PARENTS..?
THE ZERO-TYPE SAMPLE HAD PARENTS?
THE ONE KEYWORD WHICH NO ONE HAD ADVOCATED UP TILL NOW...
ZERO-TYPE POWER... TO GAIN IT...
THE ZERO-TYPE SAMPLE'S PARENTS BROKE A TABOO TO BRING ABOUT THE MUTATION NATURALLY.
TABOO..? WHAT DO YOU MEAN?
Note : It's scientifically proven that the chances of genetic mutations occuring when family members have children with each other is higher (generally bad mutations that are often fatal). This is why it was made taboo to intermarry a long time ago!
THE ZERO-TYPE SAMPLE'S PARENTS WERE...
FATHER AND DAUGHTER!

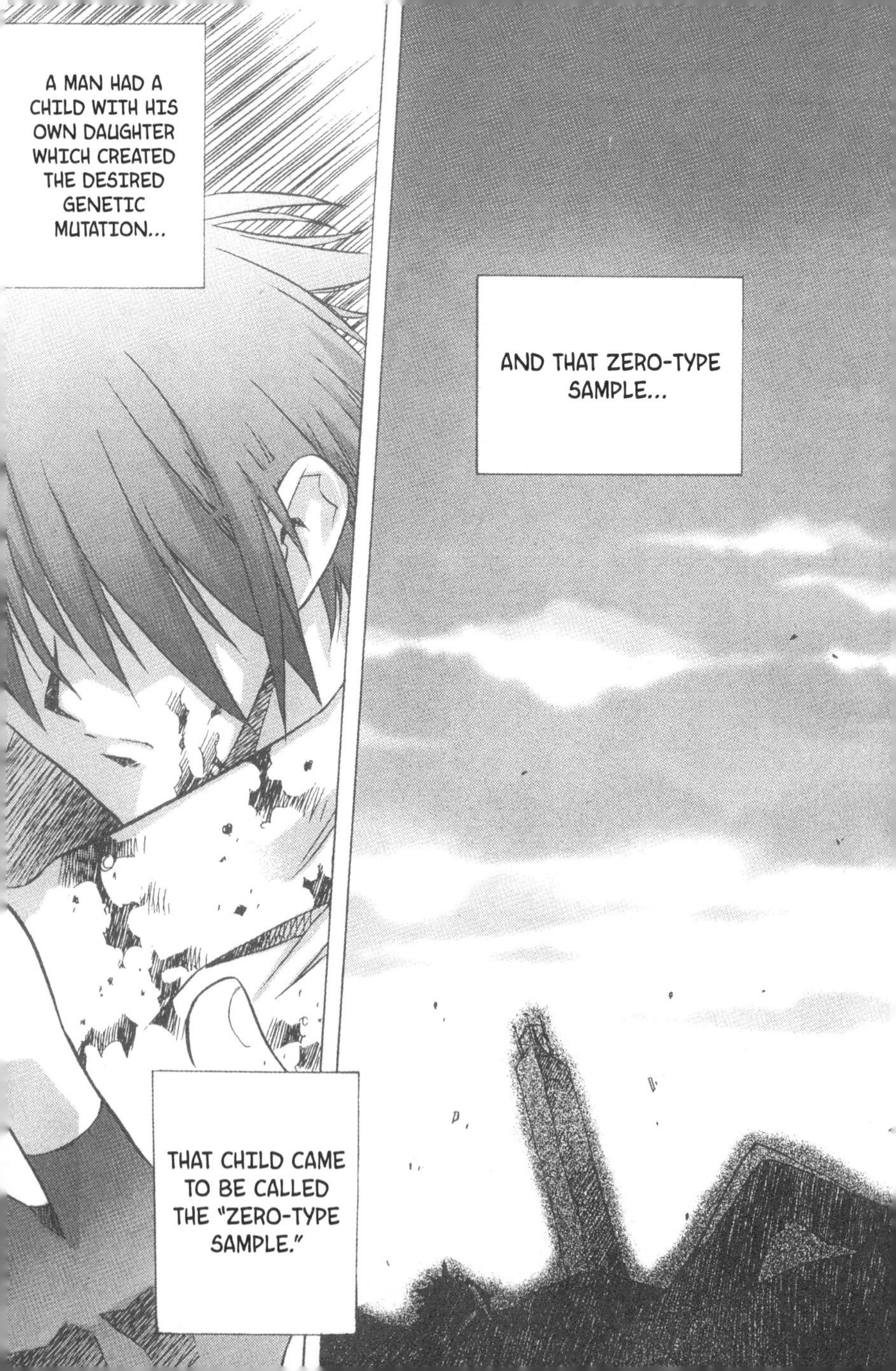

A MAN HAD A CHILD WITH HIS OWN DAUGHTER WHICH CREATED THE DESIRED GENETIC MUTATION...
THAT CHILD CAME TO BE CALLED THE "ZERO-TYPE SAMPLE."
AND THAT ZERO-TYPE SAMPLE...

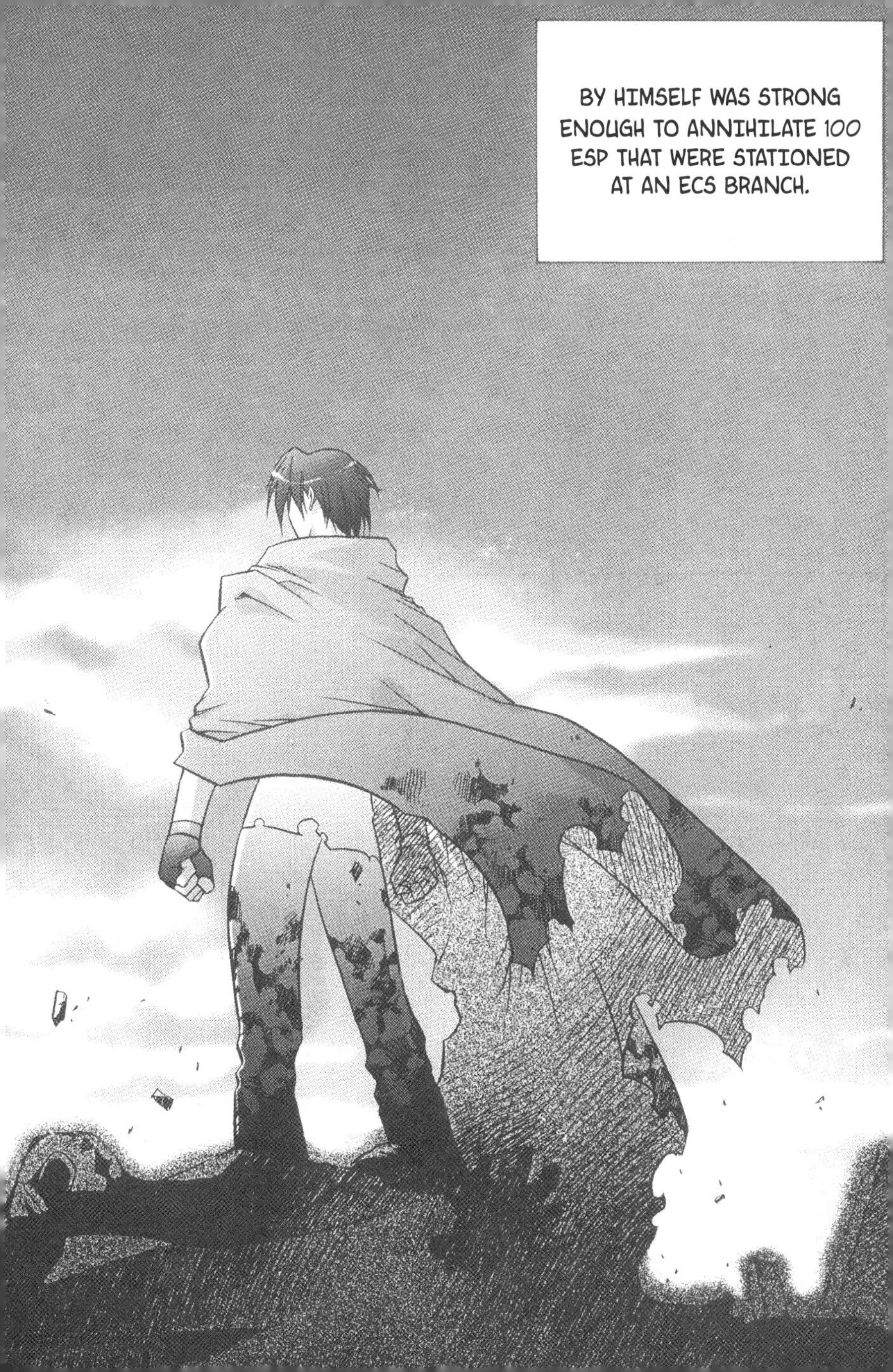
BY HIMSELF WAS STRONG ENOUGH TO ANNIHILATE 100 ESP THAT WERE STATIONED AT AN ECS BRANCH.

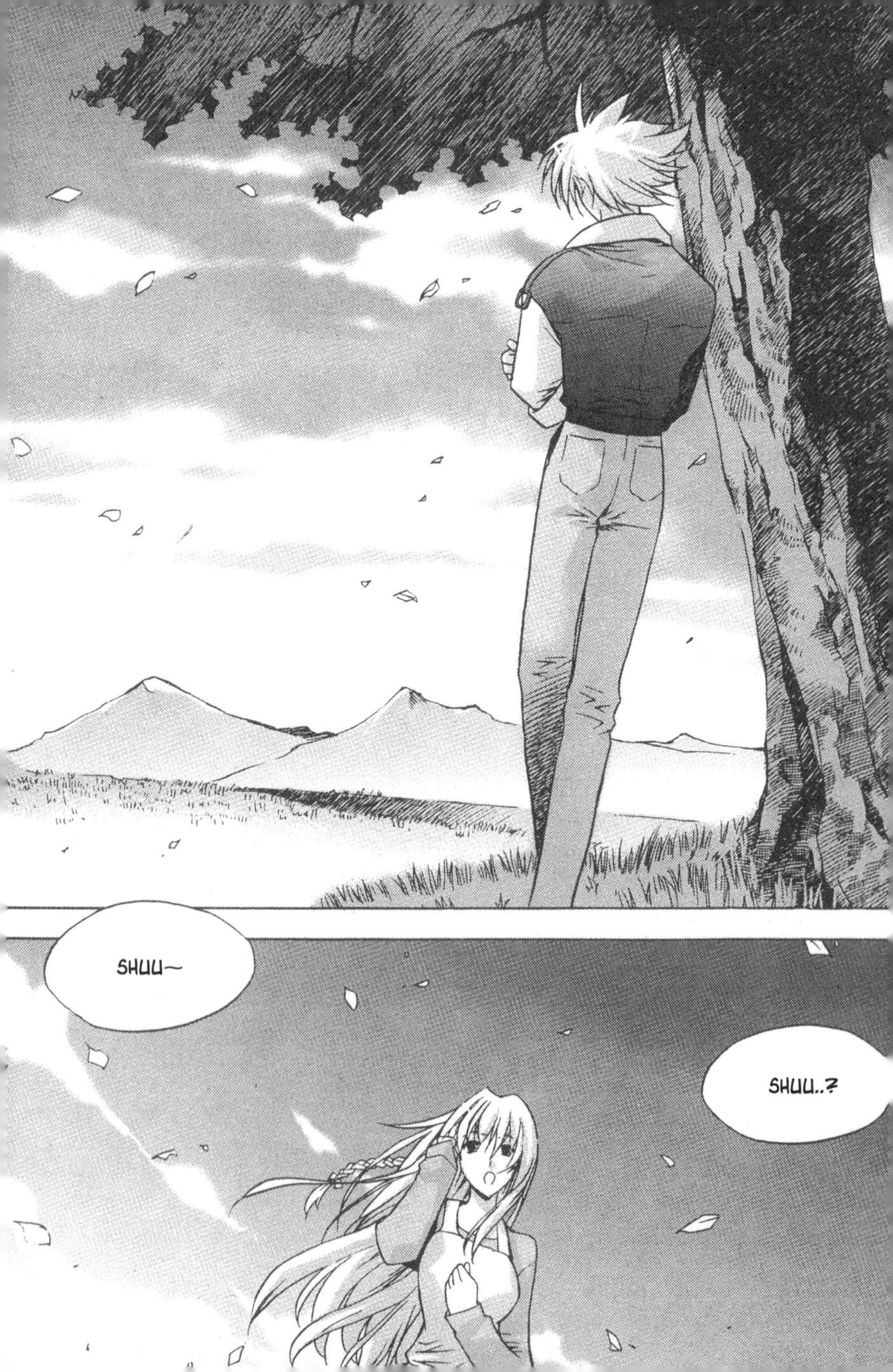
SHUU~
SHUU..?

Note : Nu-na is the word men use to address an older sister or a close elder female acquaintance. Literally, it means “older sister.”

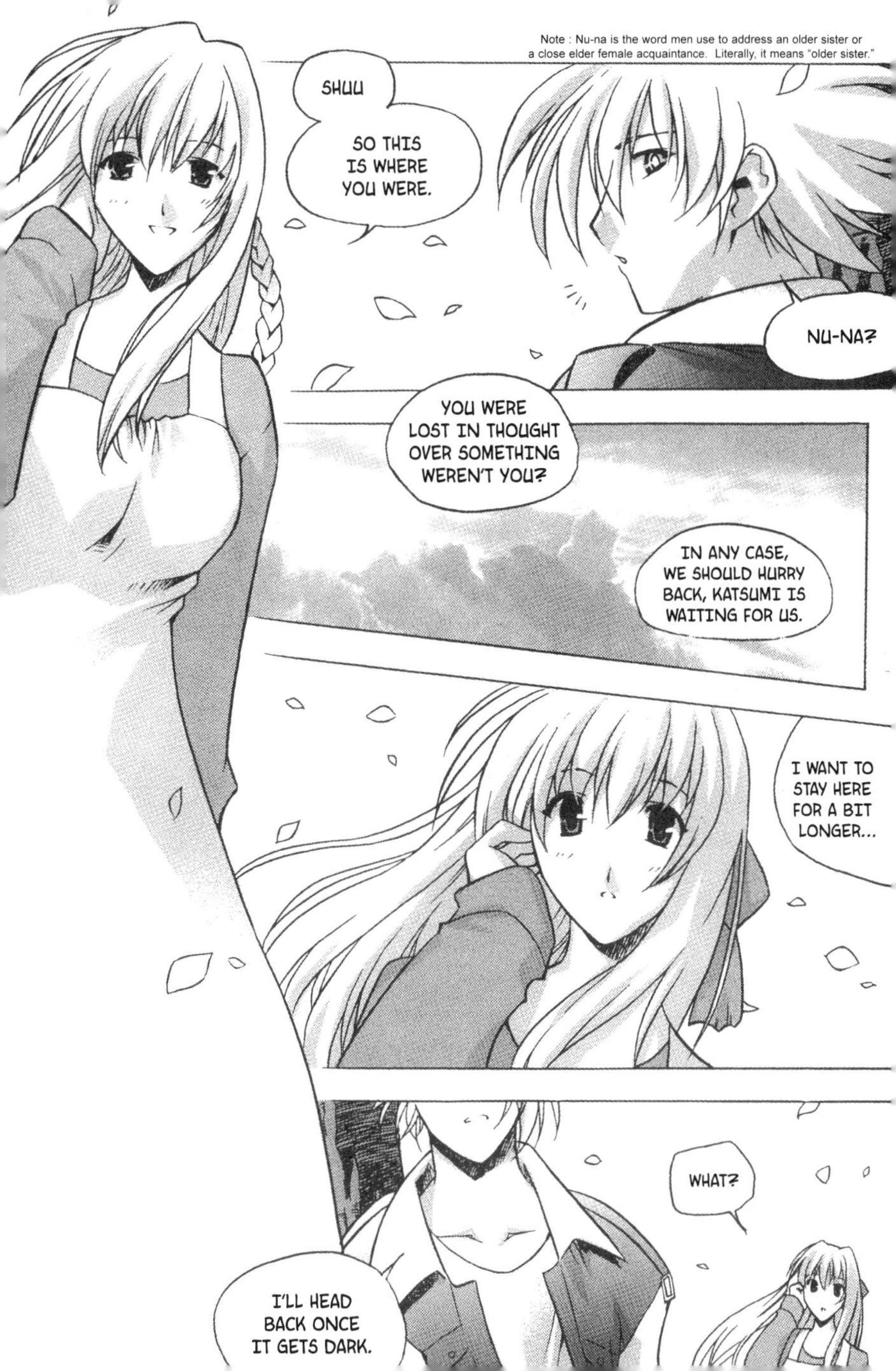
SHUU
SO THIS IS WHERE YOU WERE.
NU-NA?
YOU WERE LOST IN THOUGHT OVER SOMETHING WEREN'T YOU?
IN ANY CASE, WE SHOULD HURRY BACK, KATSUMI IS WAITING FOR US.
I WANT TO STAY HERE FOR A BIT LONGER...
WHAT?
I'LL HEAD BACK ONCE IT GETS DARK.

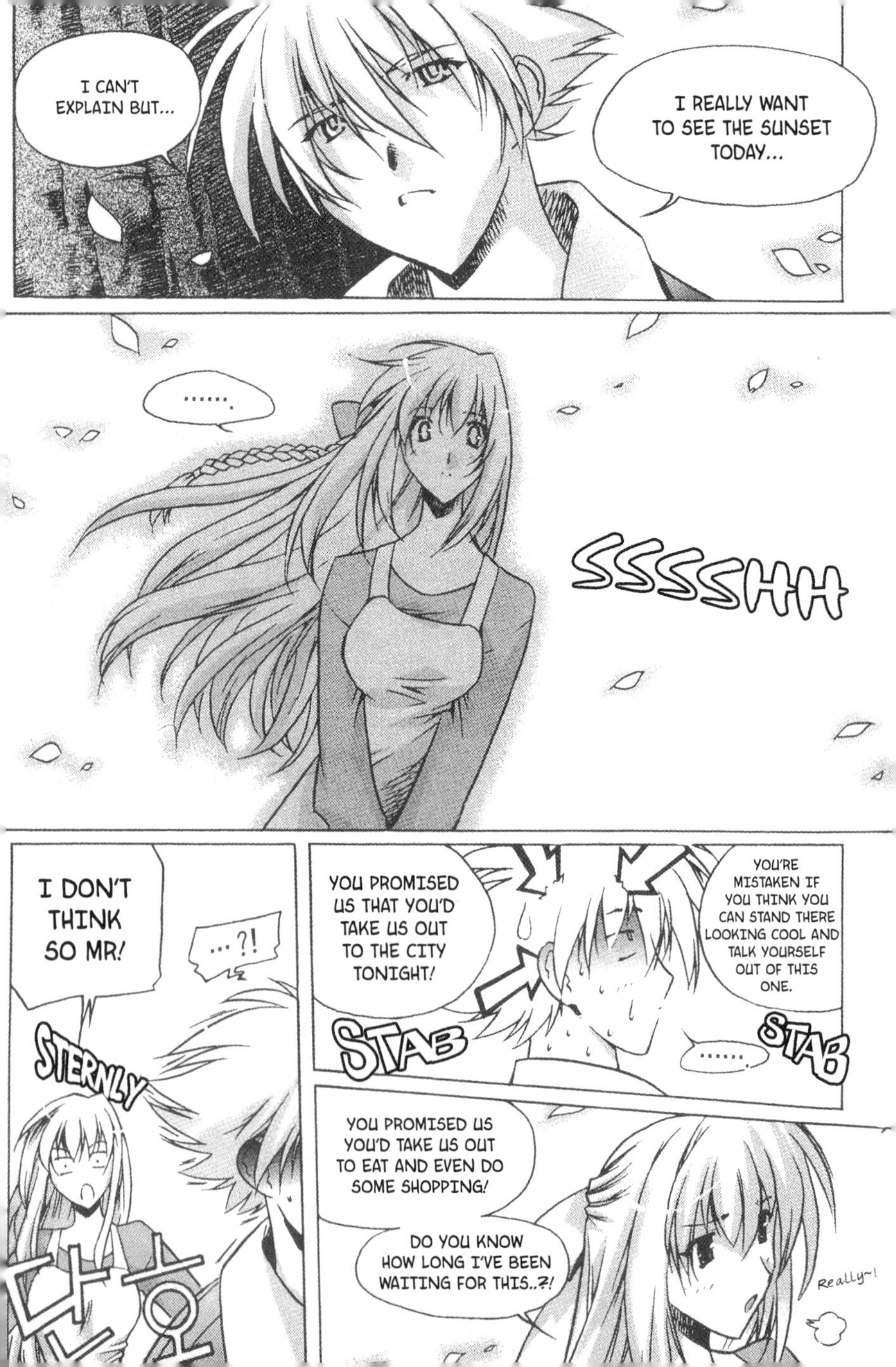
I CAN'T EXPLAIN BUT...
I REALLY WANT TO SEE THE SUNSET TODAY...
....
SSSSHH
I DON'T THINK SO MR!
...?!
STERNLY
YOU PROMISED US THAT YOU'D TAKE US OUT TO THE CITY TONIGHT!
YOU'RE MISTAKEN IF YOU THINK YOU CAN STAND THERE LOOKING COOL AND TALK YOURSELF OUT OF THIS ONE.
STAB
....
STAB
YOU PROMISED US YOU'D TAKE US OUT TO EAT AND EVEN DO SOME SHOPPING!
DO YOU KNOW HOW LONG I'VE BEEN WAITING FOR THIS..?!
Really~!

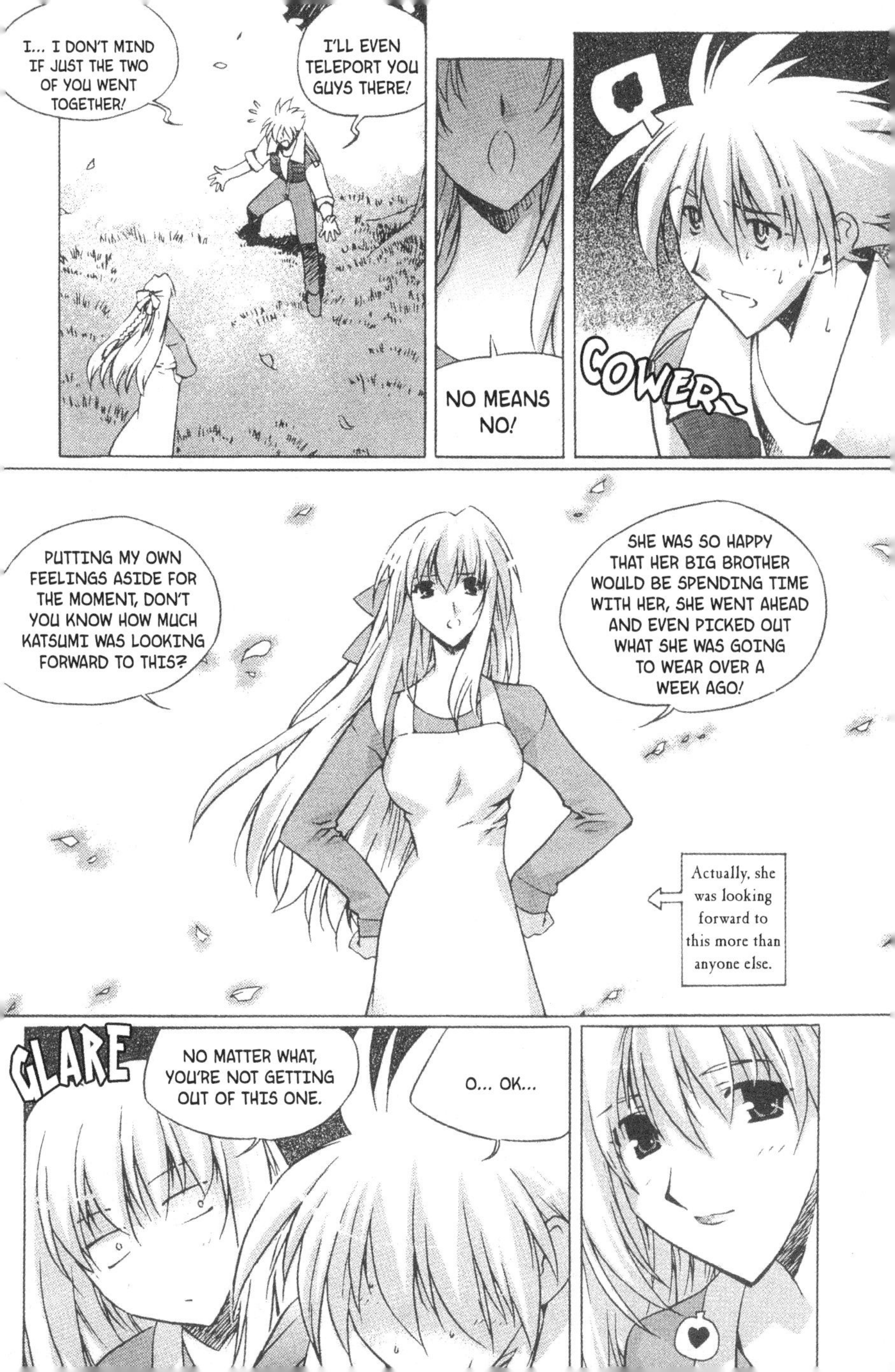
I... I DON'T MIND IF JUST THE TWO OF YOU WENT TOGETHER!
I'LL EVEN TELEPORT YOU GUYS THERE!
NO MEANS NO!
COWER~
PUTTING MY OWN FEELINGS ASIDE FOR THE MOMENT, DON'T YOU KNOW HOW MUCH KATSUMI WAS LOOKING FORWARD TO THIS?
SHE WAS SO HAPPY THAT HER BIG BROTHER WOULD BE SPENDING TIME WITH HER, SHE WENT AHEAD AND EVEN PICKED OUT WHAT SHE WAS GOING TO WEAR OVER A WEEK AGO!
Actually, she was looking forward to this more than anyone else.
GLARE
NO MATTER WHAT, YOU'RE NOT GETTING OUT OF THIS ONE.
O... OK...

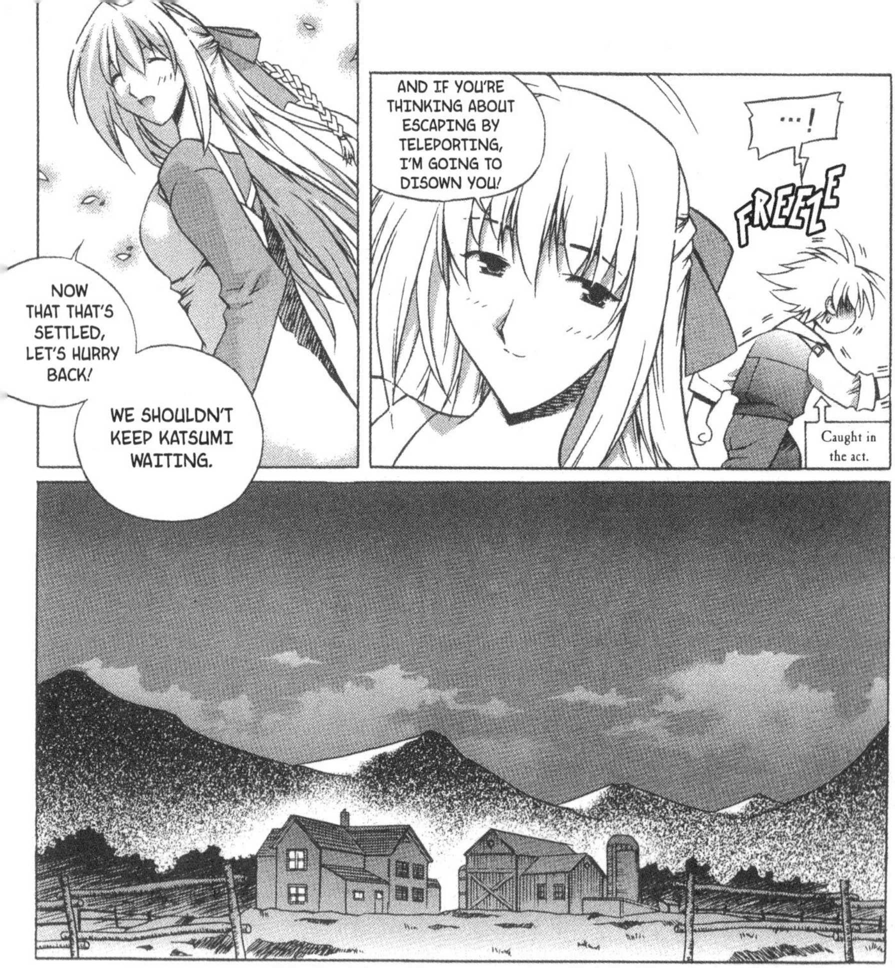
NOW THAT THAT'S SETTLED, LET'S HURRY BACK!
WE SHOULDN'T KEEP KATSUMI WAITING.
AND IF YOU'RE THINKING ABOUT ESCAPING BY TELEPORTING, I'M GOING TO DISOWN YOU!
...!
FREEZE
Caught in the act.

Note : Ohpa is the word Korean women use to say "big brother." It can also be used to mean "boyfriend."

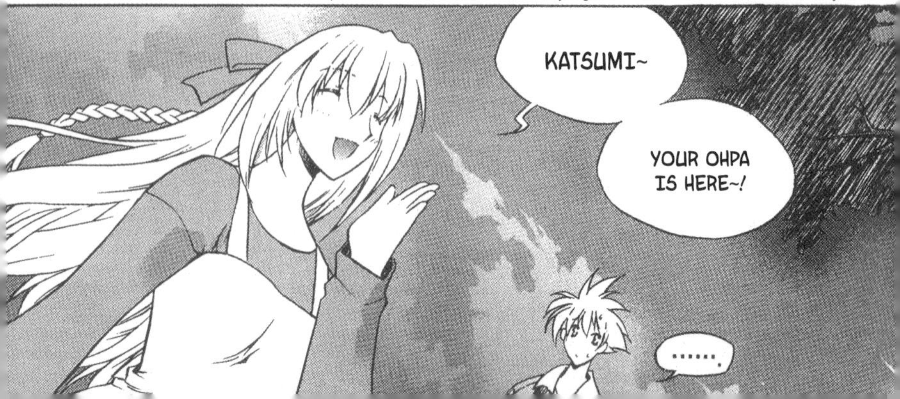
KATSUMI~
YOUR OHPA IS HERE~!
......

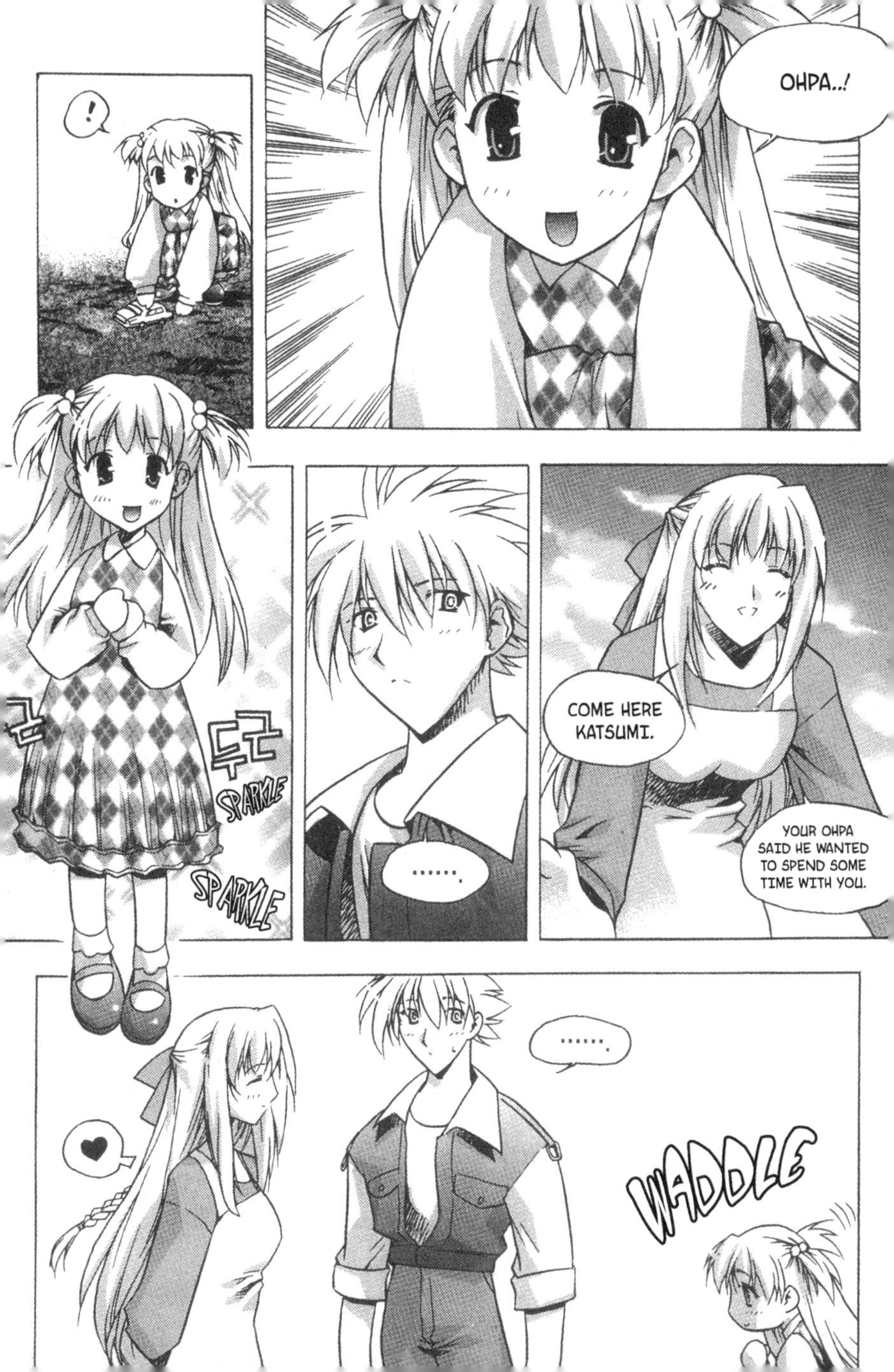
!
OHPA..!
두근
SPARKLE
SPARKLE
......
COME HERE KATSUMI.
YOUR OHPA SAID HE WANTED TO SPEND SOME TIME WITH YOU.
......
WADDLE

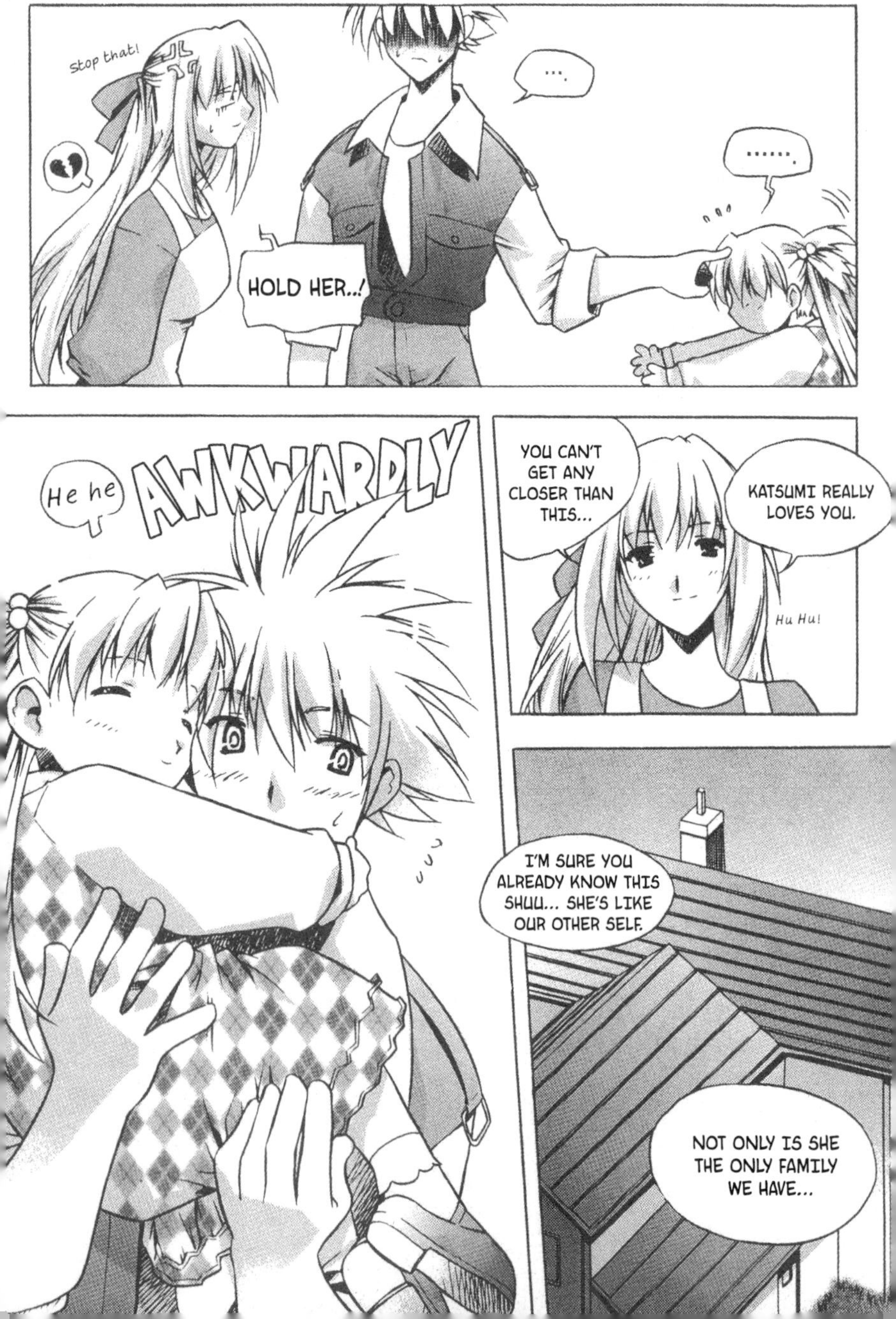

Stop that!
...
HOLD HER..!
....
He he
AWKWARDLY
YOU CAN'T GET ANY CLOSER THAN THIS...
KATSUMI REALLY LOVES YOU.
Hu Hu!
I'M SURE YOU ALREADY KNOW THIS SHUU... SHE'S LIKE OUR OTHER SELF.
NOT ONLY IS SHE THE ONLY FAMILY WE HAVE...

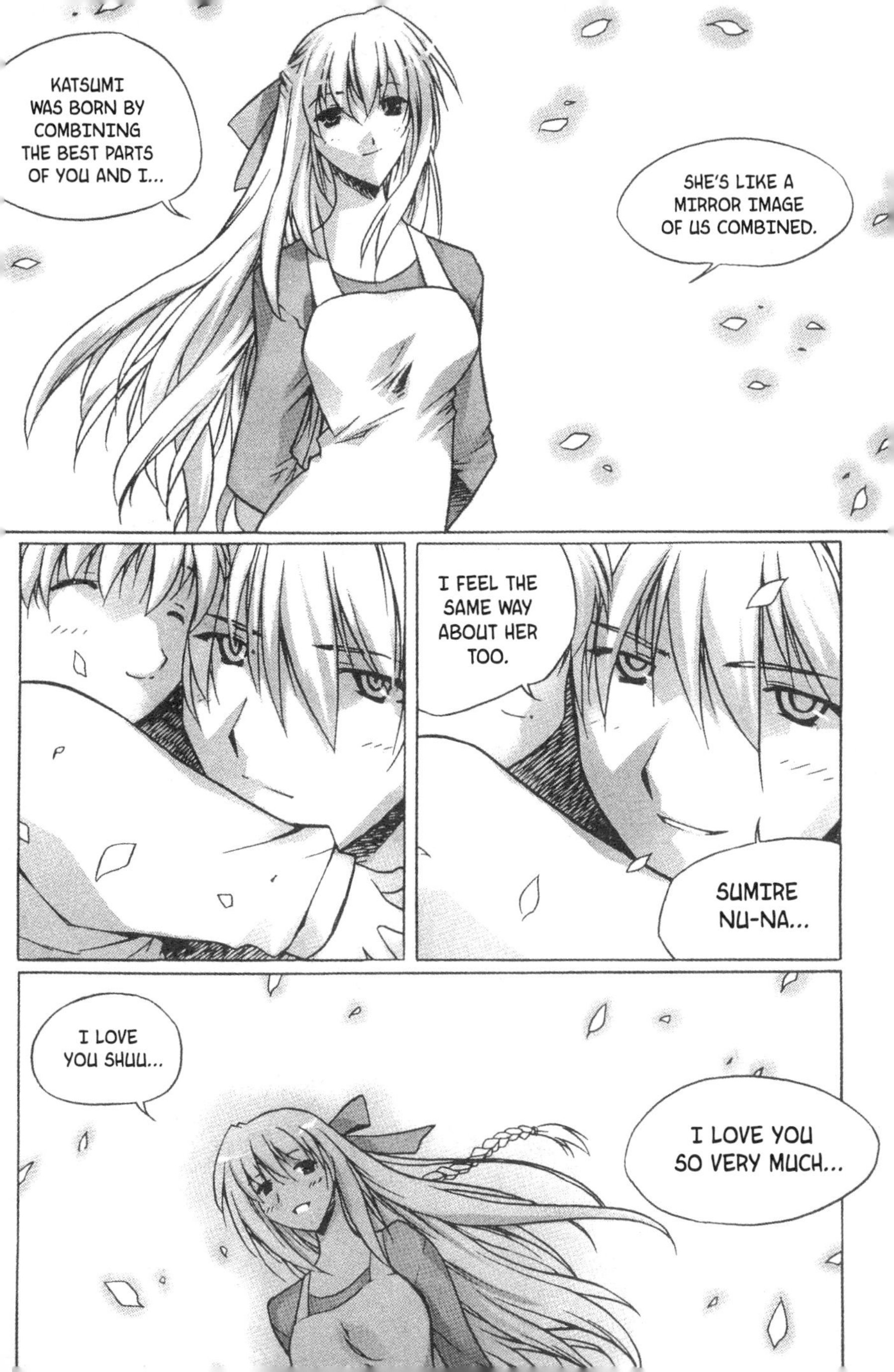
KATSUMI WAS BORN BY COMBINING THE BEST PARTS OF YOU AND I...
SHE'S LIKE A MIRROR IMAGE OF US COMBINED.
I FEEL THE SAME WAY ABOUT HER TOO.
SUMIRE NU-NA...
I LOVE YOU SHUU...
I LOVE YOU SO VERY MUCH...

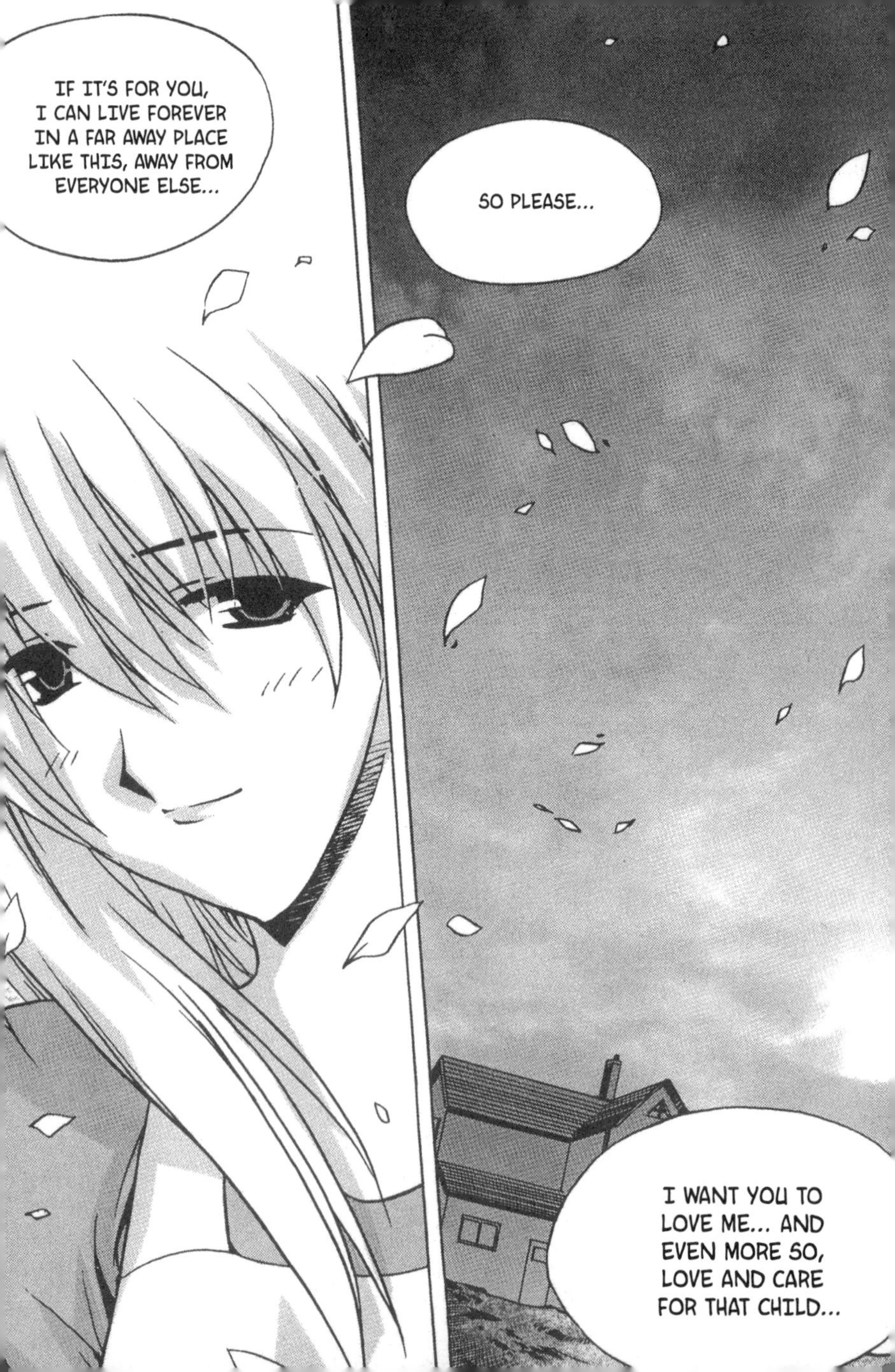
IF IT'S FOR YOU, I CAN LIVE FOREVER IN A FAR AWAY PLACE LIKE THIS, AWAY FROM EVERYONE ELSE...
SO PLEASE...
I WANT YOU TO LOVE ME... AND EVEN MORE SO, LOVE AND CARE FOR THAT CHILD...

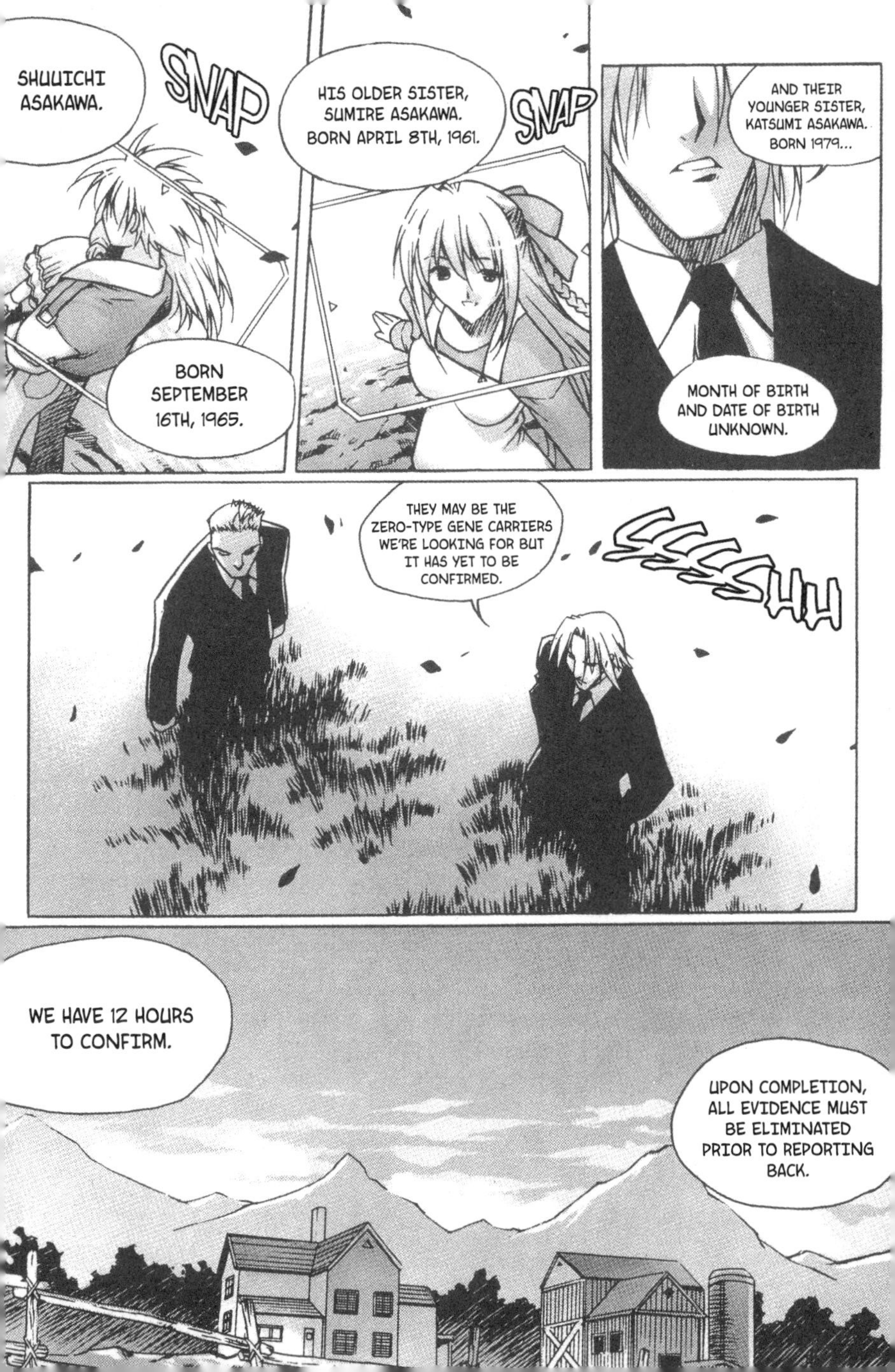
SHUUICHI ASAKAWA.
SNAP
BORN SEPTEMBER 16TH, 1965.
HIS OLDER SISTER, SUMIRE ASAKAWA. BORN APRIL 8TH, 1961.
SNAP
AND THEIR YOUNGER SISTER, KATSUMI ASAKAWA. BORN 1979...
MONTH OF BIRTH AND DATE OF BIRTH UNKNOWN.
THEY MAY BE THE ZERO-TYPE GENE CARRIERS WE'RE LOOKING FOR BUT IT HAS YET TO BE CONFIRMED.
SSSSHH
WE HAVE 12 HOURS TO CONFIRM.
UPON COMPLETION, ALL EVIDENCE MUST BE ELIMINATED PRIOR TO REPORTING BACK.

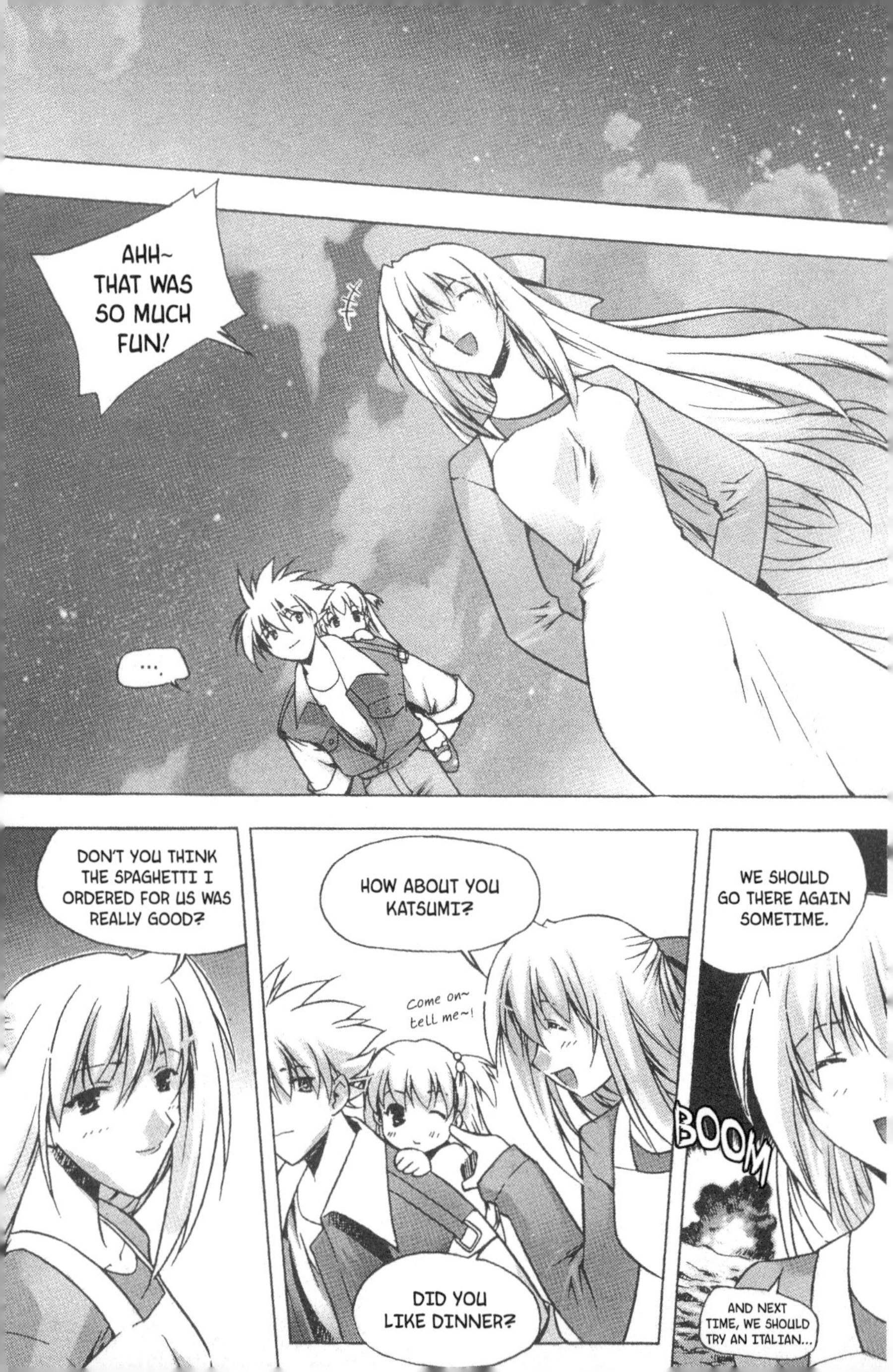

AHH~ THAT WAS SO MUCH FUN!
...
DON'T YOU THINK THE SPAGHETTI I ORDERED FOR US WAS REALLY GOOD?
HOW ABOUT YOU KATSUMI?
Come on~ tell me~!
DID YOU LIKE DINNER?
WE SHOULD GO THERE AGAIN SOMETIME.
BOOM
AND NEXT TIME, WE SHOULD TRY AN ITALIAN...

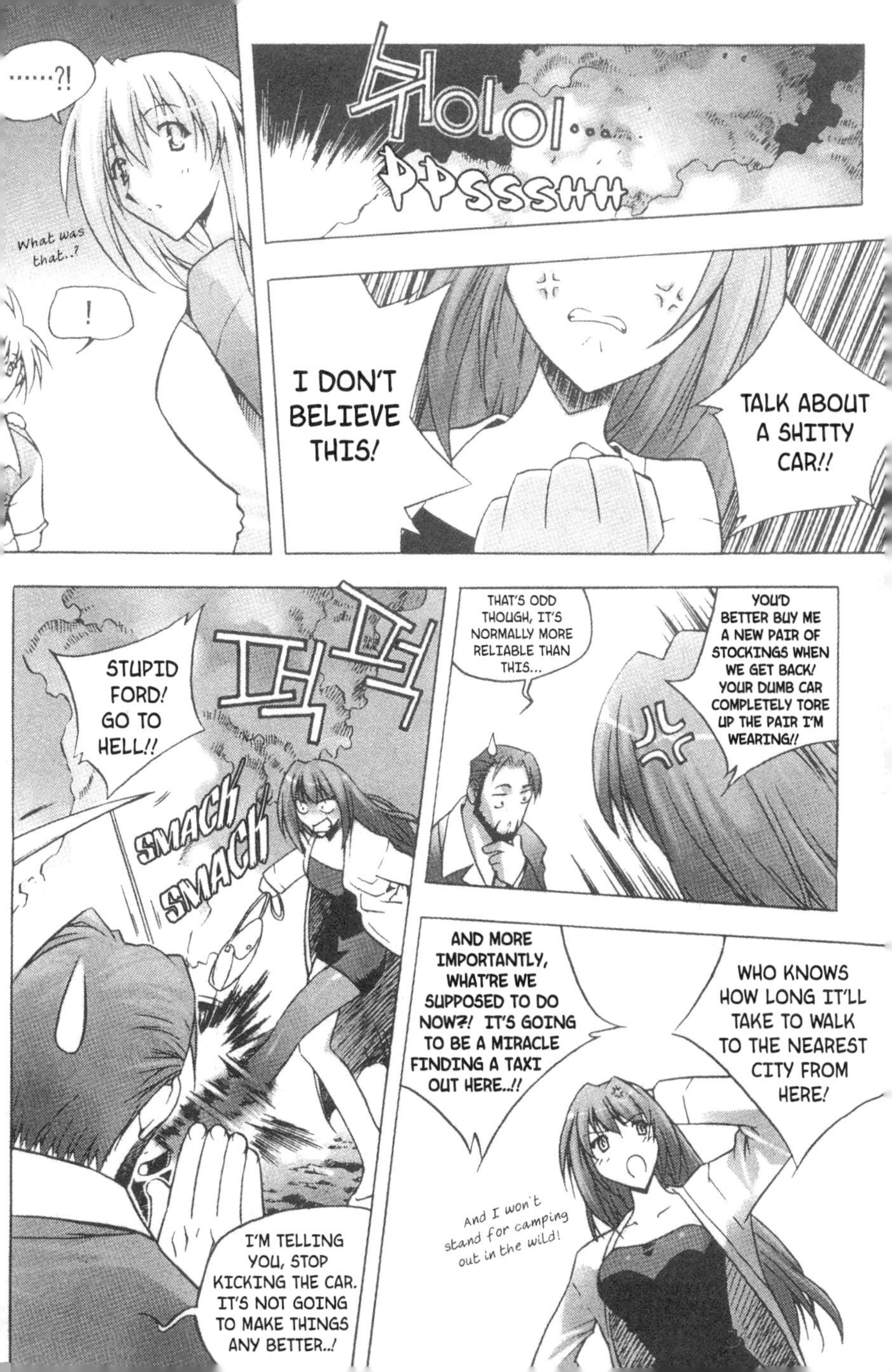

......?!
What was that..?
!
PPSSSSHH
I DON'T BELIEVE THIS!
TALK ABOUT A SHITTY CAR!!
STUPID FORD! GO TO HELL!!
퍽 퍽
SMACK SMACK
I'M TELLING YOU, STOP KICKING THE CAR. IT'S NOT GOING TO MAKE THINGS ANY BETTER..!
THAT'S ODD THOUGH, IT'S NORMALLY MORE RELIABLE THAN THIS...
YOU'D BETTER BUY ME A NEW PAIR OF STOCKINGS WHEN WE GET BACK! YOUR DUMB CAR COMPLETELY TORE UP THE PAIR I'M WEARING!!
AND MORE IMPORTANTLY, WHAT'RE WE SUPPOSED TO DO NOW?! IT'S GOING TO BE A MIRACLE FINDING A TAXI OUT HERE..!!
WHO KNOWS HOW LONG IT'LL TAKE TO WALK TO THE NEAREST CITY FROM HERE!
And I won't stand for camping out in the wild!

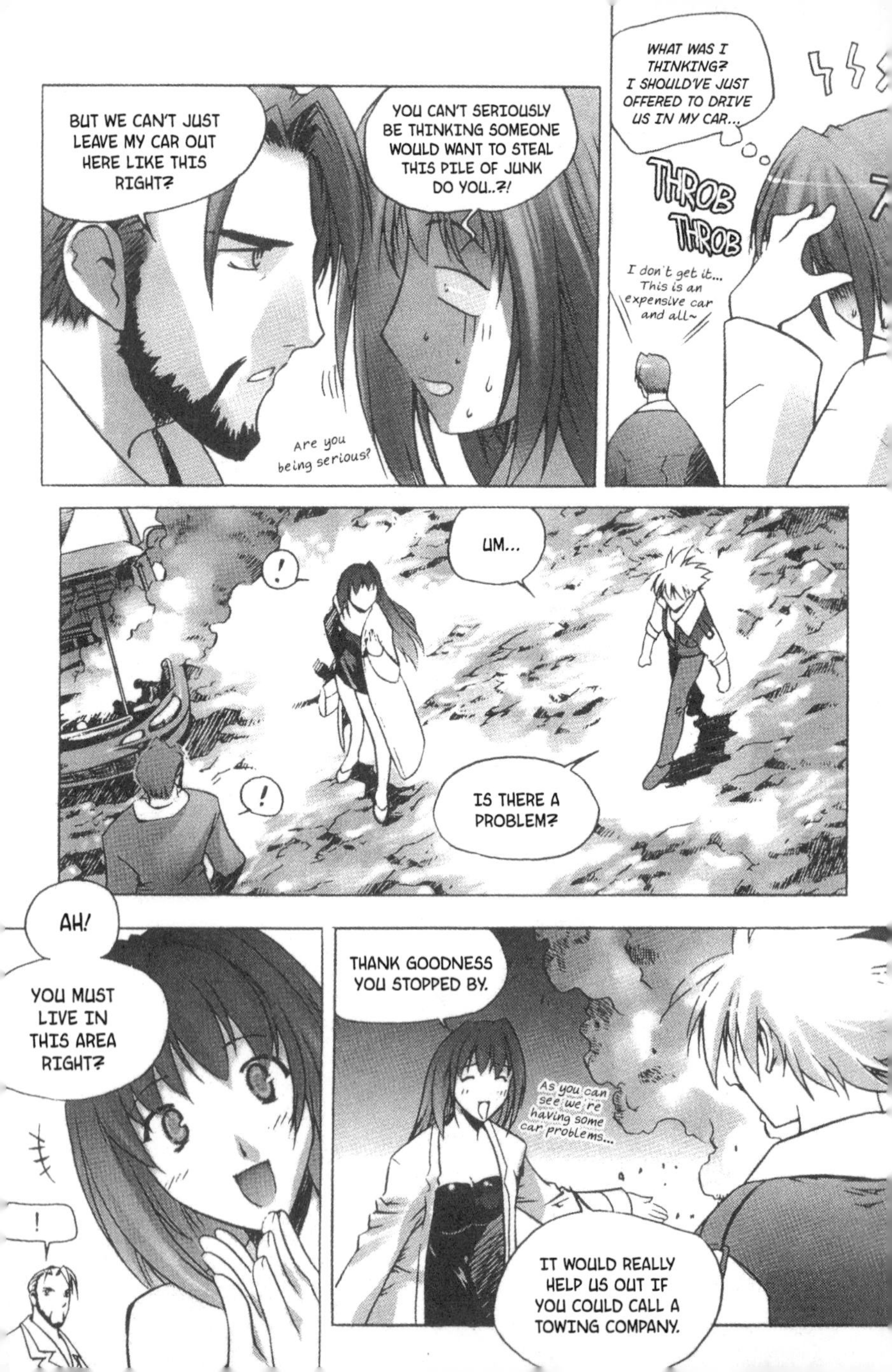
BUT WE CAN'T JUST LEAVE MY CAR OUT HERE LIKE THIS RIGHT?
YOU CAN'T SERIOUSLY BE THINKING SOMEONE WOULD WANT TO STEAL THIS PILE OF JUNK DO YOU..?!
Are you being serious?
WHAT WAS I THINKING? I SHOULD'VE JUST OFFERED TO DRIVE US IN MY CAR...
THROB THROB
I don't get it... This is an expensive car and all~
!
UM...
!
IS THERE A PROBLEM?
AH!
YOU MUST LIVE IN THIS AREA RIGHT?
!
THANK GOODNESS YOU STOPPED BY.
As you can see we're having some car problems...
IT WOULD REALLY HELP US OUT IF YOU COULD CALL A TOWING COMPANY.

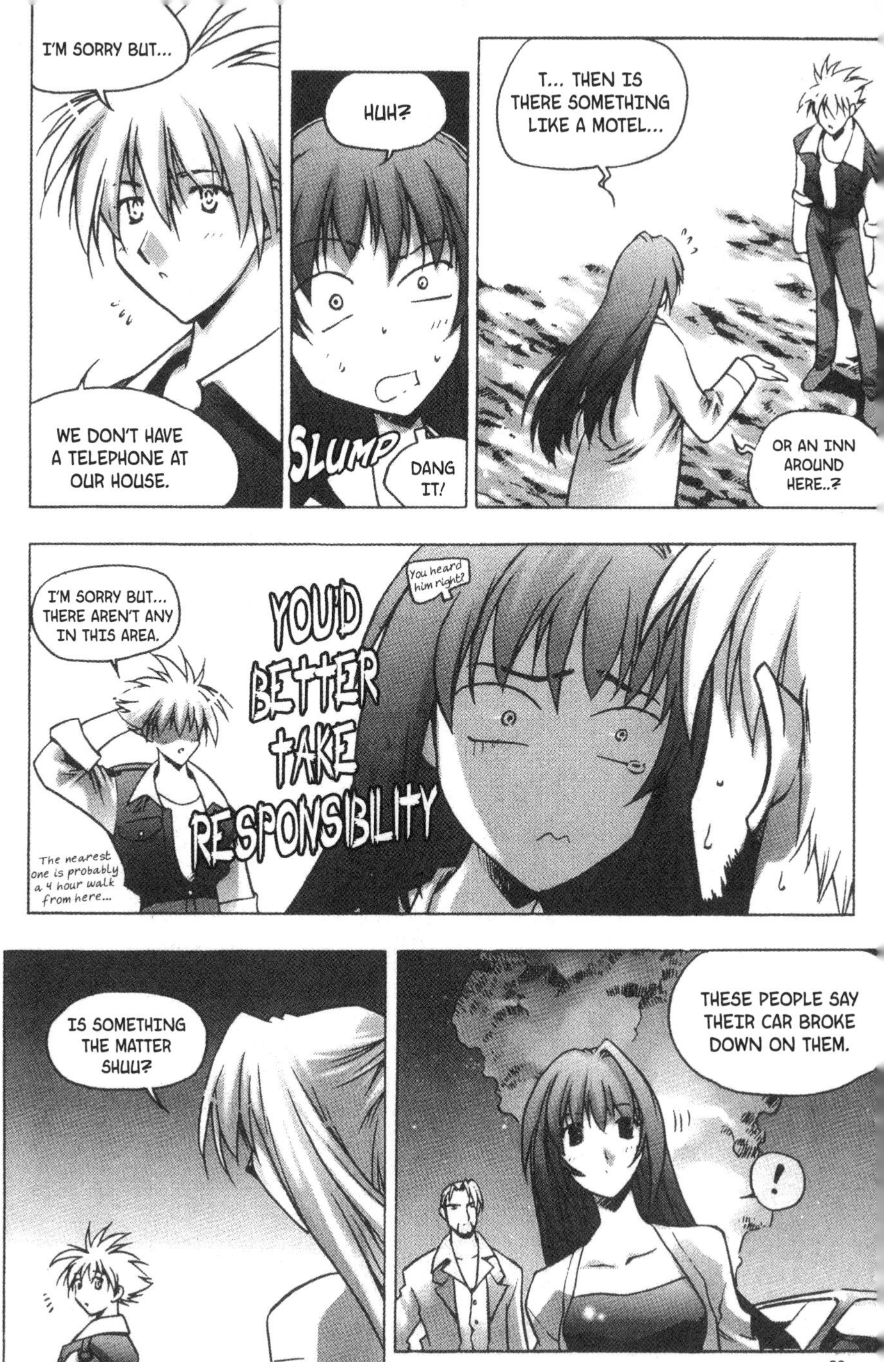
I'M SORRY BUT...
WE DON'T HAVE A TELEPHONE AT OUR HOUSE.
HUH?
SLUMP
DANG IT!
T... THEN IS THERE SOMETHING LIKE A MOTEL...
OR AN INN AROUND HERE..?
I'M SORRY BUT... THERE AREN'T ANY IN THIS AREA.
You heard him right?
YOU'D BETTER TAKE RESPONSIBLITY
The nearest one is probably a 4 hour walk from here...
IS SOMETHING THE MATTER SHUU?
THESE PEOPLE SAY THEIR CAR BROKE DOWN ON THEM.
!

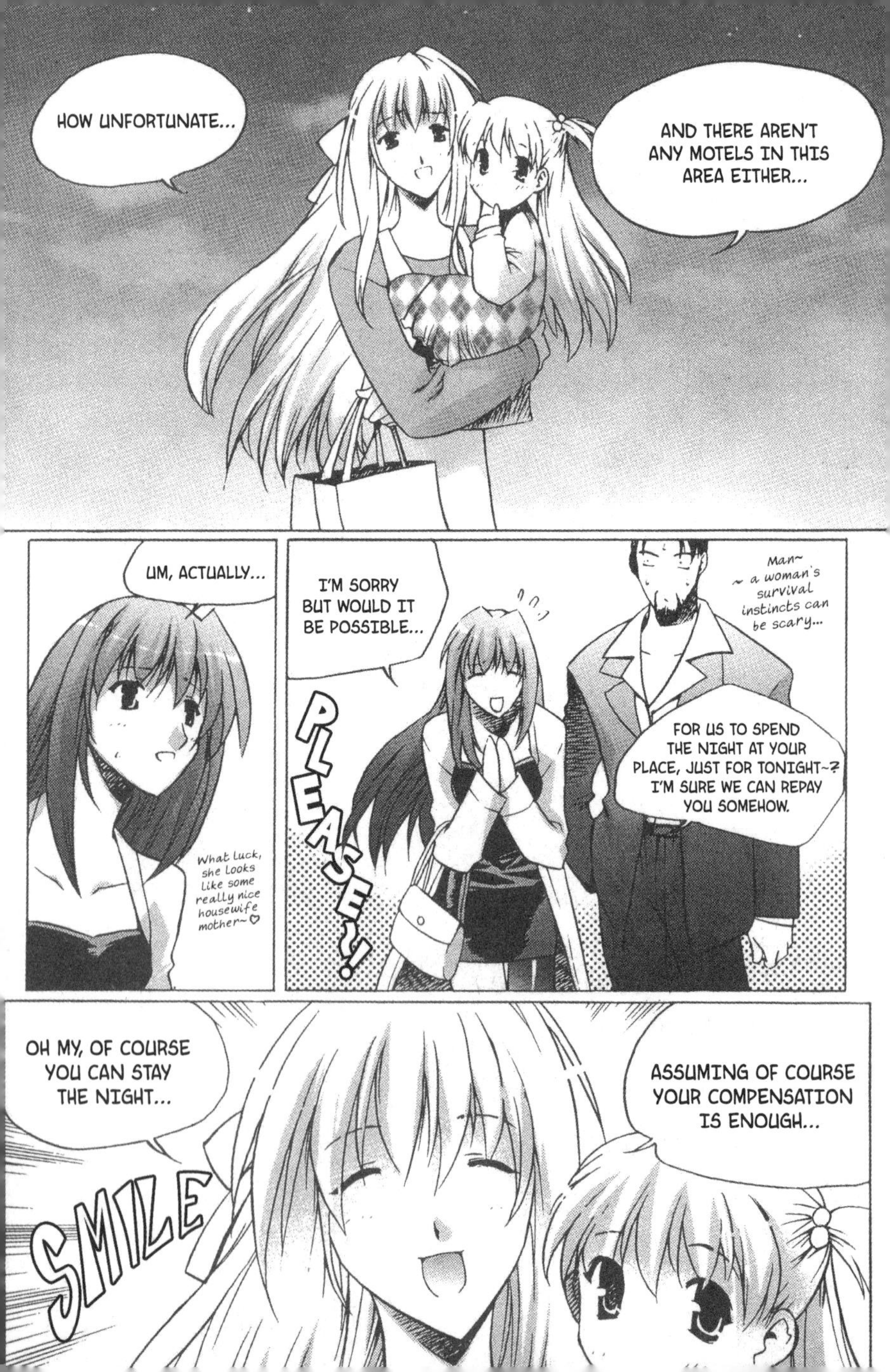
HOW UNFORTUNATE...
AND THERE AREN'T ANY MOTELS IN THIS AREA EITHER...
UM, ACTUALLY...
What luck, she looks like some really nice housewife mother~♡
I'M SORRY BUT WOULD IT BE POSSIBLE...
Man~ ~ a woman's survival instincts can be scary...
PLEASE~!
FOR US TO SPEND THE NIGHT AT YOUR PLACE, JUST FOR TONIGHT~? I'M SURE WE CAN REPAY YOU SOMEHOW.
OH MY, OF COURSE YOU CAN STAY THE NIGHT...
SMILE
ASSUMING OF COURSE YOUR COMPENSATION IS ENOUGH...

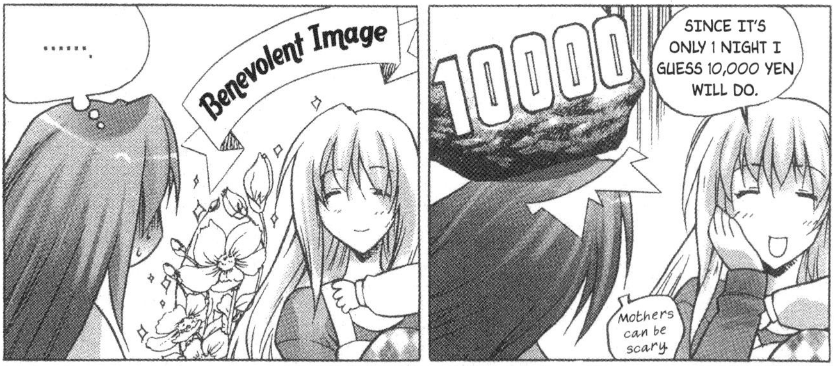
....
Benevolent Image
10000
SINCE IT'S ONLY 1 NIGHT I GUESS 10,000 YEN WILL DO.
Mothers can be scary.

Note : 10,000 yen = $100 (this is also in the 1980's when things were cheaper)

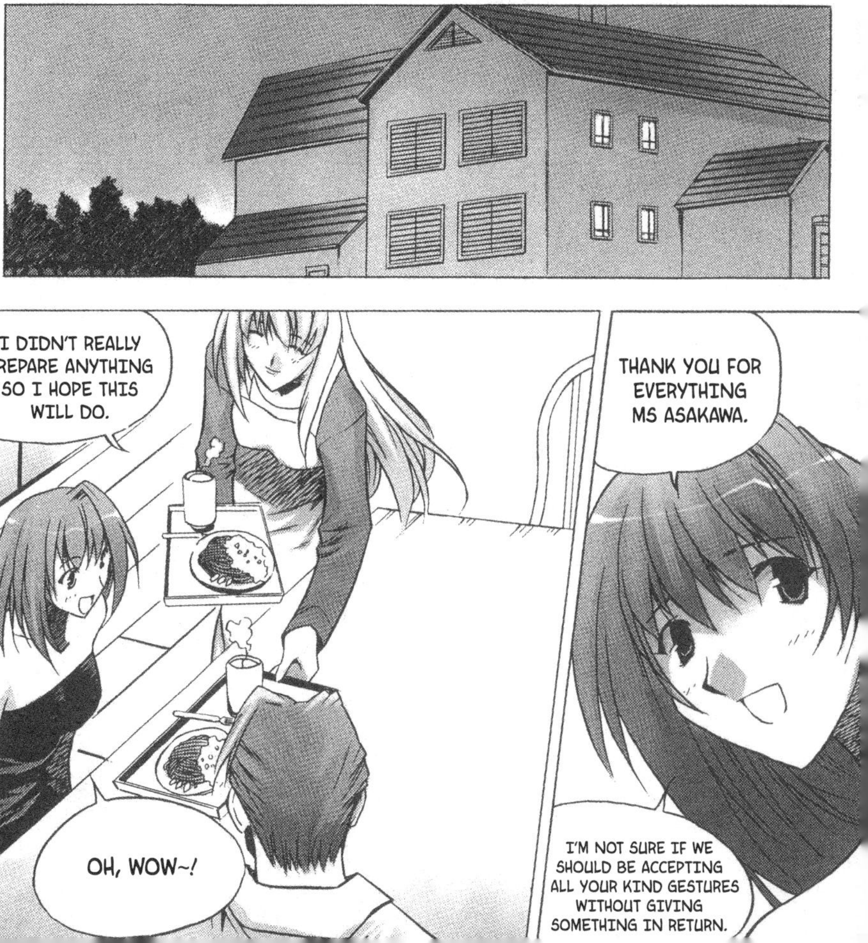
I DIDN'T REALLY PREPARE ANYTHING SO I HOPE THIS WILL DO.
OH, WOW~!
THANK YOU FOR EVERYTHING MS ASAKAWA.
I'M NOT SURE IF WE SHOULD BE ACCEPTING ALL YOUR KIND GESTURES WITHOUT GIVING SOMETHING IN RETURN.

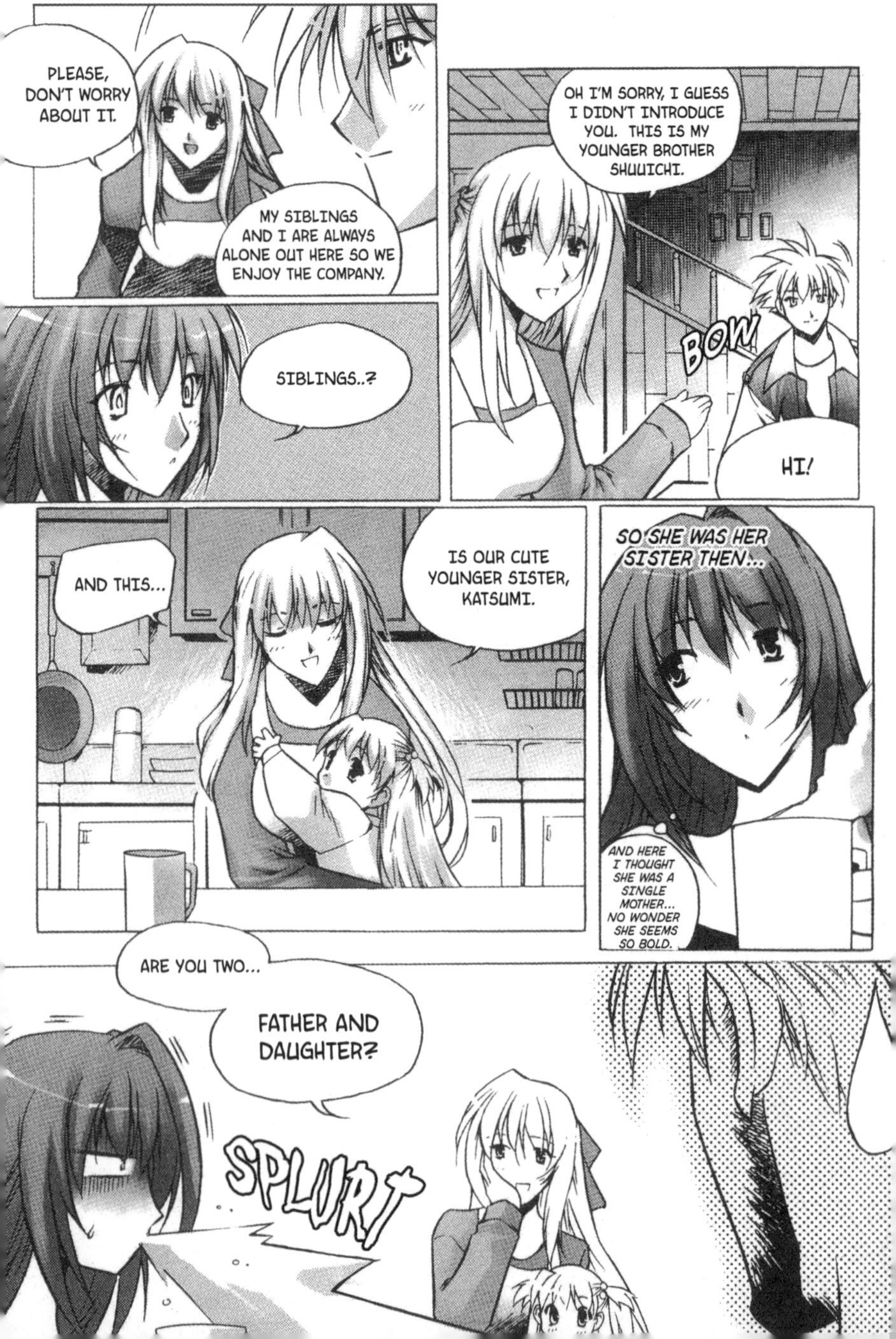
PLEASE, DON'T WORRY ABOUT IT.
MY SIBLINGS AND I ARE ALWAYS ALONE OUT HERE SO WE ENJOY THE COMPANY.
OH I'M SORRY, I GUESS I DIDN'T INTRODUCE YOU. THIS IS MY YOUNGER BROTHER SHUUICHI.
BOW
HI!
SIBLINGS..?
AND THIS...
IS OUR CUTE YOUNGER SISTER, KATSUMI.
SO SHE WAS HER SISTER THEN...
AND HERE I THOUGHT SHE WAS A SINGLE MOTHER... NO WONDER SHE SEEMS SO BOLD.
ARE YOU TWO...
FATHER AND DAUGHTER?
SPLURT

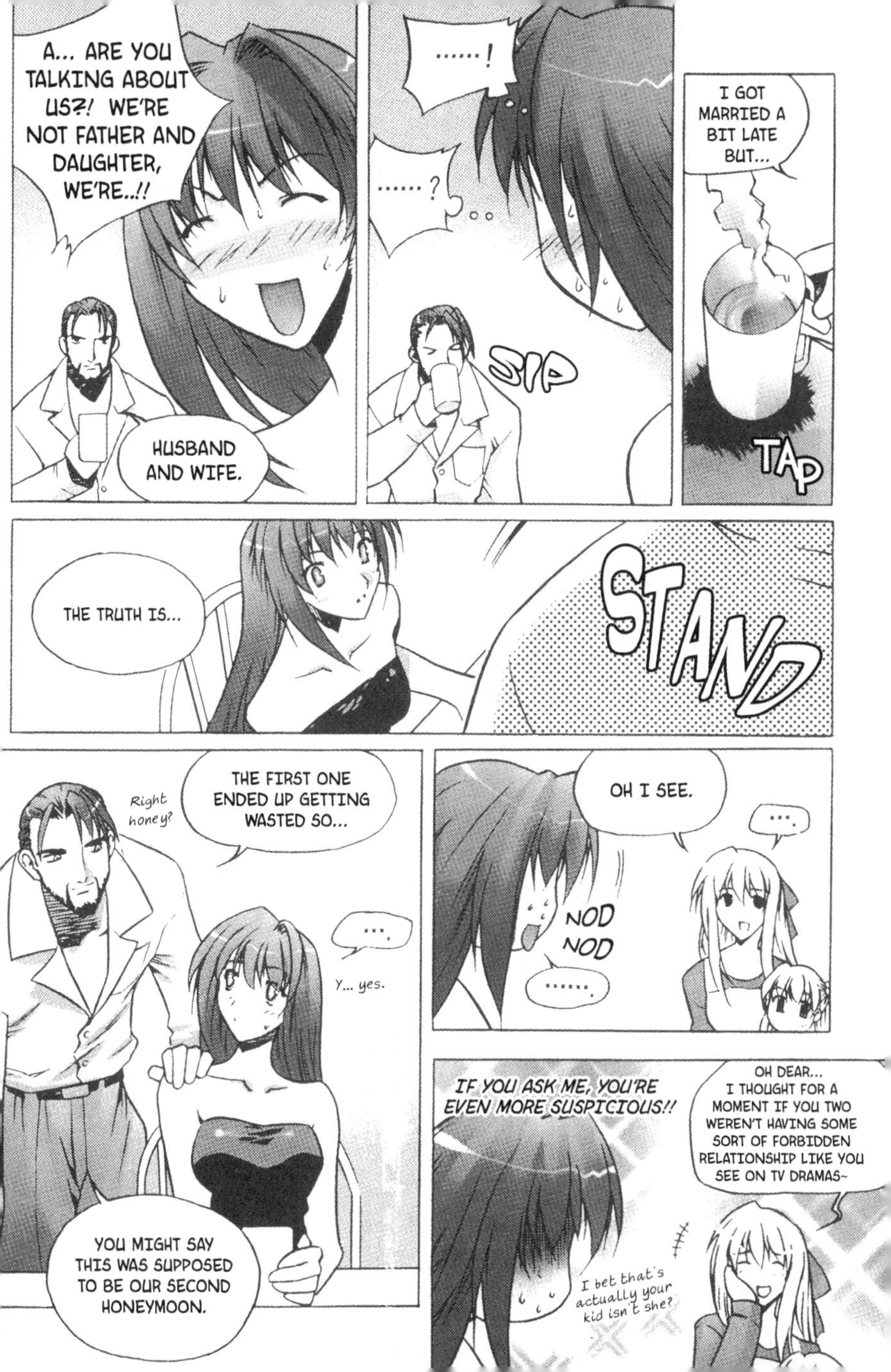

A... ARE YOU TALKING ABOUT US?! WE'RE NOT FATHER AND DAUGHTER, WE'RE..!!
HUSBAND AND WIFE.
......!
......?
SIP
I GOT MARRIED A BIT LATE BUT...
TAP
THE TRUTH IS...
STAND
Right honey?
THE FIRST ONE ENDED UP GETTING WASTED SO...
....
Y... yes.
YOU MIGHT SAY THIS WAS SUPPOSED TO BE OUR SECOND HONEYMOON.
OH I SEE.
....
NOD NOD
....
IF YOU ASK ME, YOU'RE EVEN MORE SUSPICIOUS!!
OH DEAR... I THOUGHT FOR A MOMENT IF YOU TWO WEREN'T HAVING SOME SORT OF FORBIDDEN RELATIONSHIP LIKE YOU SEE ON TV DRAMAS~
I bet that's actually your kid isn't she?

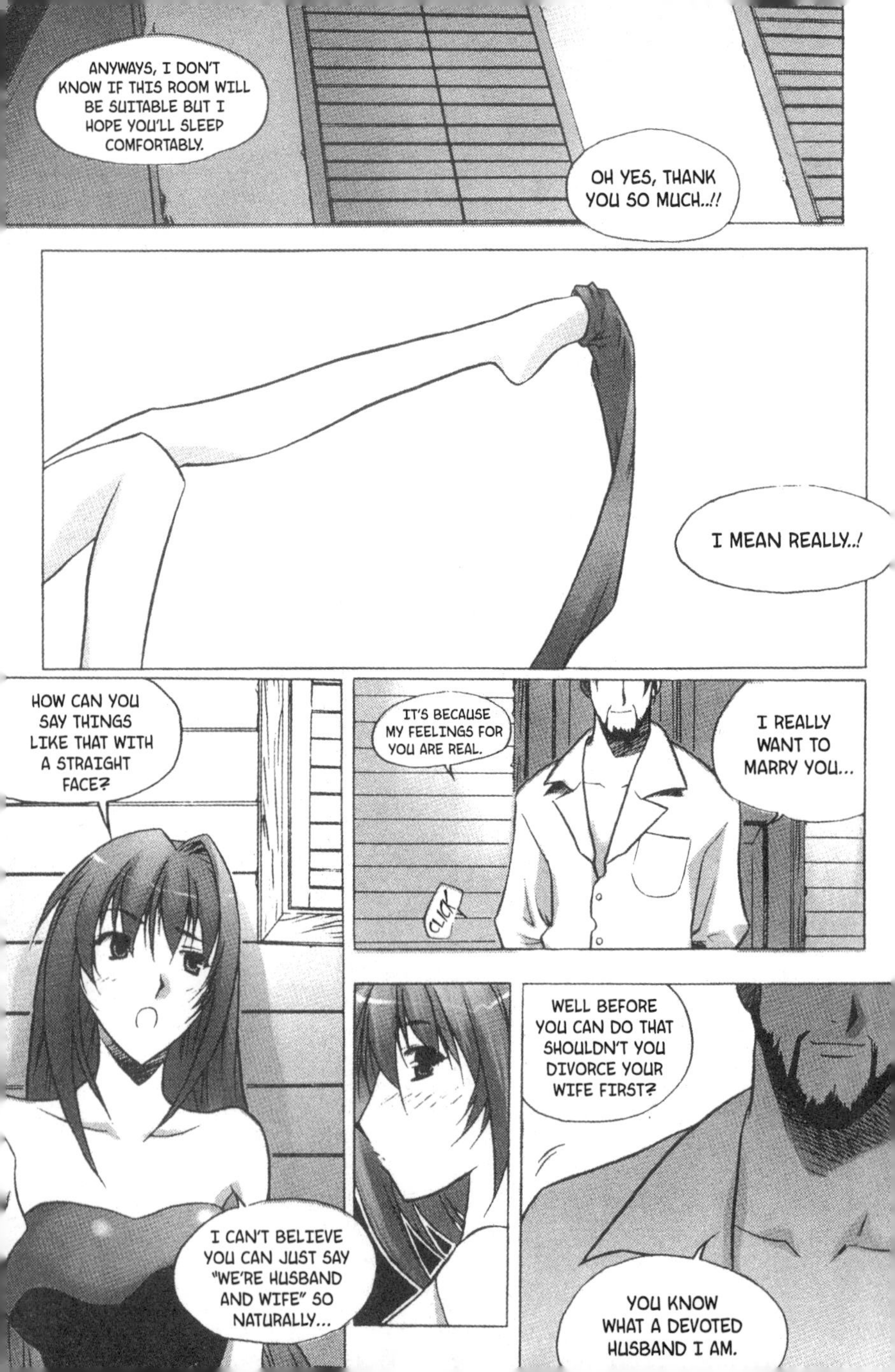
ANYWAYS, I DON'T KNOW IF THIS ROOM WILL BE SUITABLE BUT I HOPE YOU'LL SLEEP COMFORTABLY.
OH YES, THANK YOU SO MUCH..!!
I MEAN REALLY..!
HOW CAN YOU SAY THINGS LIKE THAT WITH A STRAIGHT FACE?
IT'S BECAUSE MY FEELINGS FOR YOU ARE REAL.
I REALLY WANT TO MARRY YOU...
CLICK
WELL BEFORE YOU CAN DO THAT SHOULDN'T YOU DIVORCE YOUR WIFE FIRST?
I CAN'T BELIEVE YOU CAN JUST SAY "WE'RE HUSBAND AND WIFE" SO NATURALLY...
YOU KNOW WHAT A DEVOTED HUSBAND I AM.

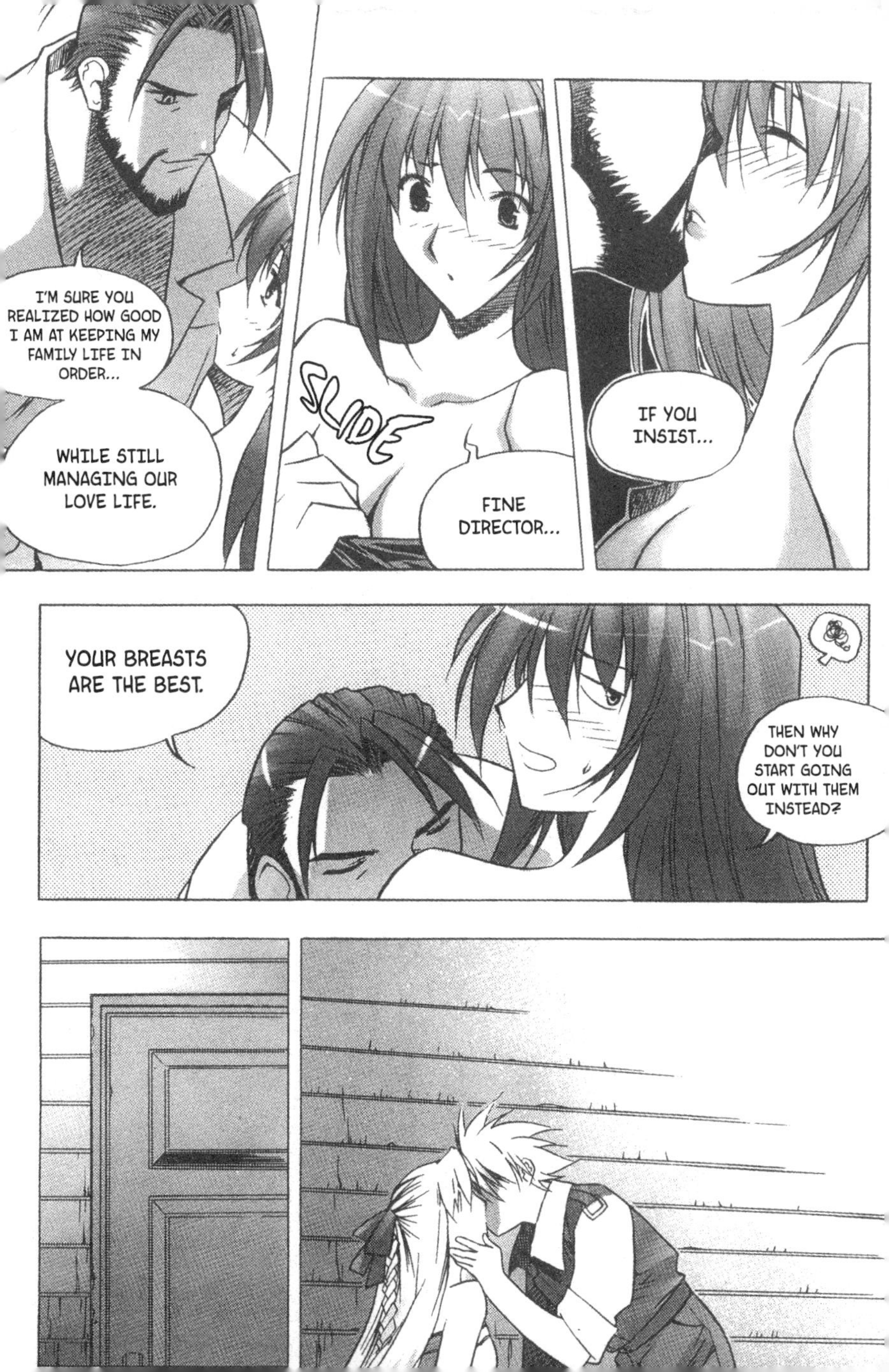
I'M SURE YOU REALIZED HOW GOOD I AM AT KEEPING MY FAMILY LIFE IN ORDER...
WHILE STILL MANAGING OUR LOVE LIFE.
SLIDE
FINE DIRECTOR...
IF YOU INSIST...
YOUR BREASTS ARE THE BEST.
THEN WHY DON'T YOU START GOING OUT WITH THEM INSTEAD?

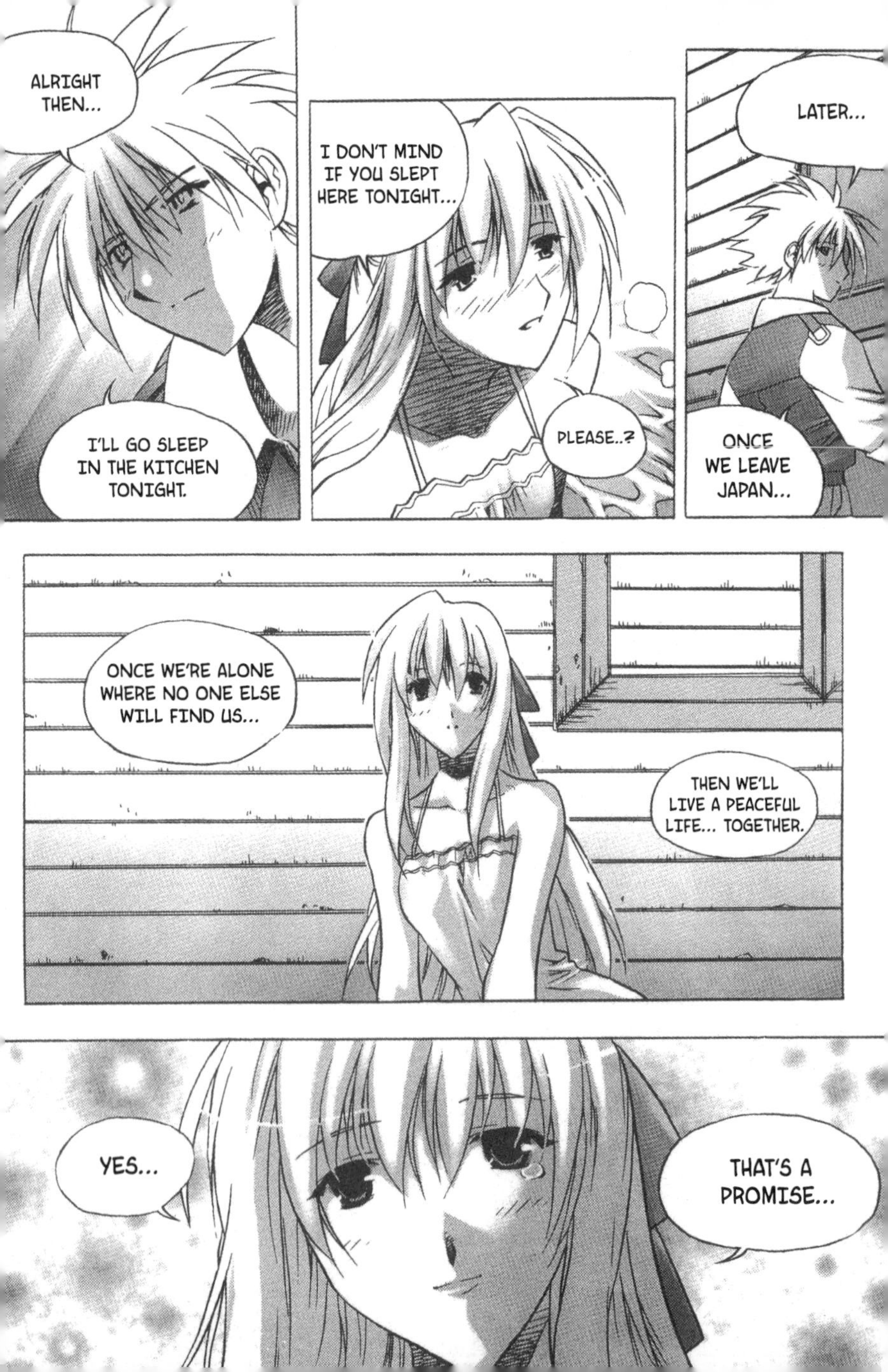
ALRIGHT THEN...
I'LL GO SLEEP IN THE KITCHEN TONIGHT.
I DON'T MIND IF YOU SLEPT HERE TONIGHT...
PLEASE..?
LATER...
ONCE WE LEAVE JAPAN...
ONCE WE'RE ALONE WHERE NO ONE ELSE WILL FIND US...
THEN WE'LL LIVE A PEACEFUL LIFE... TOGETHER.
YES...
THAT'S A PROMISE...

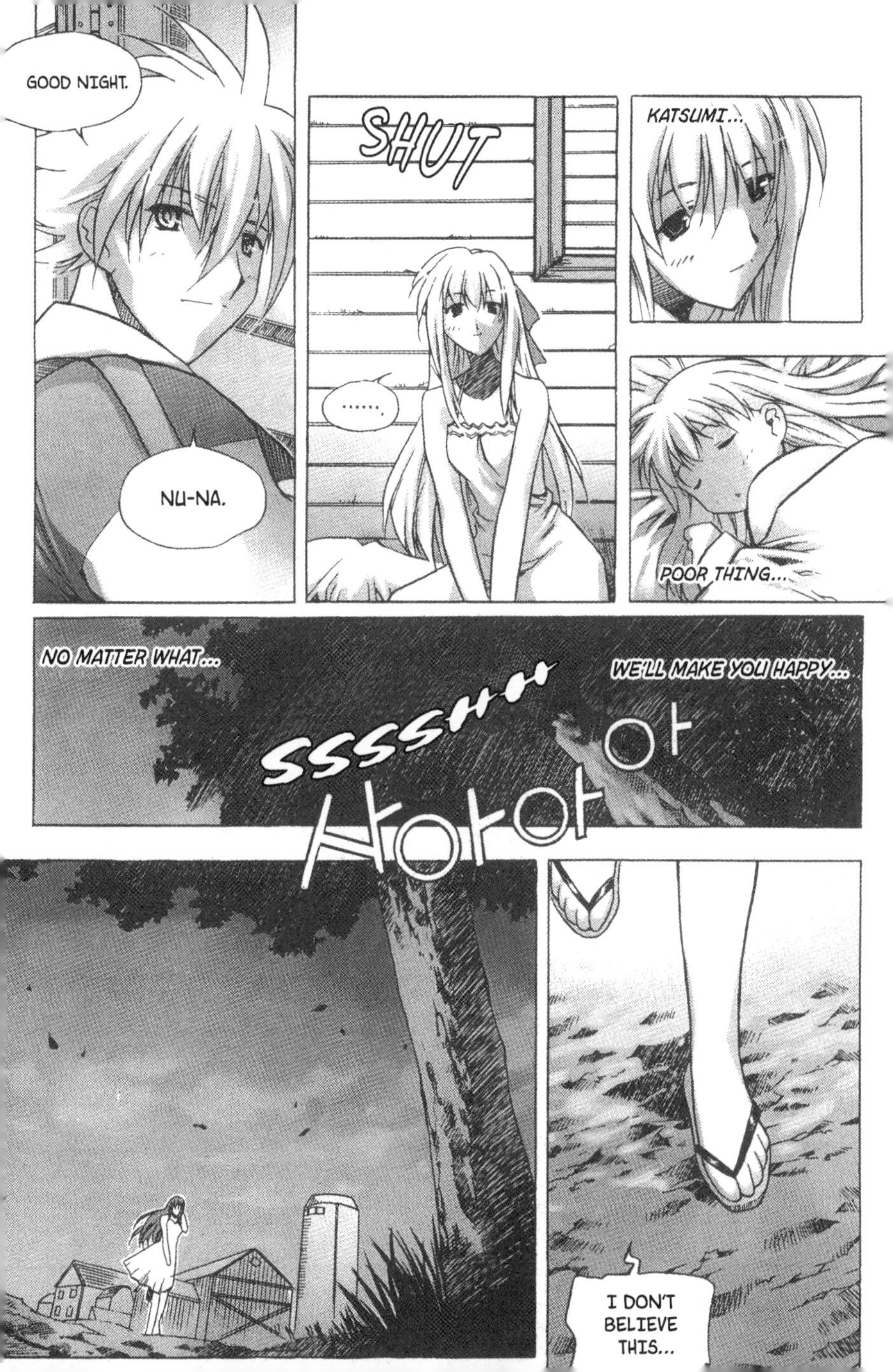
GOOD NIGHT.
NU-NA.
SHUT
......
KATSUMI...
POOR THING...
NO MATTER WHAT...
WE'LL MAKE YOU HAPPY...
SSSSHHH
사아아아
I DON'T BELIEVE THIS...

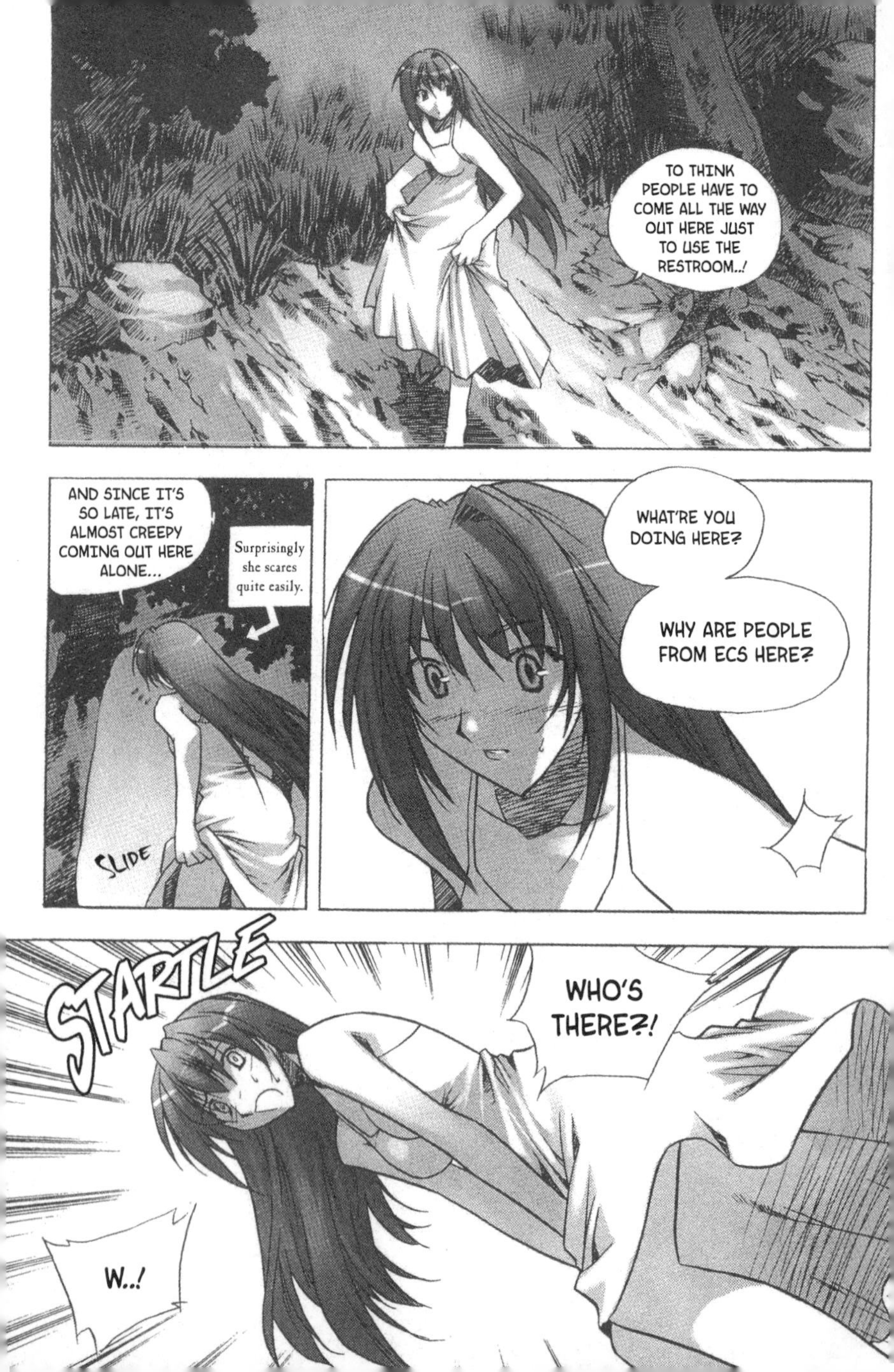

TO THINK PEOPLE HAVE TO COME ALL THE WAY OUT HERE JUST TO USE THE RESTROOM..!
AND SINCE IT'S SO LATE, IT'S ALMOST CREEPY COMING OUT HERE ALONE...
Surprisingly she scares quite easily.
SLIDE
WHAT'RE YOU DOING HERE?
WHY ARE PEOPLE FROM ECS HERE?
STARTLE
WHO'S THERE?!
W..!

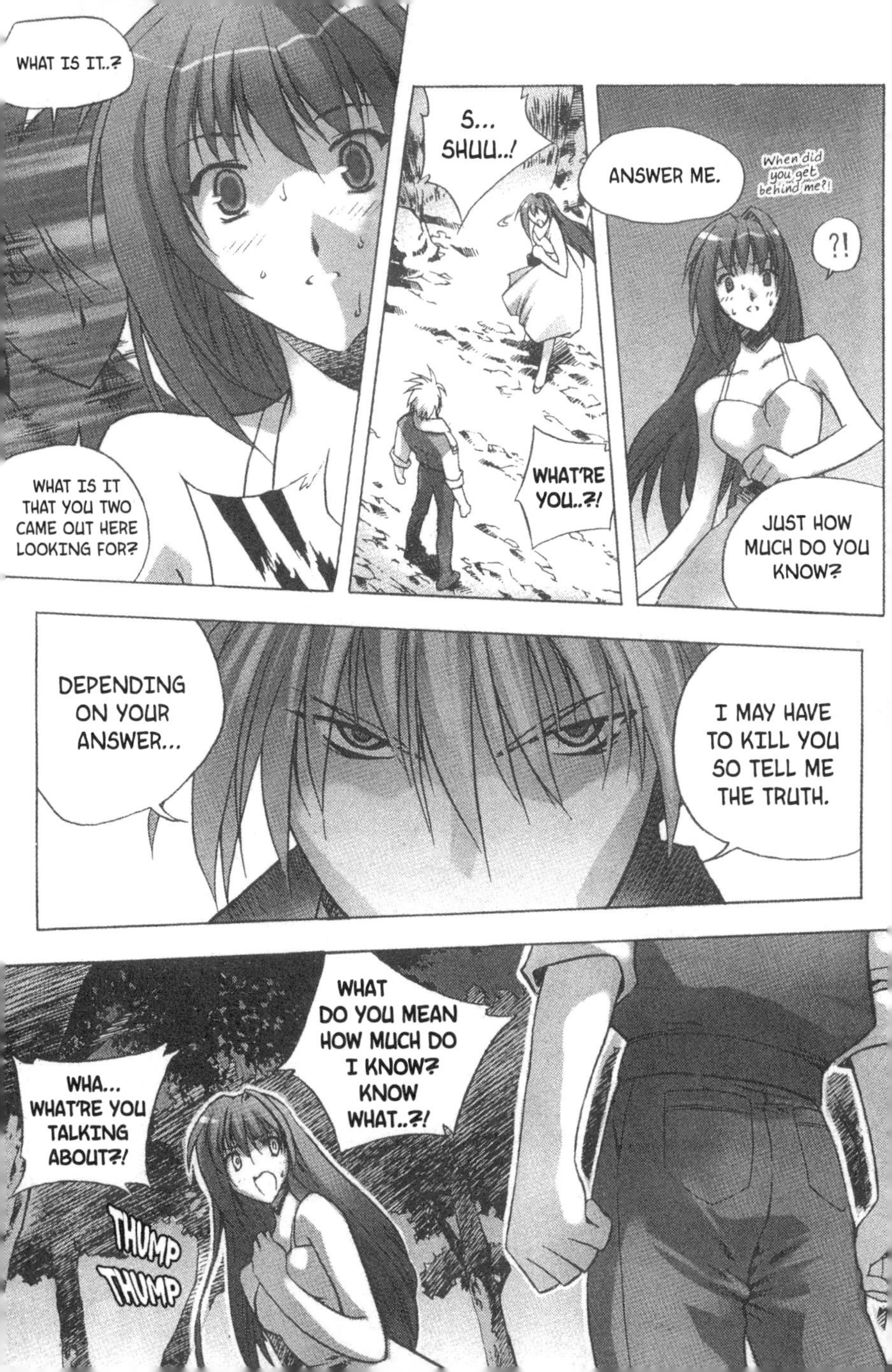
WHAT IS IT..?
WHAT IS IT THAT YOU TWO CAME OUT HERE LOOKING FOR?
S... SHUU..!
WHAT'RE YOU..?!
ANSWER ME.
When did you get behind me?!
?!
JUST HOW MUCH DO YOU KNOW?
DEPENDING ON YOUR ANSWER...
I MAY HAVE TO KILL YOU SO TELL ME THE TRUTH.
WHA... WHAT'RE YOU TALKING ABOUT?!
WHAT DO YOU MEAN HOW MUCH DO I KNOW? KNOW WHAT..?!
THUMP THUMP

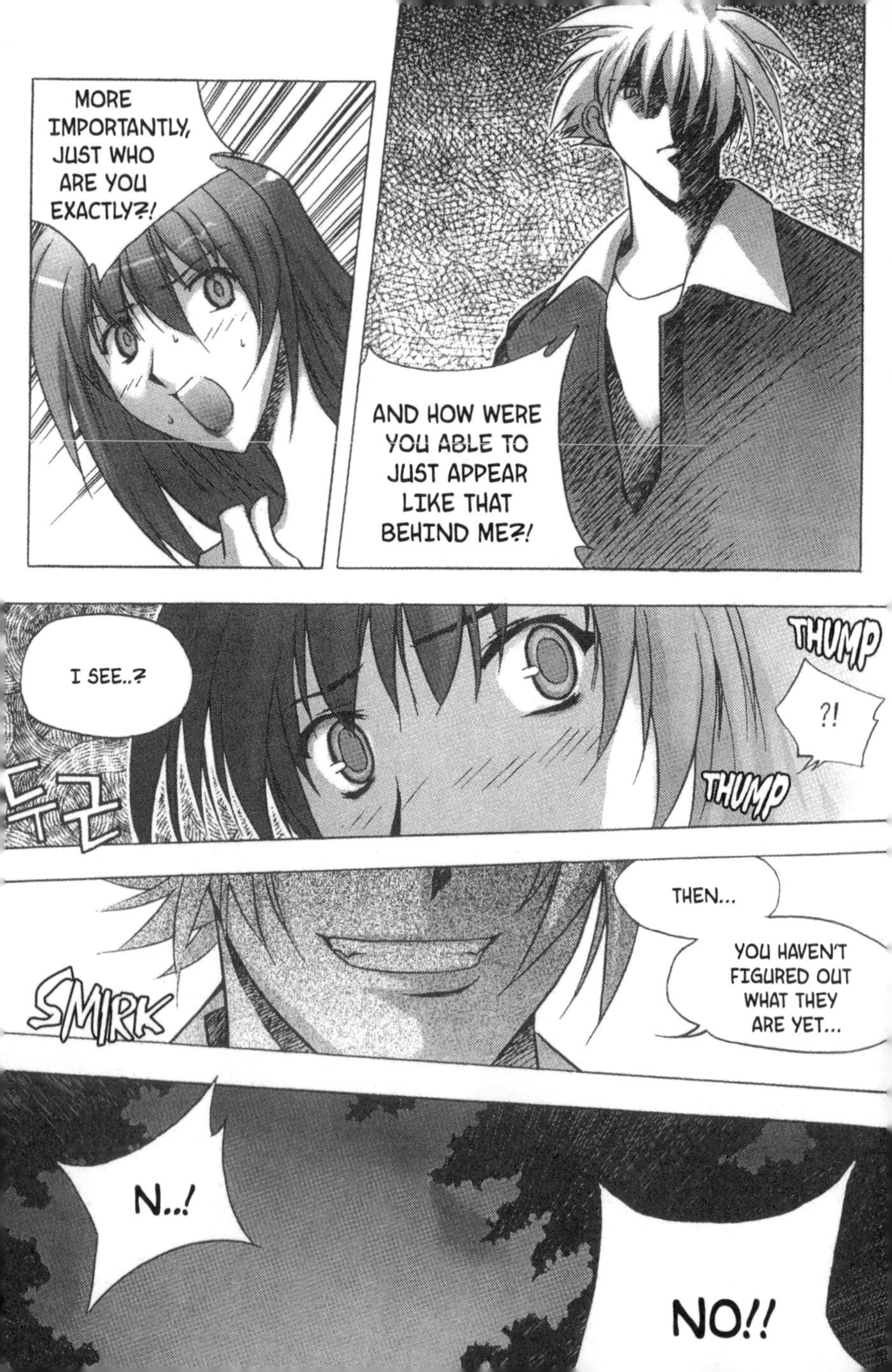
MORE IMPORTANTLY, JUST WHO ARE YOU EXACTLY?!
AND HOW WERE YOU ABLE TO JUST APPEAR LIKE THAT BEHIND ME?!
I SEE..?
THUMP
?!
THUMP
SMIRK
THEN...
YOU HAVEN'T FIGURED OUT WHAT THEY ARE YET...
N..!
NO!!

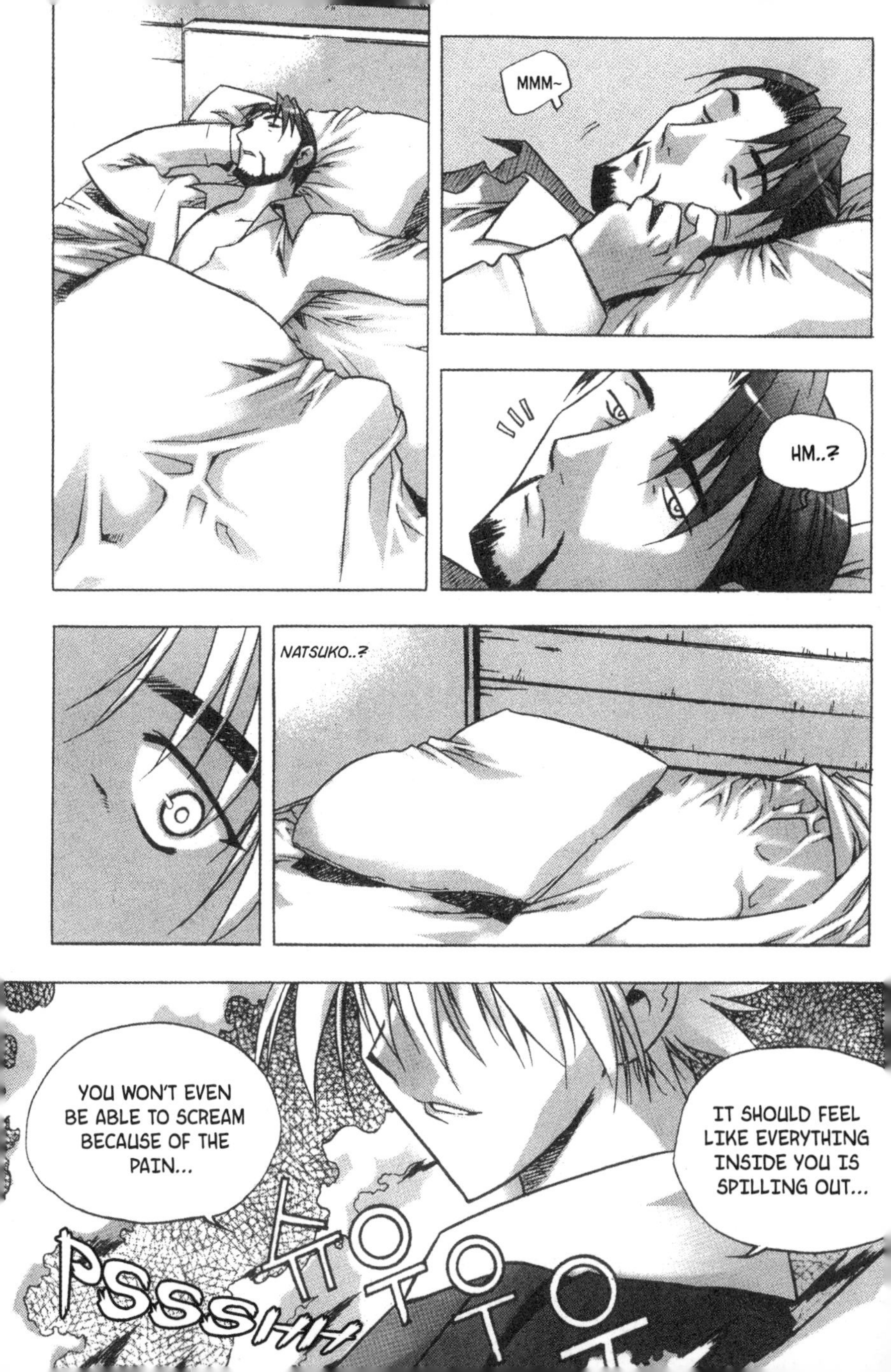
MMM~
HM..?
NATSUKO..?
YOU WON'T EVEN BE ABLE TO SCREAM BECAUSE OF THE PAIN...
IT SHOULD FEEL LIKE EVERYTHING INSIDE YOU IS SPILLING OUT...
PSSSHH

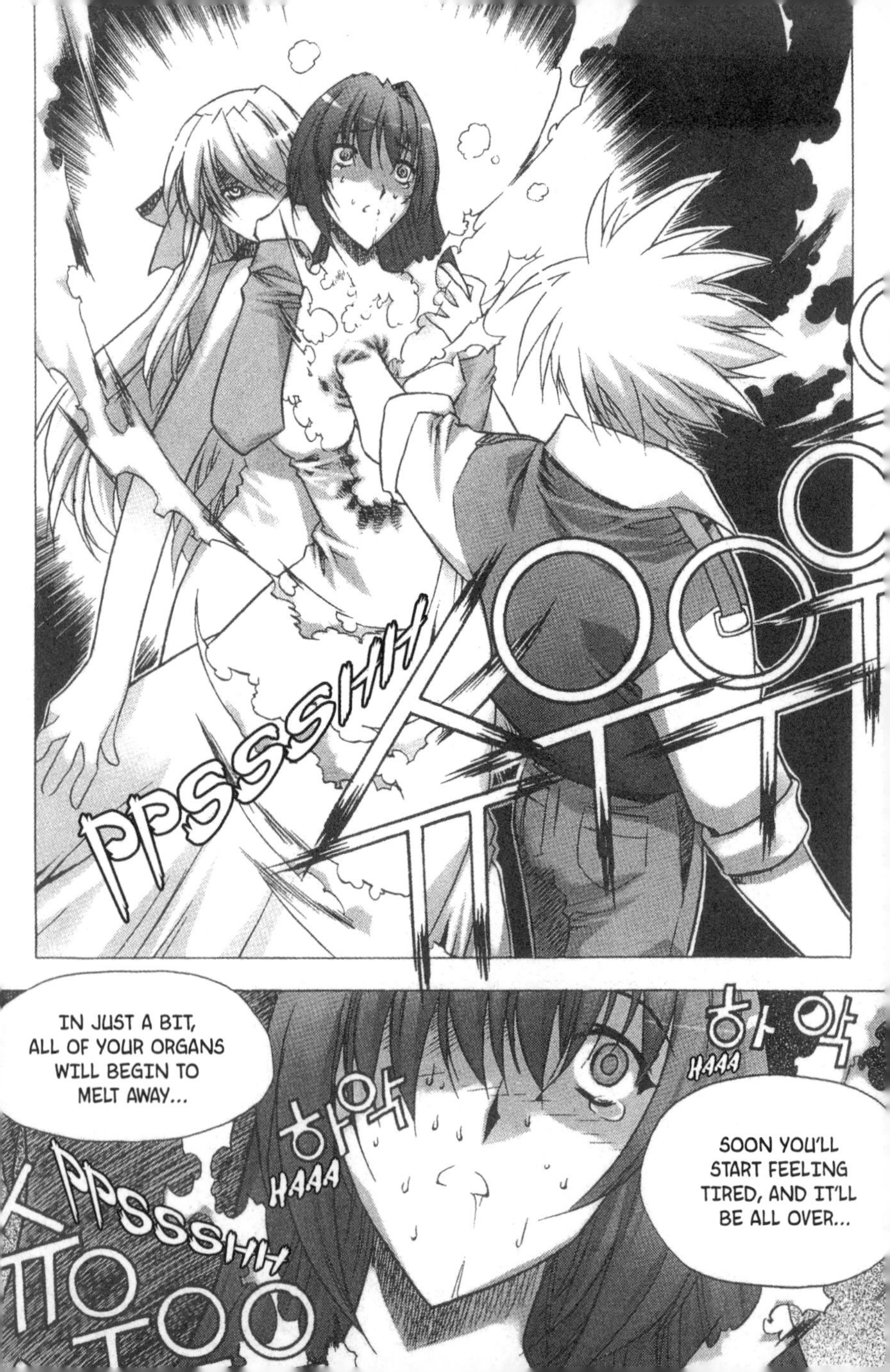
PPSSSSHH
IN JUST A BIT, ALL OF YOUR ORGANS WILL BEGIN TO MELT AWAY...
하악
HAAA
하악
HAAA
PPSSSSHH
SOON YOU'LL START FEELING TIRED, AND IT'LL BE ALL OVER...

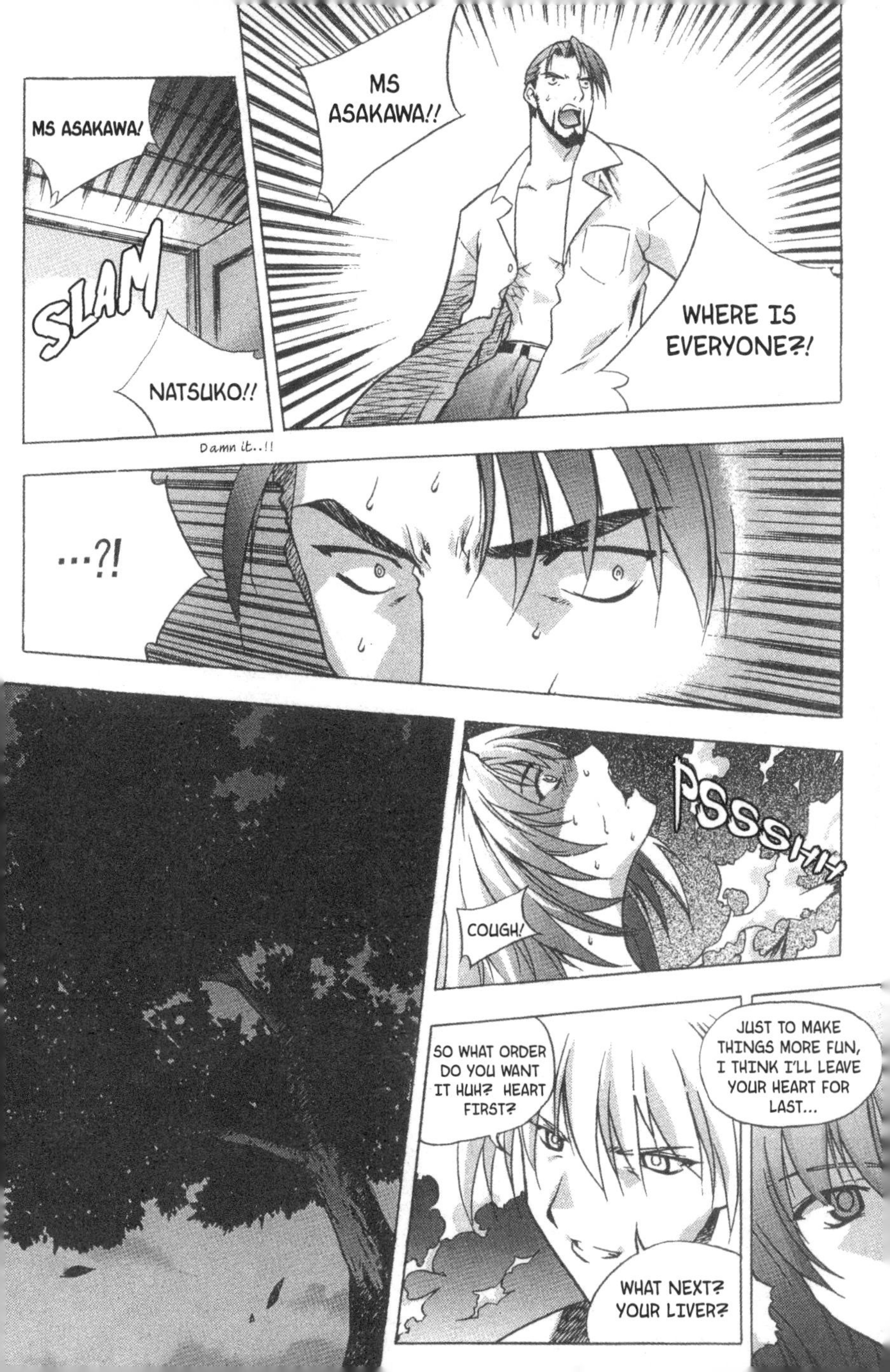
MS ASAKAWA!
SLAM
NATSUKO!!
MS ASAKAWA!!
WHERE IS EVERYONE?!
Damn it..!!
...?!
PSSSHHH
COUGH!
SO WHAT ORDER DO YOU WANT IT HUH? HEART FIRST?
WHAT NEXT? YOUR LIVER?
JUST TO MAKE THINGS MORE FUN, I THINK I'LL LEAVE YOUR HEART FOR LAST...

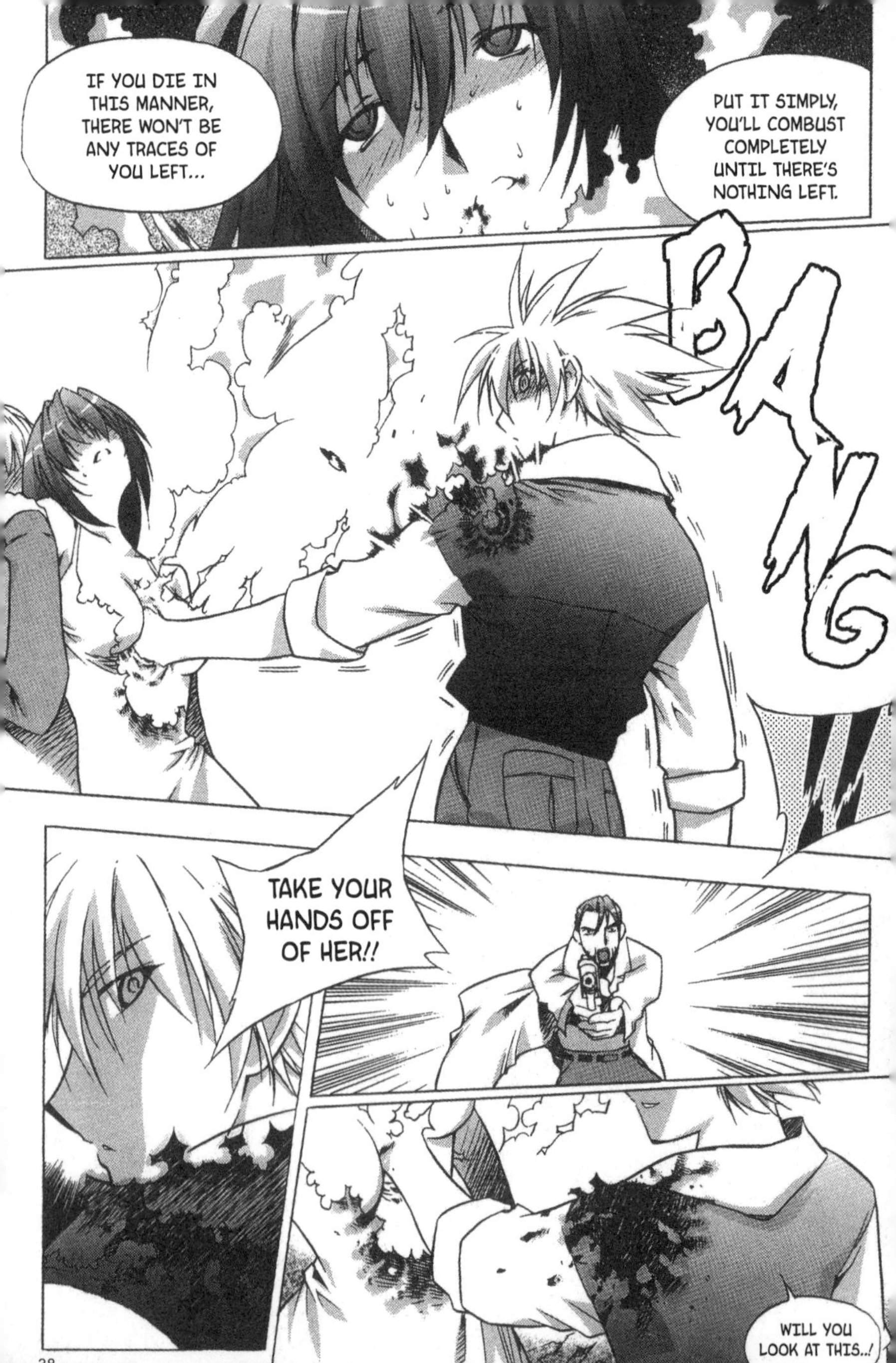
IF YOU DIE IN THIS MANNER, THERE WON'T BE ANY TRACES OF YOU LEFT...
PUT IT SIMPLY, YOU'LL COMBUST COMPLETELY UNTIL THERE'S NOTHING LEFT.
BANG
TAKE YOUR HANDS OFF OF HER!!
WILL YOU LOOK AT THIS..!

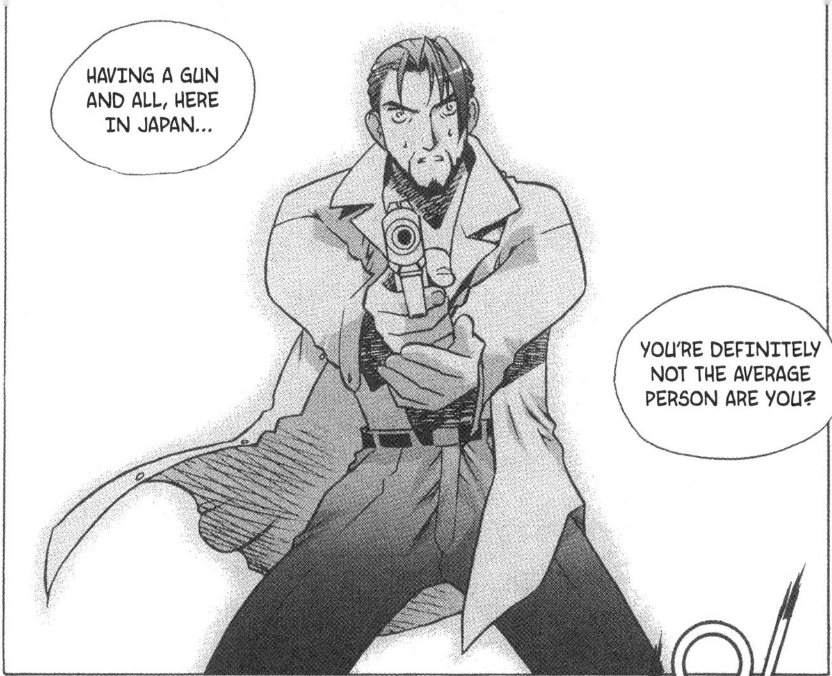
HAVING A GUN AND ALL, HERE IN JAPAN...
YOU'RE DEFINITELY NOT THE AVERAGE PERSON ARE YOU?

Note : Guns are not illegal in Japan, however, the stringent gun control makes it very difficult to own a gun in Japan.

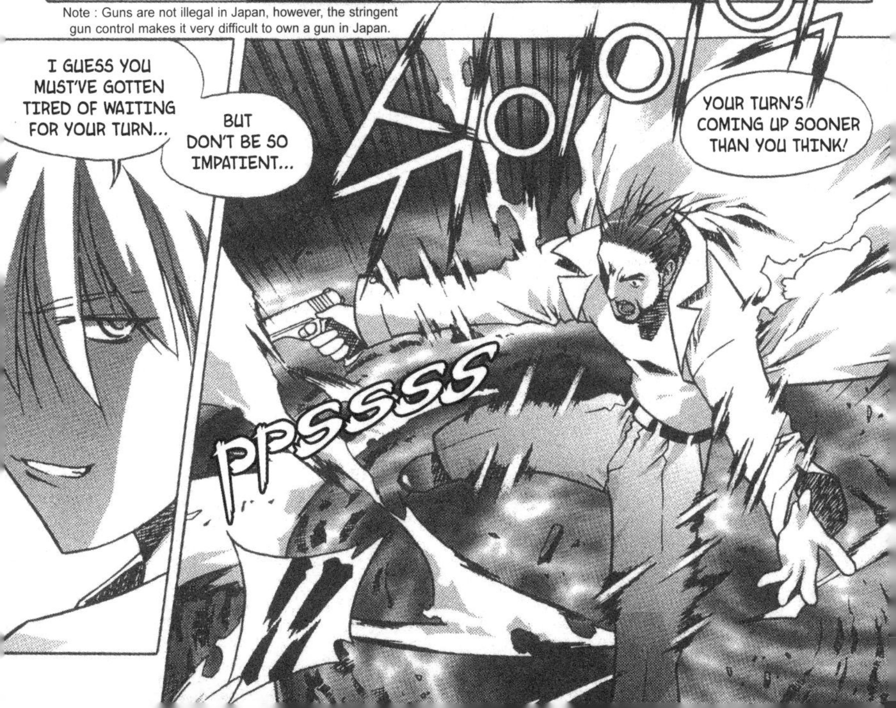
I GUESS YOU MUST'VE GOTTEN TIRED OF WAITING FOR YOUR TURN...
BUT DON'T BE SO IMPATIENT...
YOUR TURN'S COMING UP SOONER THAN YOU THINK!
PPSSSSS

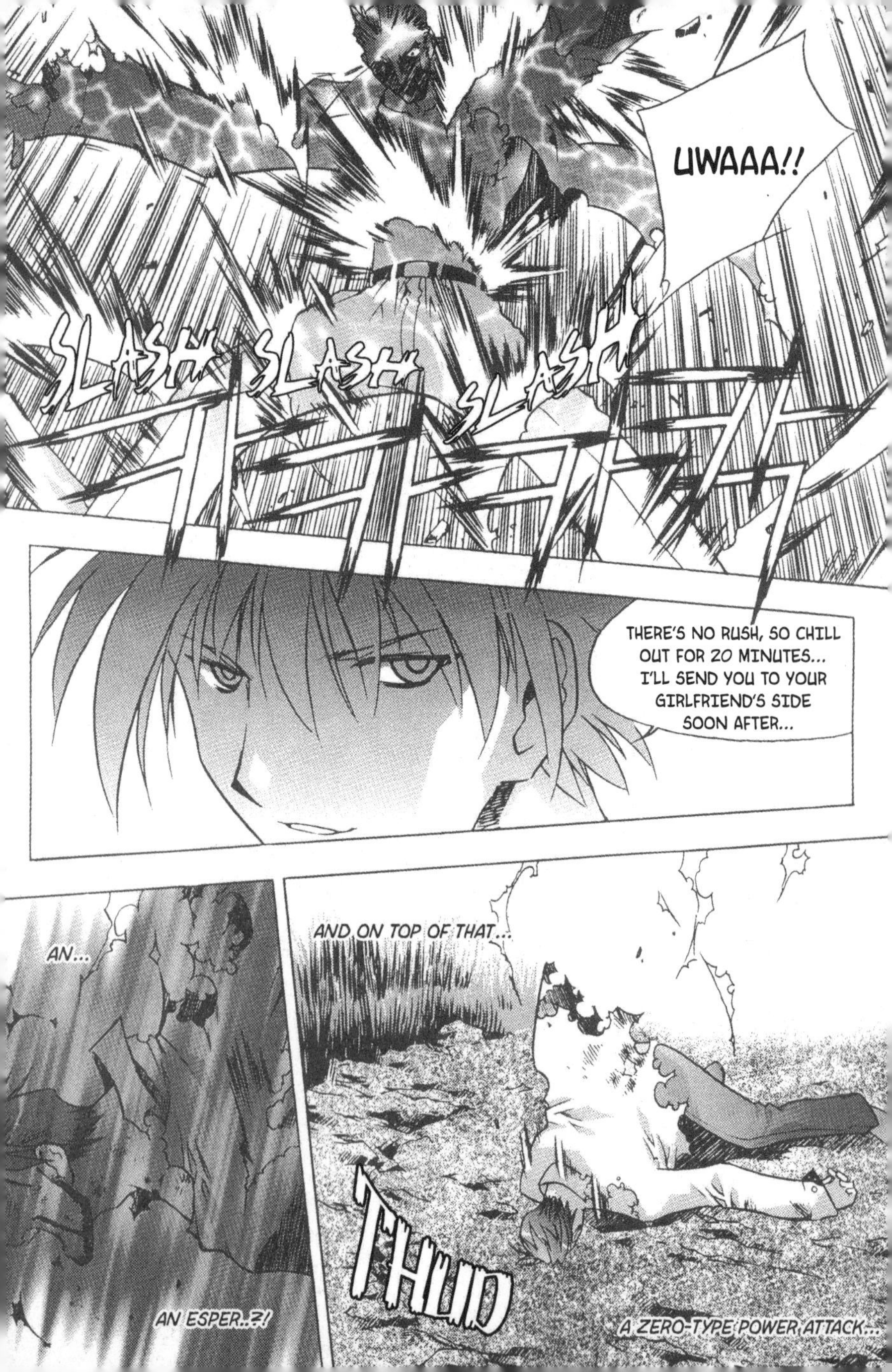
UWAAA!!
SLASH SLASH SLASH
THERE'S NO RUSH, SO CHILL OUT FOR 20 MINUTES... I'LL SEND YOU TO YOUR GIRLFRIEND'S SIDE SOON AFTER...
AN...
AN ESPER..?!
AND ON TOP OF THAT...
THUD
A ZERO-TYPE POWER ATTACK...

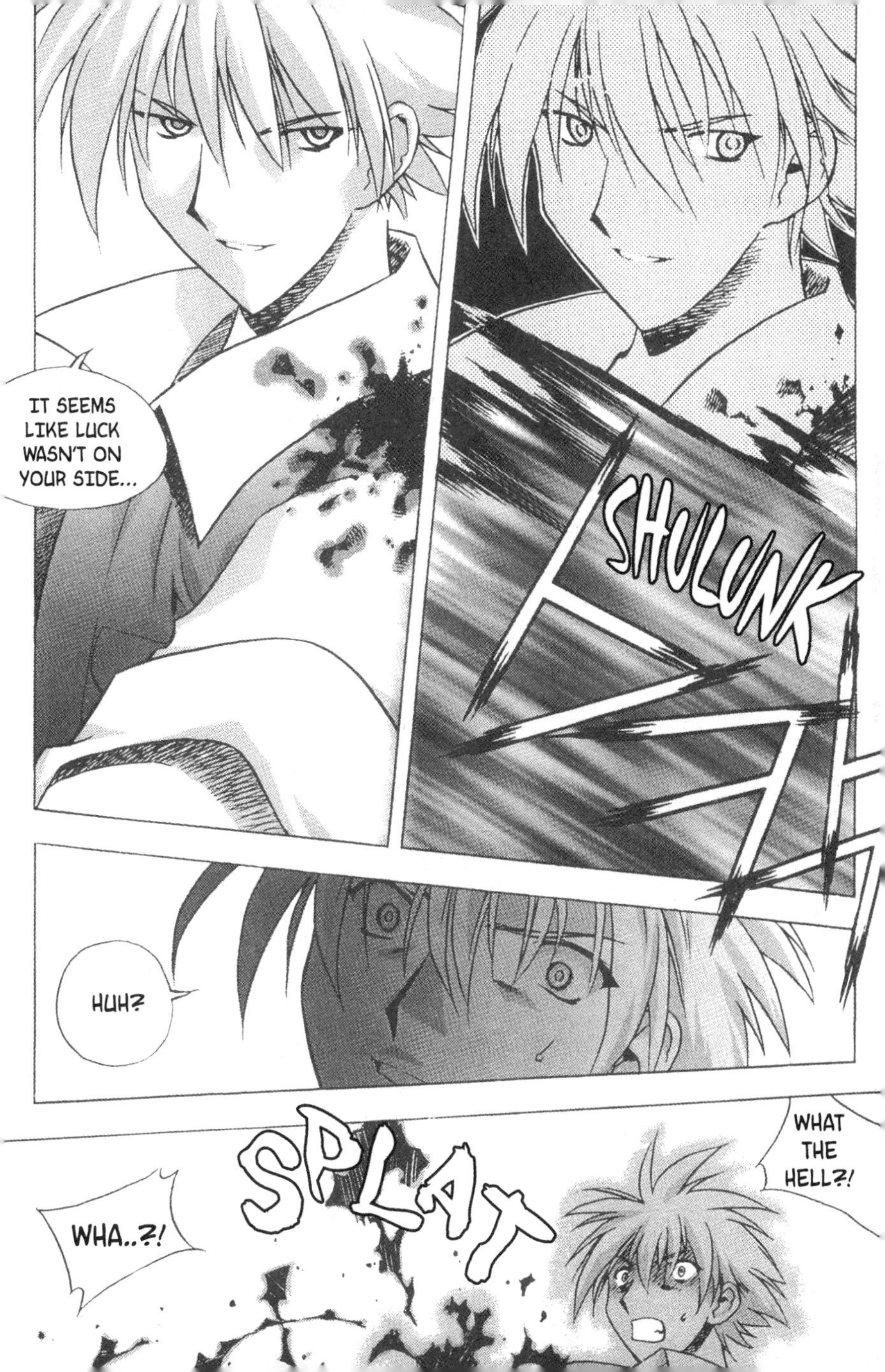
IT SEEMS LIKE LUCK WASN'T ON YOUR SIDE...
SHULUNK
HUH?
WHA..?!
SPLAT
WHAT THE HELL?!

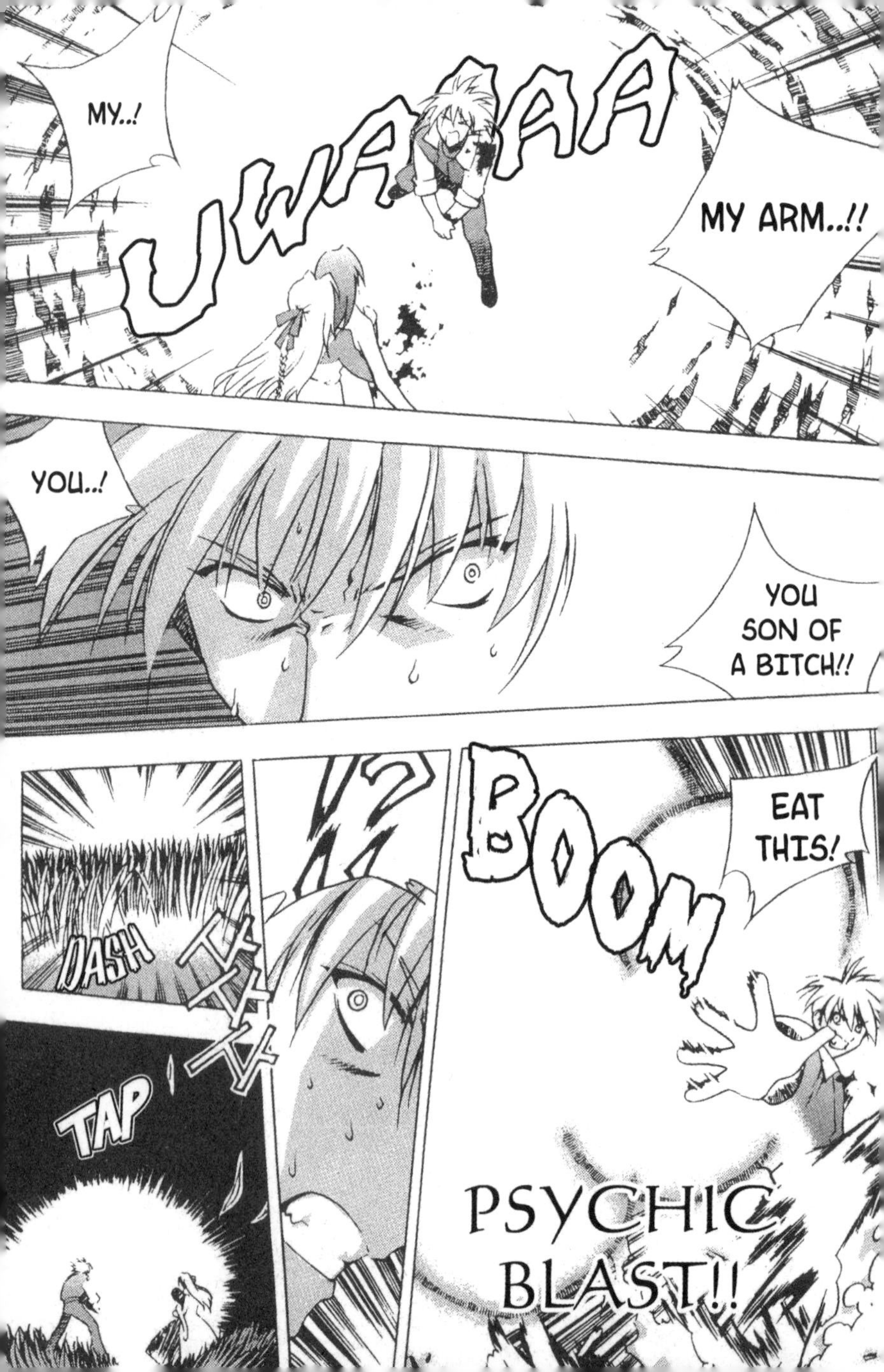
MY..!
UWAAAA
MY ARM..!!
YOU..!
YOU SON OF A BITCH!!
DASH
TAP
!?
BOOM
EAT THIS!
PSYCHIC BLAST!!

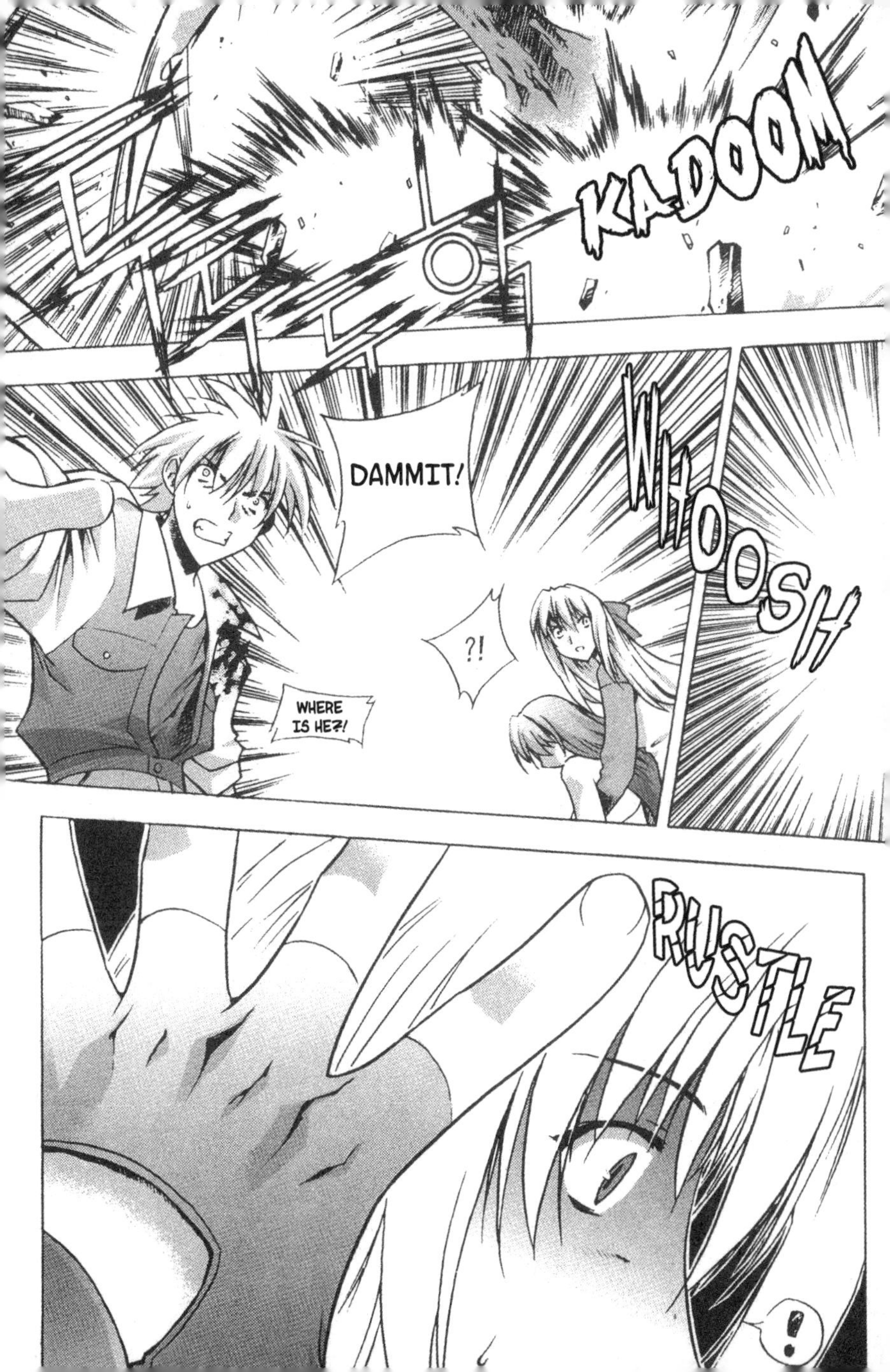
KADOOM
DAMMIT!
WHERE IS HE?!
?!
WHOOSH
RUSTLE
!

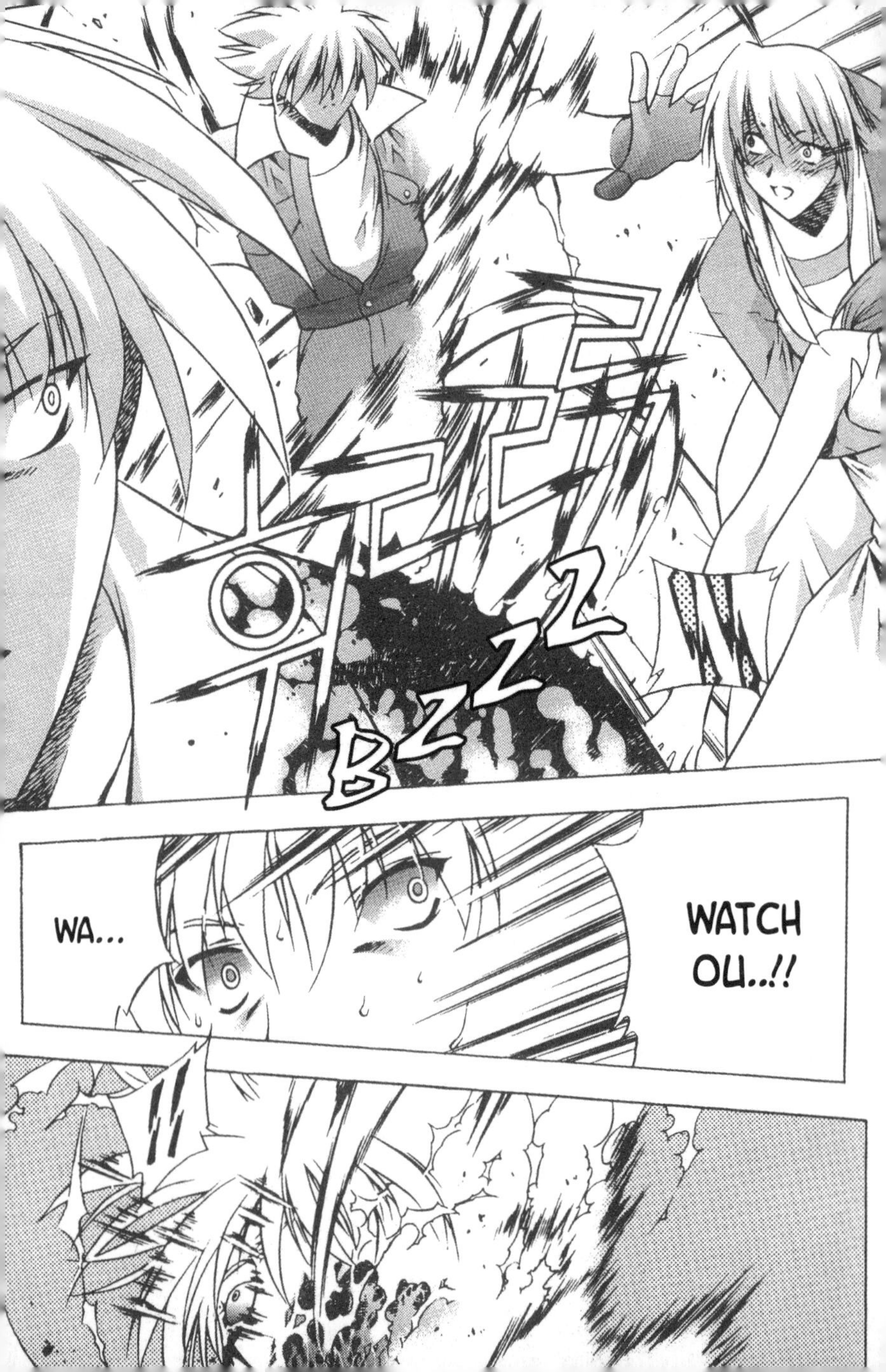
BZZZZ
WA...
WATCH OU..!!

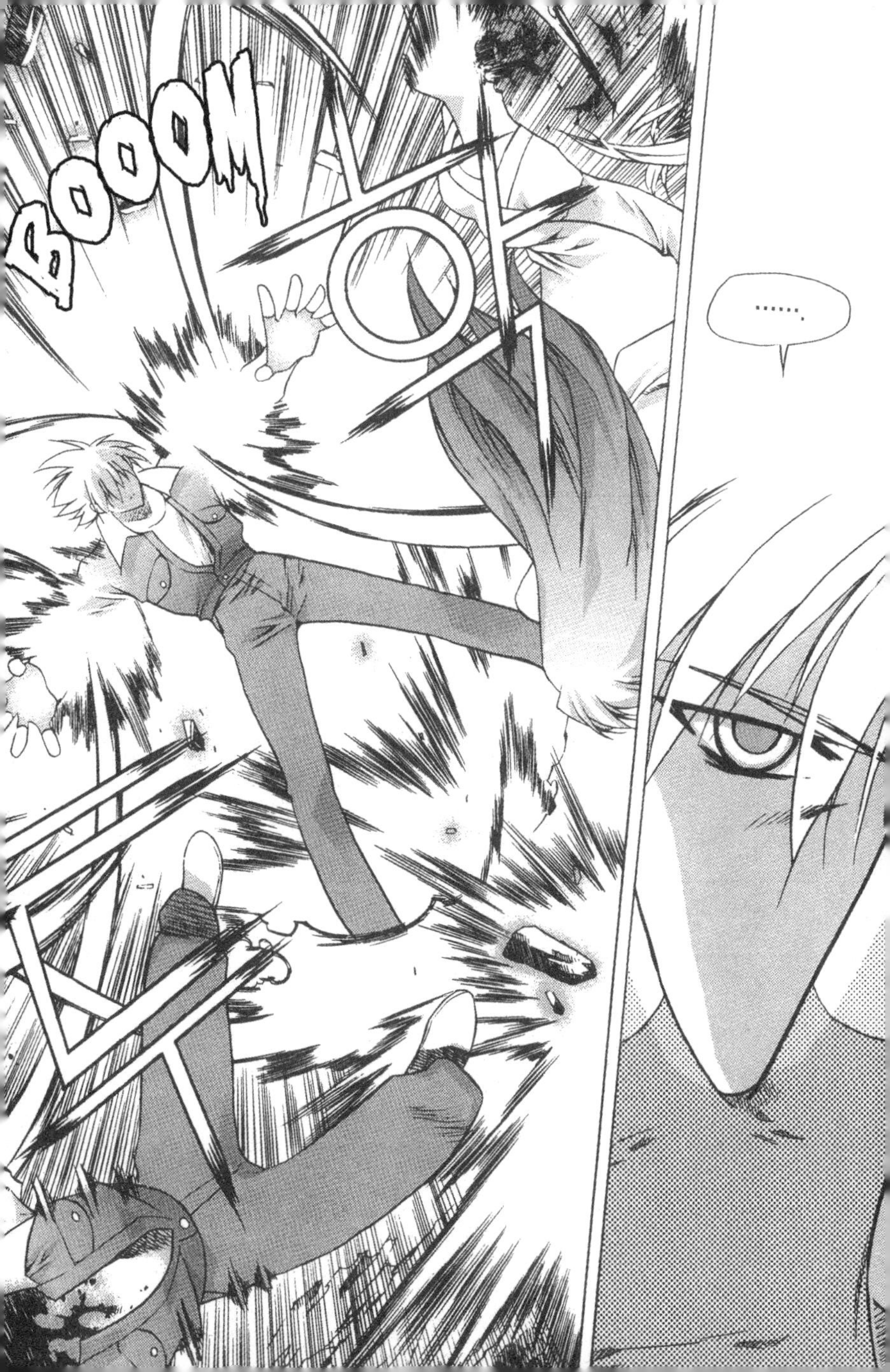
BOOOOM
......

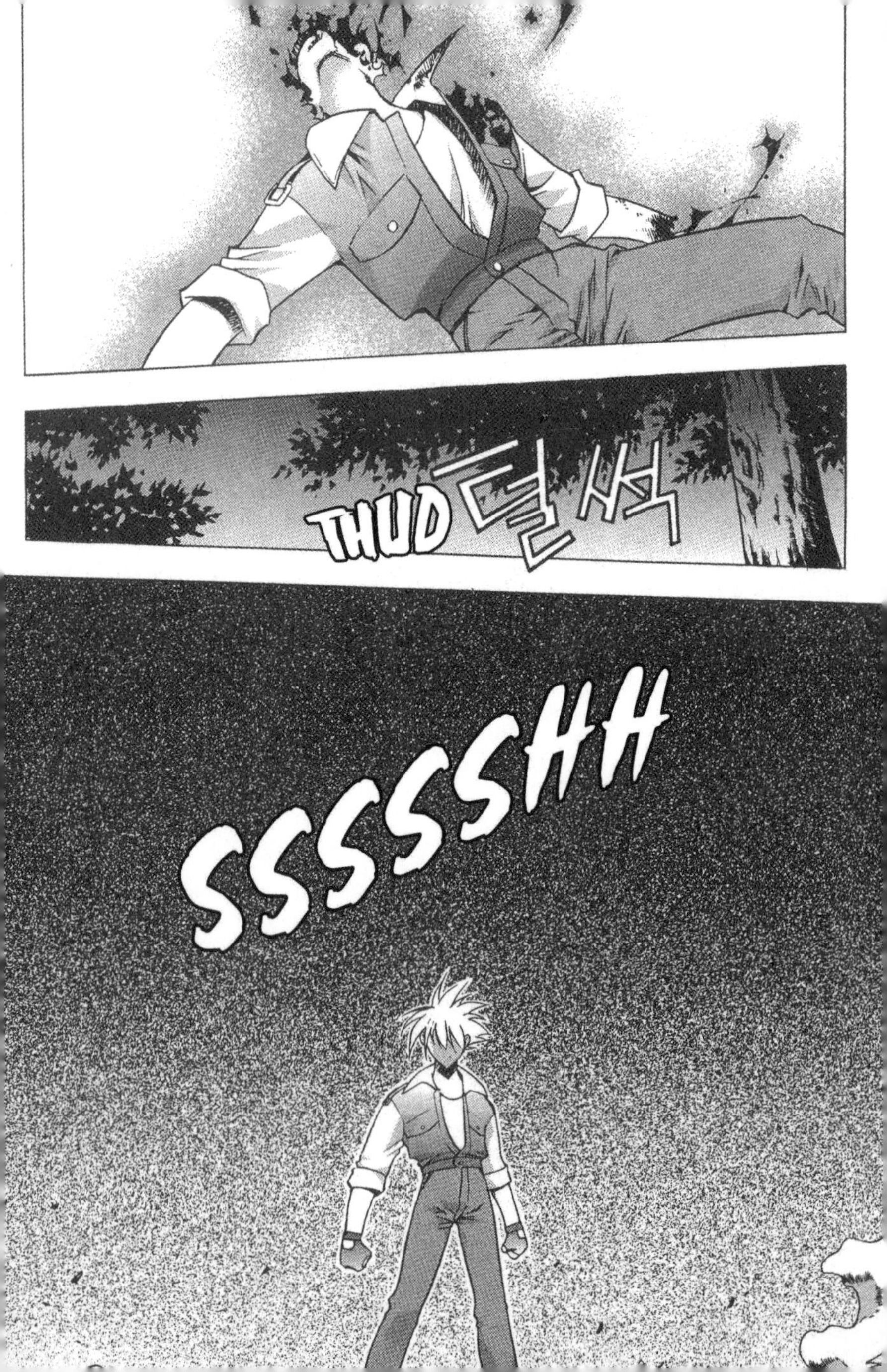
THUD
털썩
SSSSSHH

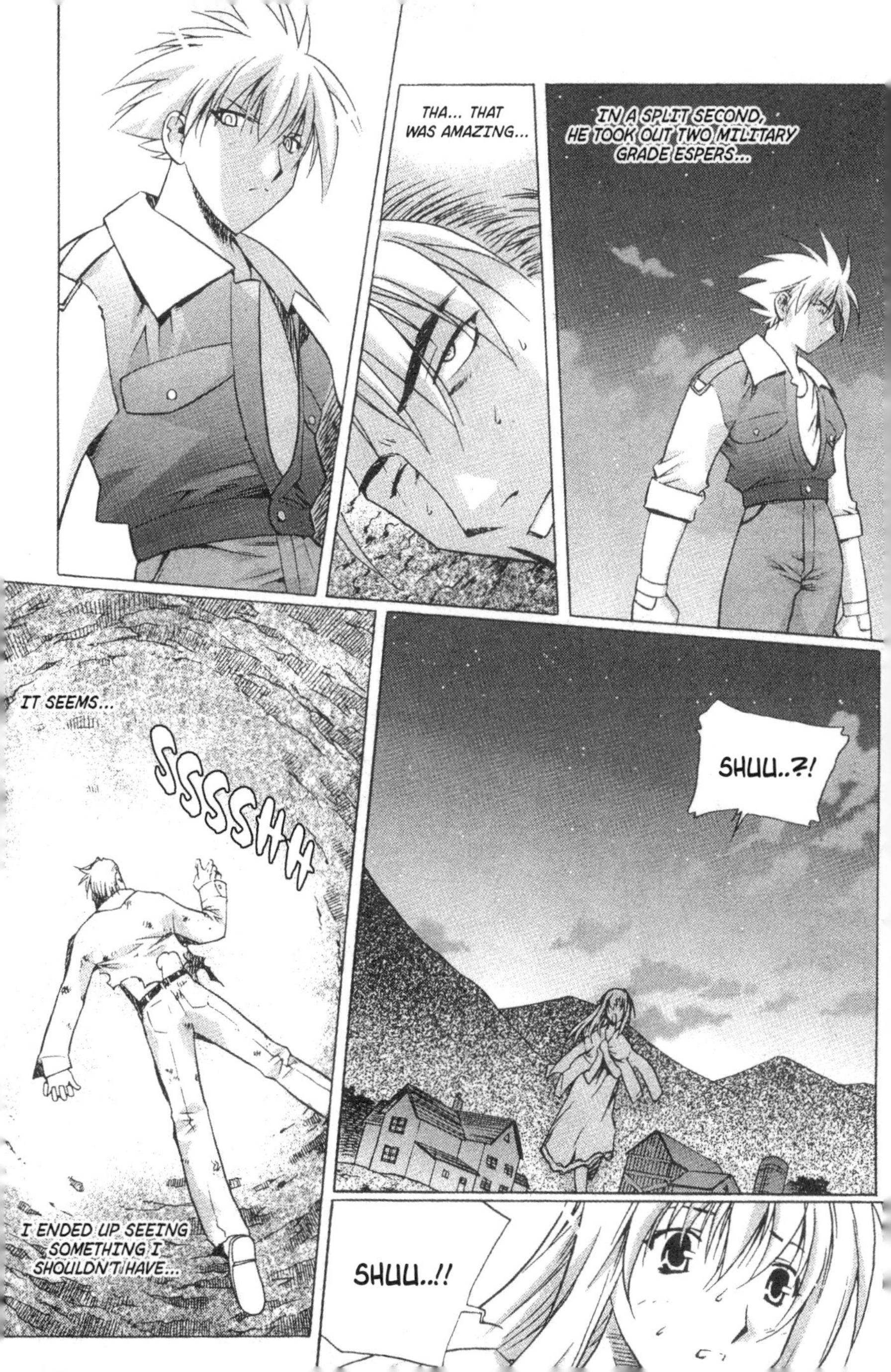
THA... THAT WAS AMAZING...
IN A SPLIT SECOND, HE TOOK OUT TWO MILITARY GRADE ESPERS...
IT SEEMS...
SSSSHH
I ENDED UP SEEING SOMETHING I SHOULDN'T HAVE...
SHUU..?!
SHUU..!!

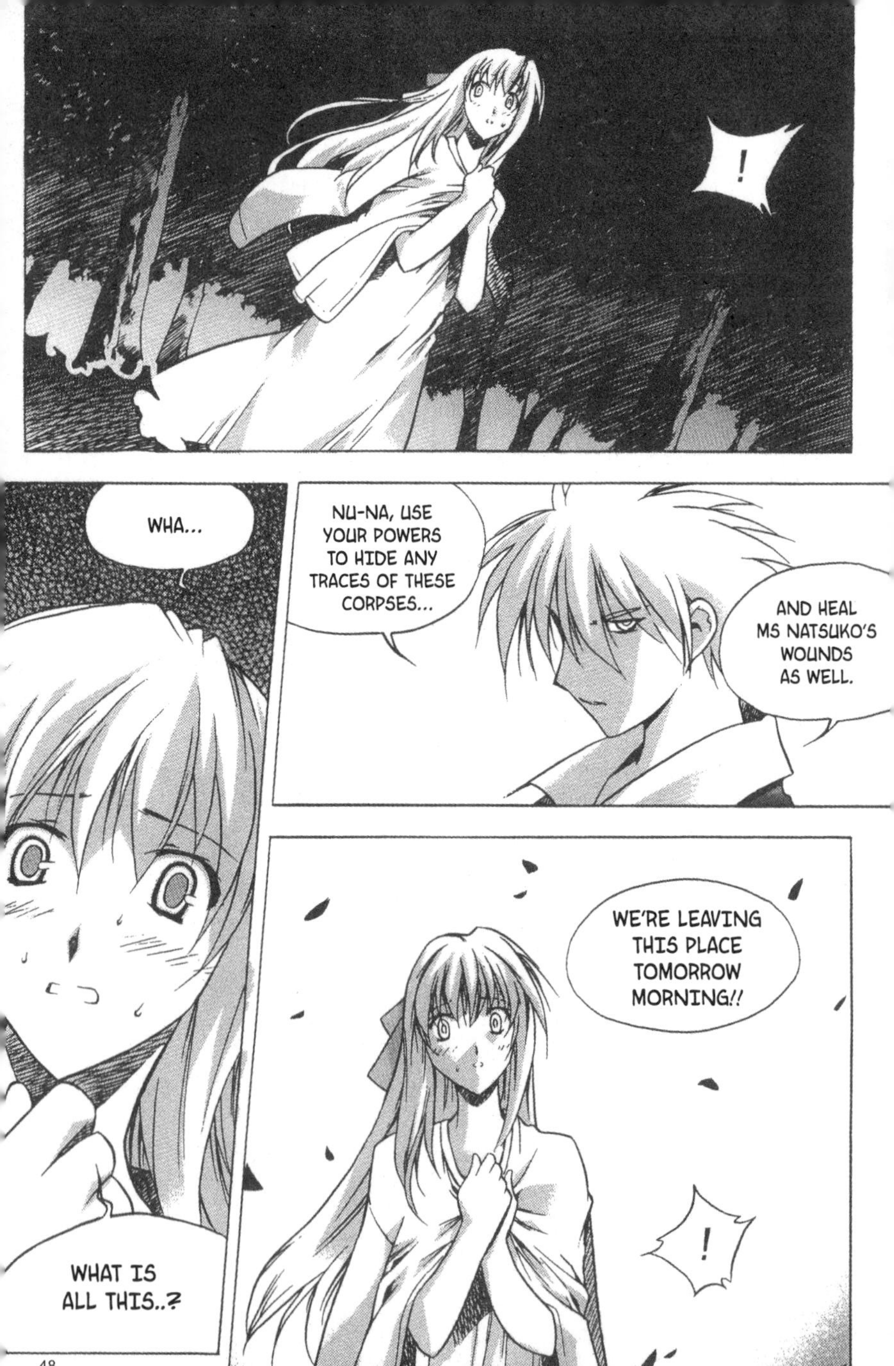
!
WHA...
WHAT IS ALL THIS..?
NU-NA, USE YOUR POWERS TO HIDE ANY TRACES OF THESE CORPSES...
AND HEAL MS NATSUKO'S WOUNDS AS WELL.
WE'RE LEAVING THIS PLACE TOMORROW MORNING!!
!

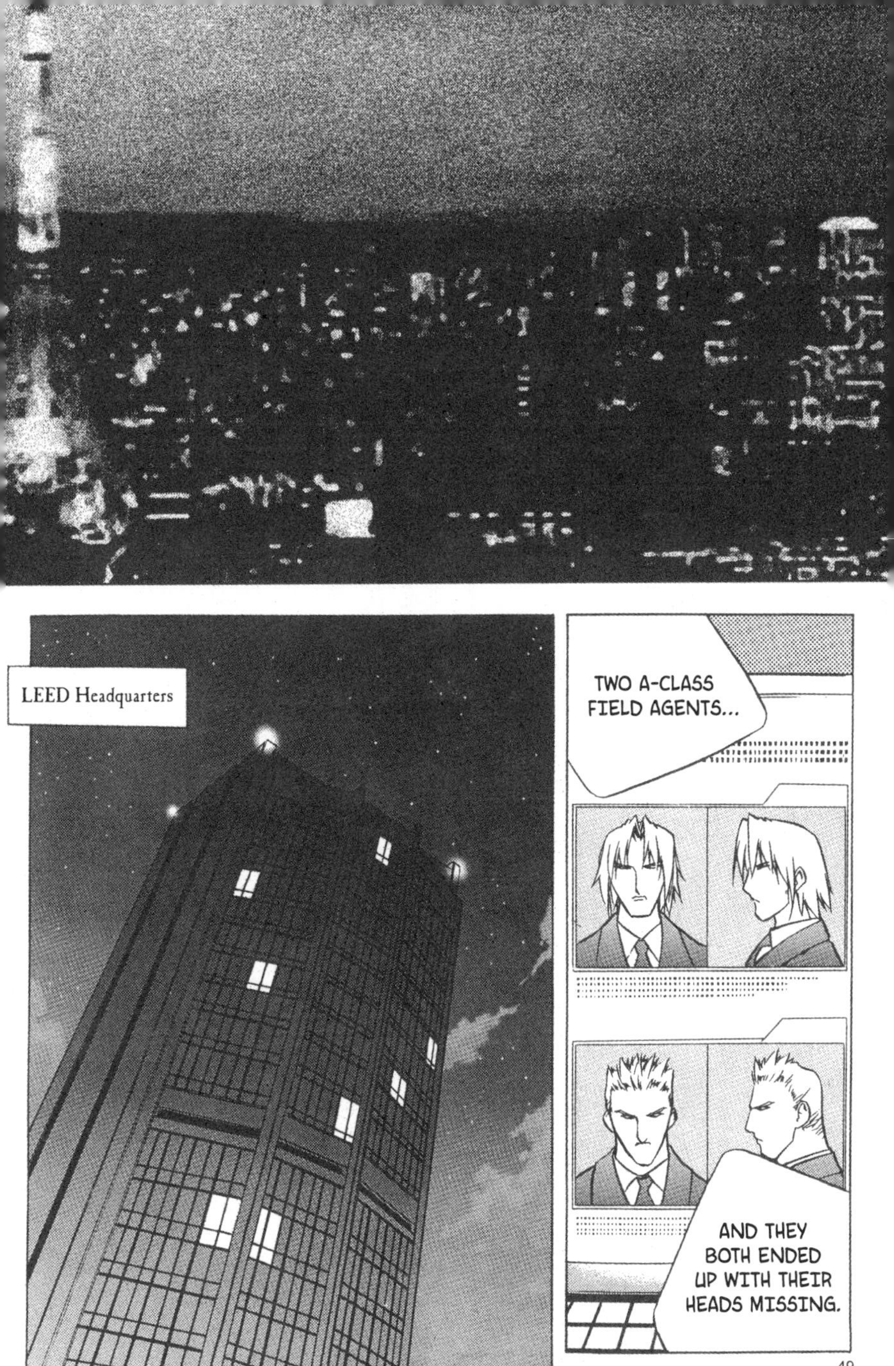
LEED Headquarters
TWO A-CLASS FIELD AGENTS...
AND THEY BOTH ENDED UP WITH THEIR HEADS MISSING.

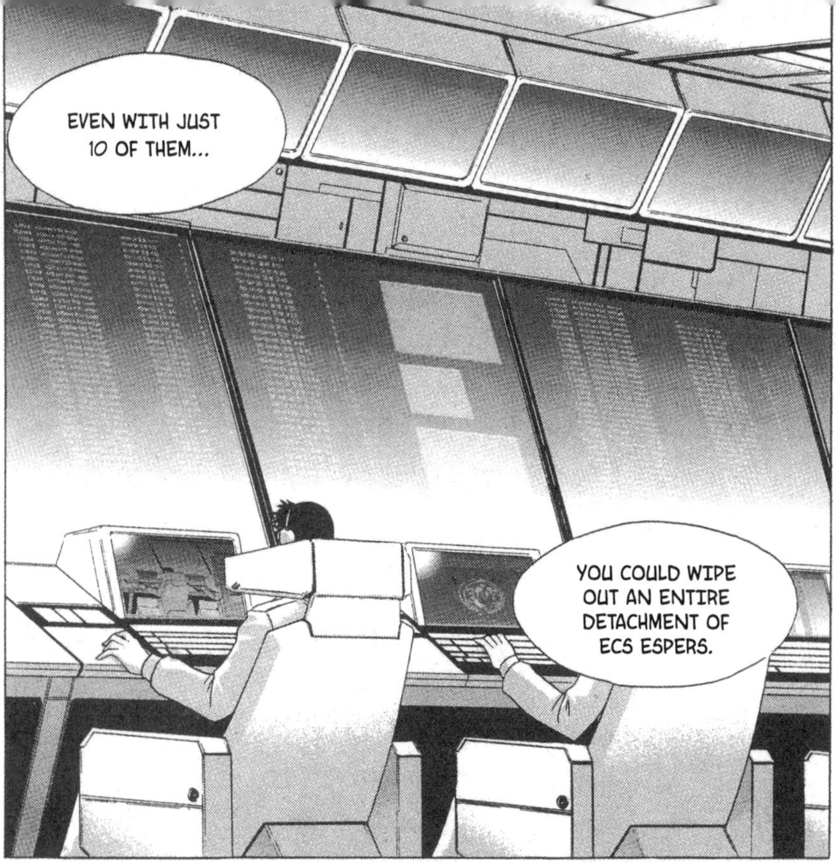
EVEN WITH JUST 10 OF THEM...
YOU COULD WIPE OUT AN ENTIRE DETACHMENT OF ECS ESPERS.

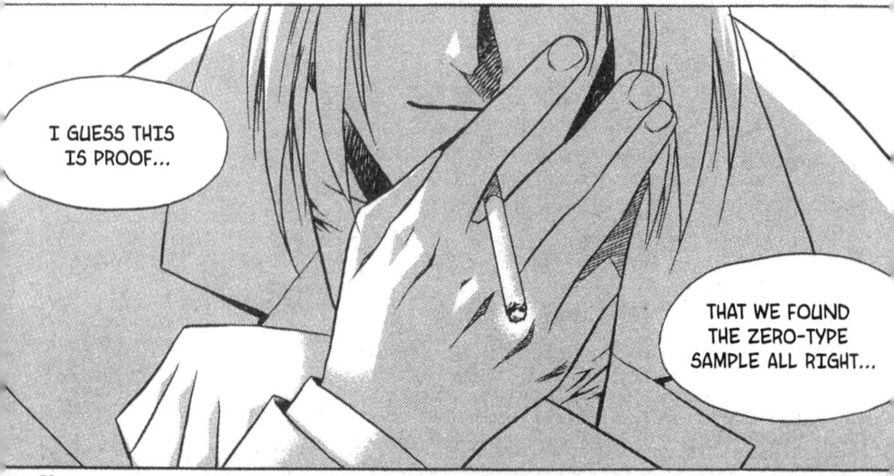
I GUESS THIS IS PROOF...
THAT WE FOUND THE ZERO-TYPE SAMPLE ALL RIGHT...

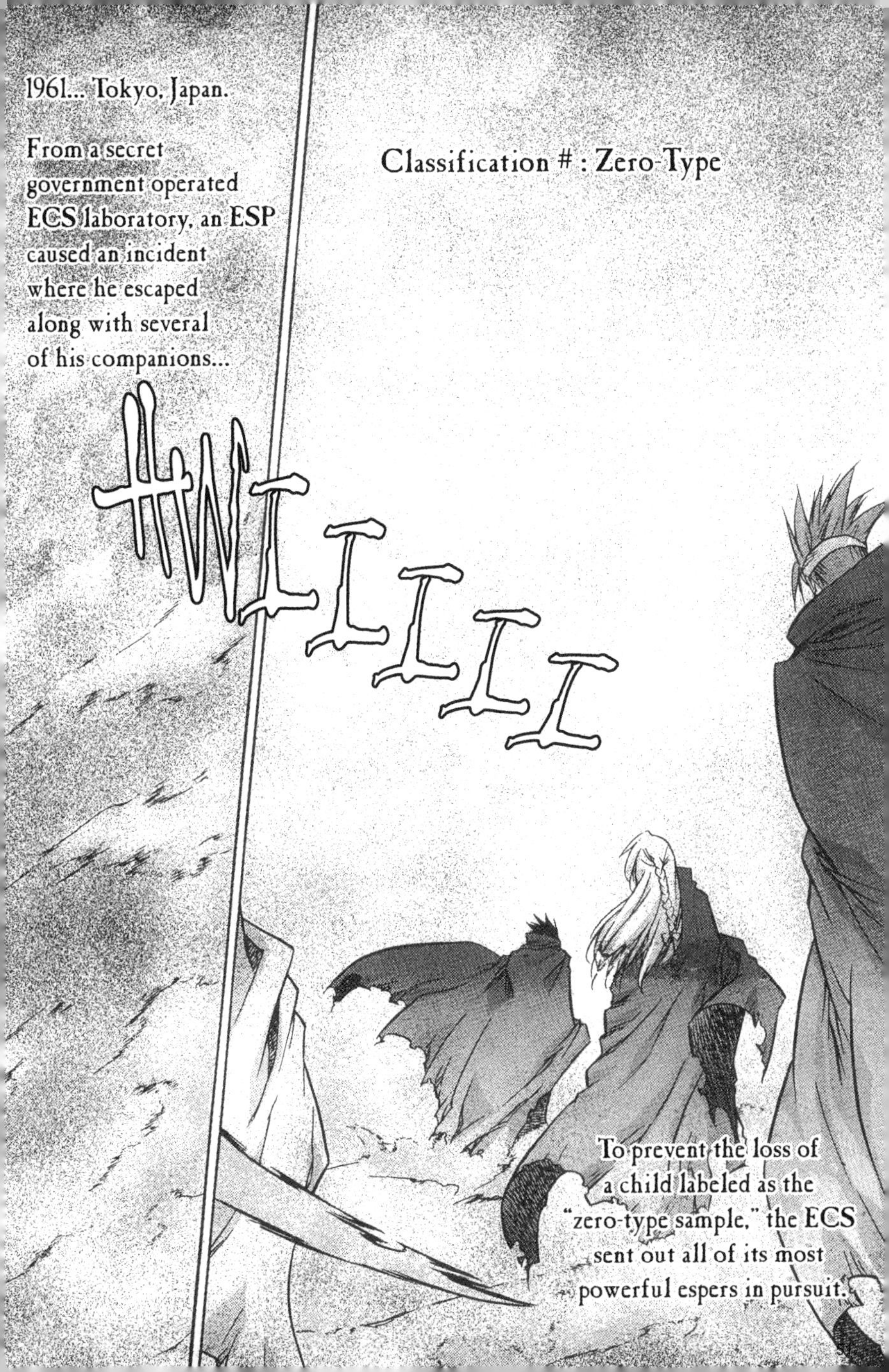
1961... Tokyo, Japan.
From a secret government operated ECS laboratory, an ESP caused an incident where he escaped along with several of his companions...
Classification # : Zero-Type
HWIIIII
To prevent the loss of a child labeled as the "zero-type sample," the ECS sent out all of its most powerful espers in pursuit.

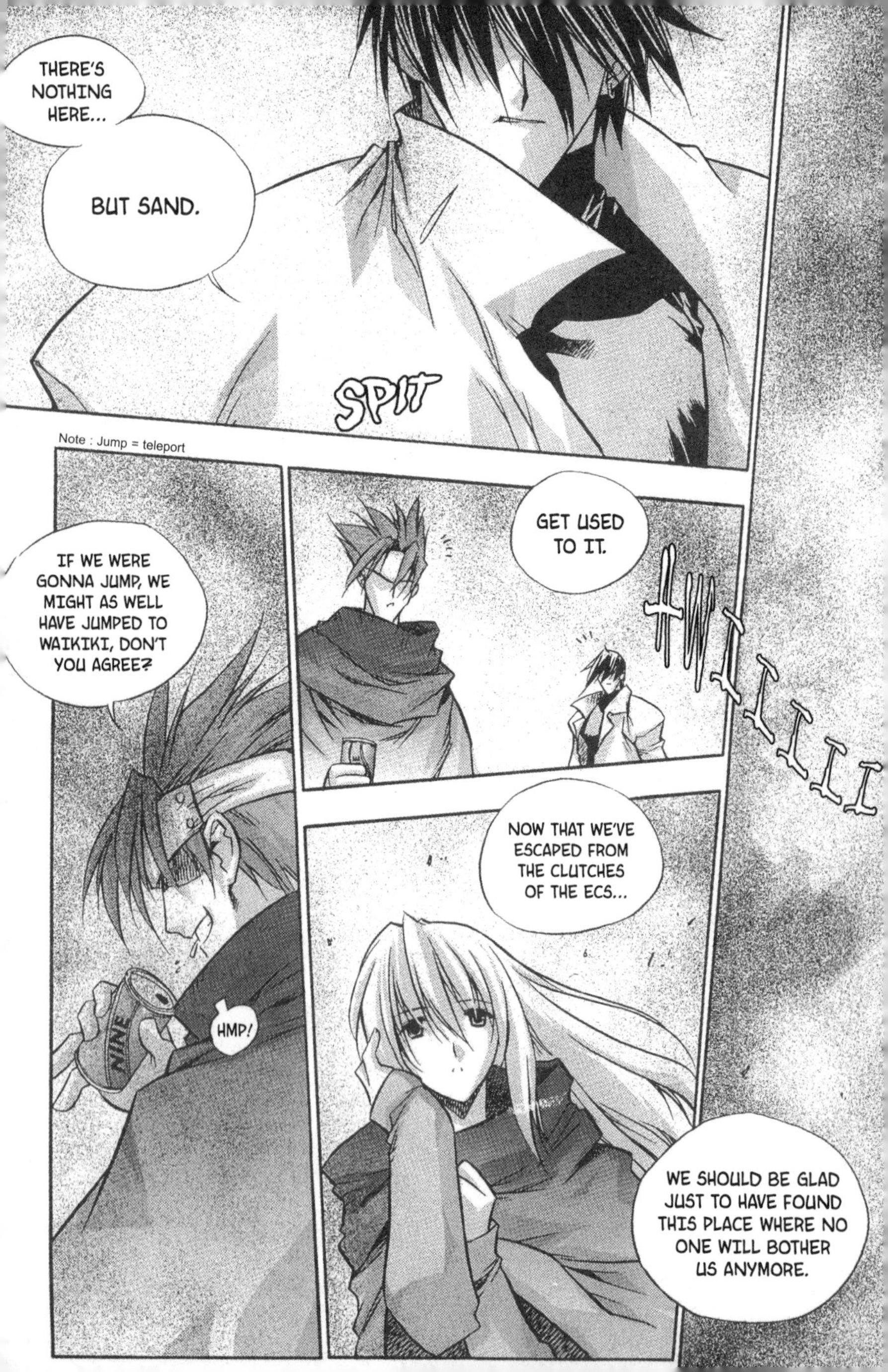
THERE'S NOTHING HERE...
BUT SAND.
SPIT
Note : Jump = teleport
IF WE WERE GONNA JUMP, WE MIGHT AS WELL HAVE JUMPED TO WAIKIKI, DON'T YOU AGREE?
NINE
HMP!
GET USED TO IT.
HWIIIIII
NOW THAT WE'VE ESCAPED FROM THE CLUTCHES OF THE ECS...
WE SHOULD BE GLAD JUST TO HAVE FOUND THIS PLACE WHERE NO ONE WILL BOTHER US ANYMORE.

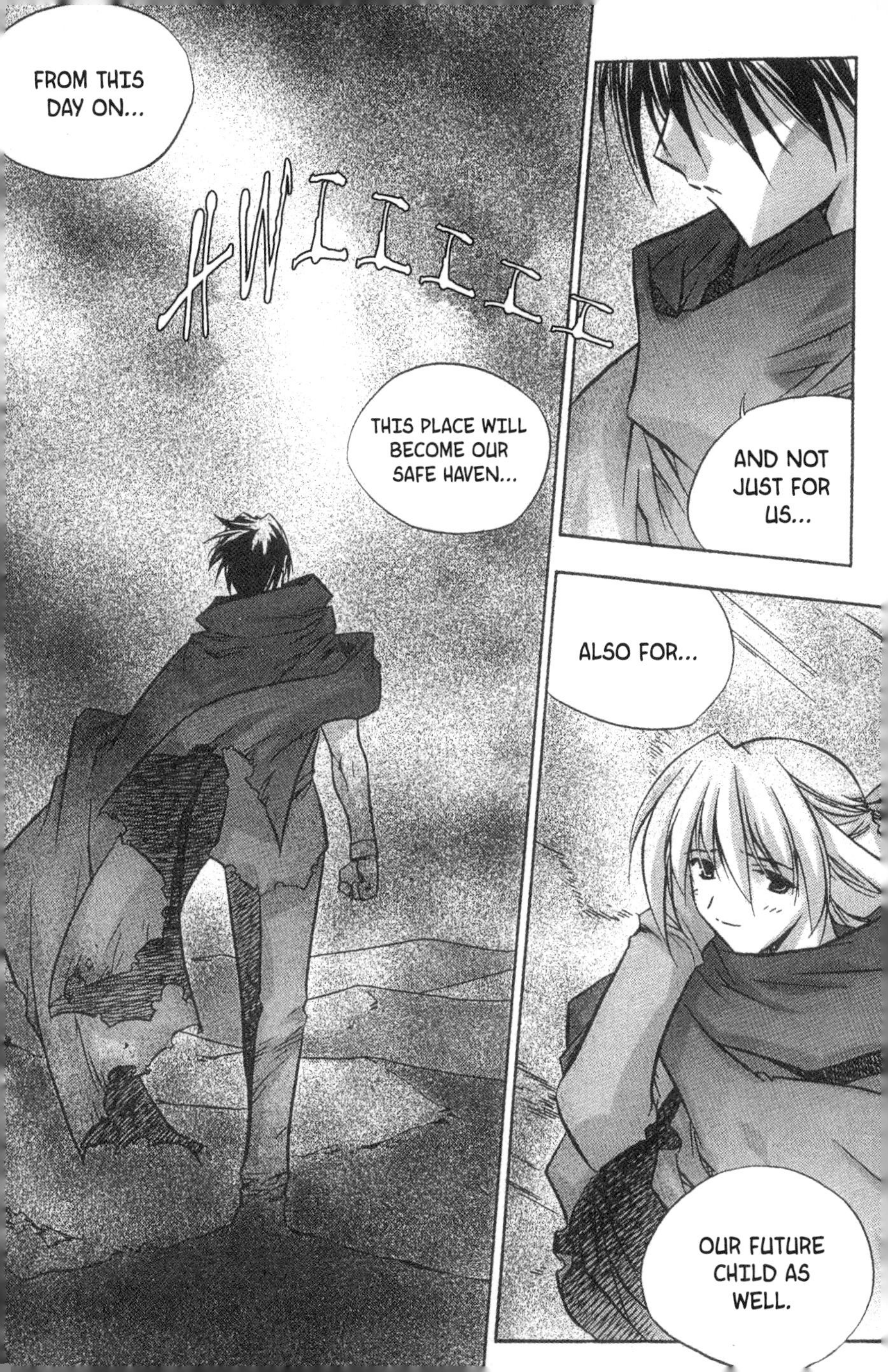
FROM THIS DAY ON...
AWIIIII
THIS PLACE WILL BECOME OUR SAFE HAVEN...
AND NOT JUST FOR US...
ALSO FOR...
OUR FUTURE CHILD AS WELL.

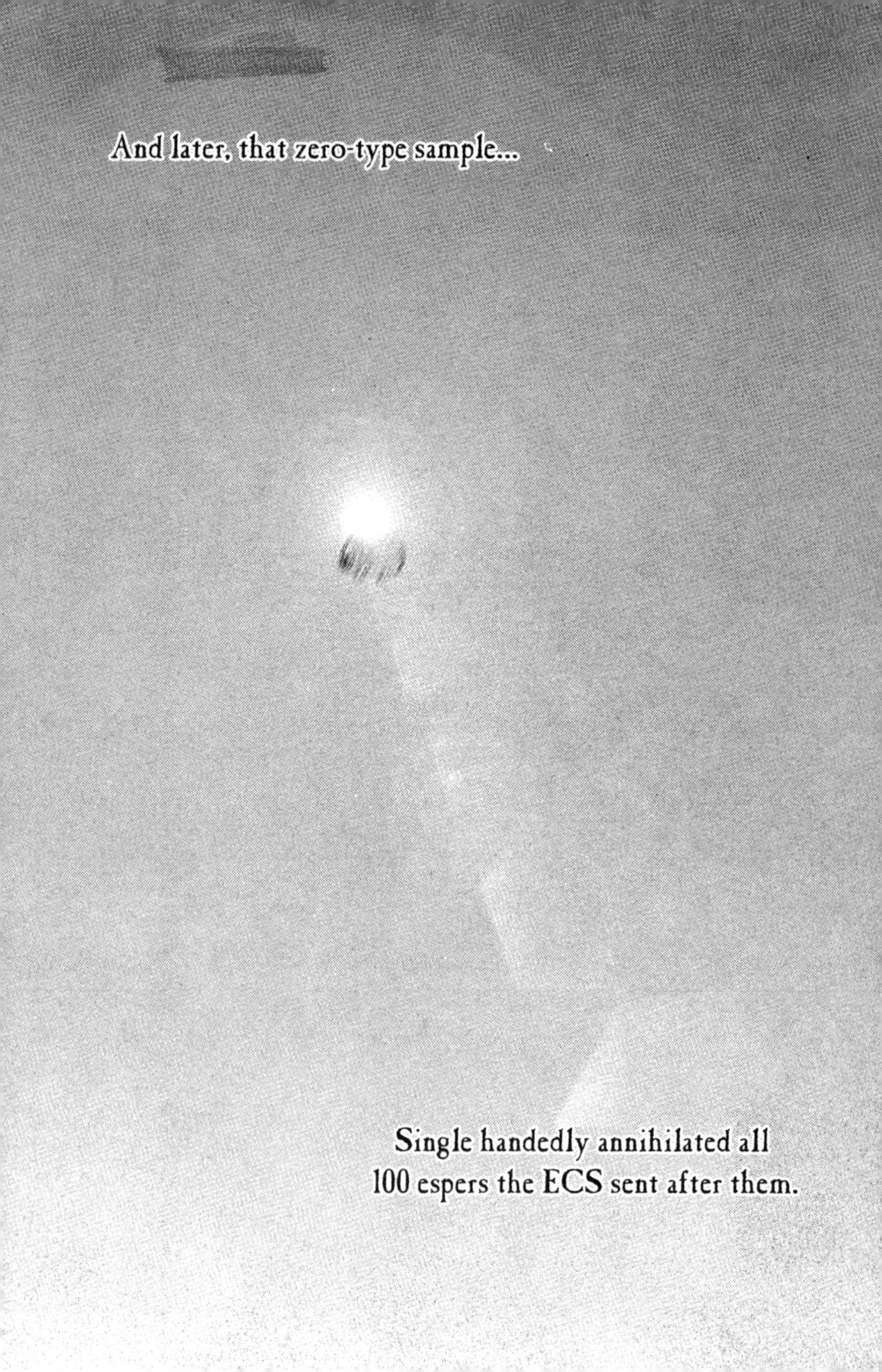
And later, that zero-type sample...
Single handedly annihilated all
100 espers the ECS sent after them.

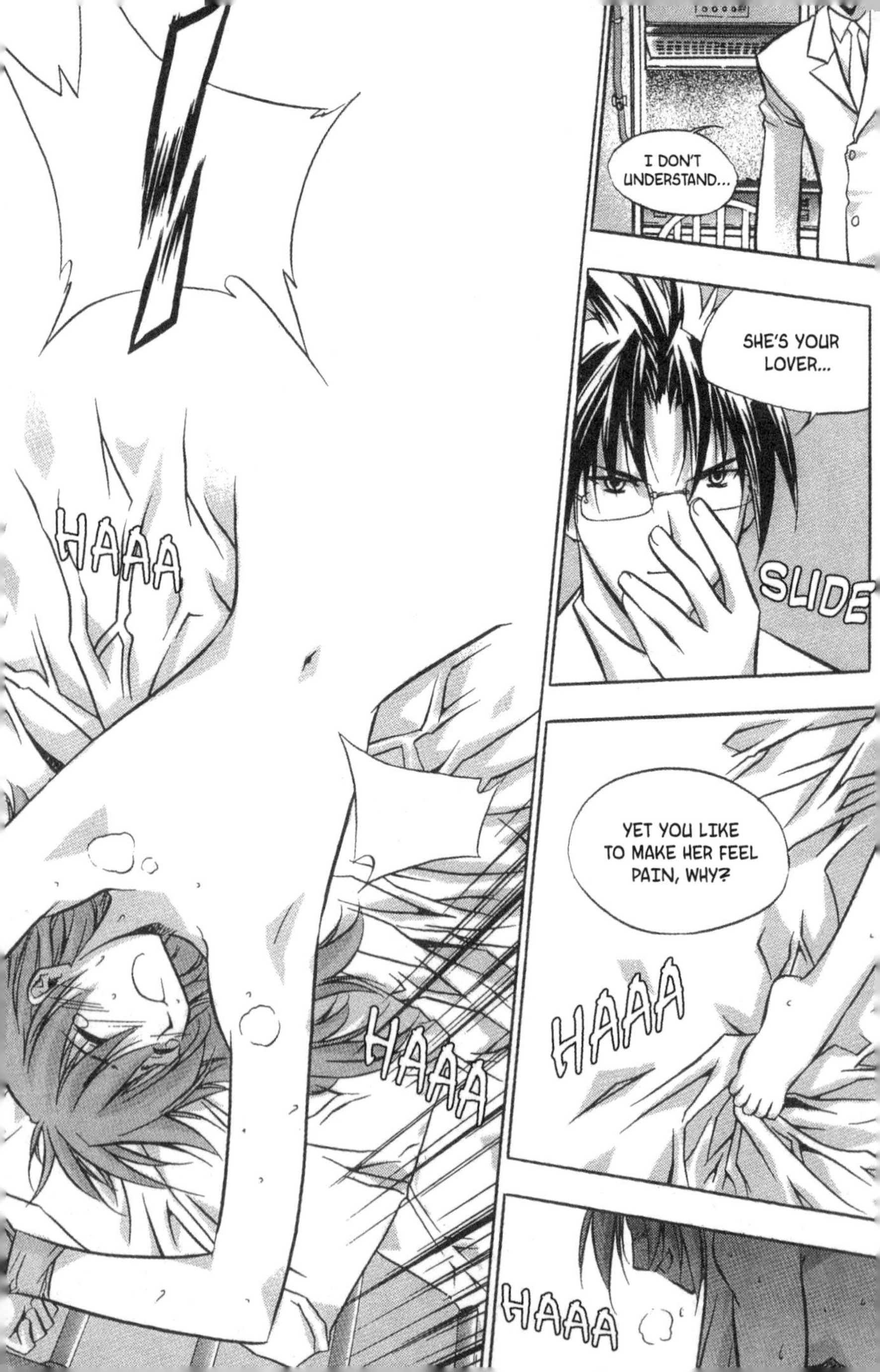
HAAA
HAAA
I DON'T UNDERSTAND...
SHE'S YOUR LOVER...
SLIDE
YET YOU LIKE TO MAKE HER FEEL PAIN, WHY?
HAAA
HAAA

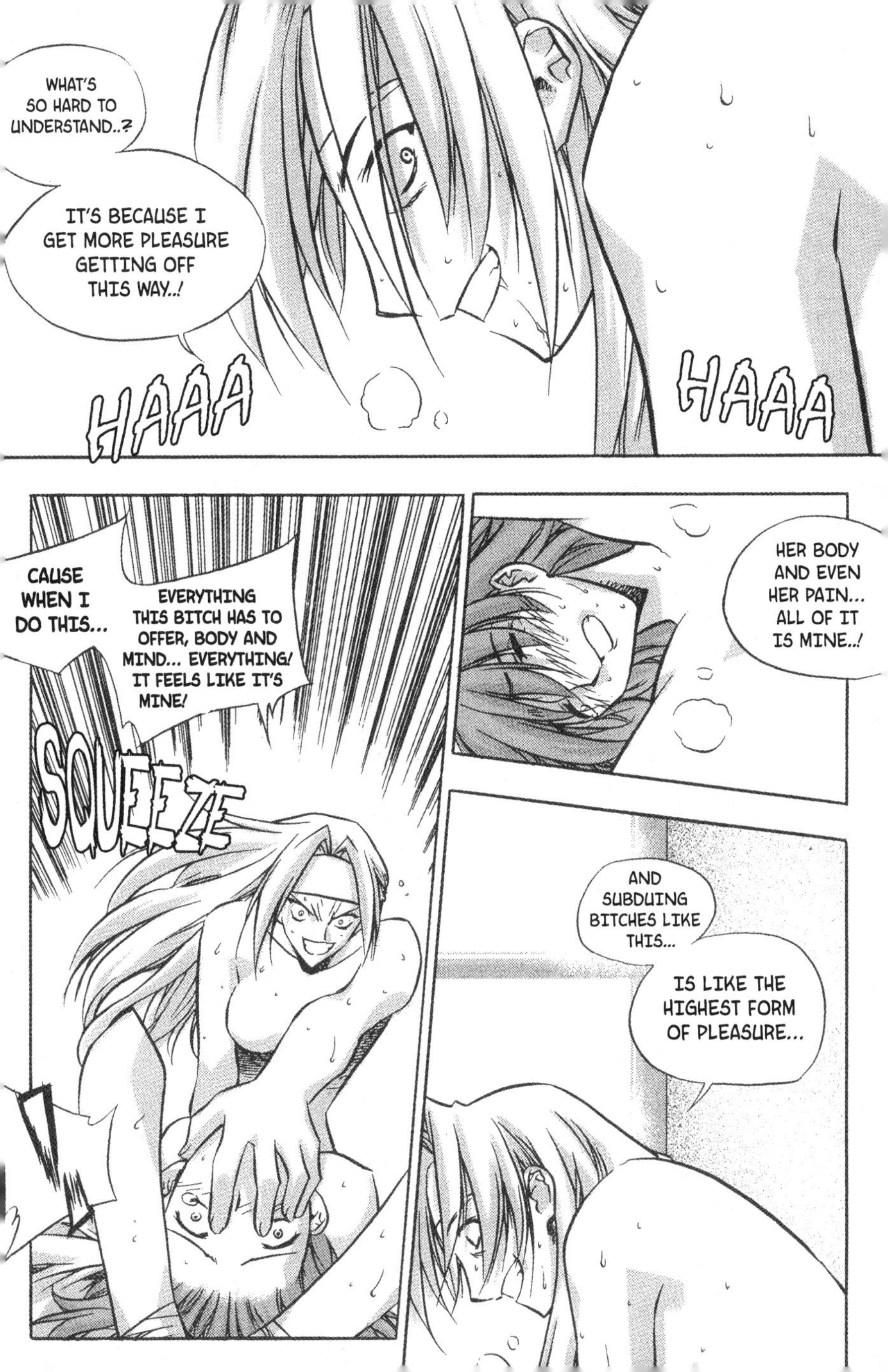
WHAT'S SO HARD TO UNDERSTAND..?
IT'S BECAUSE I GET MORE PLEASURE GETTING OFF THIS WAY..!
HAAA
HAAA
CAUSE WHEN I DO THIS...
EVERYTHING THIS BITCH HAS TO OFFER, BODY AND MIND... EVERYTHING! IT FEELS LIKE IT'S MINE!
SQUEEZE
HER BODY AND EVEN HER PAIN... ALL OF IT IS MINE..!
AND SUBDUING BITCHES LIKE THIS...
IS LIKE THE HIGHEST FORM OF PLEASURE...

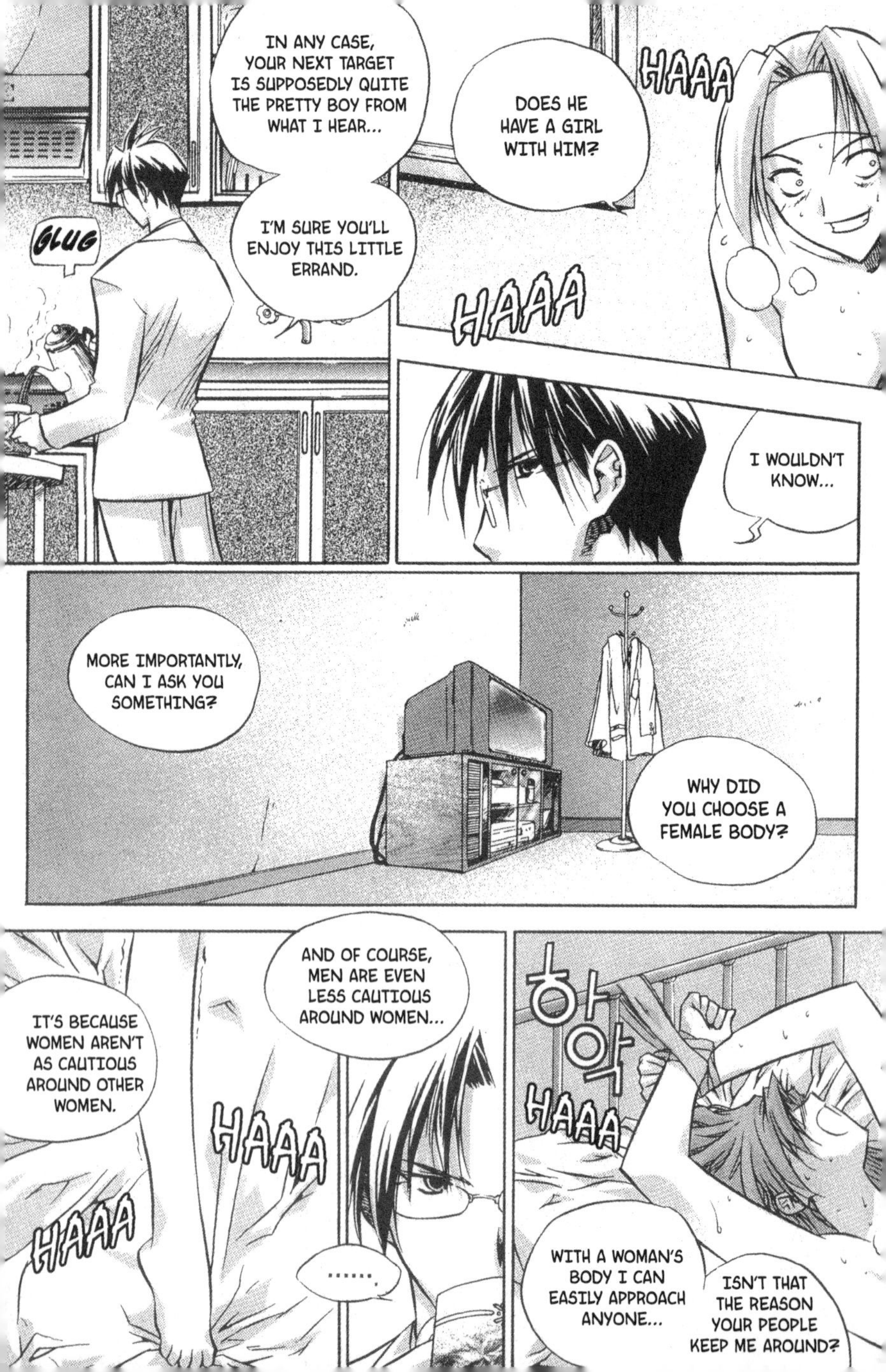
GLUG
IN ANY CASE, YOUR NEXT TARGET IS SUPPOSEDLY QUITE THE PRETTY BOY FROM WHAT I HEAR...
I'M SURE YOU'LL ENJOY THIS LITTLE ERRAND.
DOES HE HAVE A GIRL WITH HIM?
HAAA
HAAA
I WOULDN'T KNOW...
MORE IMPORTANTLY, CAN I ASK YOU SOMETHING?
WHY DID YOU CHOOSE A FEMALE BODY?
IT'S BECAUSE WOMEN AREN'T AS CAUTIOUS AROUND OTHER WOMEN.
HAAA
HAAA
AND OF COURSE, MEN ARE EVEN LESS CAUTIOUS AROUND WOMEN...
......
하악
HAAA
WITH A WOMAN'S BODY I CAN EASILY APPROACH ANYONE...
ISN'T THAT THE REASON YOUR PEOPLE KEEP ME AROUND?

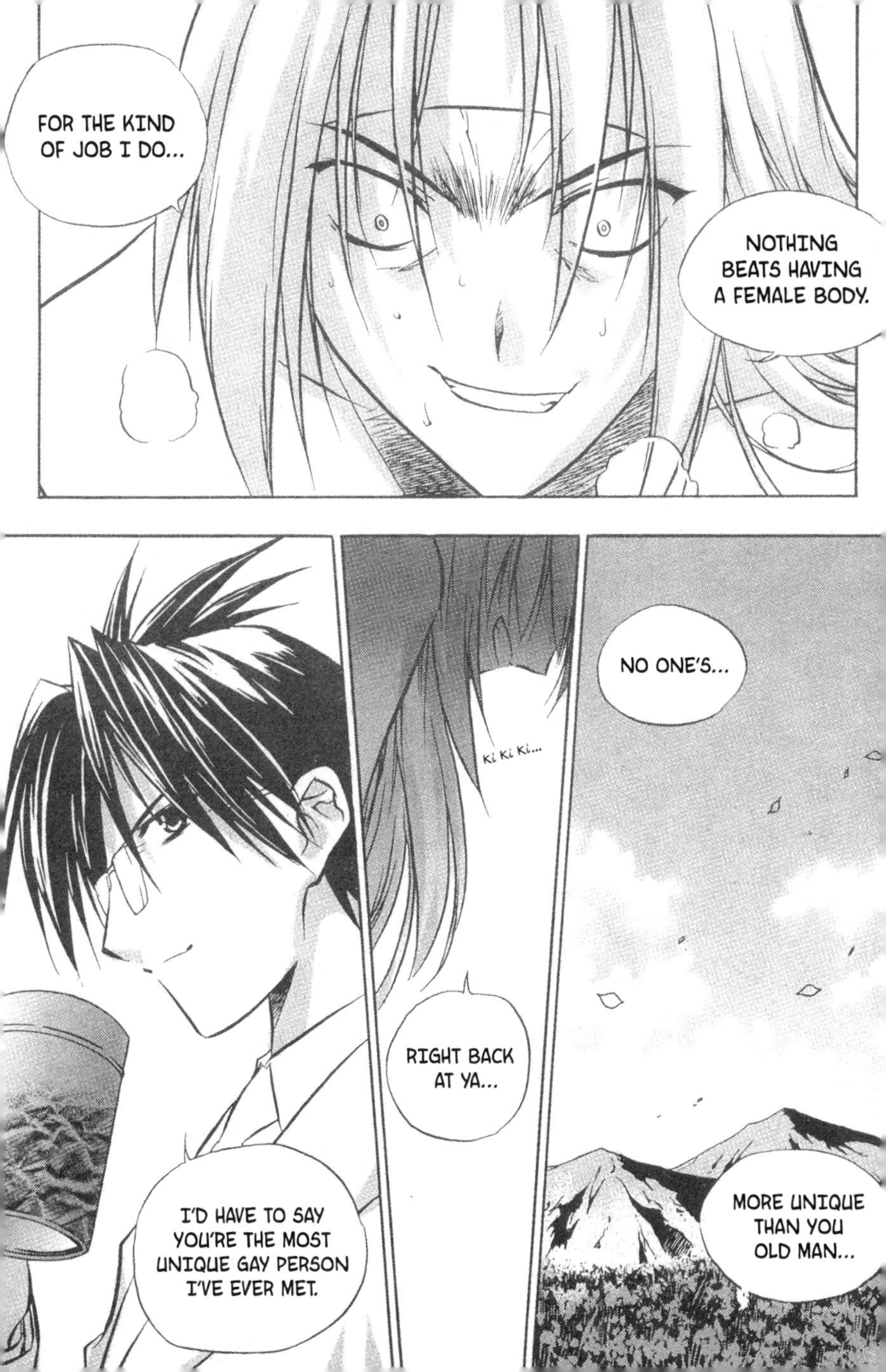
FOR THE KIND OF JOB I DO...
NOTHING BEATS HAVING A FEMALE BODY.
I'D HAVE TO SAY YOU'RE THE MOST UNIQUE GAY PERSON I'VE EVER MET.
Ki Ki Ki...
RIGHT BACK AT YA...
NO ONE'S...
MORE UNIQUE THAN YOU OLD MAN...

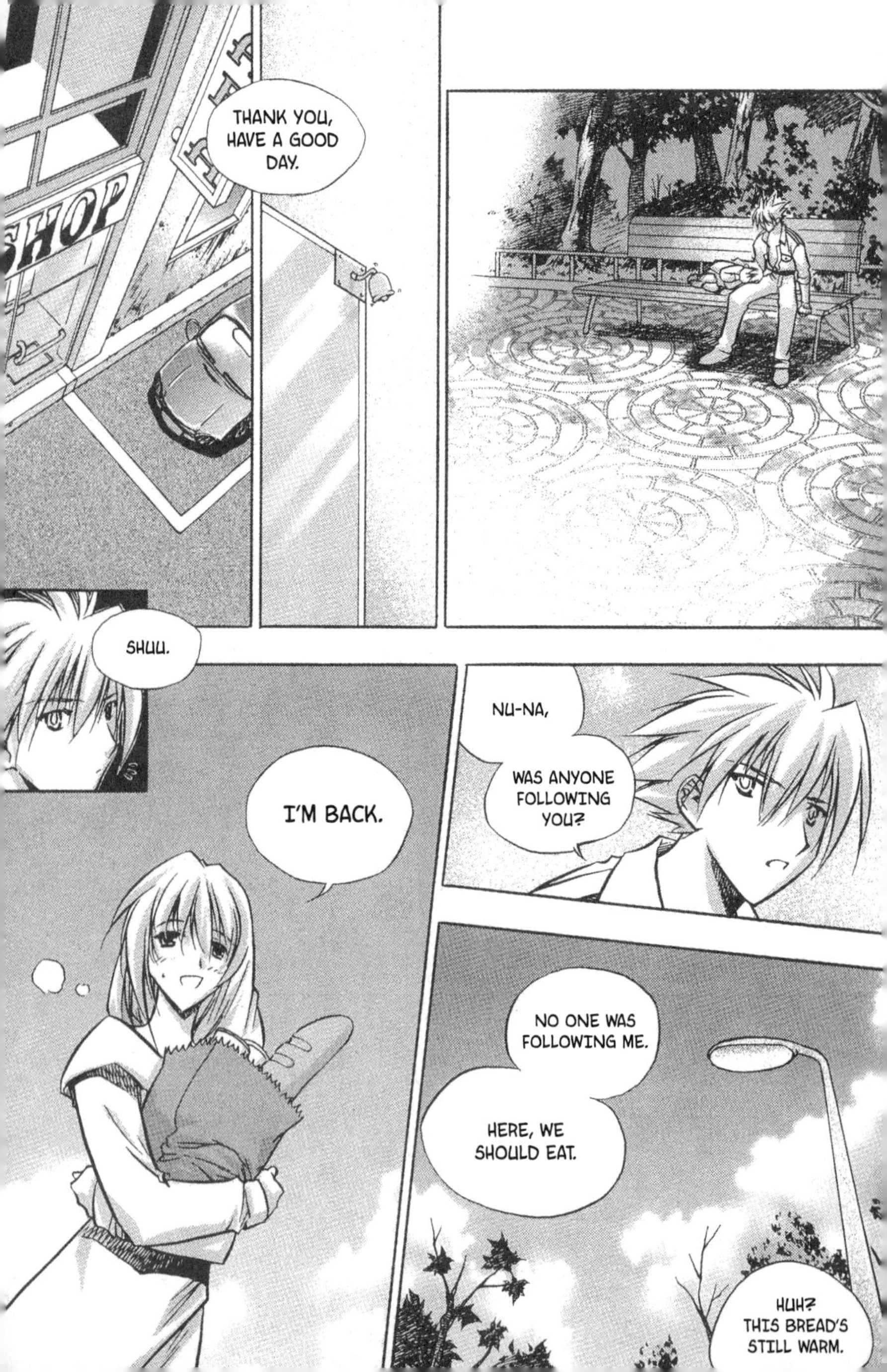
THANK YOU, HAVE A GOOD DAY.
SHOP
SHUU.
I'M BACK.
NU-NA,
WAS ANYONE FOLLOWING YOU?
NO ONE WAS FOLLOWING ME.
HERE, WE SHOULD EAT.
HUH? THIS BREAD'S STILL WARM.

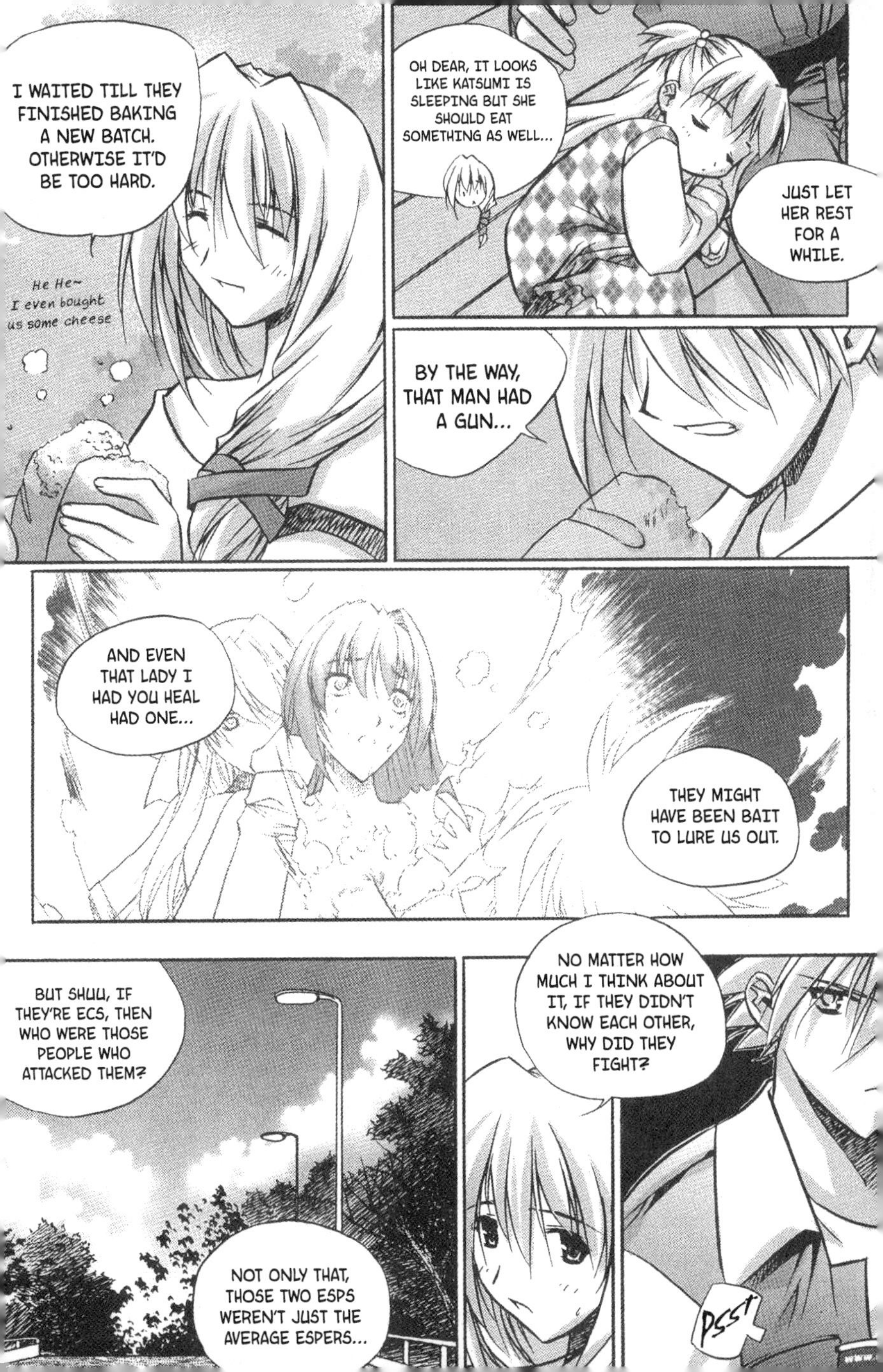
I WAITED TILL THEY FINISHED BAKING A NEW BATCH. OTHERWISE IT'D BE TOO HARD.
He He~ I even bought us some cheese
OH DEAR, IT LOOKS LIKE KATSUMI IS SLEEPING BUT SHE SHOULD EAT SOMETHING AS WELL...
JUST LET HER REST FOR A WHILE.
BY THE WAY, THAT MAN HAD A GUN...
AND EVEN THAT LADY I HAD YOU HEAL HAD ONE...
THEY MIGHT HAVE BEEN BAIT TO LURE US OUT.
BUT SHUU, IF THEY'RE ECS, THEN WHO WERE THOSE PEOPLE WHO ATTACKED THEM?
NOT ONLY THAT, THOSE TWO ESPS WEREN'T JUST THE AVERAGE ESPERS...
NO MATTER HOW MUCH I THINK ABOUT IT, IF THEY DIDN'T KNOW EACH OTHER, WHY DID THEY FIGHT?
PSST

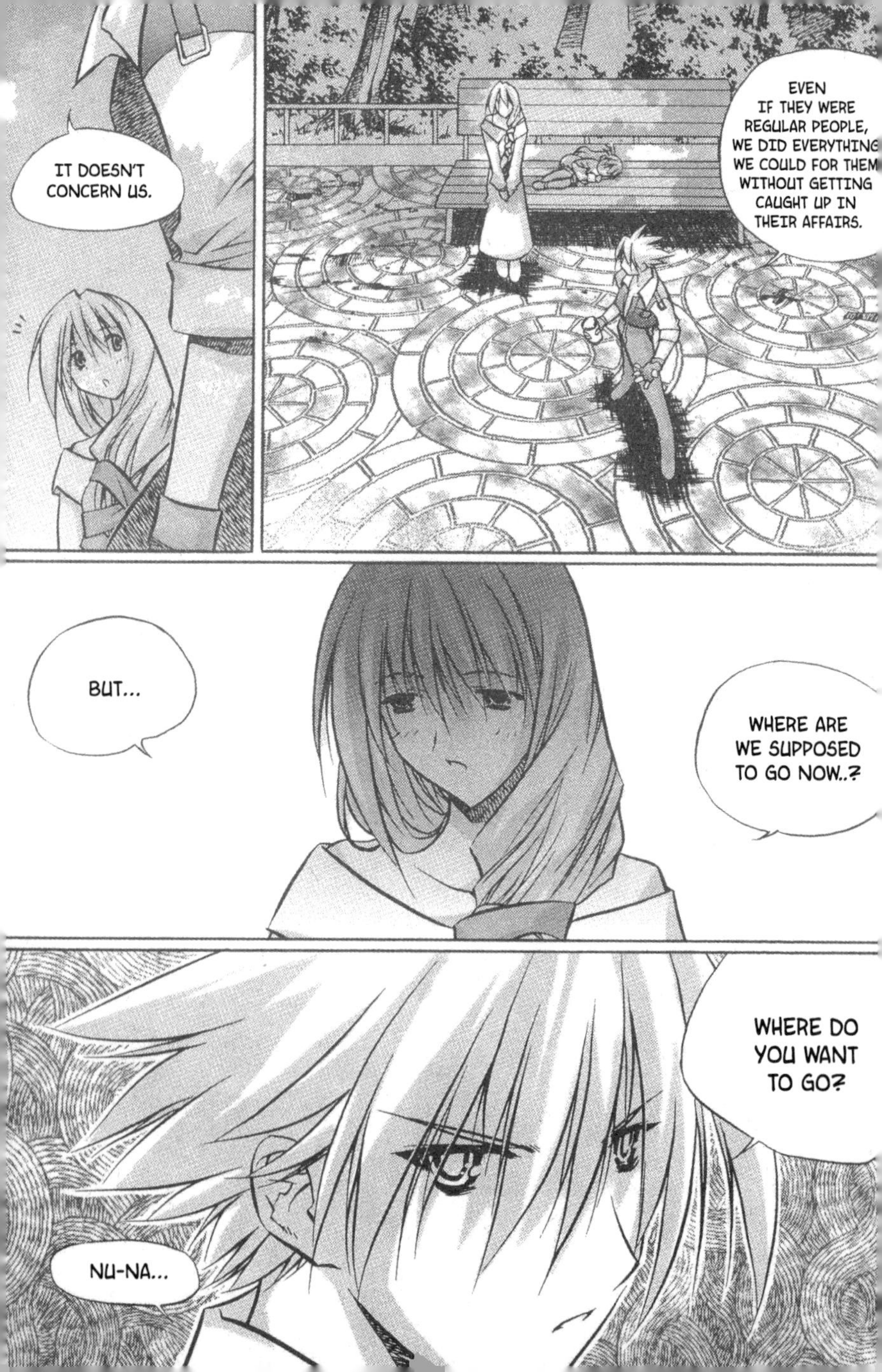
IT DOESN'T CONCERN US.
EVEN IF THEY WERE REGULAR PEOPLE, WE DID EVERYTHING WE COULD FOR THEM WITHOUT GETTING CAUGHT UP IN THEIR AFFAIRS.
BUT...
WHERE ARE WE SUPPOSED TO GO NOW..?
WHERE DO YOU WANT TO GO?
NU-NA...

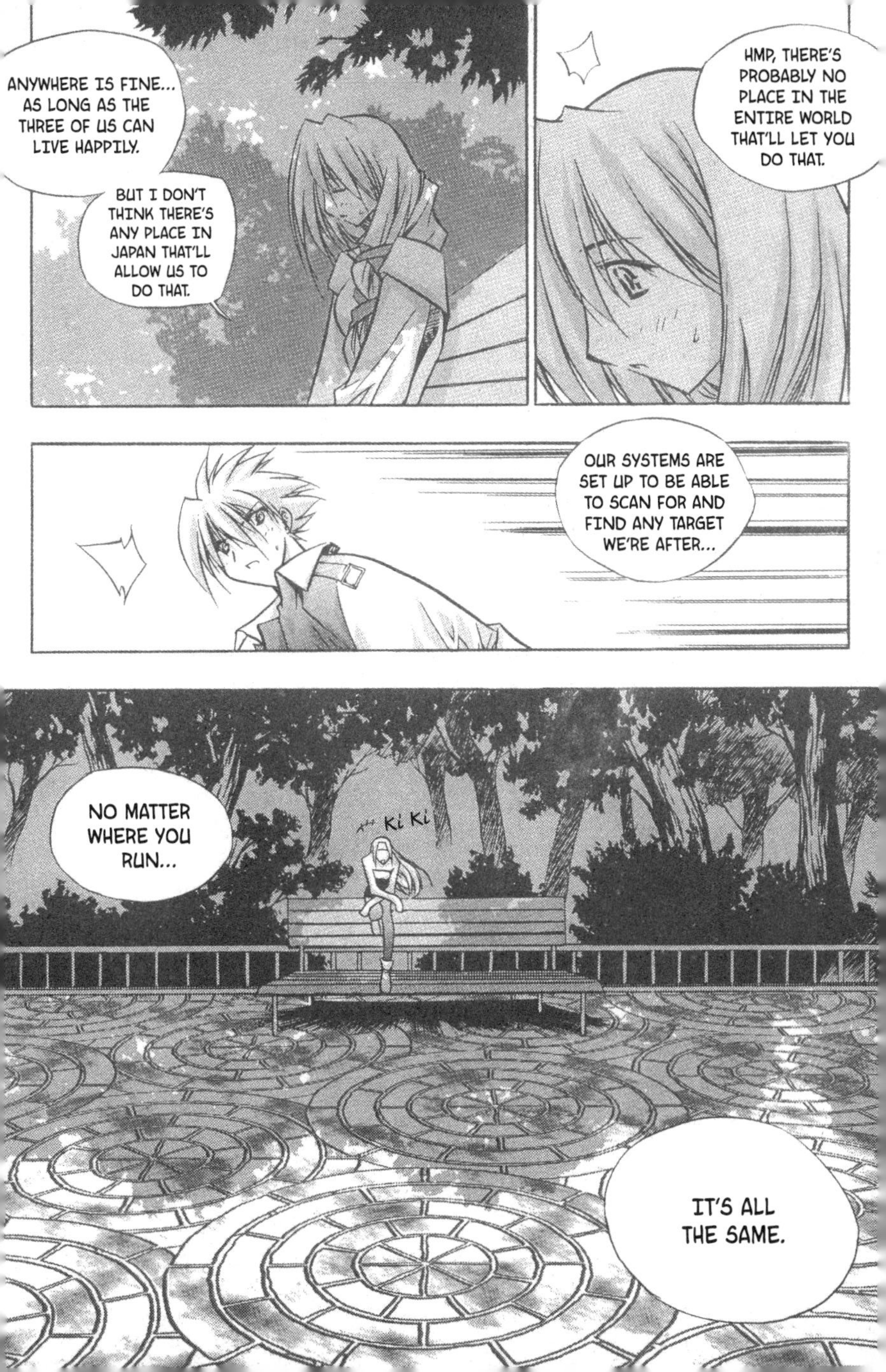
ANYWHERE IS FINE... AS LONG AS THE THREE OF US CAN LIVE HAPPILY.
BUT I DON'T THINK THERE'S ANY PLACE IN JAPAN THAT'LL ALLOW US TO DO THAT.
HMP, THERE'S PROBABLY NO PLACE IN THE ENTIRE WORLD THAT'LL LET YOU DO THAT.
OUR SYSTEMS ARE SET UP TO BE ABLE TO SCAN FOR AND FIND ANY TARGET WE'RE AFTER...
NO MATTER WHERE YOU RUN...
Ki Ki
IT'S ALL THE SAME.

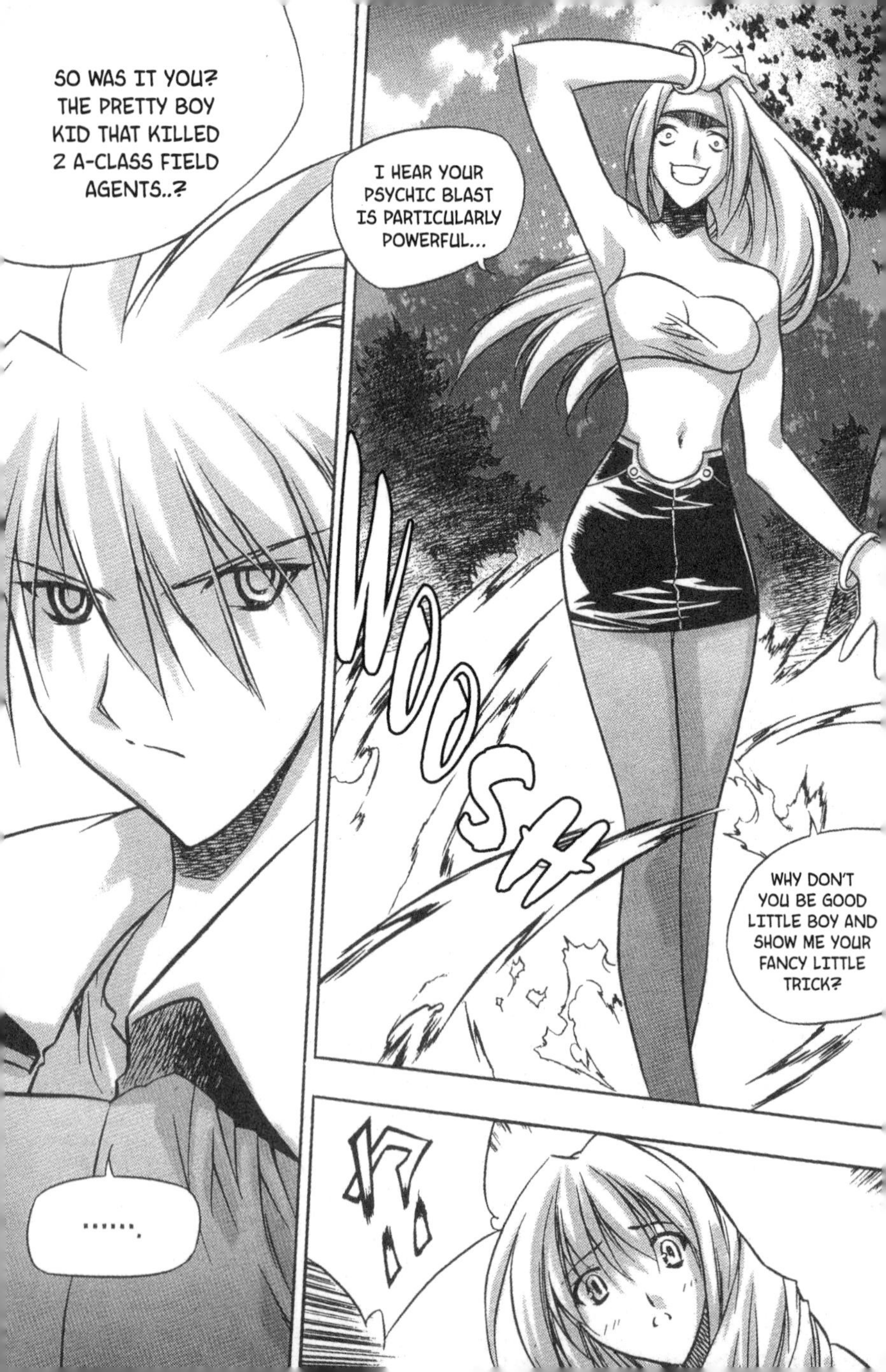
SO WAS IT YOU? THE PRETTY BOY KID THAT KILLED 2 A-CLASS FIELD AGENTS..?
......
I HEAR YOUR PSYCHIC BLAST IS PARTICULARLY POWERFUL...
WOOSH
WHY DON'T YOU BE GOOD LITTLE BOY AND SHOW ME YOUR FANCY LITTLE TRICK?

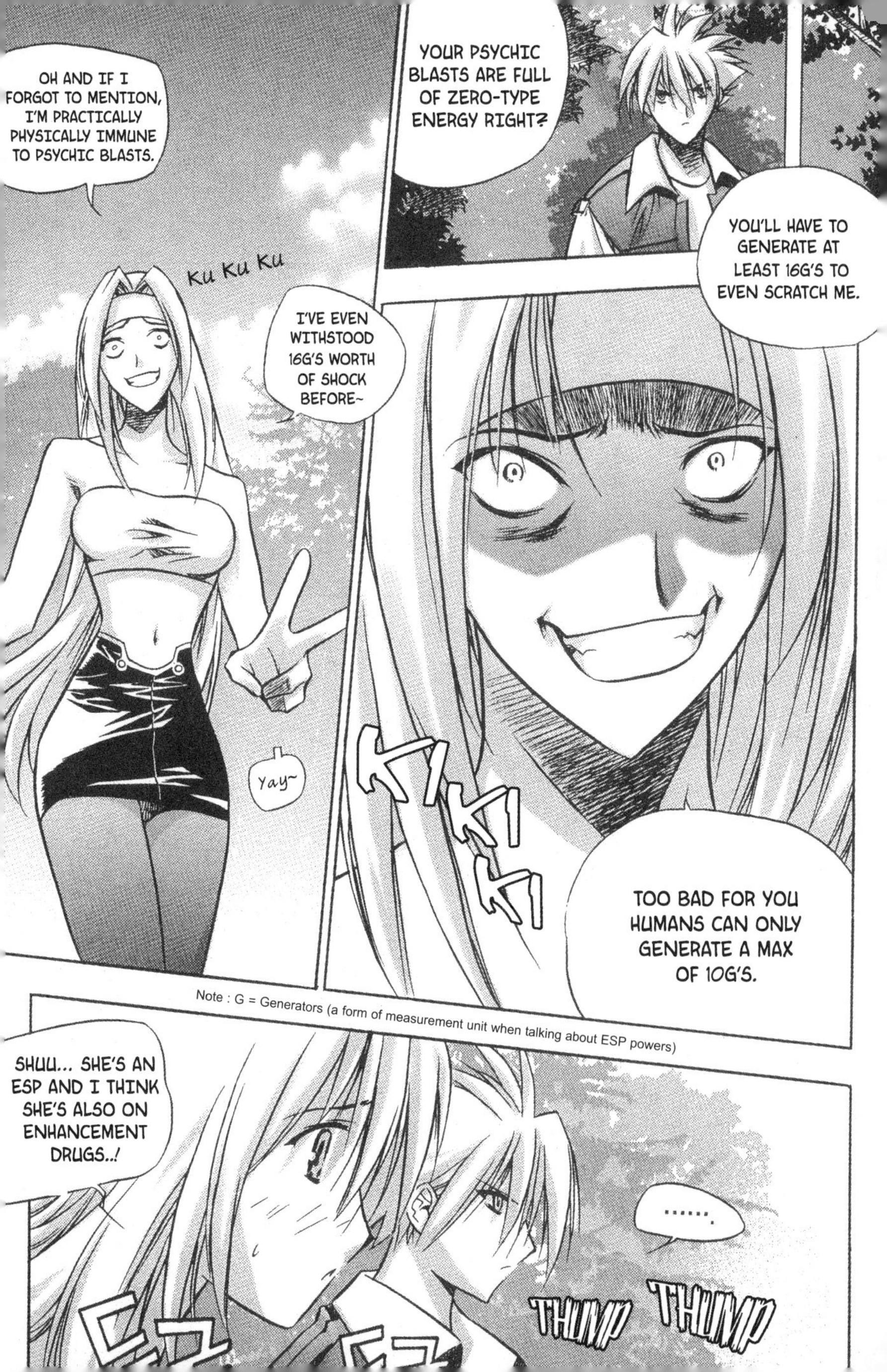
OH AND IF I FORGOT TO MENTION, I'M PRACTICALLY PHYSICALLY IMMUNE TO PSYCHIC BLASTS.
Ku Ku Ku
I'VE EVEN WITHSTOOD 16G'S WORTH OF SHOCK BEFORE~
Yay~
YOUR PSYCHIC BLASTS ARE FULL OF ZERO-TYPE ENERGY RIGHT?
YOU'LL HAVE TO GENERATE AT LEAST 16G'S TO EVEN SCRATCH ME.
KI KI KI
TOO BAD FOR YOU HUMANS CAN ONLY GENERATE A MAX OF 10G'S.
Note : G = Generators (a form of measurement unit when talking about ESP powers)
SHUU... SHE'S AN ESP AND I THINK SHE'S ALSO ON ENHANCEMENT DRUGS..!
......
THUMP THUMP

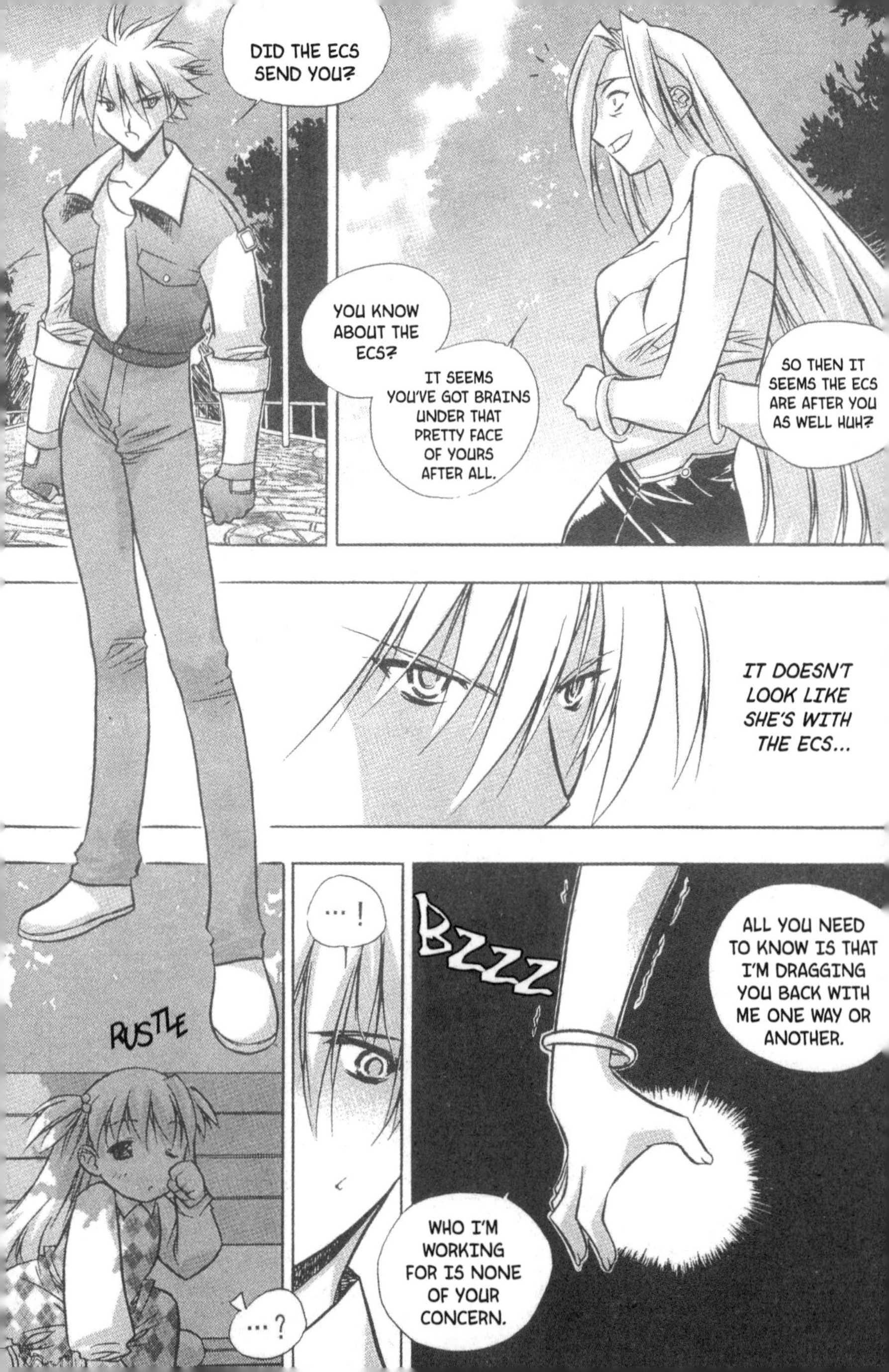
DID THE ECS SEND YOU?
YOU KNOW ABOUT THE ECS?
IT SEEMS YOU'VE GOT BRAINS UNDER THAT PRETTY FACE OF YOURS AFTER ALL.
SO THEN IT SEEMS THE ECS ARE AFTER YOU AS WELL HUH?
IT DOESN'T LOOK LIKE SHE'S WITH THE ECS...
RUSTLE
...!
BZZZ
ALL YOU NEED TO KNOW IS THAT I'M DRAGGING YOU BACK WITH ME ONE WAY OR ANOTHER.
WHO I'M WORKING FOR IS NONE OF YOUR CONCERN.
...?

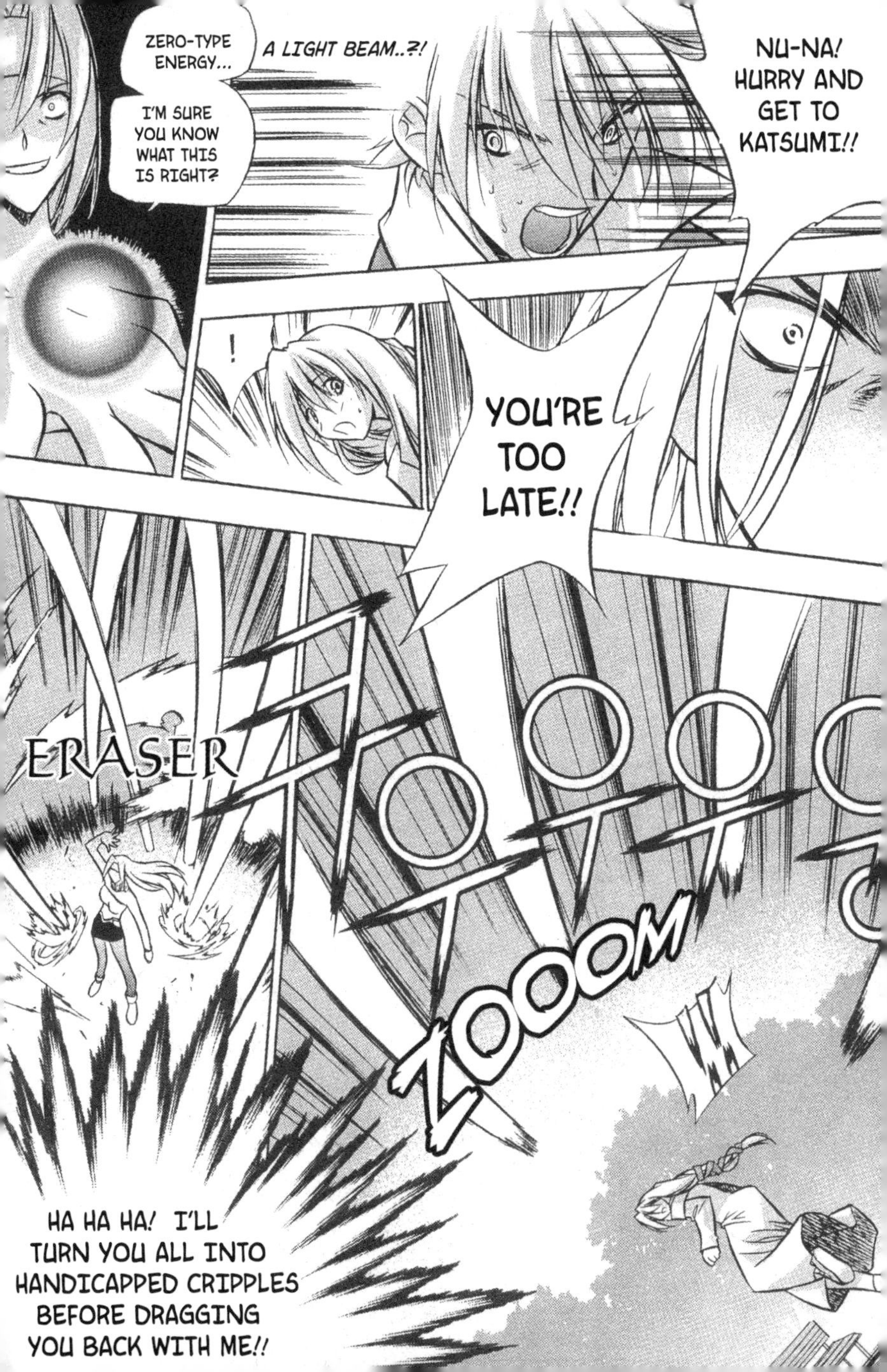
ZERO-TYPE ENERGY...
I'M SURE YOU KNOW WHAT THIS IS RIGHT?
A LIGHT BEAM..?!
NU-NA! HURRY AND GET TO KATSUMI!!
!
YOU'RE TOO LATE!!
ERASER
ZOOOM
HA HA HA! I'LL TURN YOU ALL INTO HANDICAPPED CRIPPLES BEFORE DRAGGING YOU BACK WITH ME!!

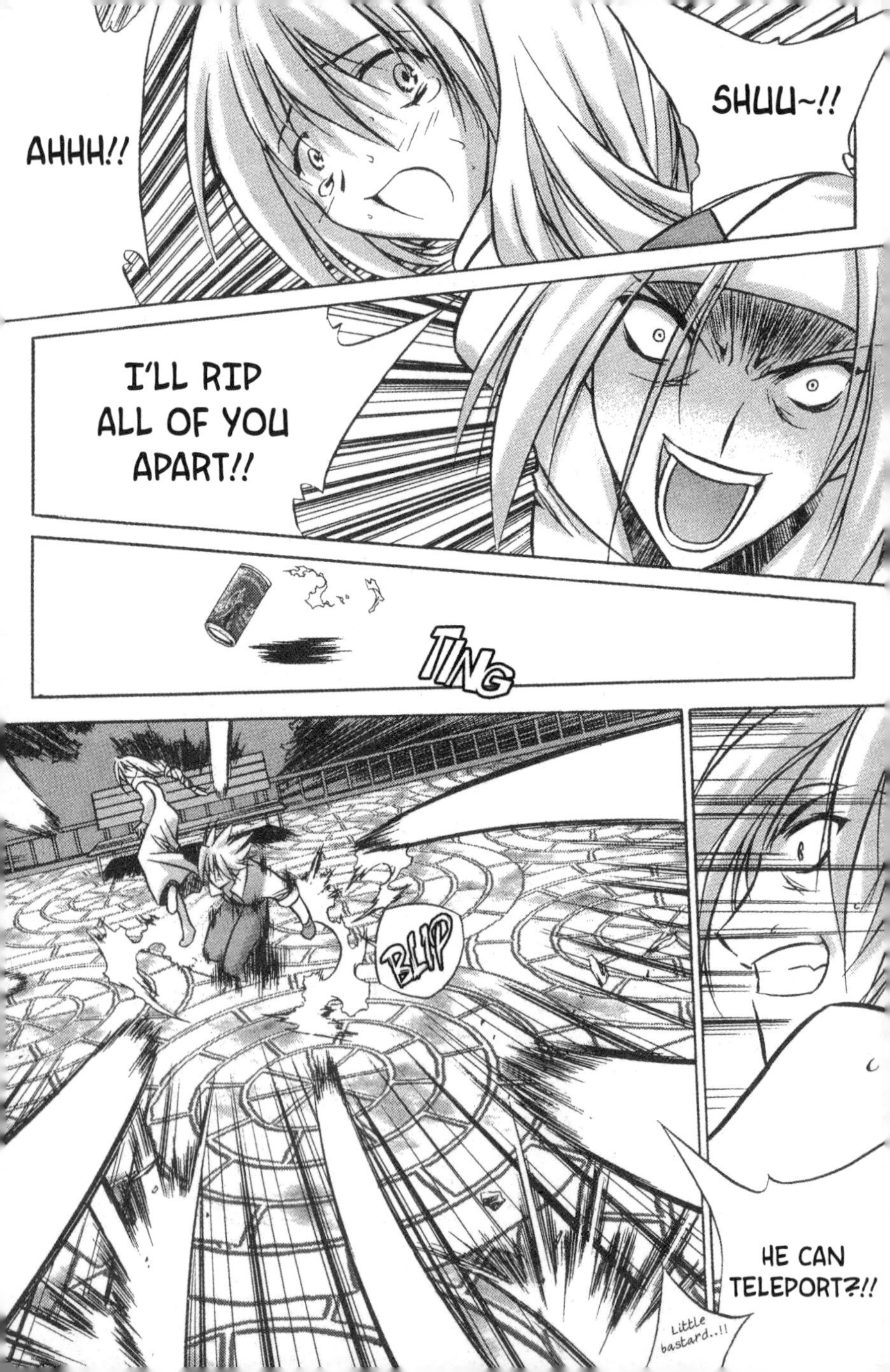
AHHH!!
SHUU~!!
I'LL RIP ALL OF YOU APART!!
TING
BLIP
HE CAN TELEPORT?!!
Little bastard..!!

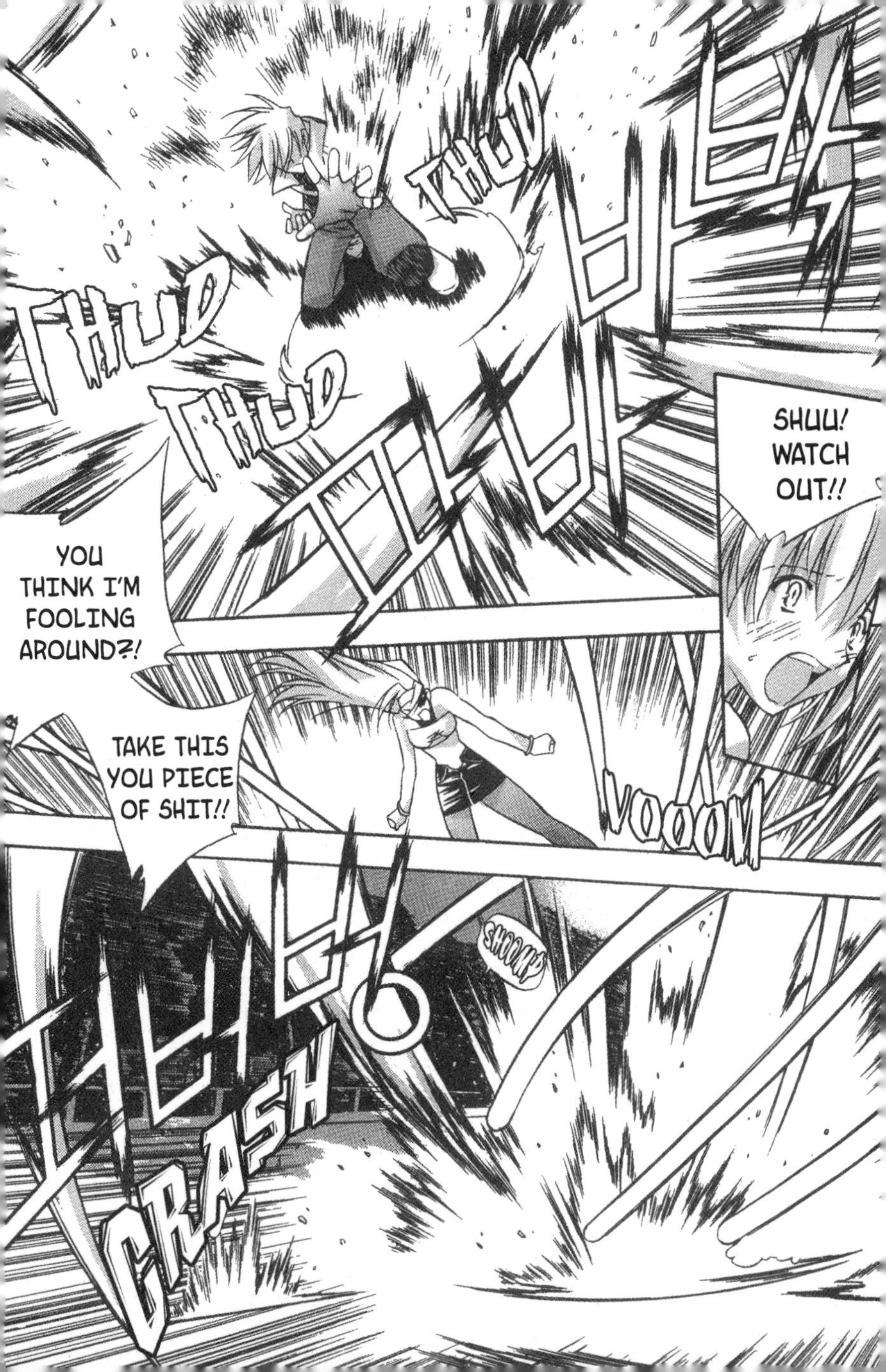
THUD
THUD
THUD
YOU THINK I'M FOOLING AROUND?!
SHUU! WATCH OUT!!
TAKE THIS YOU PIECE OF SHIT!!
VOOOM
SHOOM
CRASH

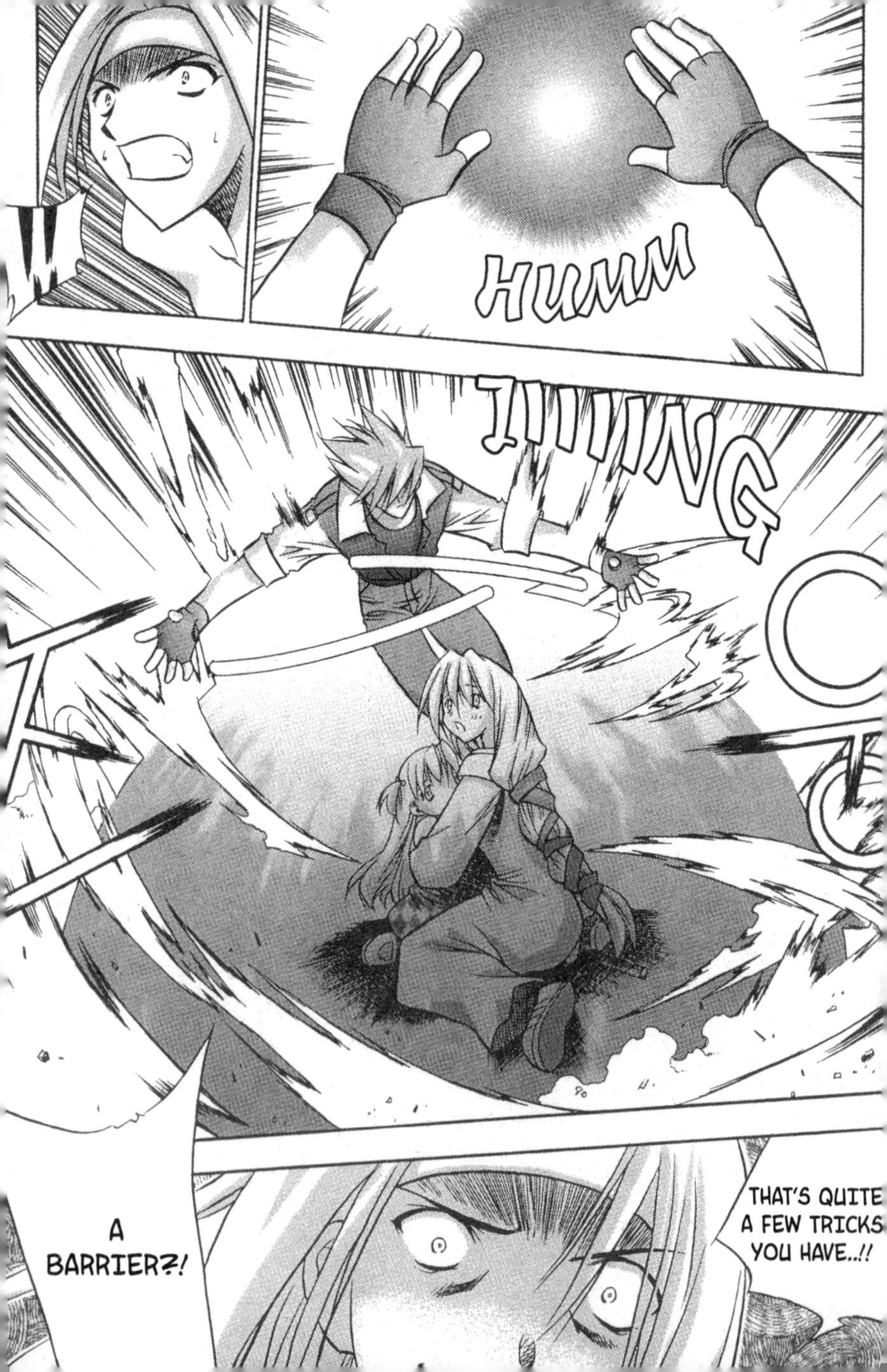
HUMM
IIIING
A BARRIER?!
THAT'S QUITE A FEW TRICKS YOU HAVE..!!

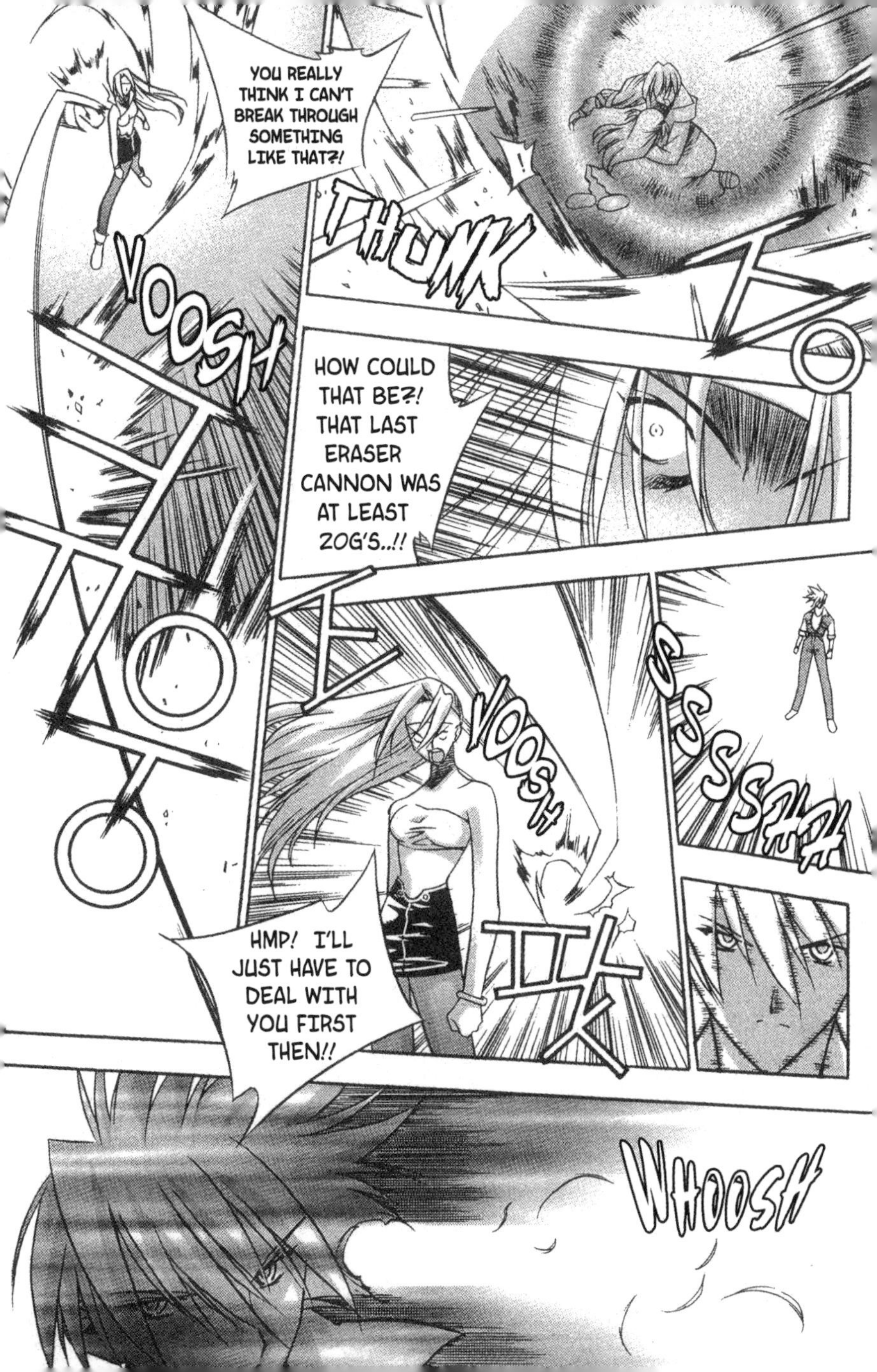
YOU REALLY THINK I CAN'T BREAK THROUGH SOMETHING LIKE THAT?!
VOOSH
THUNK
!
HOW COULD THAT BE?! THAT LAST ERASER CANNON WAS AT LEAST ZOG'S..!!
VOOSH
SSSSHA
HMP! I'LL JUST HAVE TO DEAL WITH YOU FIRST THEN!!
WHOOSH

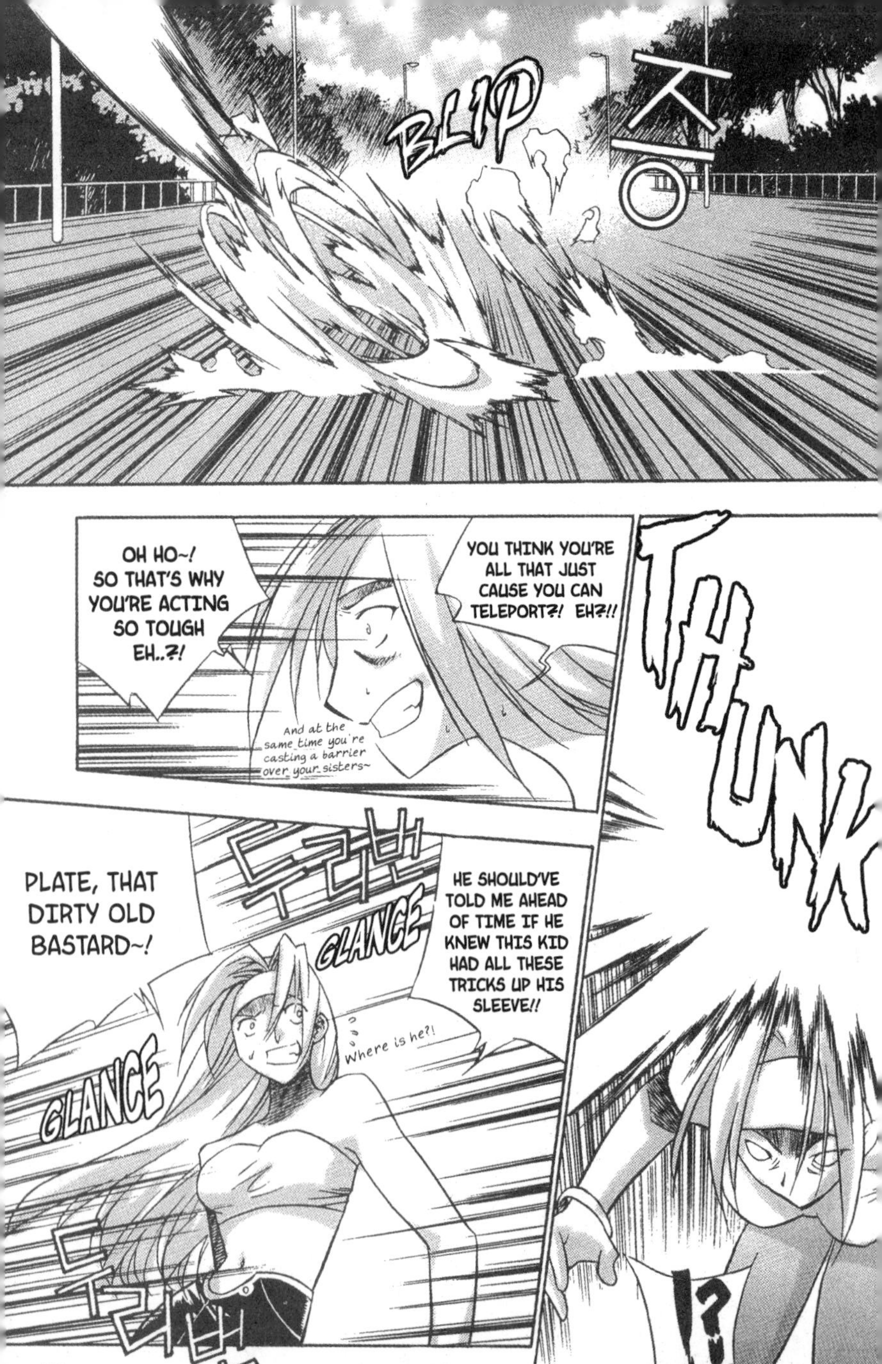
BLIP
OH HO~! SO THAT'S WHY YOU'RE ACTING SO TOUGH EH..?!
YOU THINK YOU'RE ALL THAT JUST CAUSE YOU CAN TELEPORT?! EH?!!
And at the same time you're casting a barrier over your sisters~
PLATE, THAT DIRTY OLD BASTARD~!
두리번
GLANCE
HE SHOULD'VE TOLD ME AHEAD OF TIME IF HE KNEW THIS KID HAD ALL THESE TRICKS UP HIS SLEEVE!!
Where is he?!
GLANCE
두리번
THUNK
!?

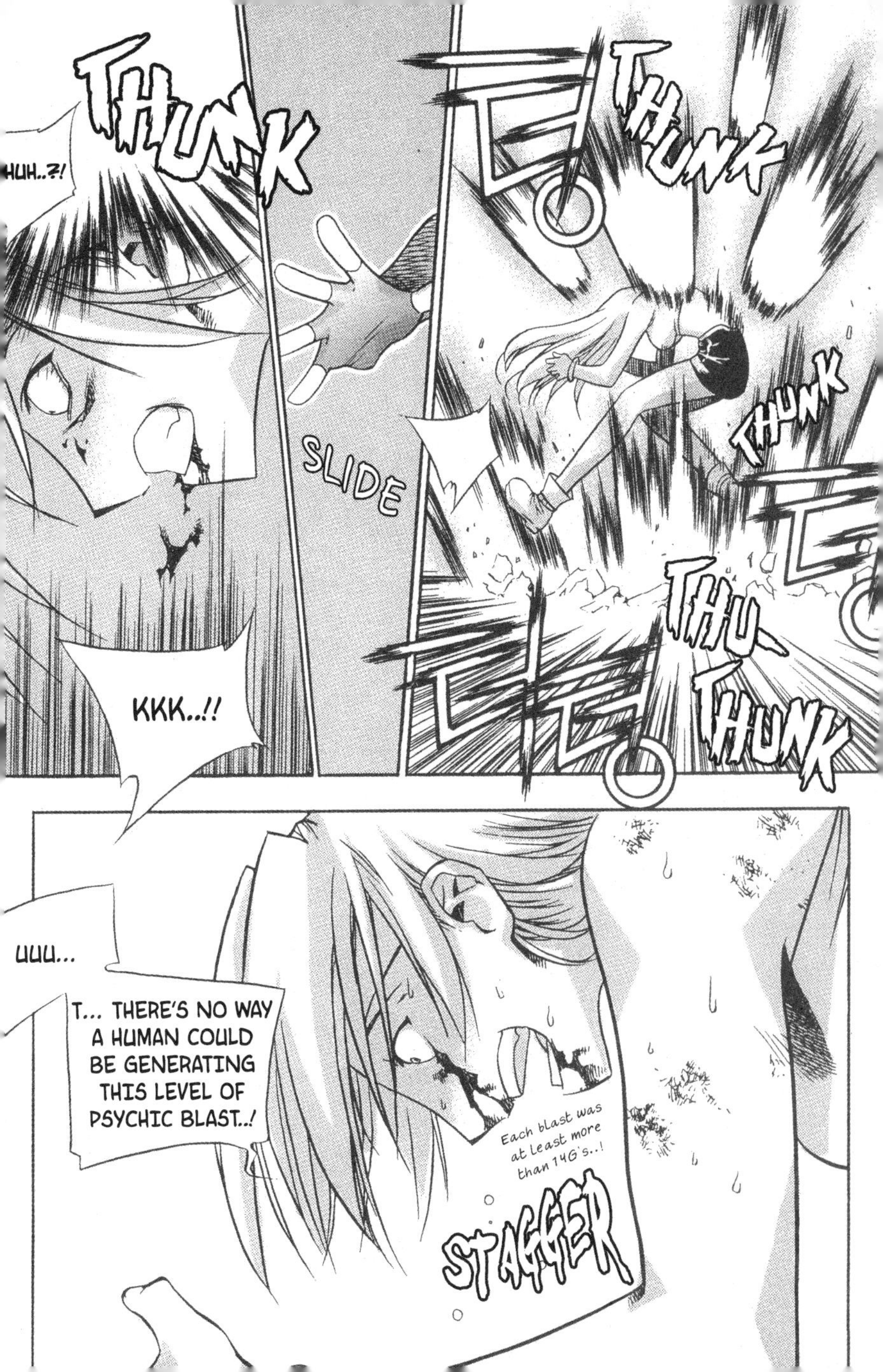
THUNK
HUH..?!
KKK..!!
SLIDE
THUNK
THUNK
THU-THUNK
UUU...
T... THERE'S NO WAY A HUMAN COULD BE GENERATING THIS LEVEL OF PSYCHIC BLAST..!
Each blast was at least more than 14G's..!
STAGGER

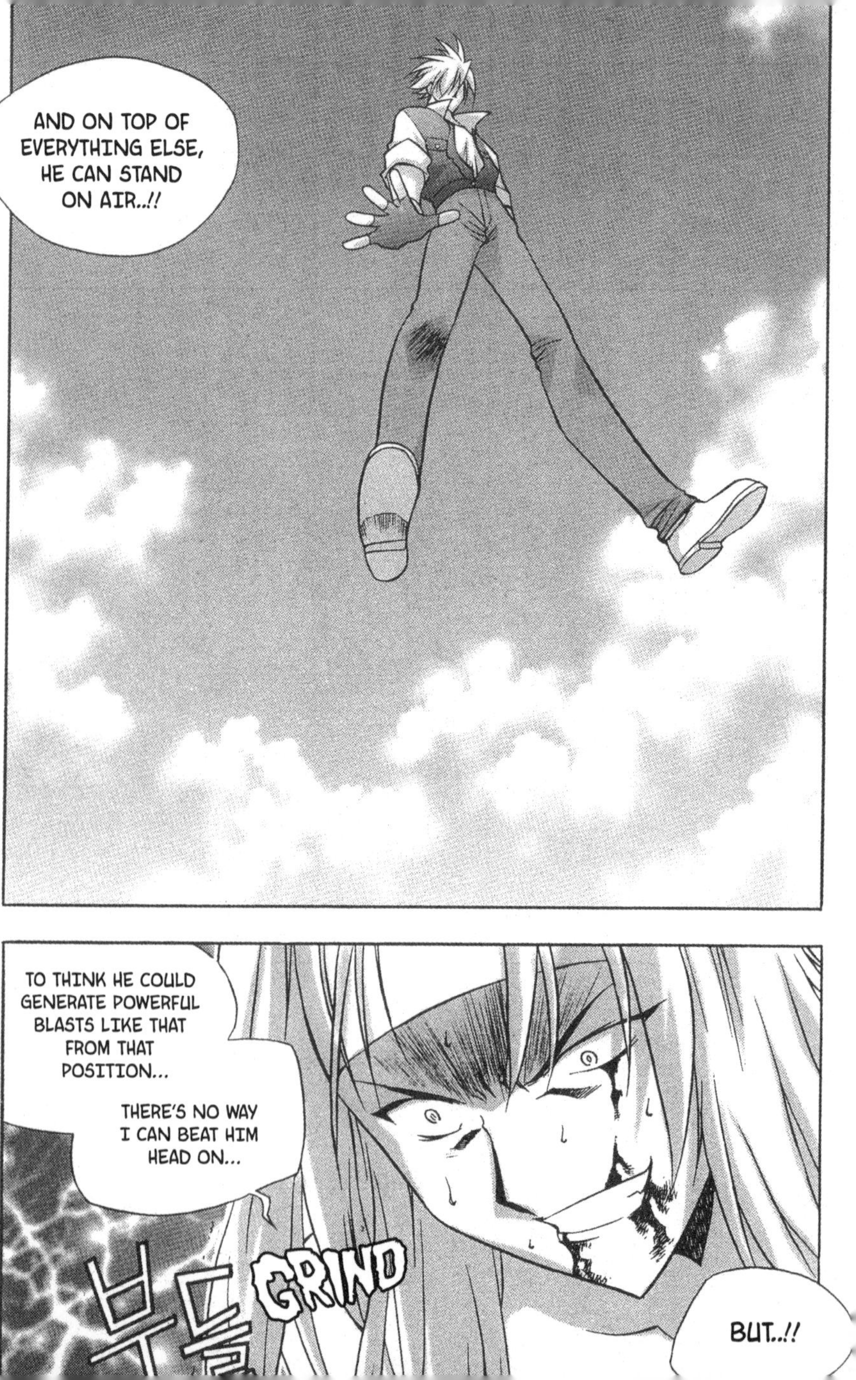
AND ON TOP OF EVERYTHING ELSE, HE CAN STAND ON AIR..!!
TO THINK HE COULD GENERATE POWERFUL BLASTS LIKE THAT FROM THAT POSITION...
THERE'S NO WAY I CAN BEAT HIM HEAD ON...
GRIND
BUT..!!

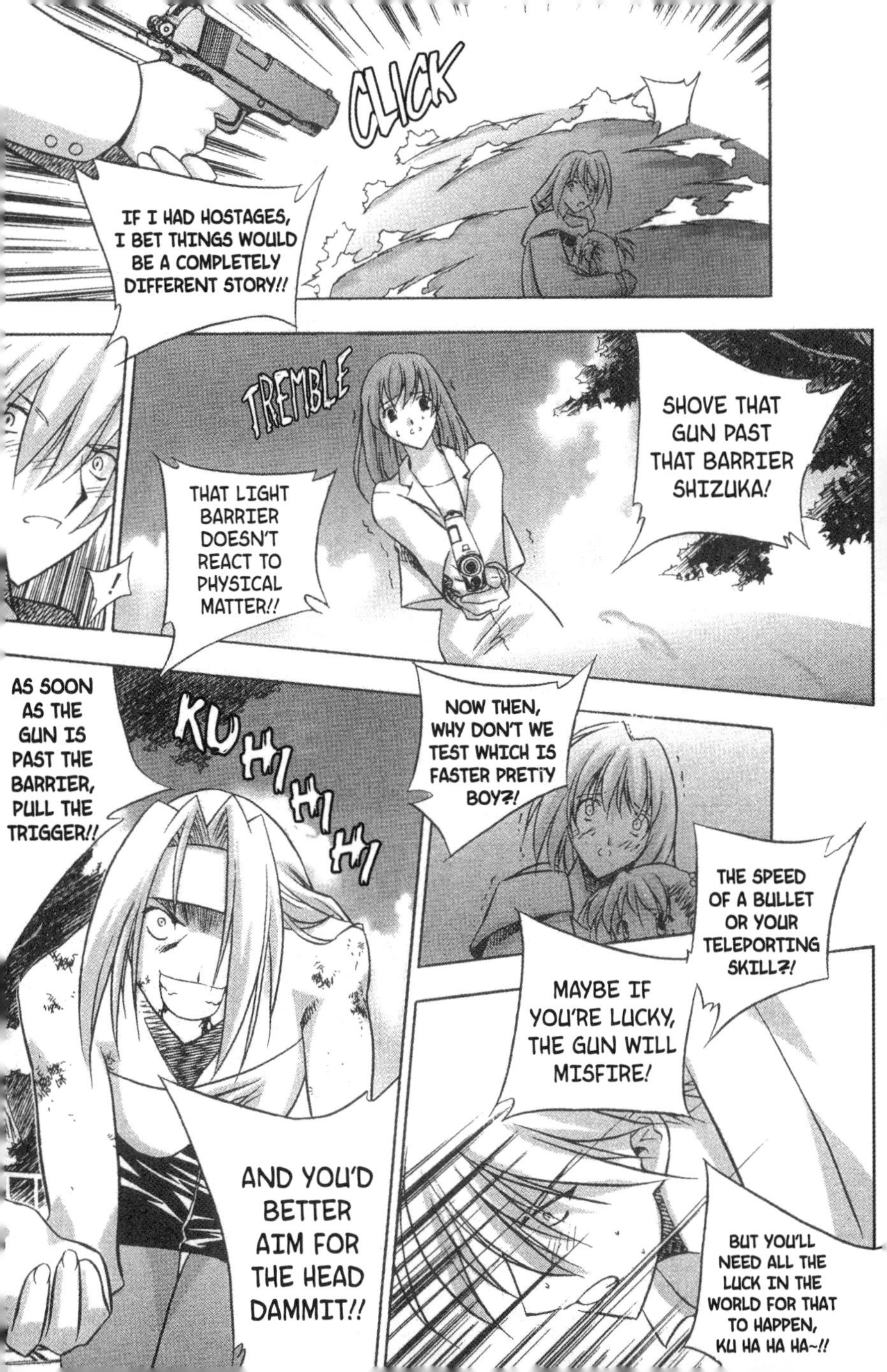
CLICK
IF I HAD HOSTAGES, I BET THINGS WOULD BE A COMPLETELY DIFFERENT STORY!!
!
TREMBLE
THAT LIGHT BARRIER DOESN'T REACT TO PHYSICAL MATTER!!
SHOVE THAT GUN PAST THAT BARRIER SHIZUKA!
AS SOON AS THE GUN IS PAST THE BARRIER, PULL THE TRIGGER!!
KUHIHIHI
AND YOU'D BETTER AIM FOR THE HEAD DAMMIT!!
NOW THEN, WHY DON'T WE TEST WHICH IS FASTER PRETTY BOY?!
THE SPEED OF A BULLET OR YOUR TELEPORTING SKILL?!
MAYBE IF YOU'RE LUCKY, THE GUN WILL MISFIRE!
BUT YOU'LL NEED ALL THE LUCK IN THE WORLD FOR THAT TO HAPPEN, KU HA HA HA~!!

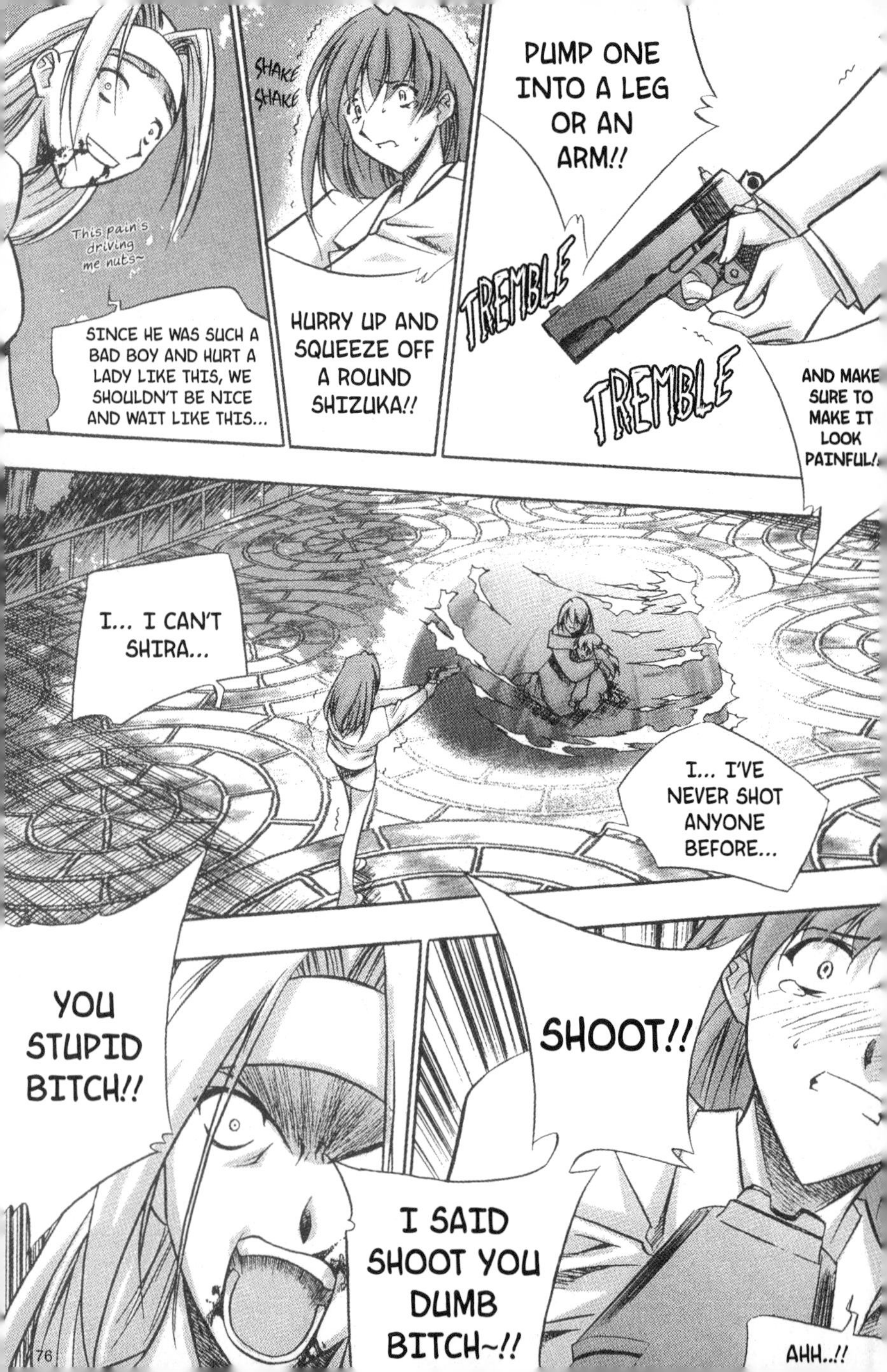
This pain's driving me nuts~
SINCE HE WAS SUCH A BAD BOY AND HURT A LADY LIKE THIS, WE SHOULDN'T BE NICE AND WAIT LIKE THIS...
SHAKE SHAKE
HURRY UP AND SQUEEZE OFF A ROUND SHIZUKA!!
PUMP ONE INTO A LEG OR AN ARM!!
TREMBLE
TREMBLE
AND MAKE SURE TO MAKE IT LOOK PAINFUL!!
I... I CAN'T SHIRA...
I... I'VE NEVER SHOT ANYONE BEFORE...
YOU STUPID BITCH!!
I SAID SHOOT YOU DUMB BITCH~!!
SHOOT!!
AHH..!!

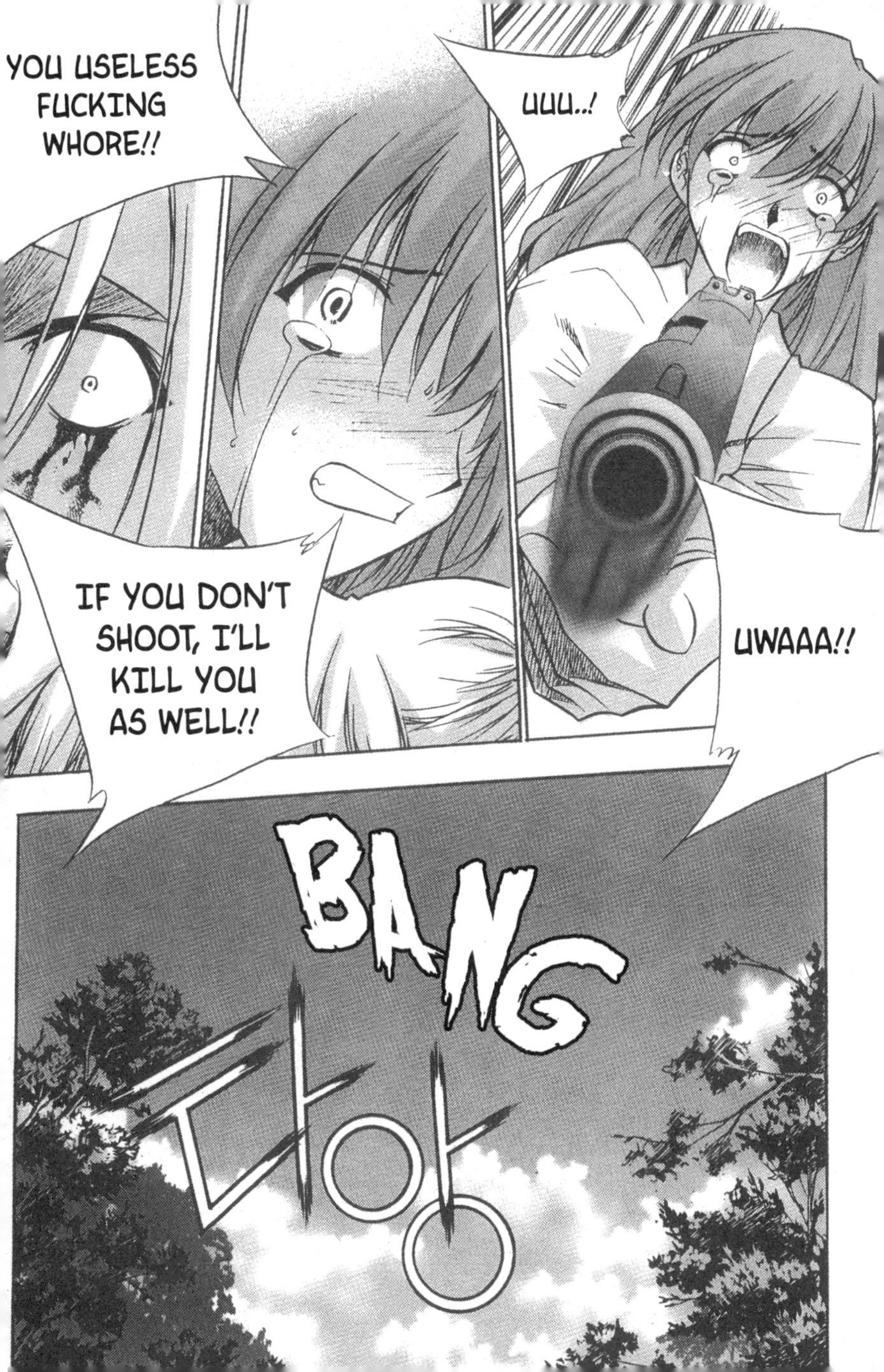
YOU USELESS FUCKING WHORE!!
IF YOU DON'T SHOOT, I'LL KILL YOU AS WELL!!
UUU..!
UWAAA!!
BANG

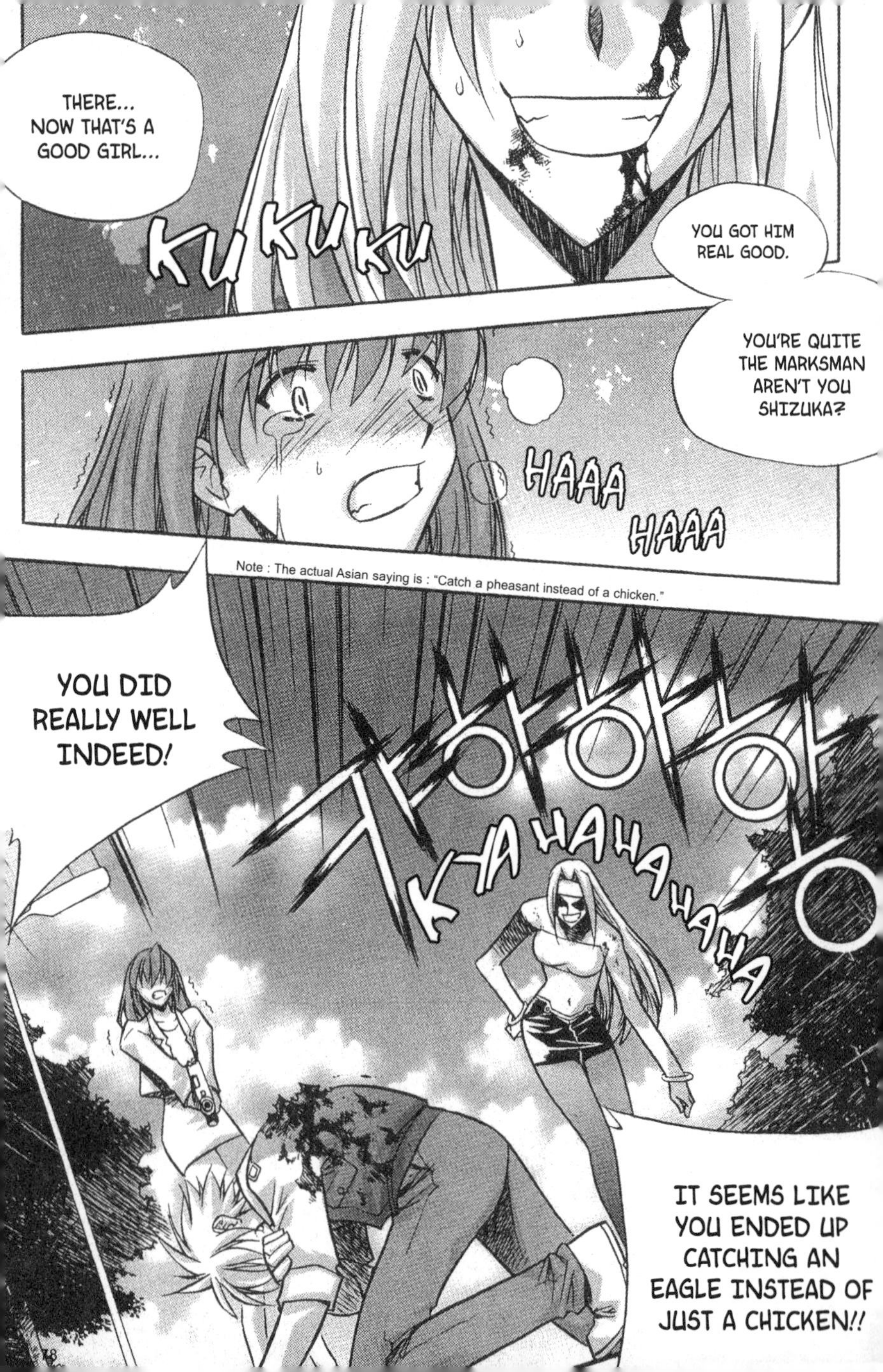
THERE... NOW THAT'S A GOOD GIRL...
KU KU KU KU
YOU GOT HIM REAL GOOD.
YOU'RE QUITE THE MARKSMAN AREN'T YOU SHIZUKA?
HAAA HAAA
Note : The actual Asian saying is : "Catch a pheasant instead of a chicken."
YOU DID REALLY WELL INDEED!
KYAHAHAHAHAHAHA
IT SEEMS LIKE YOU ENDED UP CATCHING AN EAGLE INSTEAD OF JUST A CHICKEN!!

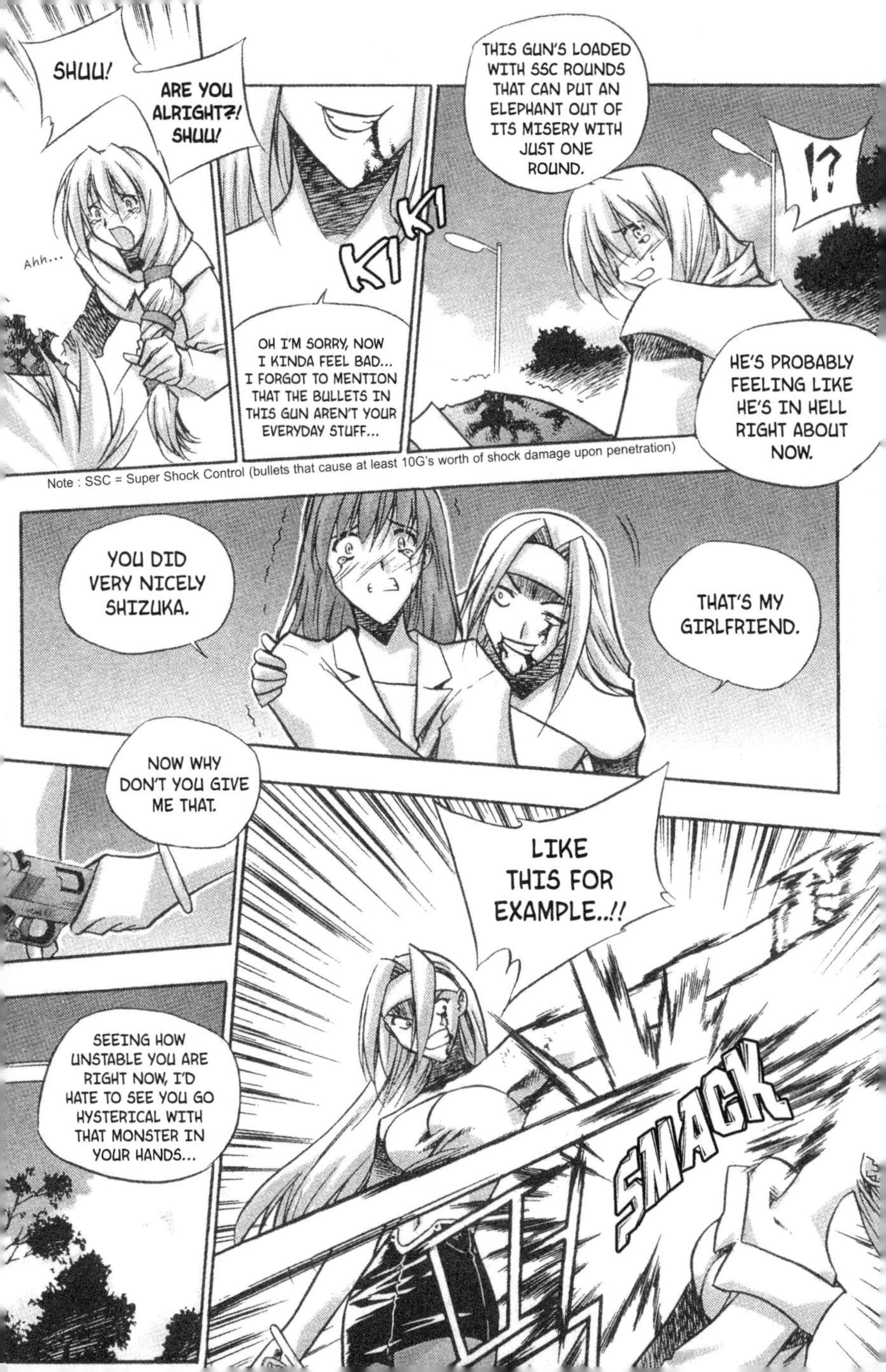

SHUU!
ARE YOU ALRIGHT?! SHUU!
Ahh...
KI KI
OH I'M SORRY, NOW I KINDA FEEL BAD... I FORGOT TO MENTION THAT THE BULLETS IN THIS GUN AREN'T YOUR EVERYDAY STUFF...
THIS GUN'S LOADED WITH SSC ROUNDS THAT CAN PUT AN ELEPHANT OUT OF ITS MISERY WITH JUST ONE ROUND.
!?
HE'S PROBABLY FEELING LIKE HE'S IN HELL RIGHT ABOUT NOW.
Note : SSC = Super Shock Control (bullets that cause at least 10G's worth of shock damage upon penetration)
YOU DID VERY NICELY SHIZUKA.
THAT'S MY GIRLFRIEND.
NOW WHY DON'T YOU GIVE ME THAT.
SEEING HOW UNSTABLE YOU ARE RIGHT NOW, I'D HATE TO SEE YOU GO HYSTERICAL WITH THAT MONSTER IN YOUR HANDS...
LIKE THIS FOR EXAMPLE..!!
SMACK

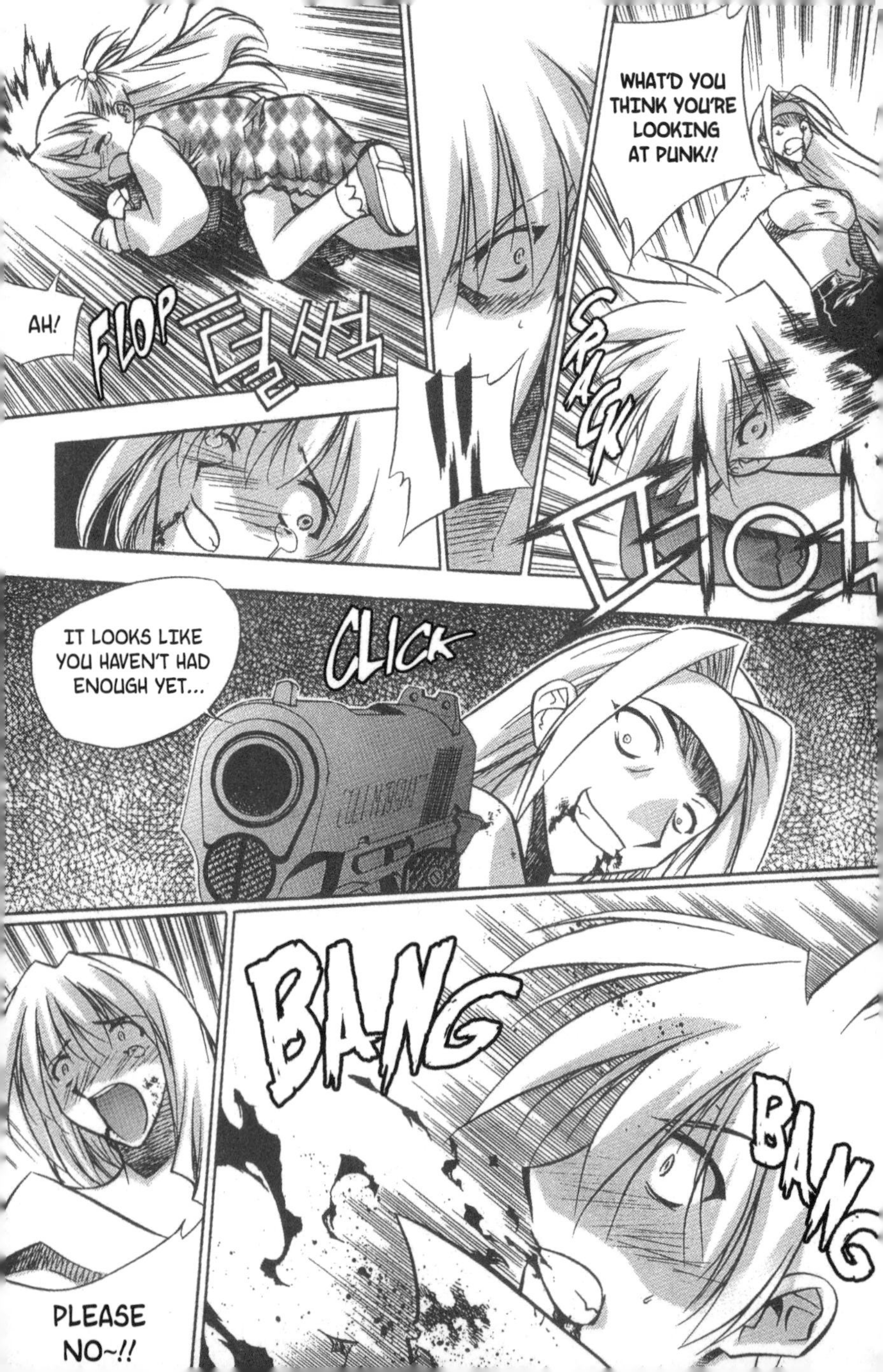
AH!
FLOP
WHAT'D YOU THINK YOU'RE LOOKING AT PUNK!!
CRACK
IT LOOKS LIKE YOU HAVEN'T HAD ENOUGH YET...
CLICK
PLEASE NO~!!
BANG
BANG
BANG

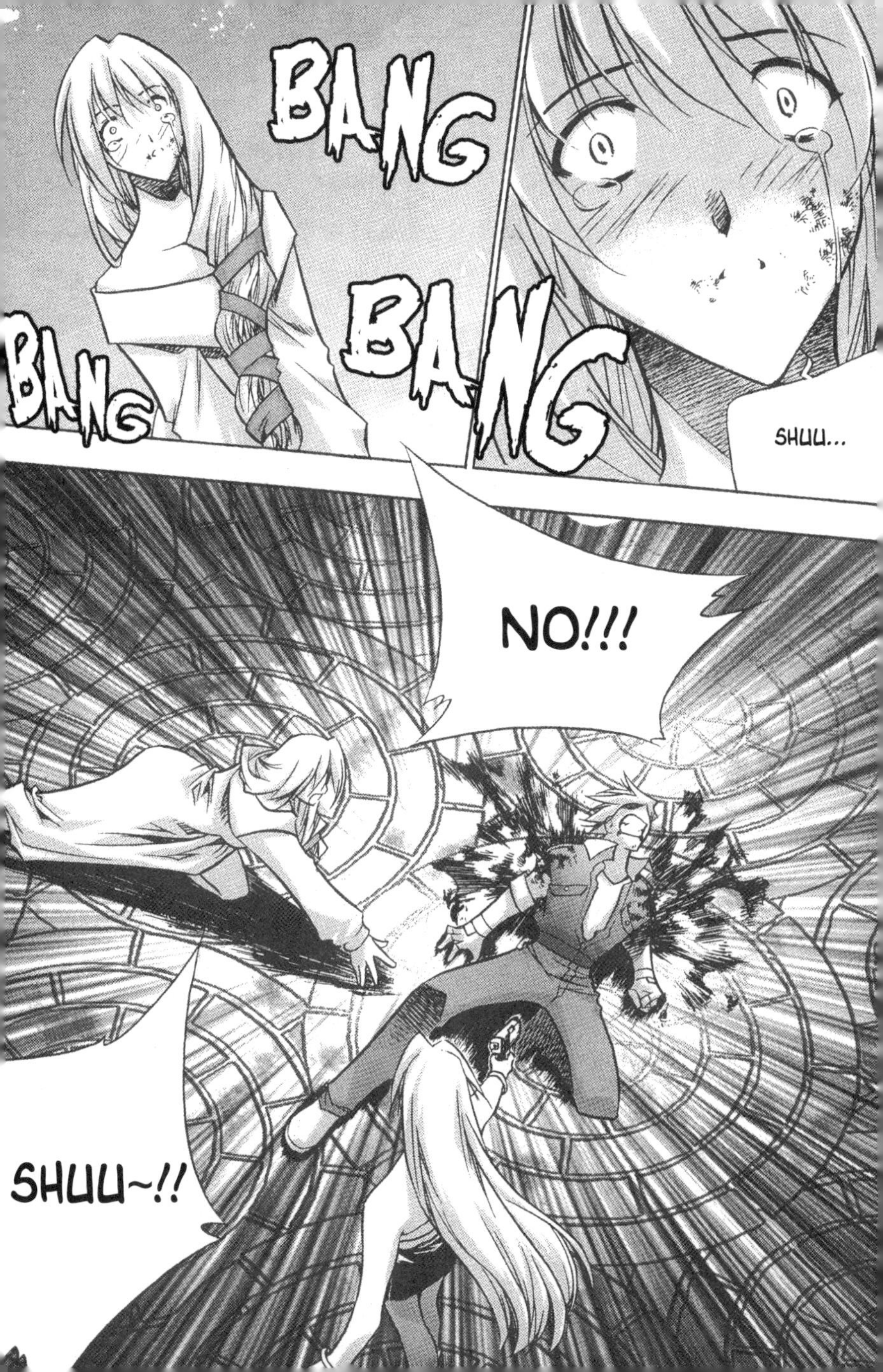
BANG
BANG
BANG
SHUU...
NO!!!
SHUU~!!

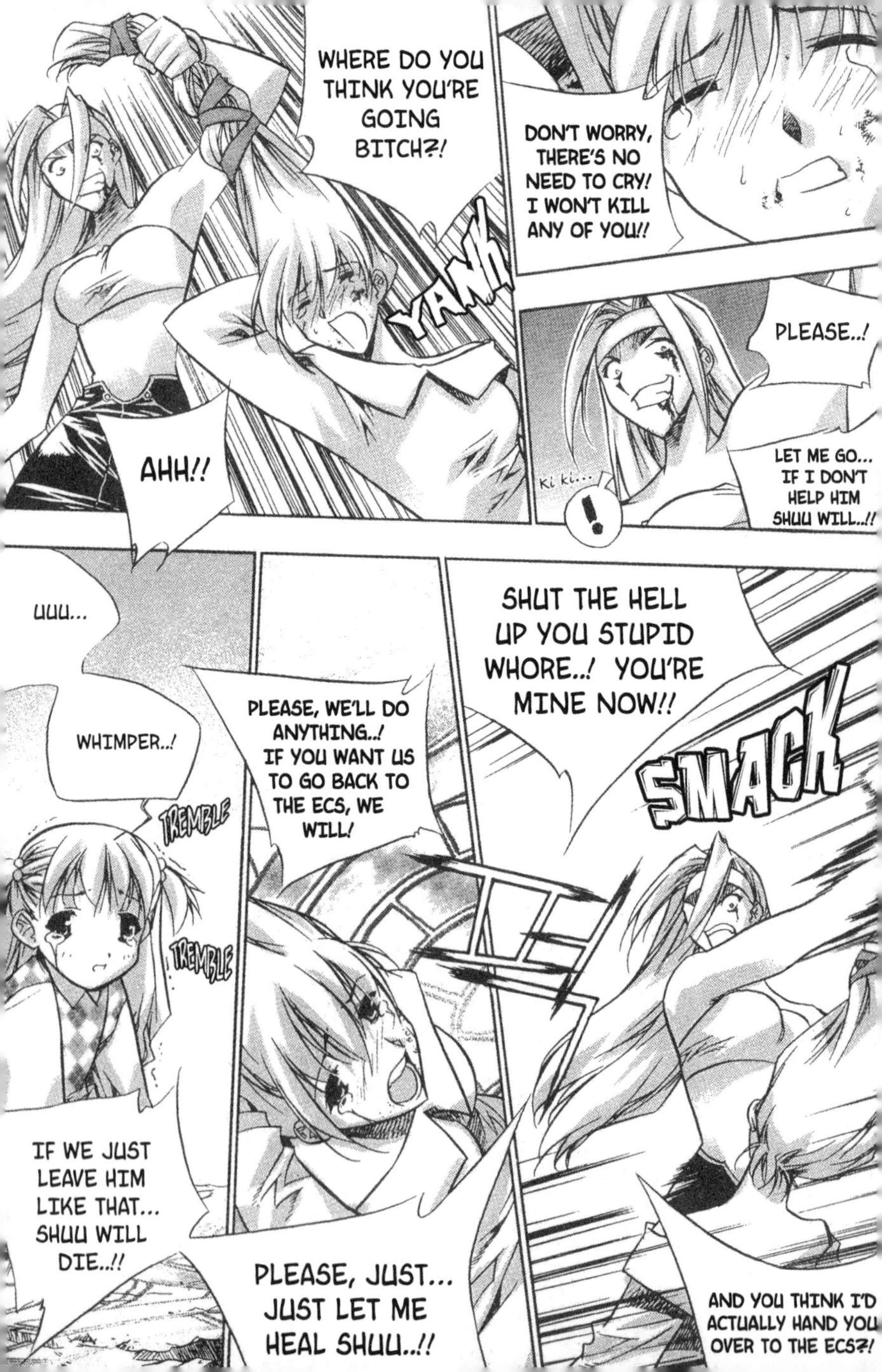

WHERE DO YOU THINK YOU'RE GOING BITCH?!
YANK
AHH!!
DON'T WORRY, THERE'S NO NEED TO CRY! I WON'T KILL ANY OF YOU!!
PLEASE..!
Ki ki...
!
LET ME GO... IF I DON'T HELP HIM SHUU WILL..!!
uuu...
WHIMPER..!
TREMBLE
TREMBLE
IF WE JUST LEAVE HIM LIKE THAT... SHUU WILL DIE..!!
PLEASE, WE'LL DO ANYTHING..! IF YOU WANT US TO GO BACK TO THE ECS, WE WILL!
PLEASE, JUST... JUST LET ME HEAL SHUU..!!
SHUT THE HELL UP YOU STUPID WHORE..! YOU'RE MINE NOW!!
SMACK
AND YOU THINK I'D ACTUALLY HAND YOU OVER TO THE ECS?!

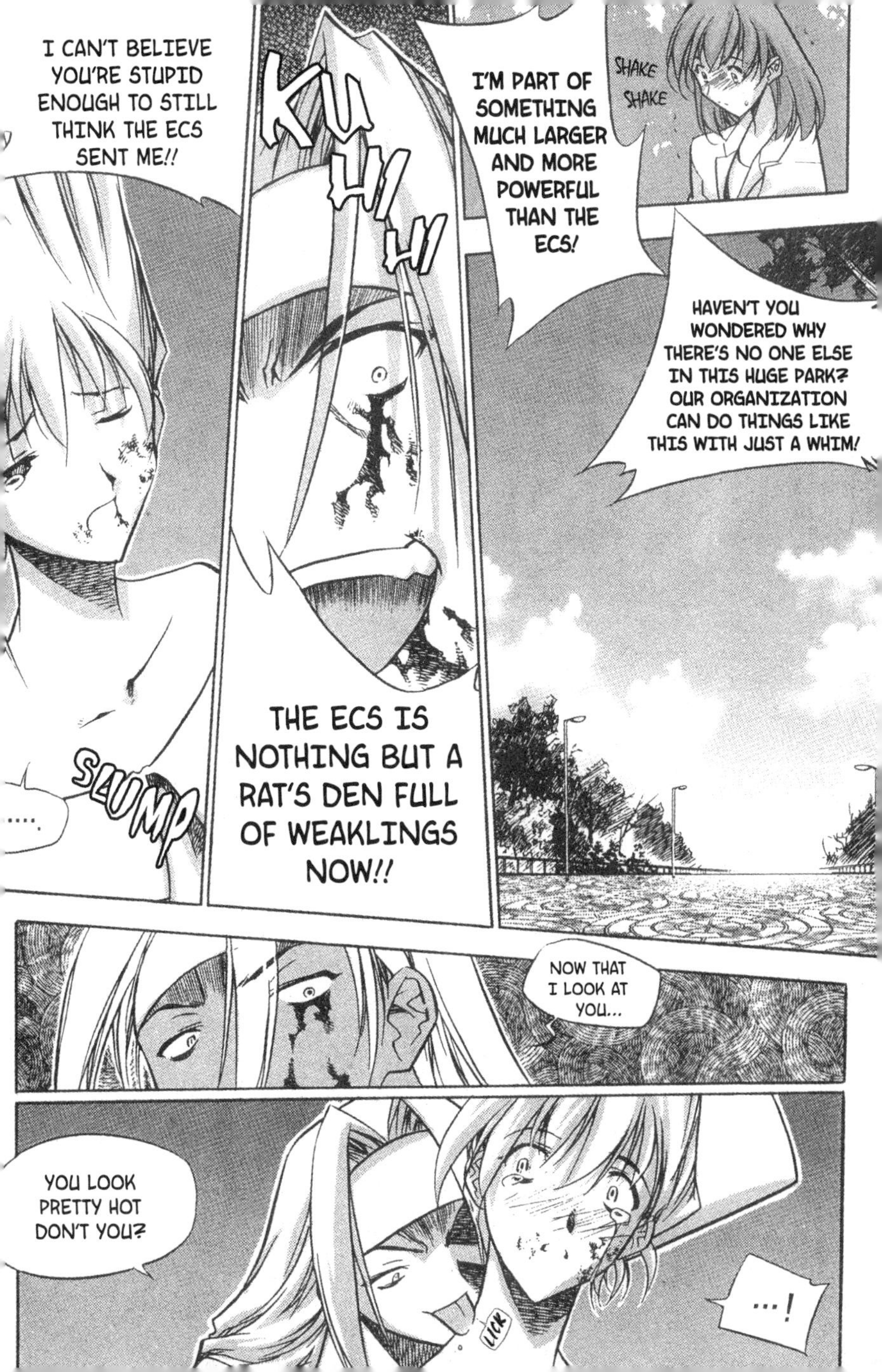
I CAN'T BELIEVE YOU'RE STUPID ENOUGH TO STILL THINK THE ECS SENT ME!!
SLUMP
.....
KU HI HI
THE ECS IS NOTHING BUT A RAT'S DEN FULL OF WEAKLINGS NOW!!
I'M PART OF SOMETHING MUCH LARGER AND MORE POWERFUL THAN THE ECS!
SHAKE SHAKE
HAVEN'T YOU WONDERED WHY THERE'S NO ONE ELSE IN THIS HUGE PARK? OUR ORGANIZATION CAN DO THINGS LIKE THIS WITH JUST A WHIM!
NOW THAT I LOOK AT YOU...
YOU LOOK PRETTY HOT DON'T YOU?
LICK
...!

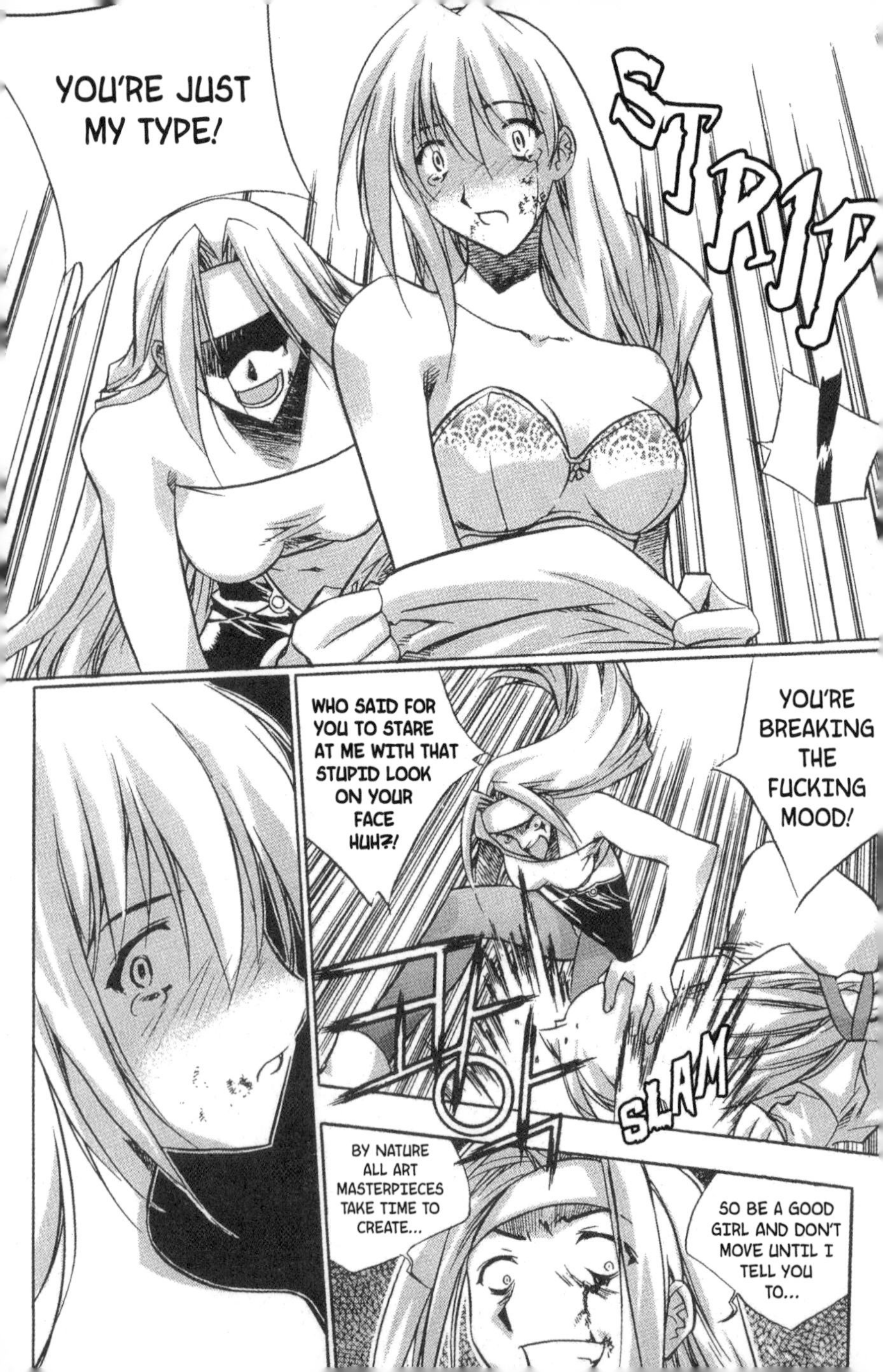
YOU'RE JUST MY TYPE!
STRIP
WHO SAID FOR YOU TO STARE AT ME WITH THAT STUPID LOOK ON YOUR FACE HUH?!
YOU'RE BREAKING THE FUCKING MOOD!
SLAM
BY NATURE ALL ART MASTERPIECES TAKE TIME TO CREATE...
SO BE A GOOD GIRL AND DON'T MOVE UNTIL I TELL YOU TO...

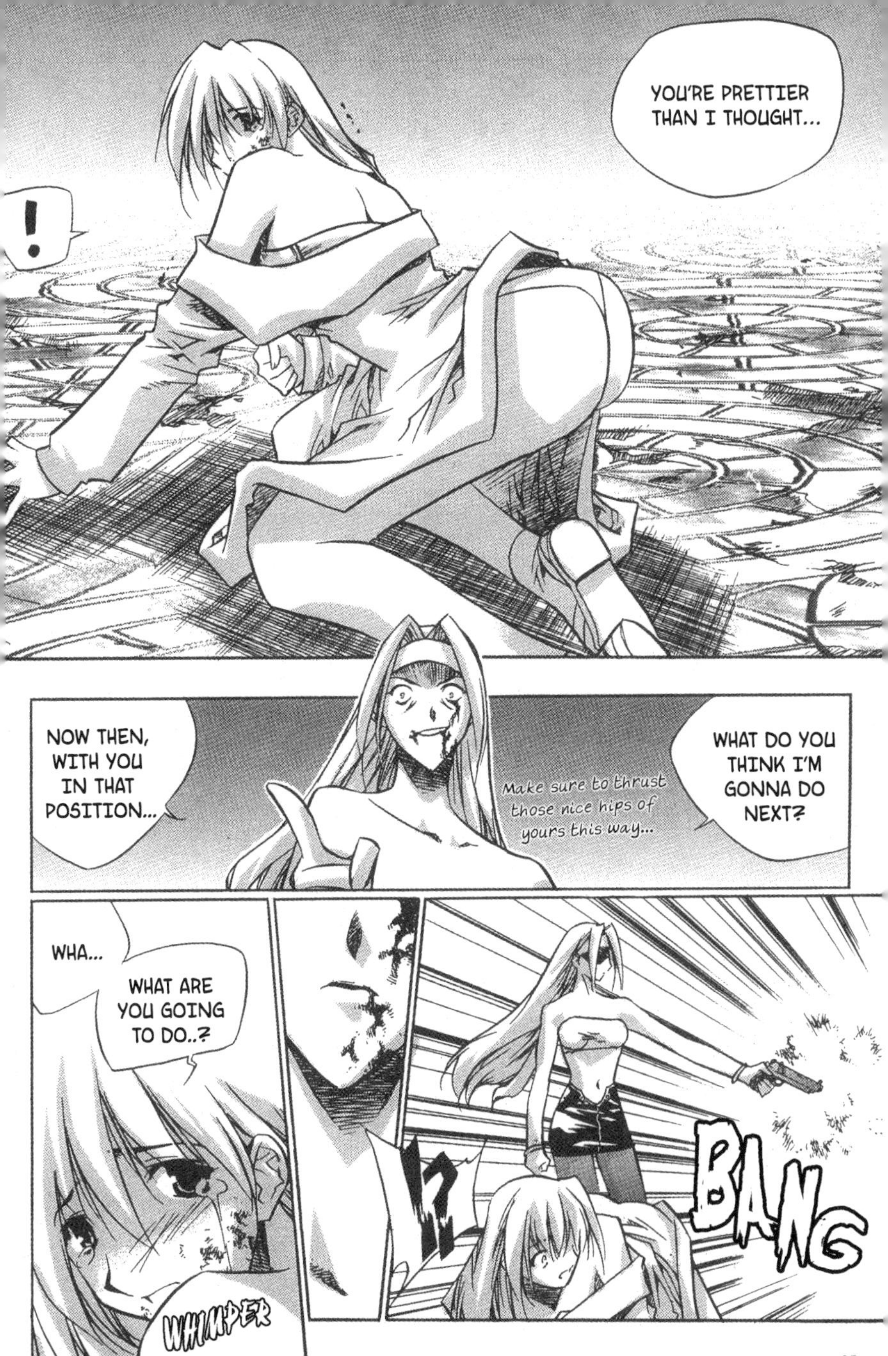
!
YOU'RE PRETTIER THAN I THOUGHT...
NOW THEN, WITH YOU IN THAT POSITION...
Make sure to thrust those nice hips of yours this way...
WHAT DO YOU THINK I'M GONNA DO NEXT?
WHA...
WHAT ARE YOU GOING TO DO..?
WHIMPER
!?
BANG

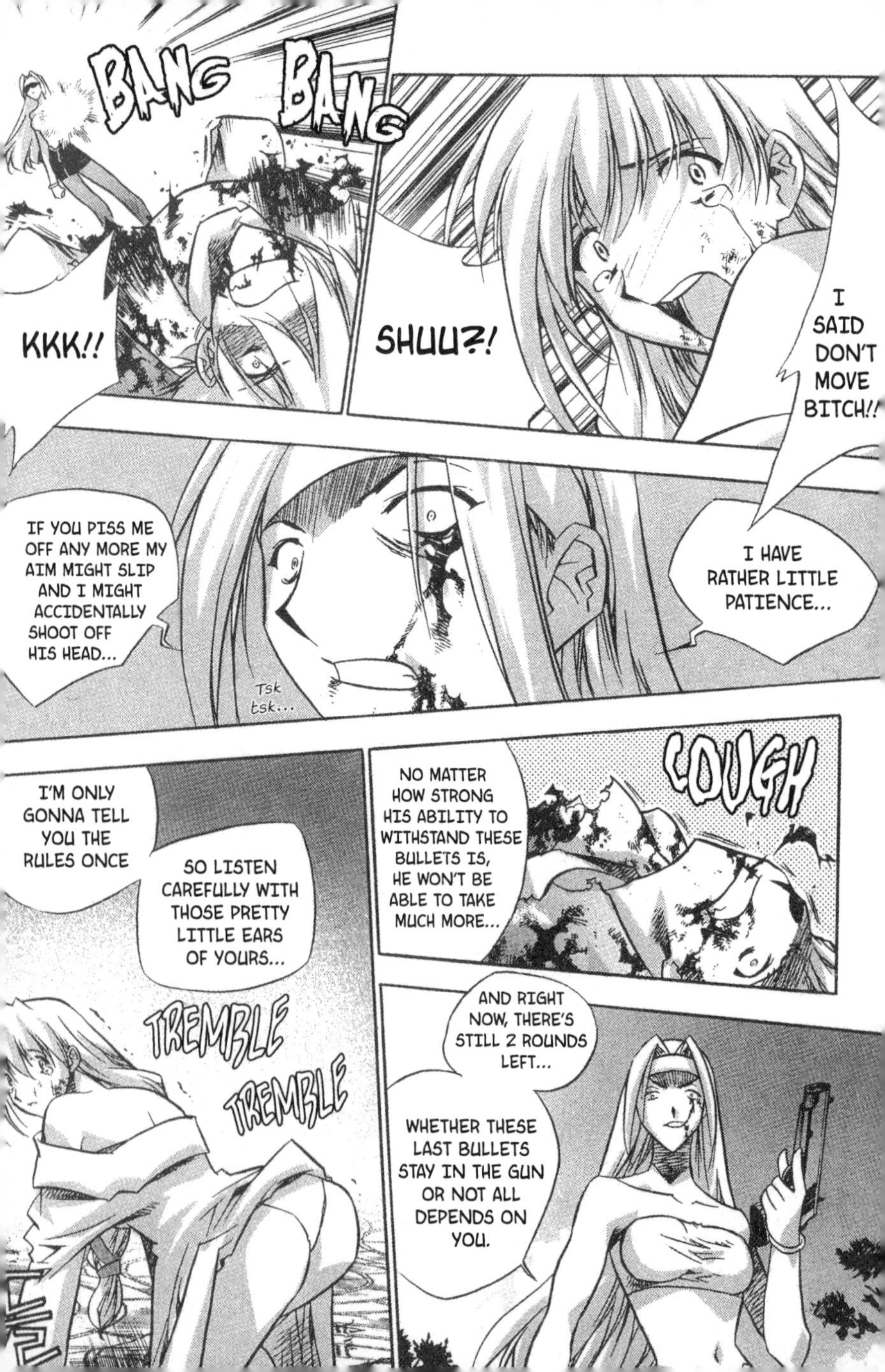
BANG BANG
KKK!!
SHUU?!
I SAID DON'T MOVE BITCH!!
IF YOU PISS ME OFF ANY MORE MY AIM MIGHT SLIP AND I MIGHT ACCIDENTALLY SHOOT OFF HIS HEAD...
Tsk tsk...
I HAVE RATHER LITTLE PATIENCE...
I'M ONLY GONNA TELL YOU THE RULES ONCE
SO LISTEN CAREFULLY WITH THOSE PRETTY LITTLE EARS OF YOURS...
TREMBLE
TREMBLE
NO MATTER HOW STRONG HIS ABILITY TO WITHSTAND THESE BULLETS IS, HE WON'T BE ABLE TO TAKE MUCH MORE...
COUGH
AND RIGHT NOW, THERE'S STILL 2 ROUNDS LEFT...
WHETHER THESE LAST BULLETS STAY IN THE GUN OR NOT ALL DEPENDS ON YOU.

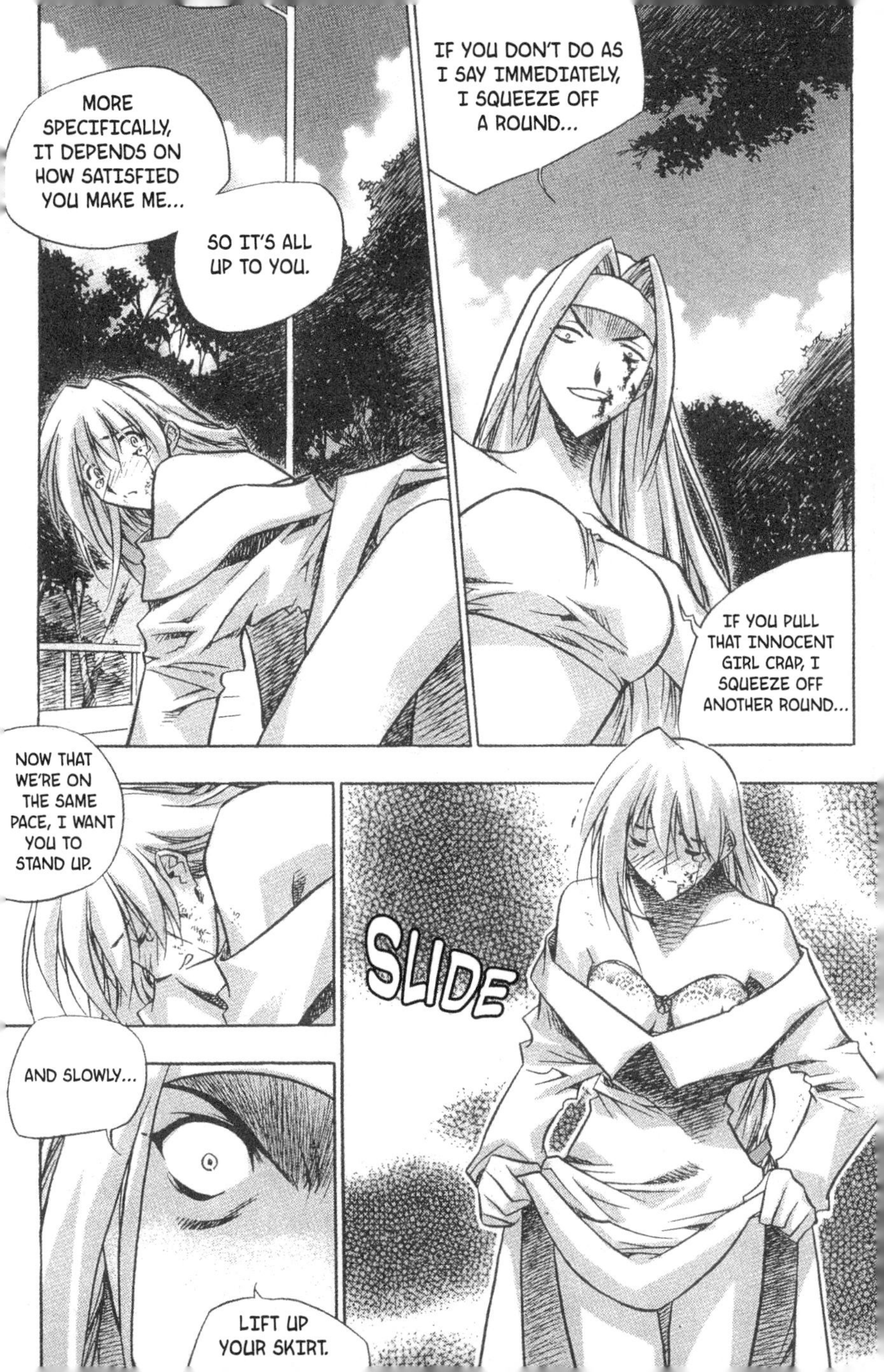
MORE SPECIFICALLY, IT DEPENDS ON HOW SATISFIED YOU MAKE ME...
SO IT'S ALL UP TO YOU.
IF YOU DON'T DO AS I SAY IMMEDIATELY, I SQUEEZE OFF A ROUND...
IF YOU PULL THAT INNOCENT GIRL CRAP, I SQUEEZE OFF ANOTHER ROUND...
NOW THAT WE'RE ON THE SAME PACE, I WANT YOU TO STAND UP.
AND SLOWLY...
LIFT UP YOUR SKIRT.
SLIDE

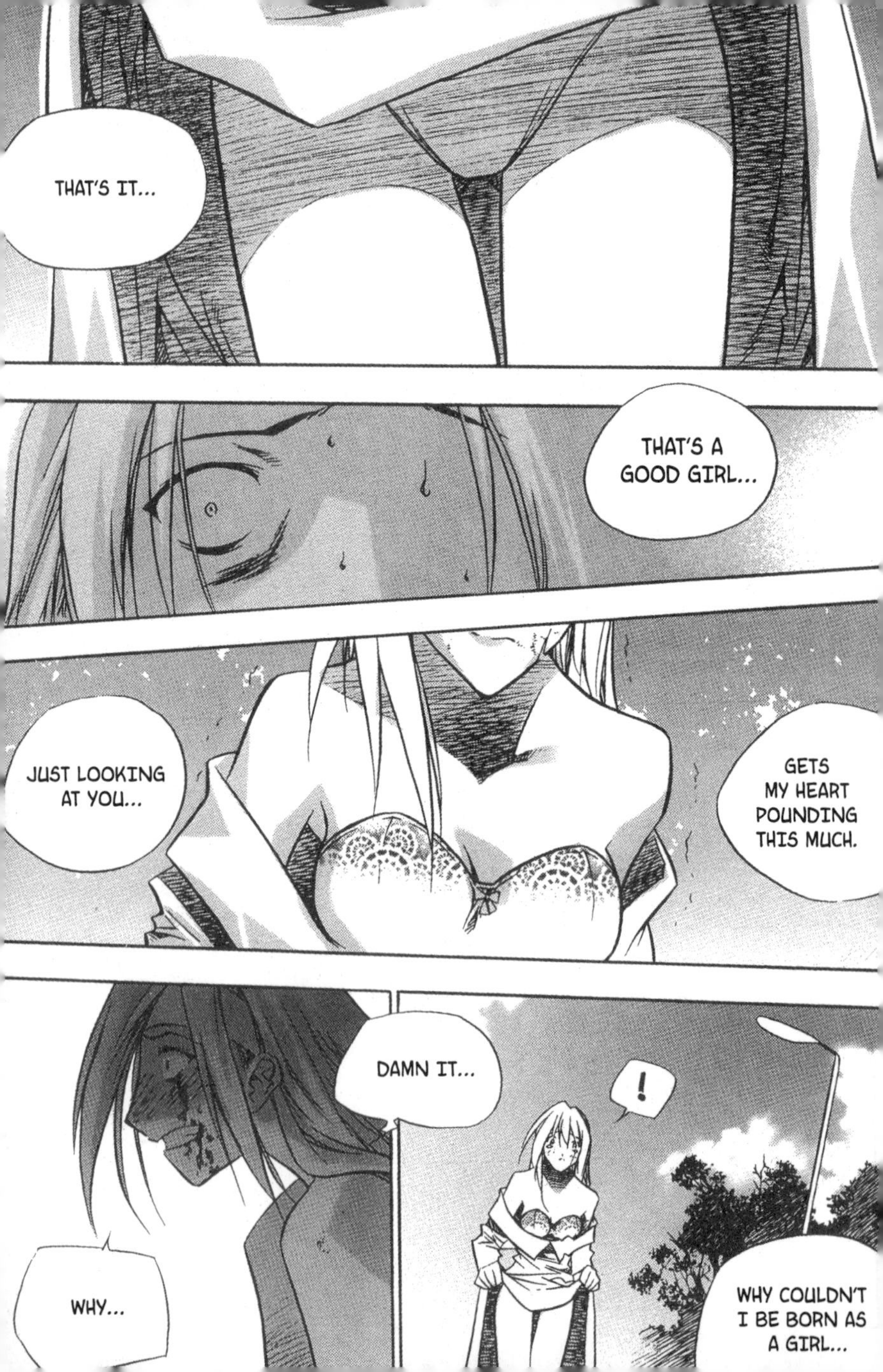
THAT'S IT...
THAT'S A GOOD GIRL...
JUST LOOKING AT YOU...
GETS MY HEART POUNDING THIS MUCH.
DAMN IT...
!
WHY...
WHY COULDN'T I BE BORN AS A GIRL...

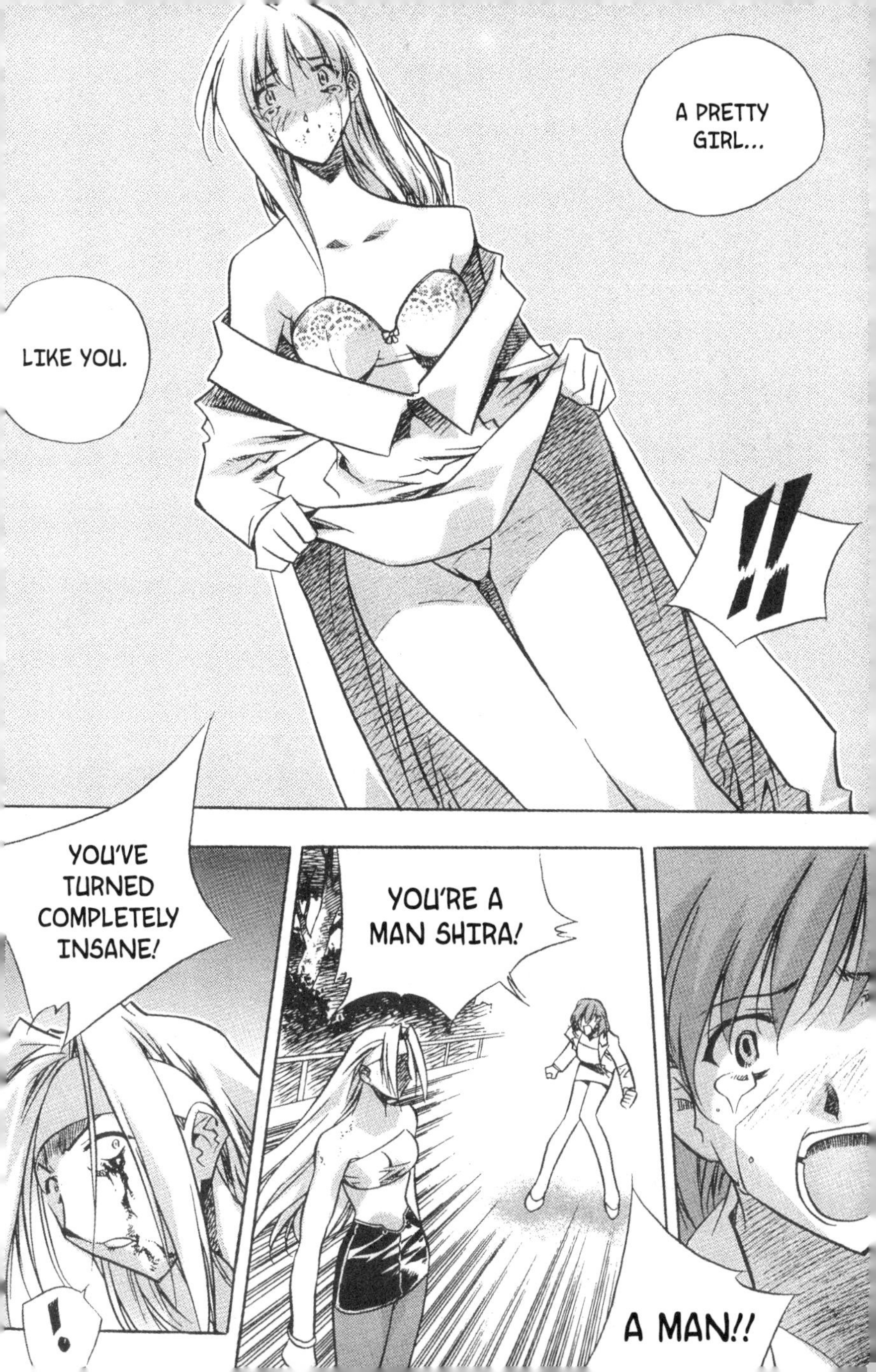
A PRETTY GIRL...
LIKE YOU.
!!
YOU'VE TURNED COMPLETELY INSANE!
!
YOU'RE A MAN SHIRA!
A MAN!!

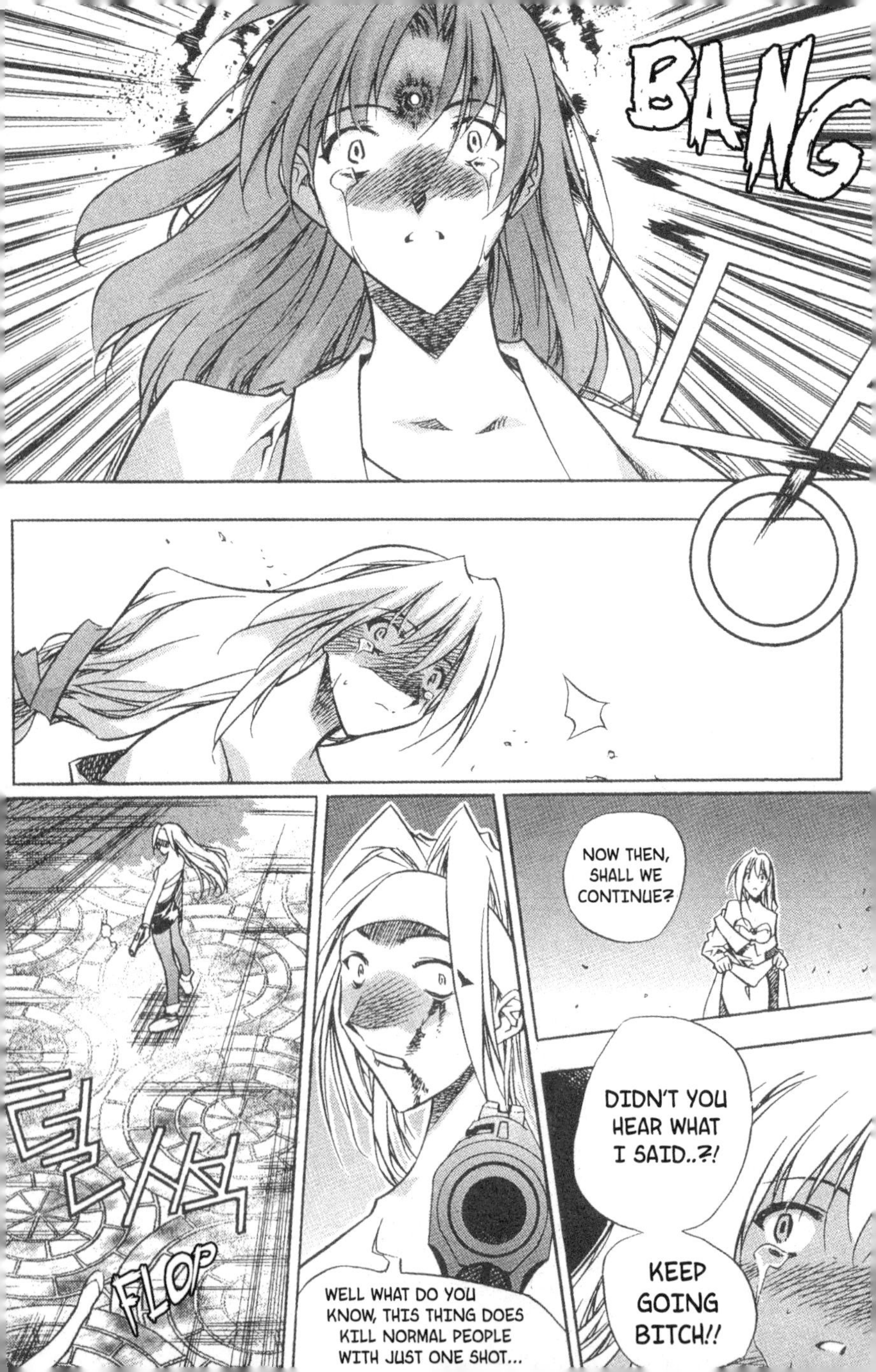
BANG
FLOP
WELL WHAT DO YOU KNOW, THIS THING DOES KILL NORMAL PEOPLE WITH JUST ONE SHOT...
NOW THEN, SHALL WE CONTINUE?
DIDN'T YOU HEAR WHAT I SAID..?!
KEEP GOING BITCH!!

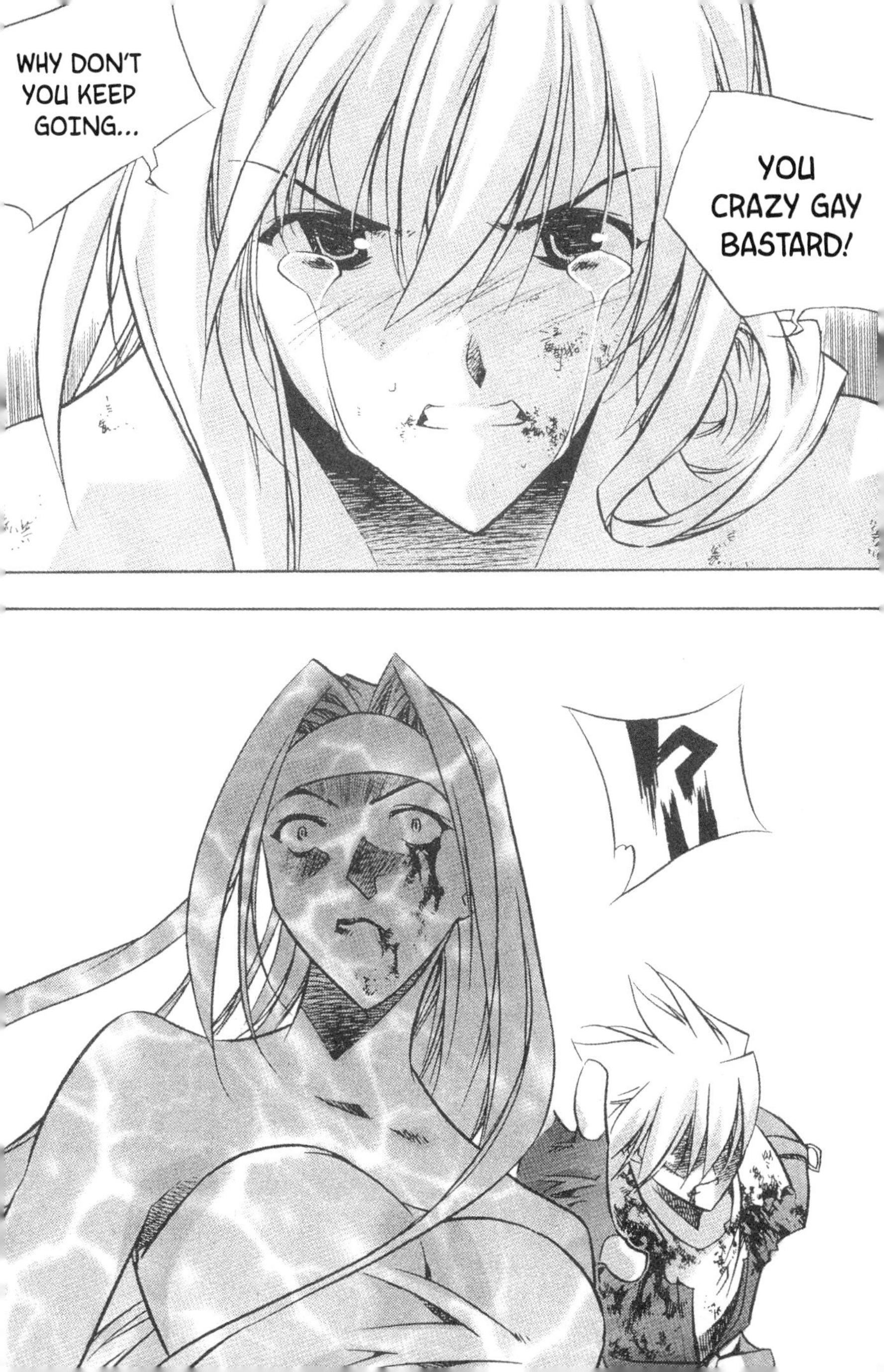
WHY DON'T YOU KEEP GOING...
YOU CRAZY GAY BASTARD!

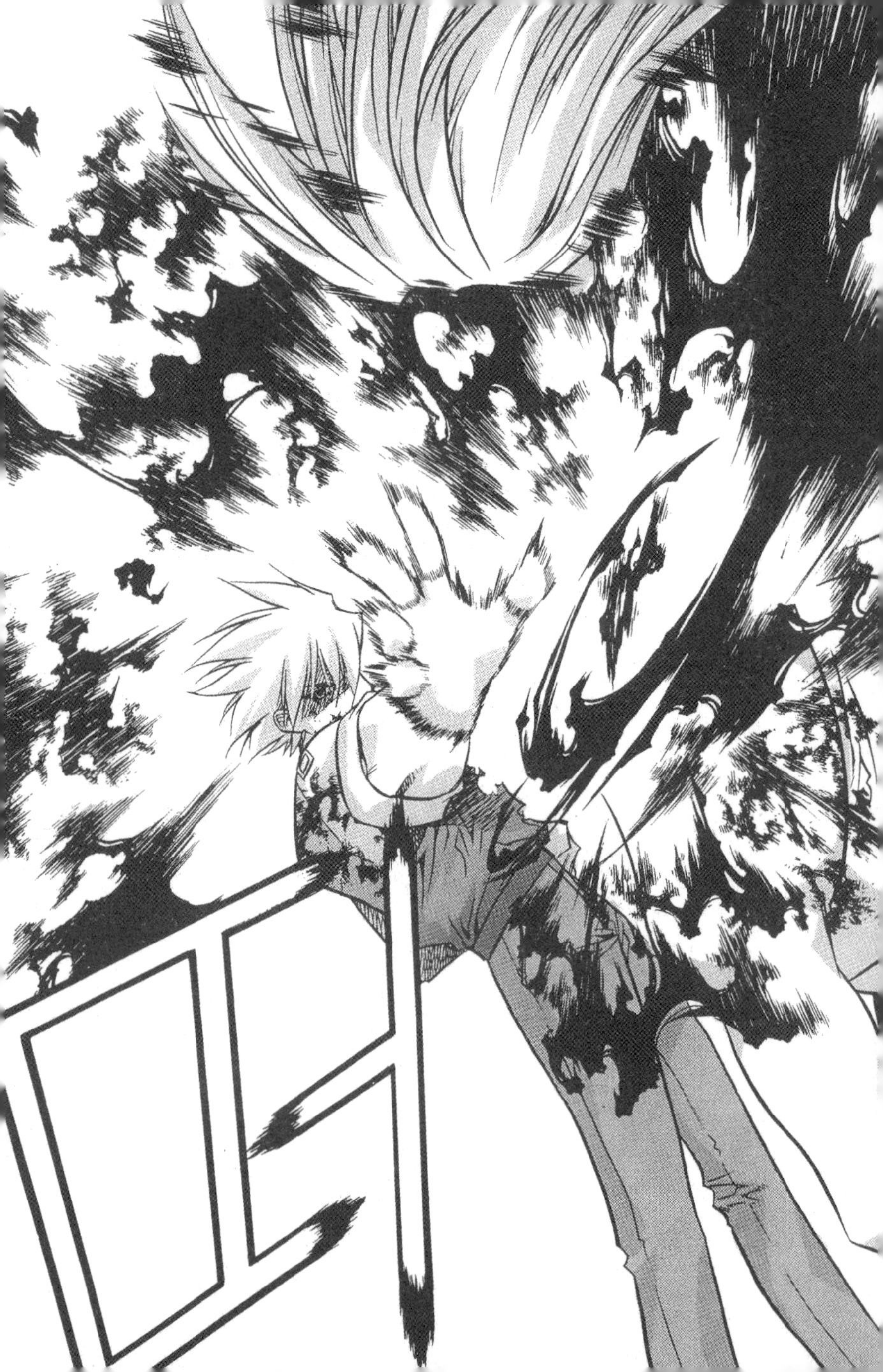

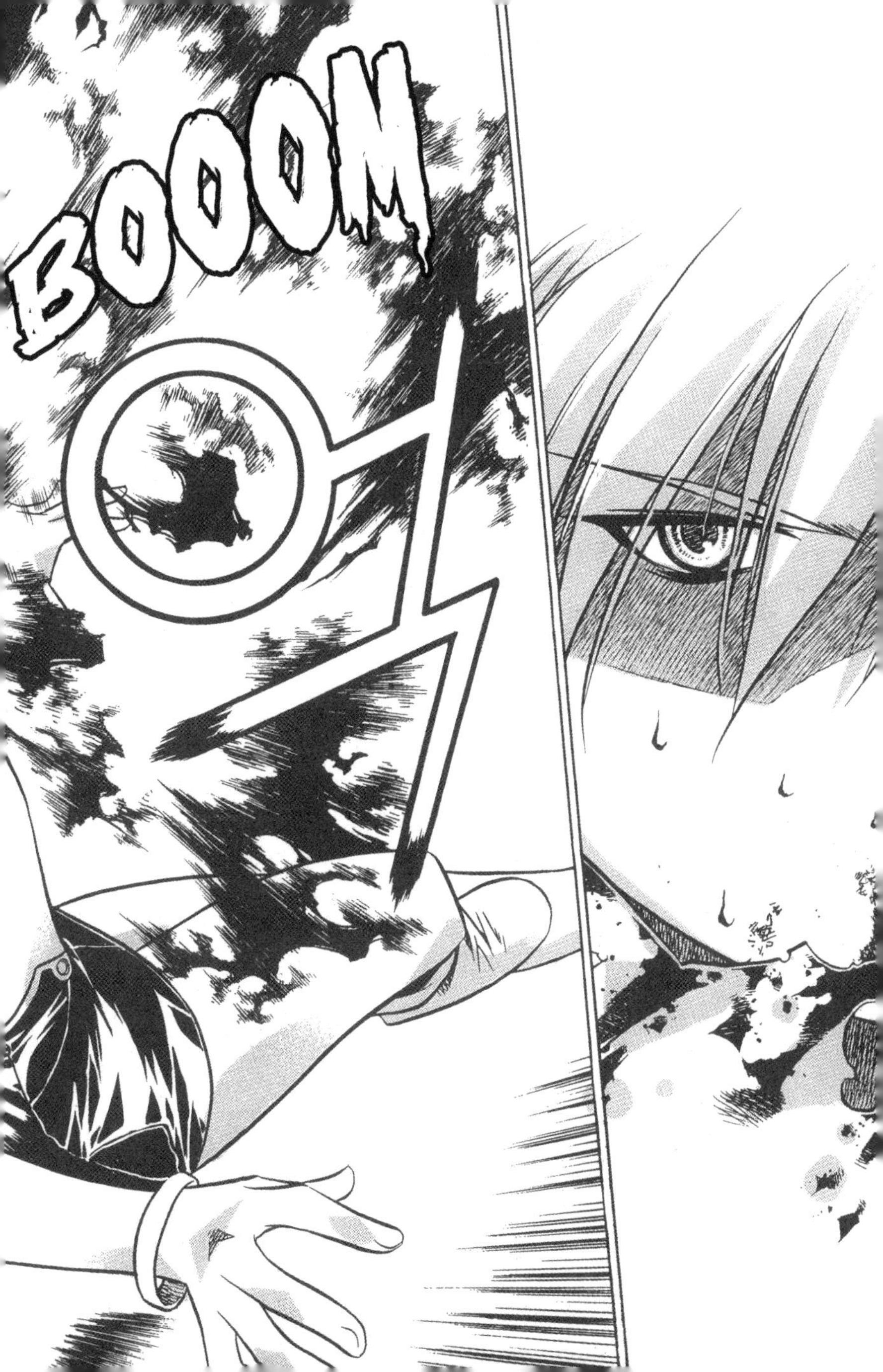
BOOOM

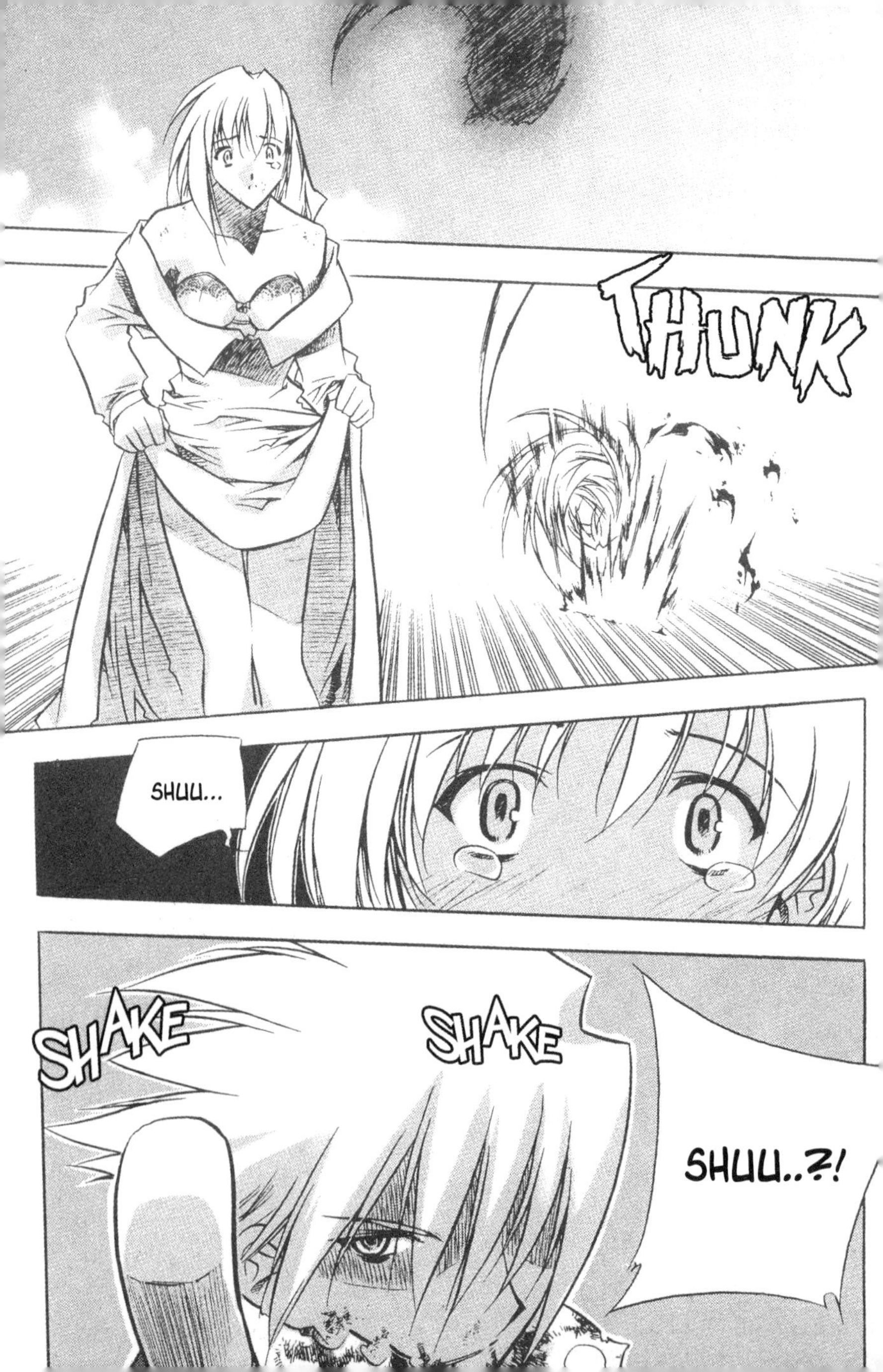
THUNK
SHUU...
SHAKE
SHAKE
SHUU..?!

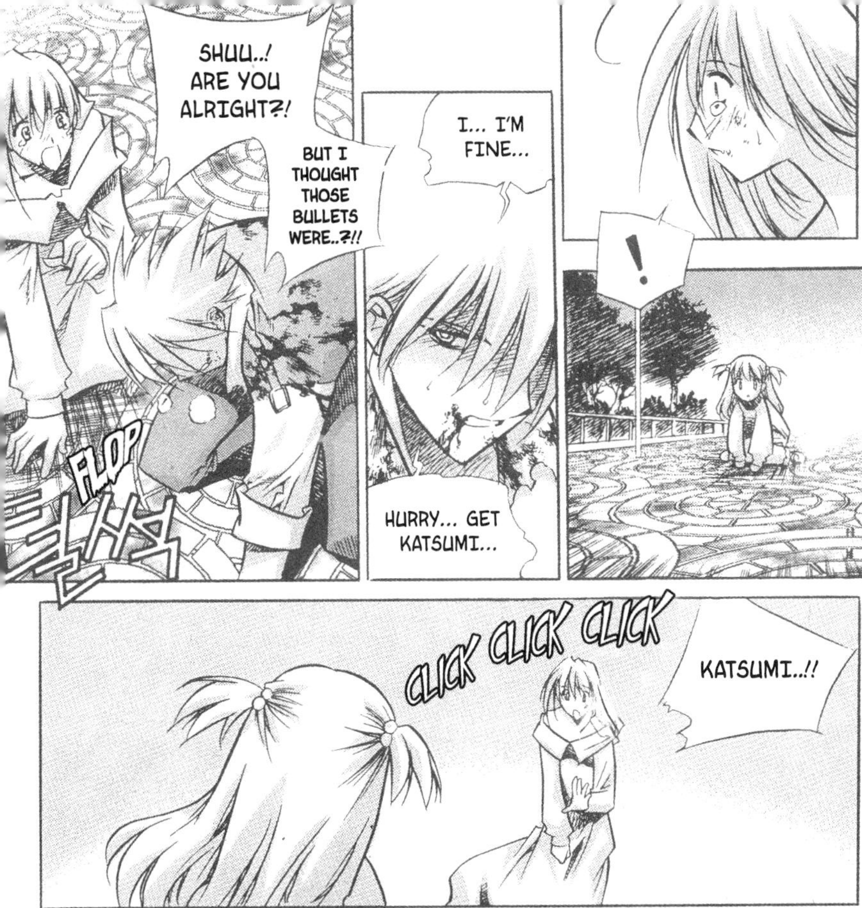
SHUU..! ARE YOU ALRIGHT?!
BUT I THOUGHT THOSE BULLETS WERE..?!!
FLOP
I... I'M FINE...
HURRY... GET KATSUMI...
!
CLICK CLICK CLICK
KATSUMI..!!

Note : Un-nee is the word women use to address an older sister or a close elder female acquaintance. Literally, it means "older sister."

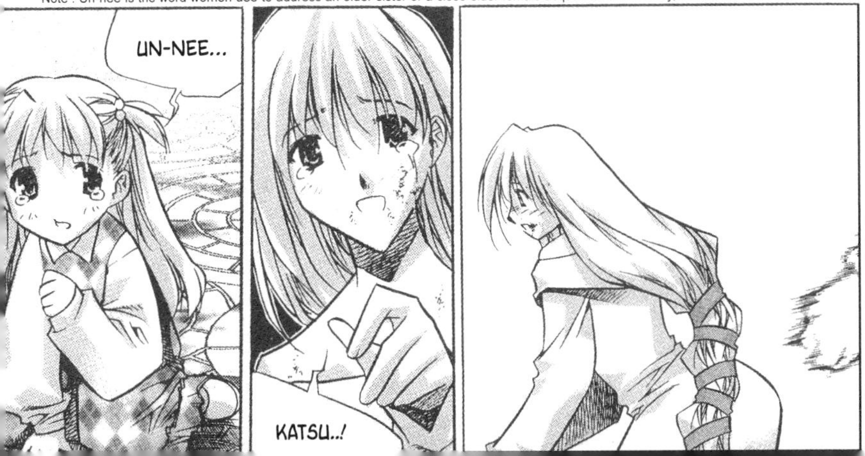
UN-NEE...
KATSU..!

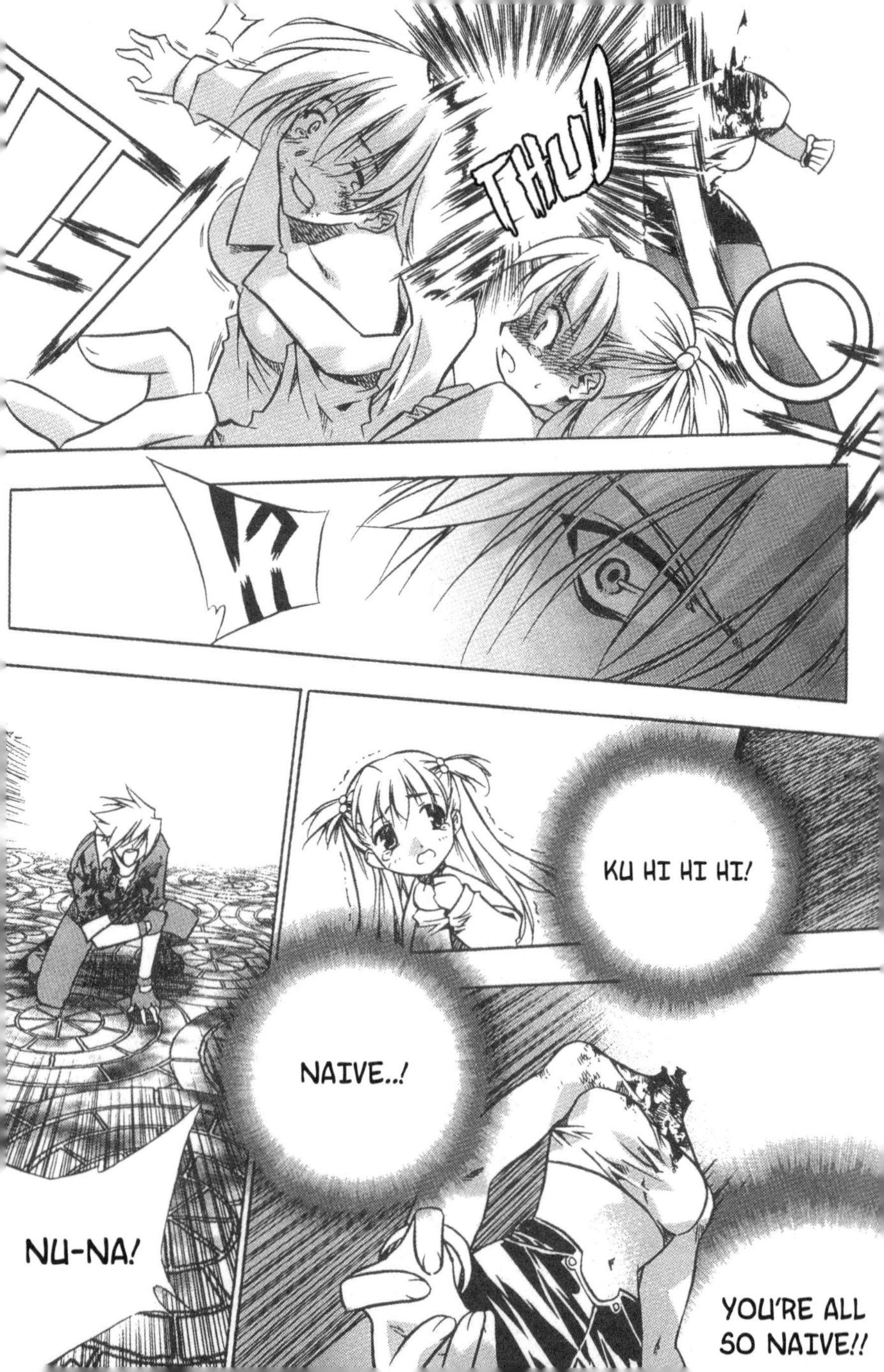
THUD
!?
NU-NA!
KU HI HI HI!
NAIVE..!
YOU'RE ALL SO NAIVE!!

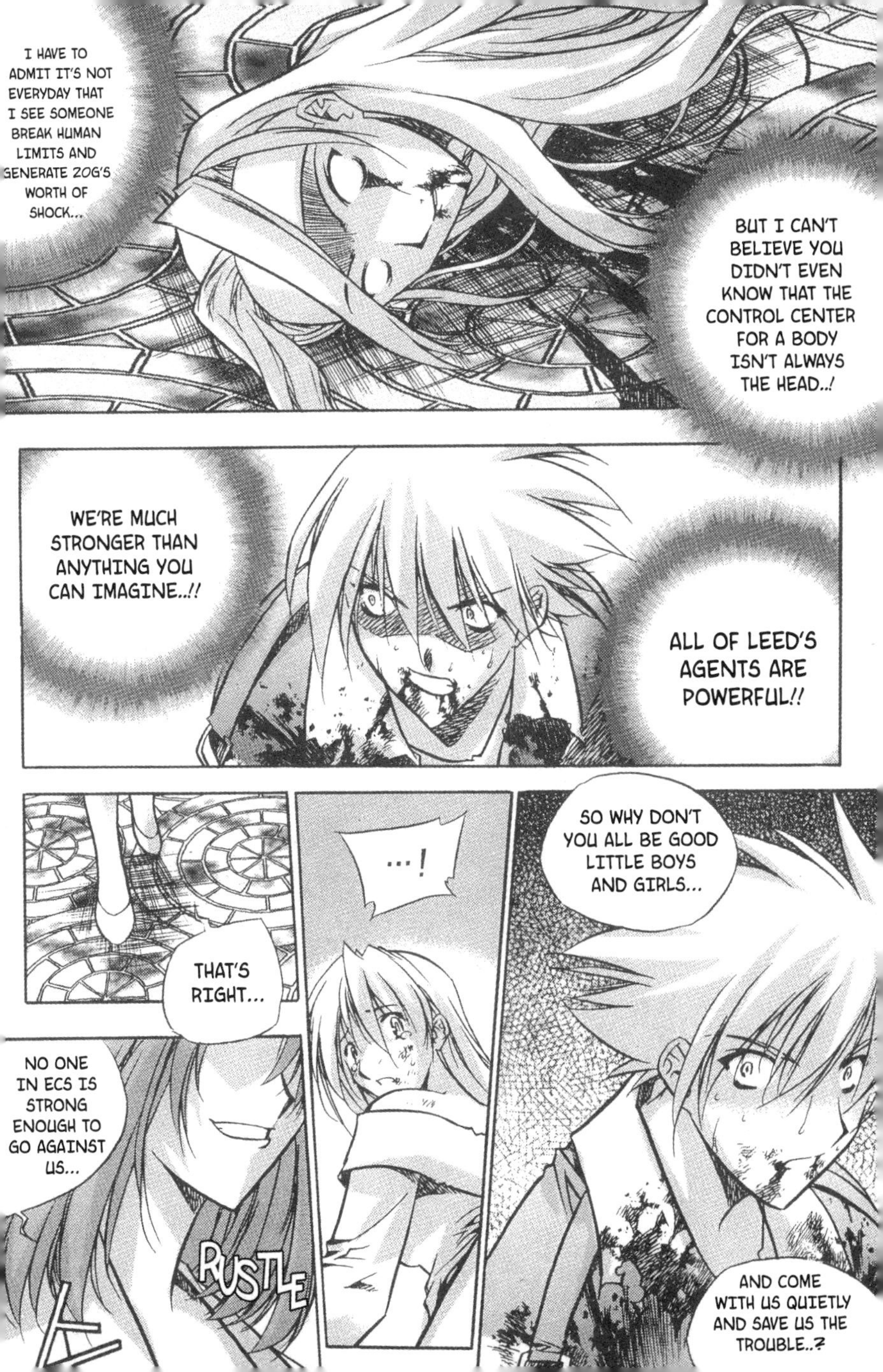
I HAVE TO ADMIT IT'S NOT EVERYDAY THAT I SEE SOMEONE BREAK HUMAN LIMITS AND GENERATE ZOG'S WORTH OF SHOCK...
BUT I CAN'T BELIEVE YOU DIDN'T EVEN KNOW THAT THE CONTROL CENTER FOR A BODY ISN'T ALWAYS THE HEAD..!
WE'RE MUCH STRONGER THAN ANYTHING YOU CAN IMAGINE..!!
ALL OF LEED'S AGENTS ARE POWERFUL!!
THAT'S RIGHT...
...!
SO WHY DON'T YOU ALL BE GOOD LITTLE BOYS AND GIRLS...
NO ONE IN ECS IS STRONG ENOUGH TO GO AGAINST US...
RUSTLE
AND COME WITH US QUIETLY AND SAVE US THE TROUBLE..?

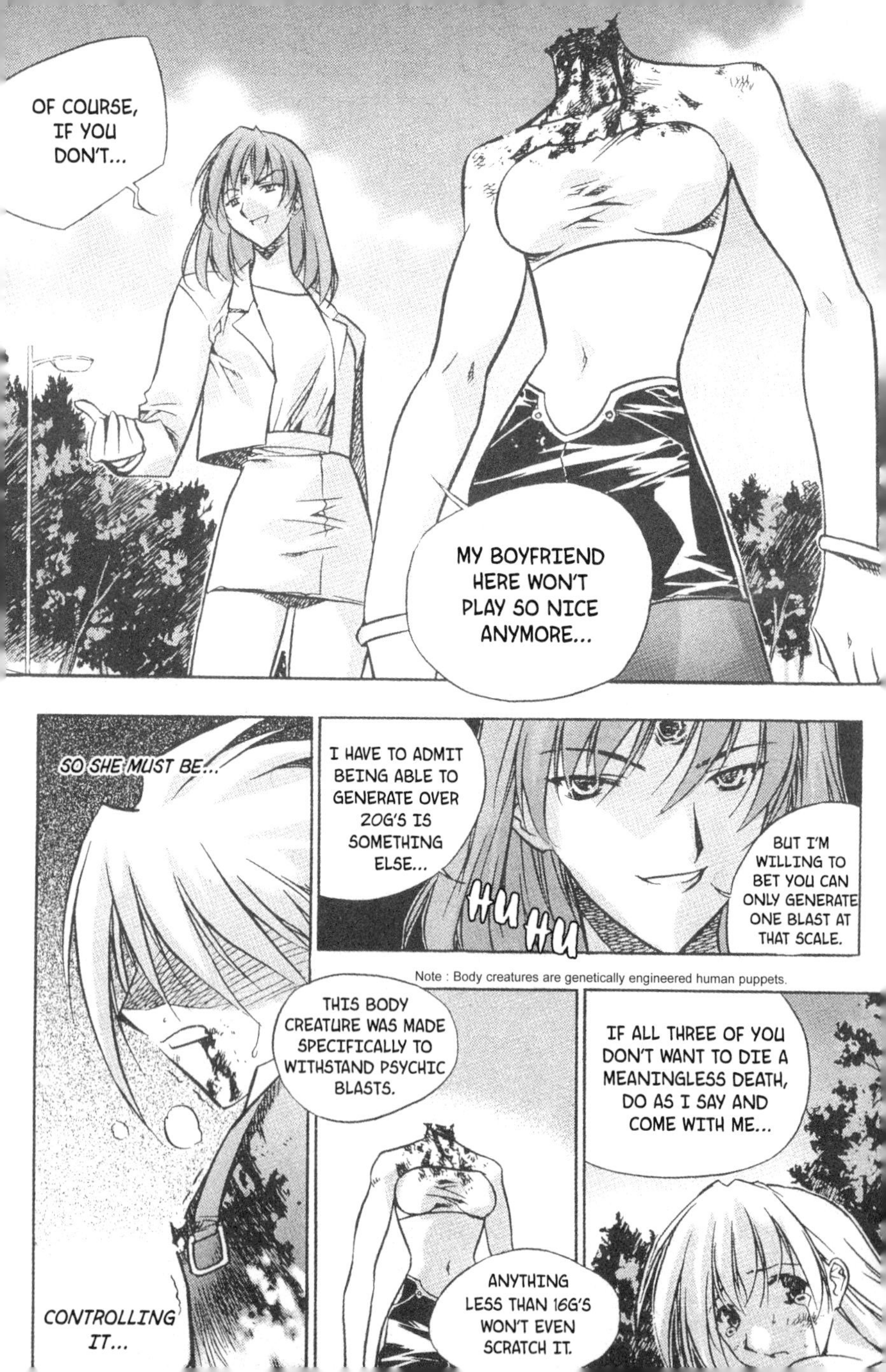
OF COURSE, IF YOU DON'T...
MY BOYFRIEND HERE WON'T PLAY SO NICE ANYMORE...
SO SHE MUST BE...
CONTROLLING IT...
I HAVE TO ADMIT BEING ABLE TO GENERATE OVER 20G'S IS SOMETHING ELSE...
HU HU
BUT I'M WILLING TO BET YOU CAN ONLY GENERATE ONE BLAST AT THAT SCALE.
THIS BODY CREATURE WAS MADE SPECIFICALLY TO WITHSTAND PSYCHIC BLASTS.
ANYTHING LESS THAN 16G'S WON'T EVEN SCRATCH IT.
IF ALL THREE OF YOU DON'T WANT TO DIE A MEANINGLESS DEATH, DO AS I SAY AND COME WITH ME...

Note : Body creatures are genetically engineered human puppets.

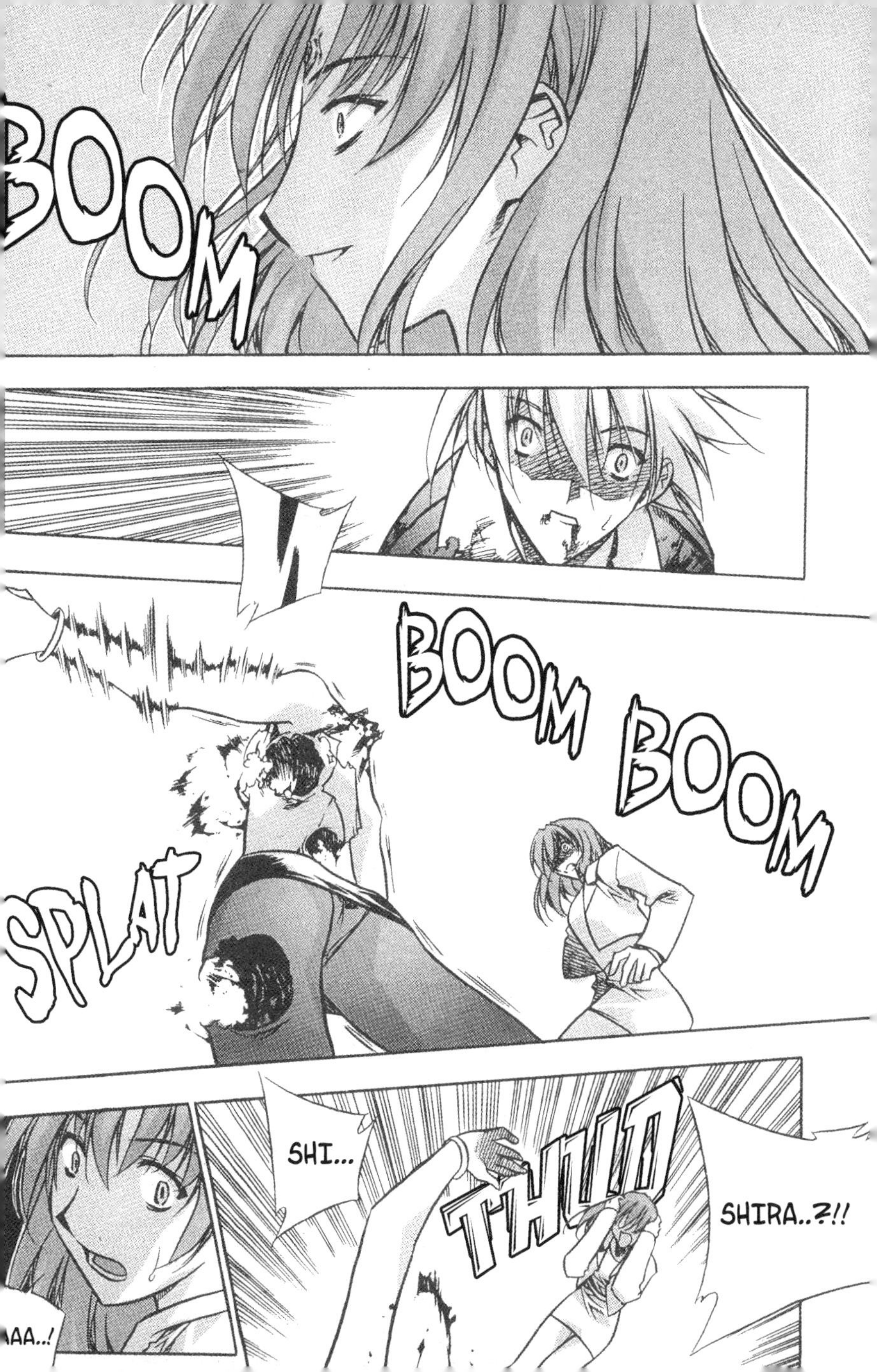
BOOM
BOOM BOOM BOOM
SPLAT
AAA..!
SHI...
THUD
SHIRA..?!!

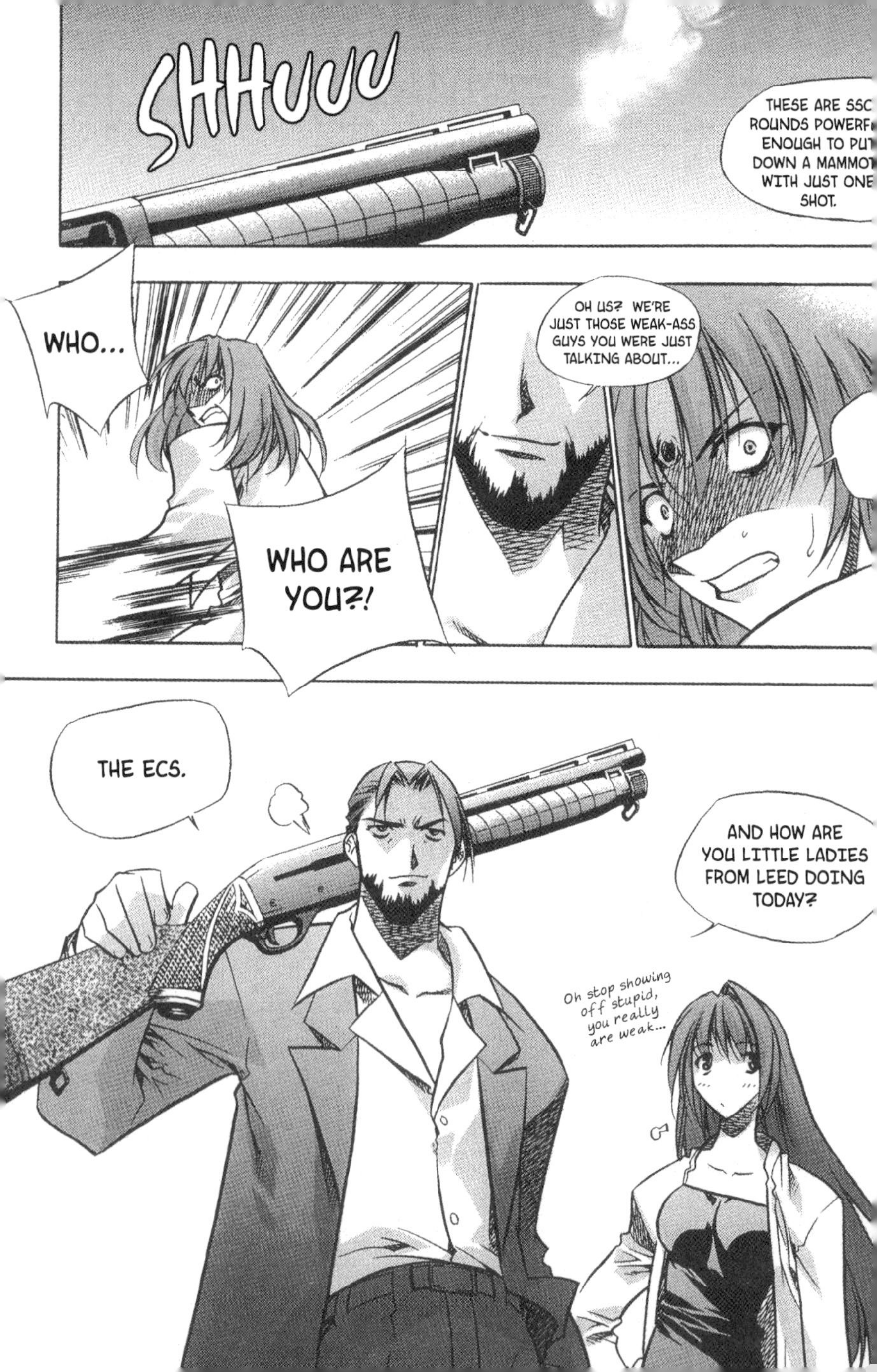
SHHUUU
THESE ARE SSC ROUNDS POWERF ENOUGH TO PUT DOWN A MAMMOT WITH JUST ONE SHOT.
WHO...
WHO ARE YOU?!
OH US? WE'RE JUST THOSE WEAK-ASS GUYS YOU WERE JUST TALKING ABOUT...
THE ECS.
AND HOW ARE YOU LITTLE LADIES FROM LEED DOING TODAY?
Oh stop showing off stupid, you really are weak...

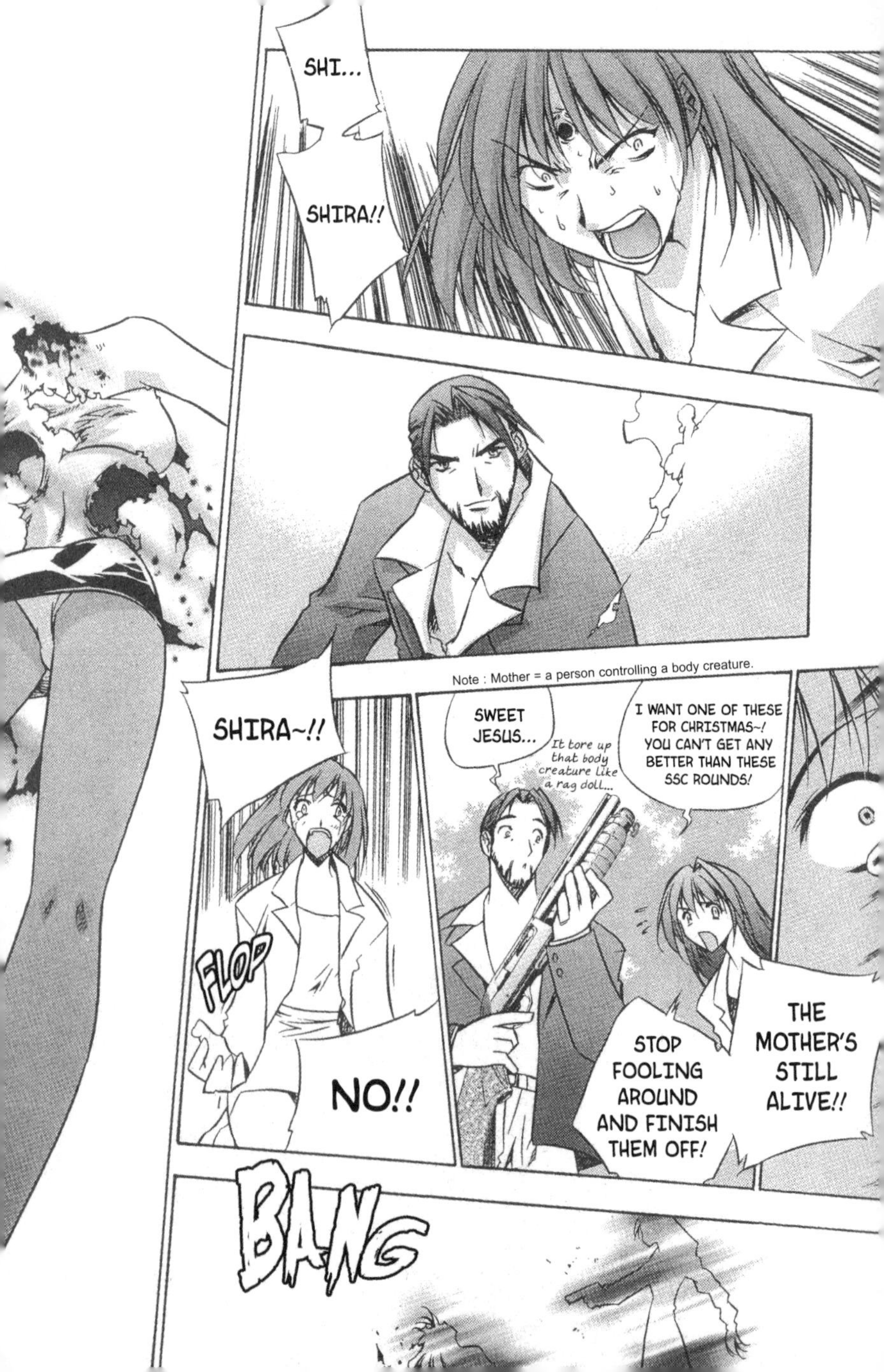
SHI...
SHIRA!!
Note : Mother = a person controlling a body creature.
SHIRA~!!
FLOP
NO!!
SWEET JESUS...
It tore up that body creature like a rag doll...
I WANT ONE OF THESE FOR CHRISTMAS~! YOU CAN'T GET ANY BETTER THAN THESE SSC ROUNDS!
STOP FOOLING AROUND AND FINISH THEM OFF!
THE MOTHER'S STILL ALIVE!!
BANG

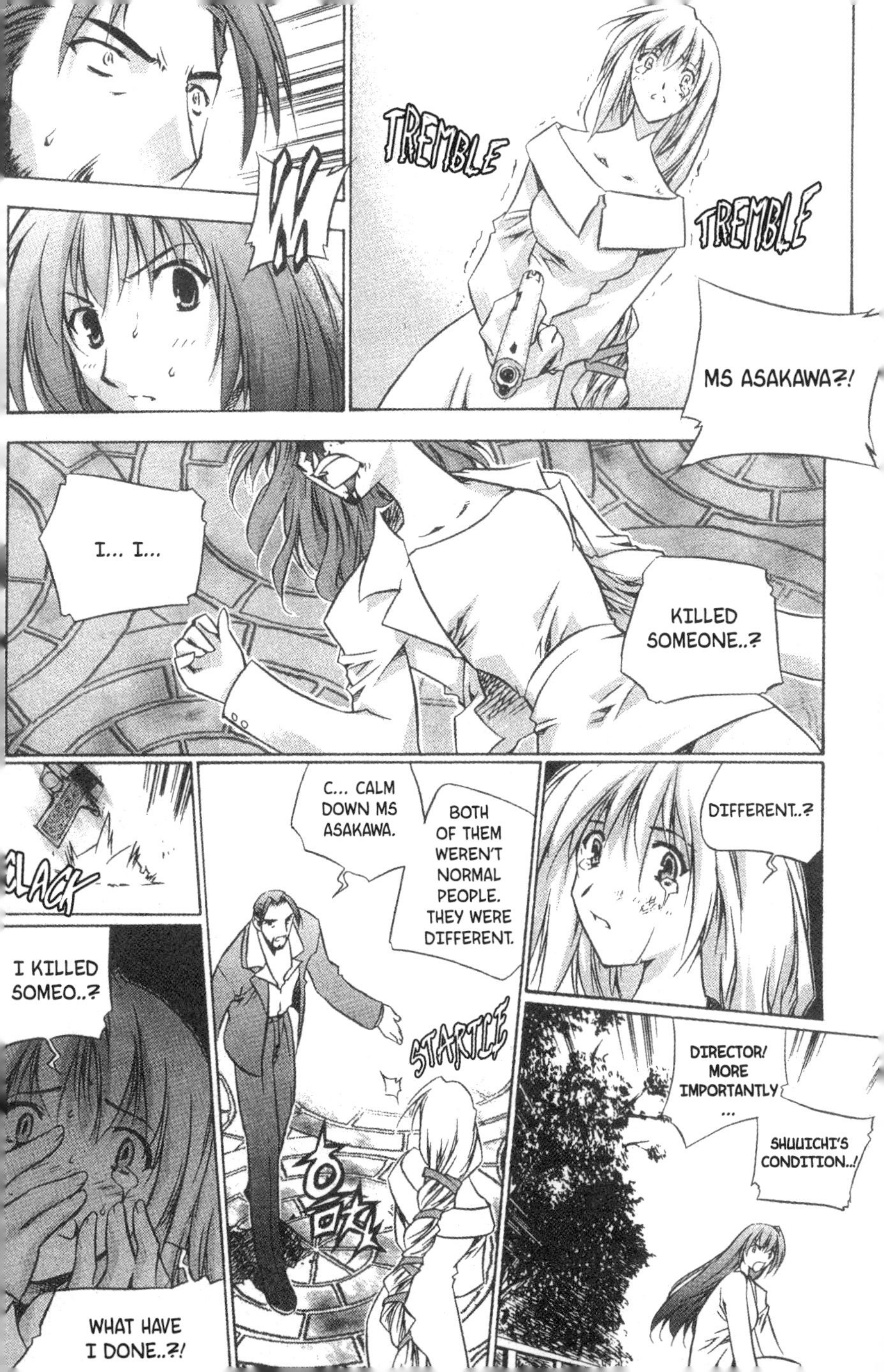

TREMBLE
TREMBLE
MS ASAKAWA?!
I... I...
KILLED SOMEONE..?
CLACK
I KILLED SOMEO..?
WHAT HAVE I DONE..?!
C... CALM DOWN MS ASAKAWA.
BOTH OF THEM WEREN'T NORMAL PEOPLE. THEY WERE DIFFERENT.
STARTLE
DIFFERENT..?
DIRECTOR! MORE IMPORTANTLY ...
SHUUICHI'S CONDITION..!

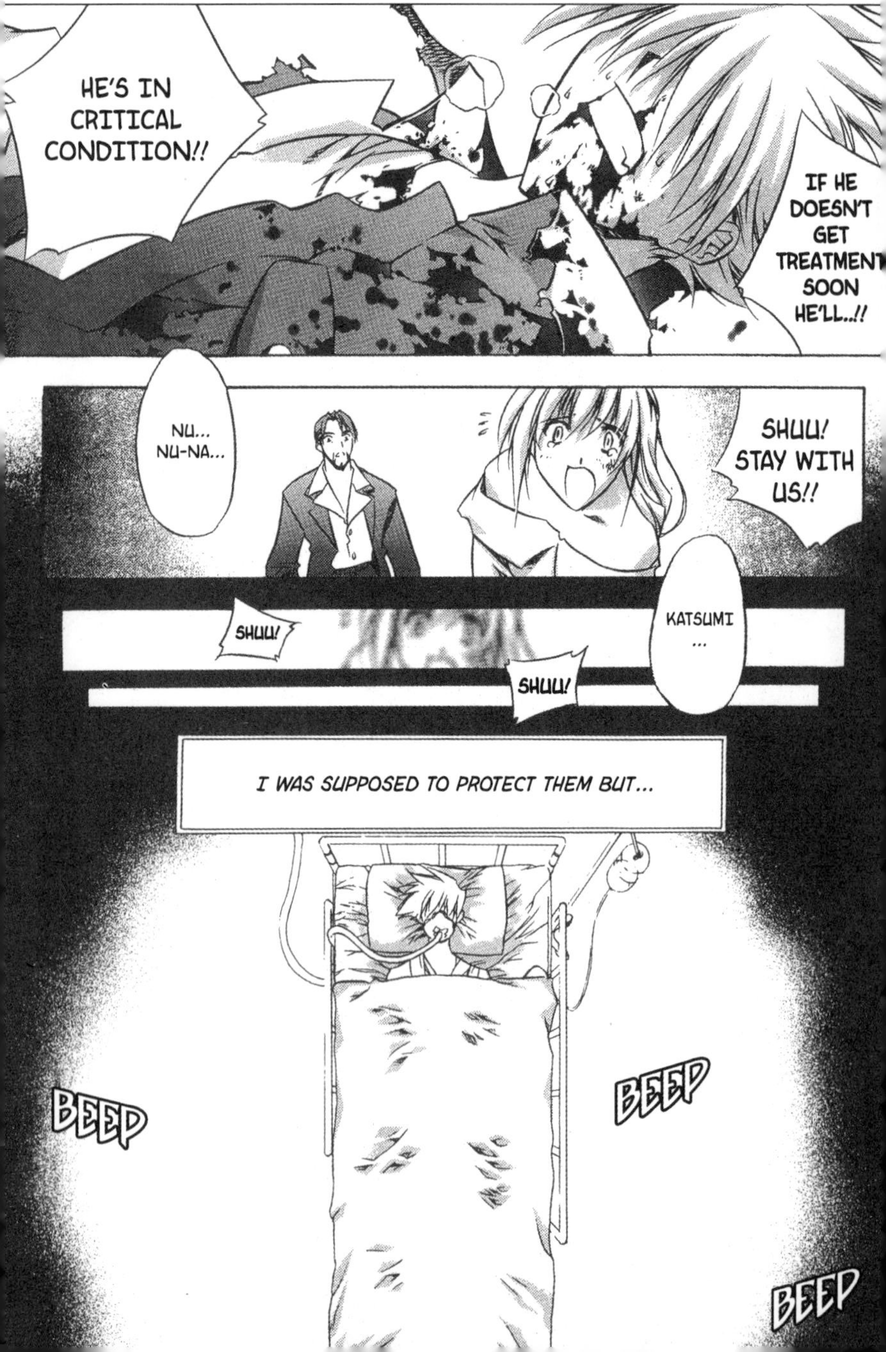
HE'S IN CRITICAL CONDITION!!
IF HE DOESN'T GET TREATMENT SOON HE'LL..!!
NU... NU-NA...
SHUU! STAY WITH US!!
SHUU!
KATSUMI ...
SHUU!
I WAS SUPPOSED TO PROTECT THEM BUT...
BEEP
BEEP
BEEP

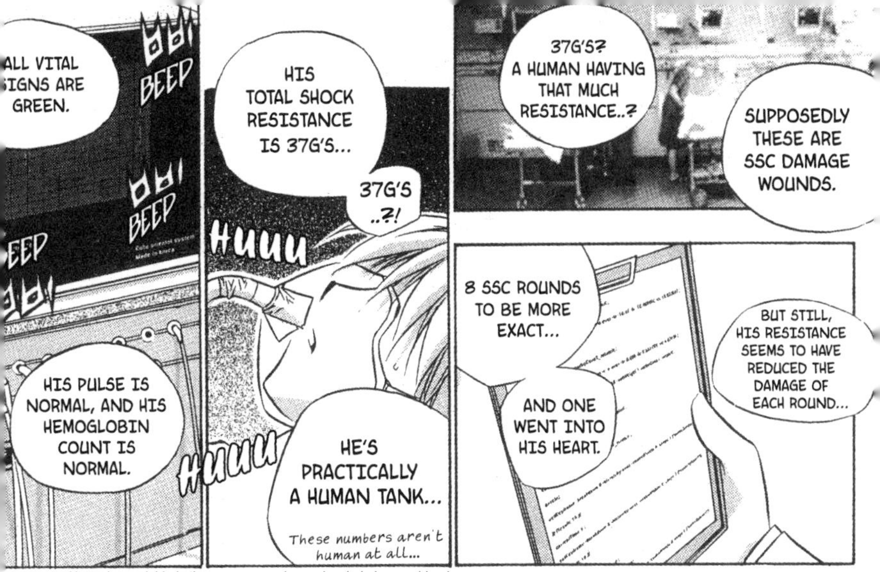
ALL VITAL SIGNS ARE GREEN.
BEEP
BEEP
BEEP
HIS PULSE IS NORMAL, AND HIS HEMOGLOBIN COUNT IS NORMAL.
HIS TOTAL SHOCK RESISTANCE IS 37G'S...
37G'S ..?!
HUUU
HUUU
HE'S PRACTICALLY A HUMAN TANK...
These numbers aren't human at all...
37G'S? A HUMAN HAVING THAT MUCH RESISTANCE..?
SUPPOSEDLY THESE ARE SSC DAMAGE WOUNDS.
8 SSC ROUNDS TO BE MORE EXACT...
AND ONE WENT INTO HIS HEART.
BUT STILL, HIS RESISTANCE SEEMS TO HAVE REDUCED THE DAMAGE OF EACH ROUND...

Note : hemoglobin is the oxygen carrying molecule in human blood.

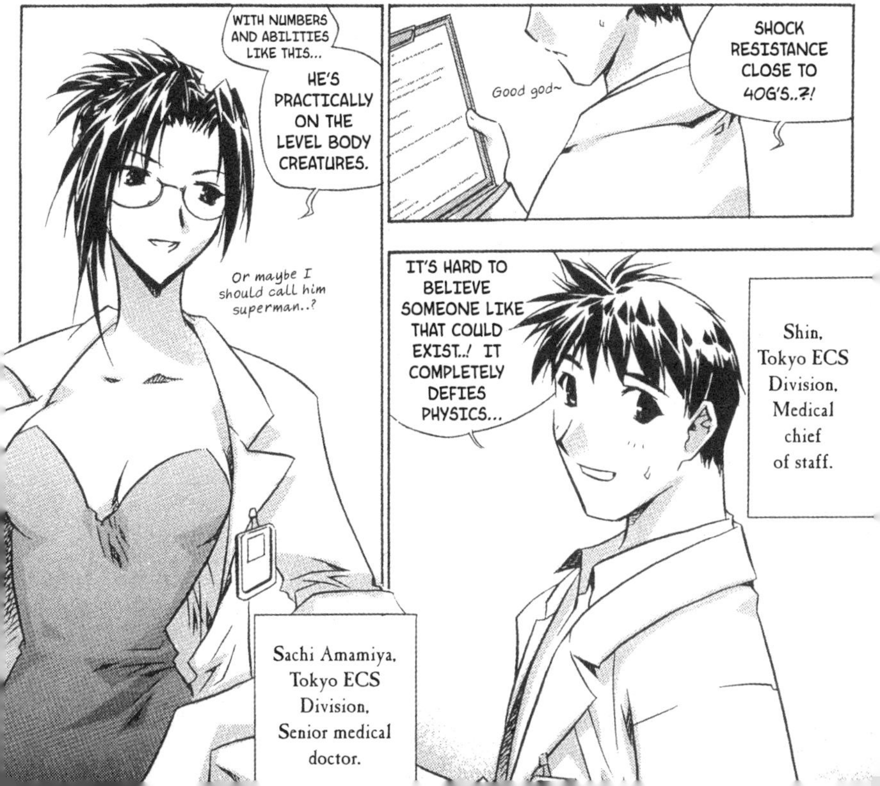
WITH NUMBERS AND ABILITIES LIKE THIS...
HE'S PRACTICALLY ON THE LEVEL BODY CREATURES.
Or maybe I should call him superman..?
Sachi Amamiya, Tokyo ECS Division, Senior medical doctor.
Good god~
SHOCK RESISTANCE CLOSE TO 40G'S..?!
IT'S HARD TO BELIEVE SOMEONE LIKE THAT COULD EXIST..! IT COMPLETELY DEFIES PHYSICS...
Shin, Tokyo ECS Division, Medical chief of staff.

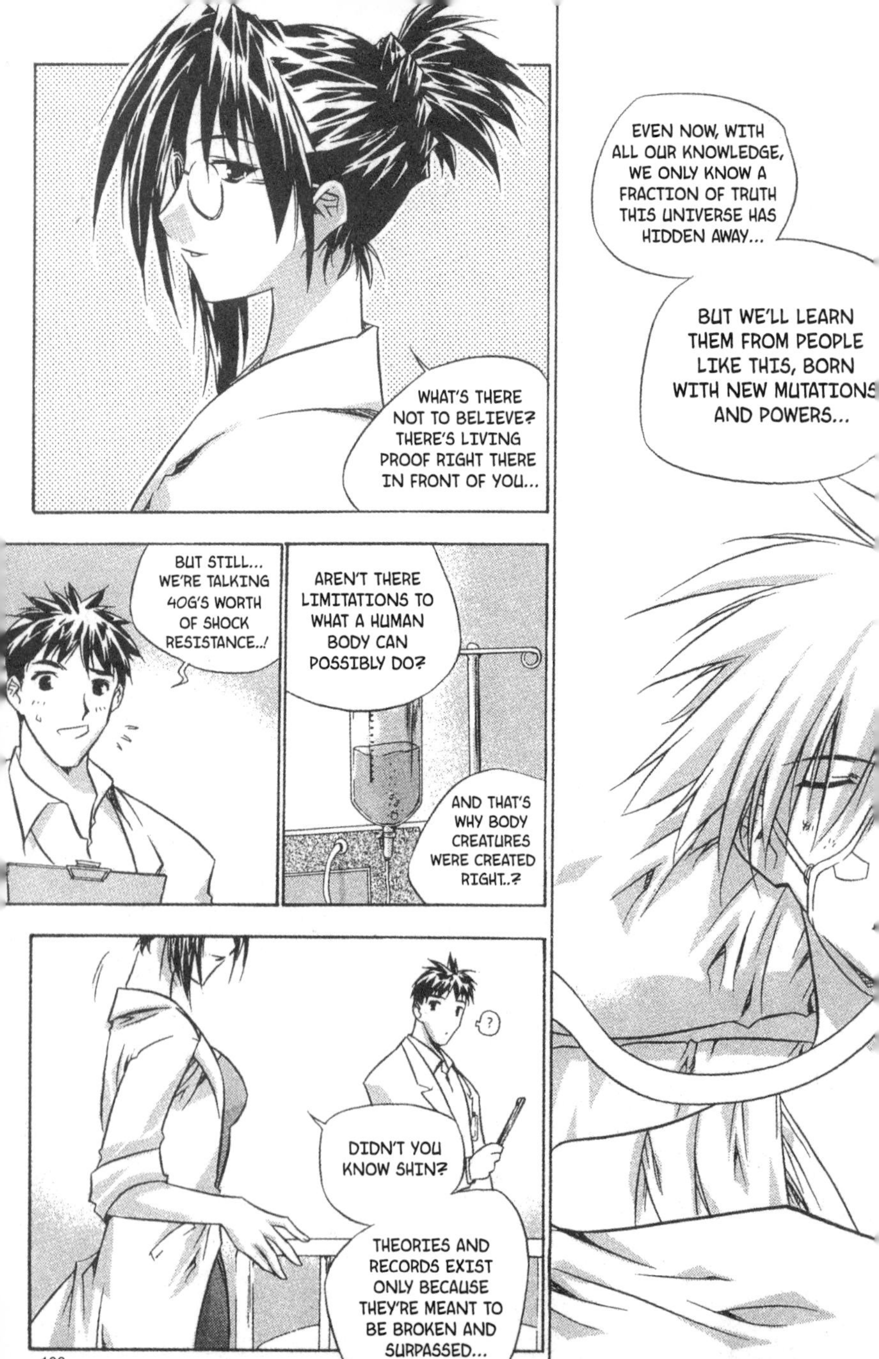
WHAT'S THERE NOT TO BELIEVE? THERE'S LIVING PROOF RIGHT THERE IN FRONT OF YOU...
BUT STILL... WE'RE TALKING 40G'S WORTH OF SHOCK RESISTANCE..!
AREN'T THERE LIMITATIONS TO WHAT A HUMAN BODY CAN POSSIBLY DO?
AND THAT'S WHY BODY CREATURES WERE CREATED RIGHT..?
?
DIDN'T YOU KNOW SHIN?
THEORIES AND RECORDS EXIST ONLY BECAUSE THEY'RE MEANT TO BE BROKEN AND SURPASSED...
EVEN NOW, WITH ALL OUR KNOWLEDGE, WE ONLY KNOW A FRACTION OF TRUTH THIS UNIVERSE HAS HIDDEN AWAY...
BUT WE'LL LEARN THEM FROM PEOPLE LIKE THIS, BORN WITH NEW MUTATIONS AND POWERS...

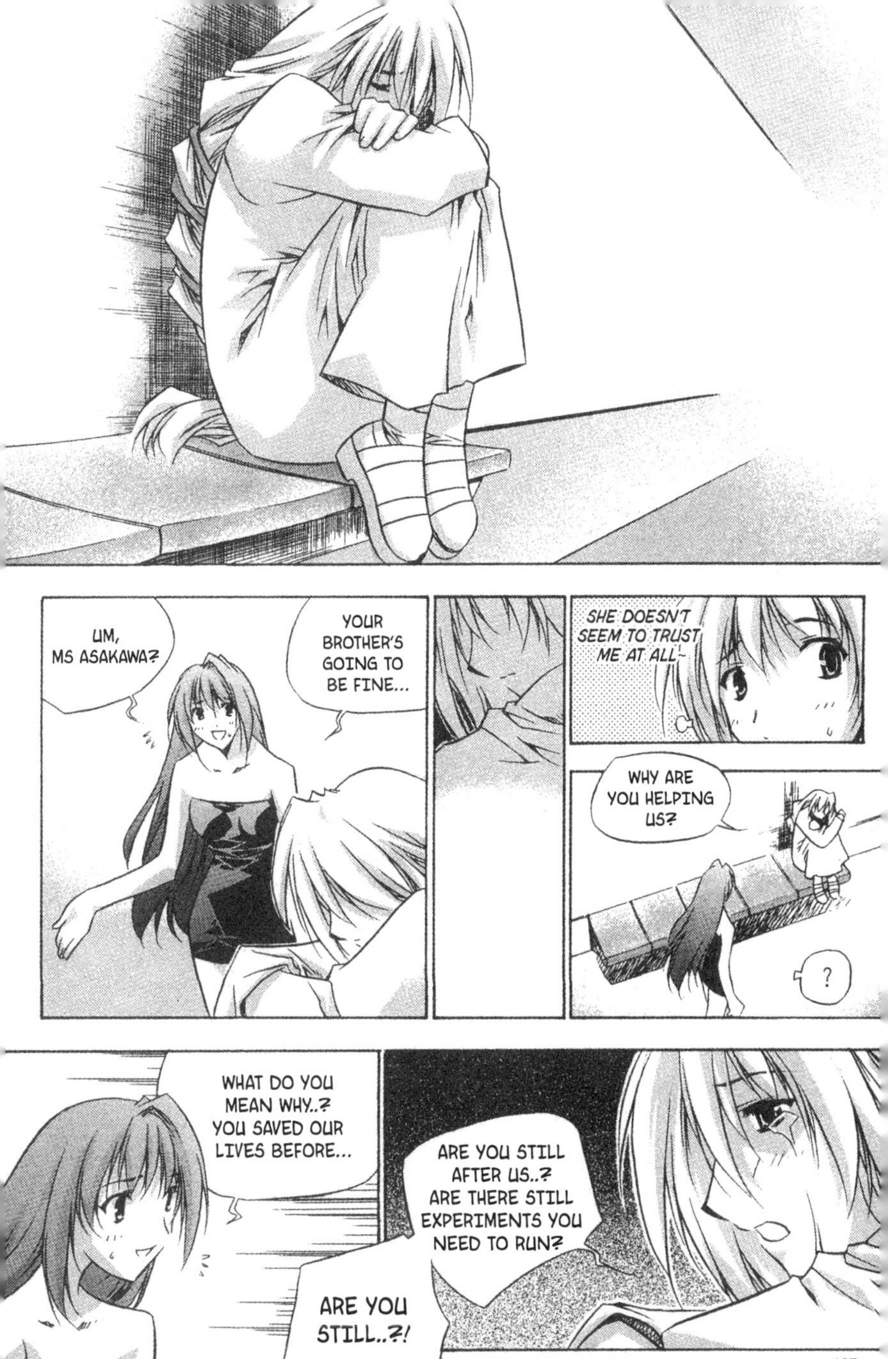
UM, MS ASAKAWA?
YOUR BROTHER'S GOING TO BE FINE...
SHE DOESN'T SEEM TO TRUST ME AT ALL~
WHY ARE YOU HELPING US?
?
WHAT DO YOU MEAN WHY..? YOU SAVED OUR LIVES BEFORE...
ARE YOU STILL AFTER US..? ARE THERE STILL EXPERIMENTS YOU NEED TO RUN?
ARE YOU STILL..?!

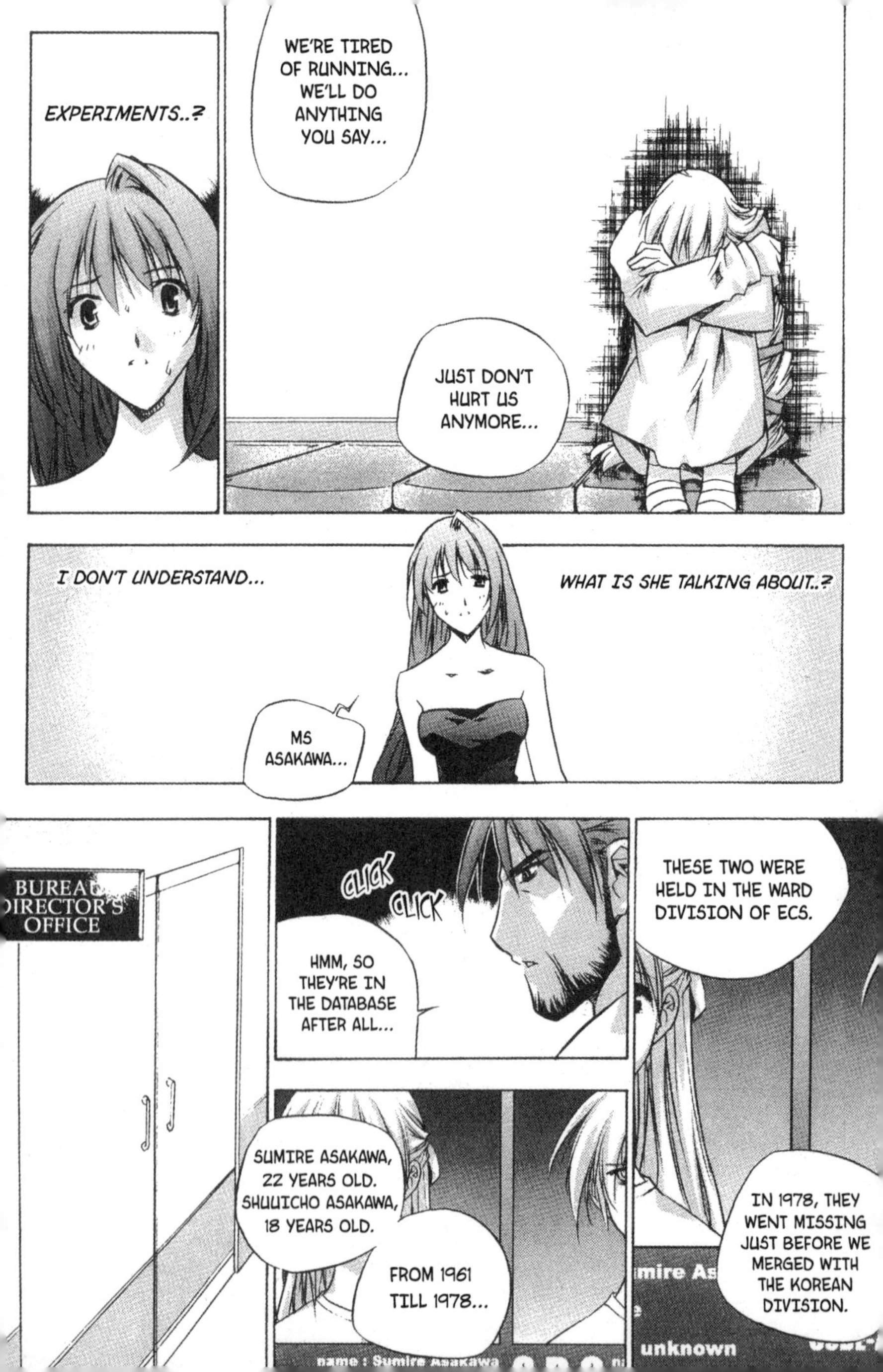
EXPERIMENTS..?
WE'RE TIRED OF RUNNING... WE'LL DO ANYTHING YOU SAY...
JUST DON'T HURT US ANYMORE...
I DON'T UNDERSTAND...
WHAT IS SHE TALKING ABOUT..?
MS ASAKAWA...
BUREA
IRECTOR'S
OFFICE
CLICK
CLICK
HMM, SO THEY'RE IN THE DATABASE AFTER ALL...
THESE TWO WERE HELD IN THE WARD DIVISION OF ECS.
SUMIRE ASAKAWA, 22 YEARS OLD. SHUUICHO ASAKAWA, 18 YEARS OLD.
FROM 1961 TILL 1978...
IN 1978, THEY WENT MISSING JUST BEFORE WE MERGED WITH THE KOREAN DIVISION.
name : Sumire Asakawa
unknown

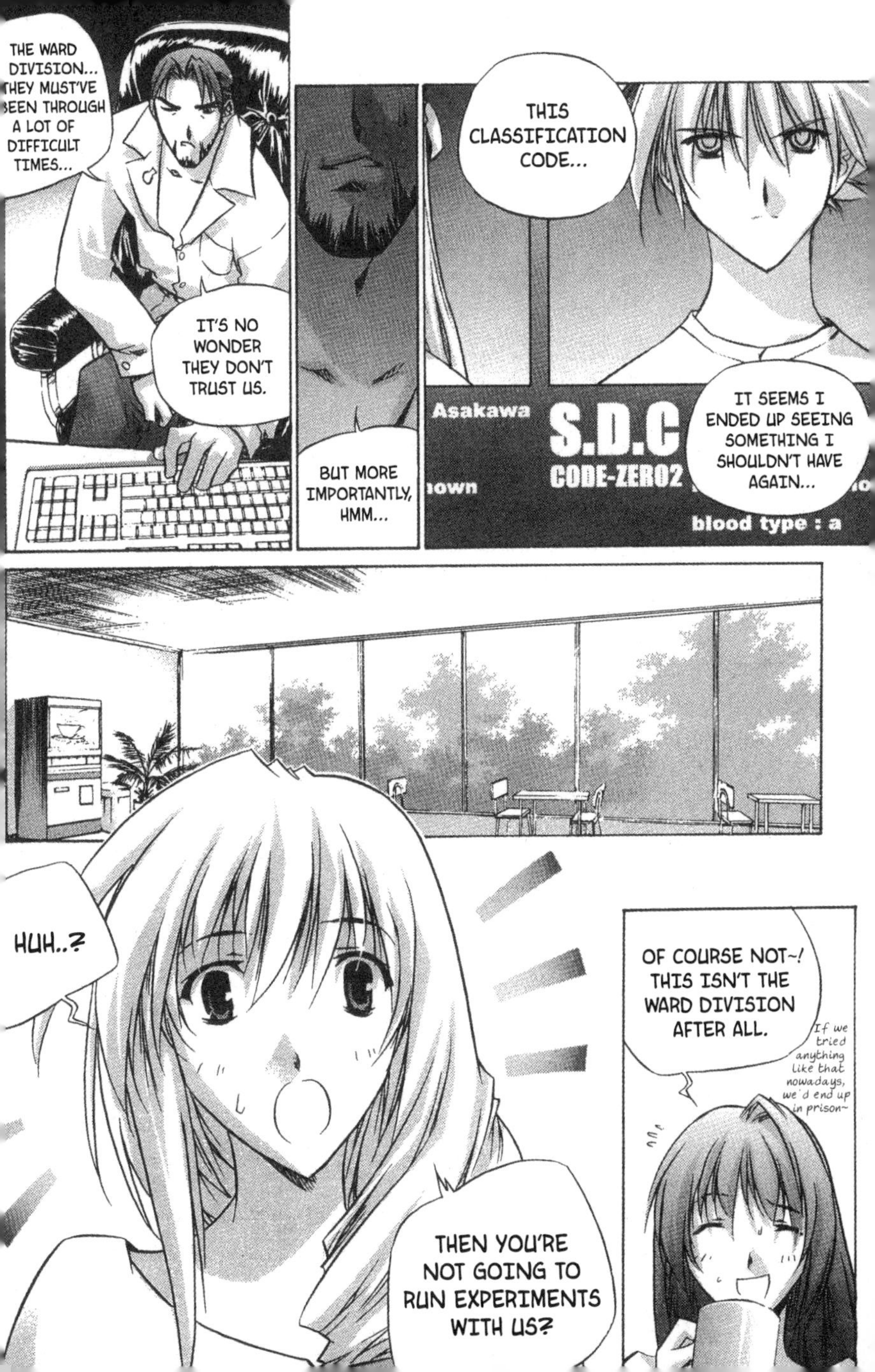
THE WARD DIVISION... THEY MUST'VE BEEN THROUGH A LOT OF DIFFICULT TIMES...
IT'S NO WONDER THEY DON'T TRUST US.
BUT MORE IMPORTANTLY, HMM...
THIS CLASSIFICATION CODE...
Asakawa
S.D.C
CODE-ZERO2
blood type : a
IT SEEMS I ENDED UP SEEING SOMETHING I SHOULDN'T HAVE AGAIN...
HUH..?
THEN YOU'RE NOT GOING TO RUN EXPERIMENTS WITH US?
OF COURSE NOT~! THIS ISN'T THE WARD DIVISION AFTER ALL.
If we tried anything like that nowadays, we'd end up in prison~

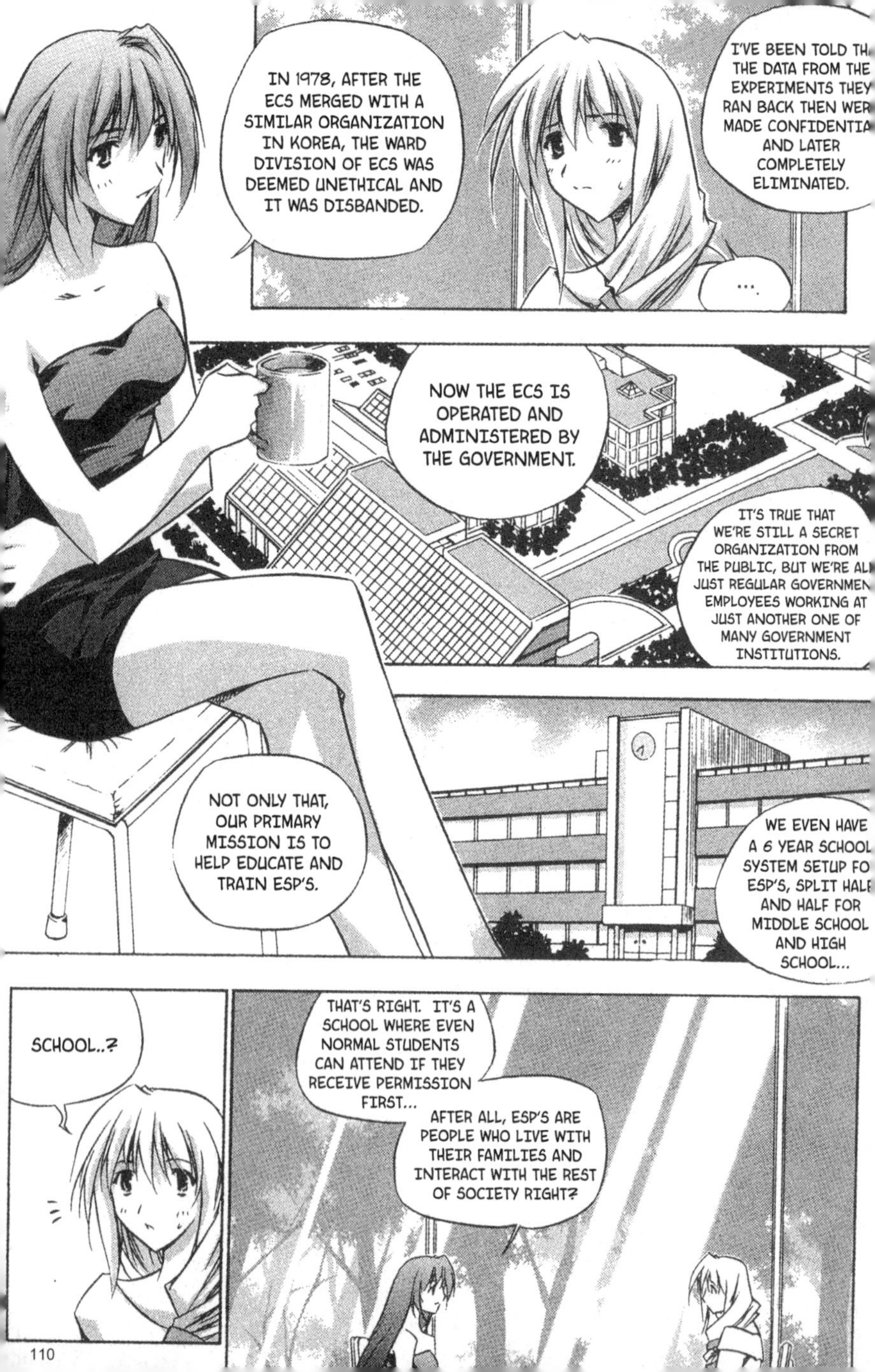
IN 1978, AFTER THE ECS MERGED WITH A SIMILAR ORGANIZATION IN KOREA, THE WARD DIVISION OF ECS WAS DEEMED UNETHICAL AND IT WAS DISBANDED.
I'VE BEEN TOLD TH THE DATA FROM THE EXPERIMENTS THEY RAN BACK THEN WER MADE CONFIDENTIA AND LATER COMPLETELY ELIMINATED.
...
NOW THE ECS IS OPERATED AND ADMINISTERED BY THE GOVERNMENT.
IT'S TRUE THAT WE'RE STILL A SECRET ORGANIZATION FROM THE PUBLIC, BUT WE'RE AL JUST REGULAR GOVERNMEN EMPLOYEES WORKING AT JUST ANOTHER ONE OF MANY GOVERNMENT INSTITUTIONS.
NOT ONLY THAT, OUR PRIMARY MISSION IS TO HELP EDUCATE AND TRAIN ESP'S.
WE EVEN HAVE A 6 YEAR SCHOOL SYSTEM SETUP FO ESP'S, SPLIT HALF AND HALF FOR MIDDLE SCHOOL AND HIGH SCHOOL...
SCHOOL..?
THAT'S RIGHT. IT'S A SCHOOL WHERE EVEN NORMAL STUDENTS CAN ATTEND IF THEY RECEIVE PERMISSION FIRST...
AFTER ALL, ESP'S ARE PEOPLE WHO LIVE WITH THEIR FAMILIES AND INTERACT WITH THE REST OF SOCIETY RIGHT?

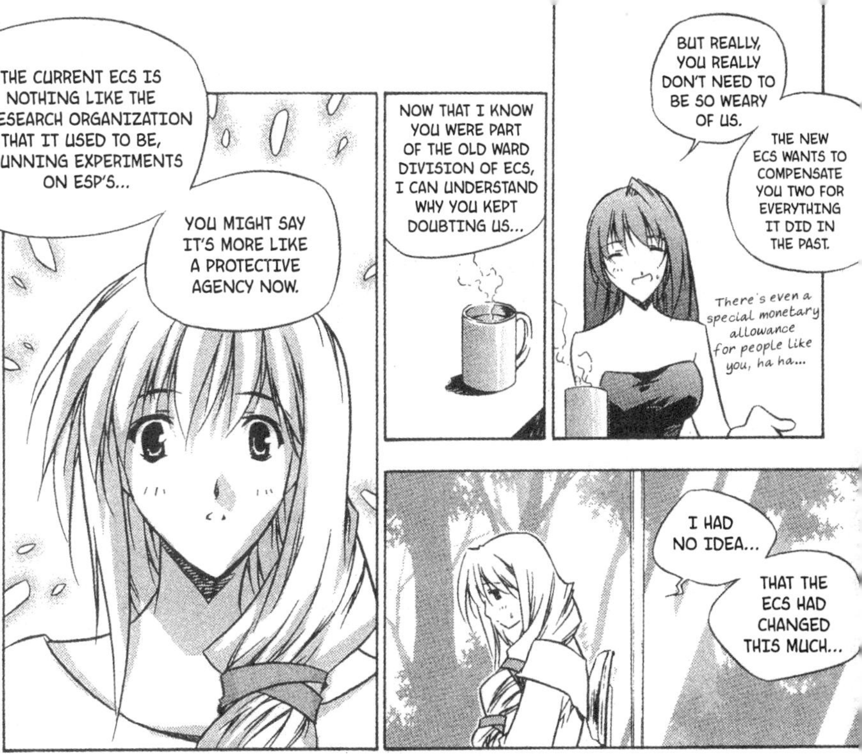
THE CURRENT ECS IS NOTHING LIKE THE RESEARCH ORGANIZATION THAT IT USED TO BE, RUNNING EXPERIMENTS ON ESP'S...
YOU MIGHT SAY IT'S MORE LIKE A PROTECTIVE AGENCY NOW.
NOW THAT I KNOW YOU WERE PART OF THE OLD WARD DIVISION OF ECS, I CAN UNDERSTAND WHY YOU KEPT DOUBTING US...
BUT REALLY, YOU REALLY DON'T NEED TO BE SO WEARY OF US.
THE NEW ECS WANTS TO COMPENSATE YOU TWO FOR EVERYTHING IT DID IN THE PAST.
There's even a special monetary allowance for people like you, ha ha...
I HAD NO IDEA...
THAT THE ECS HAD CHANGED THIS MUCH...

Note : In both Japan and Korea, high school education is not compulsory and there is a required tuition fee even for public schools.

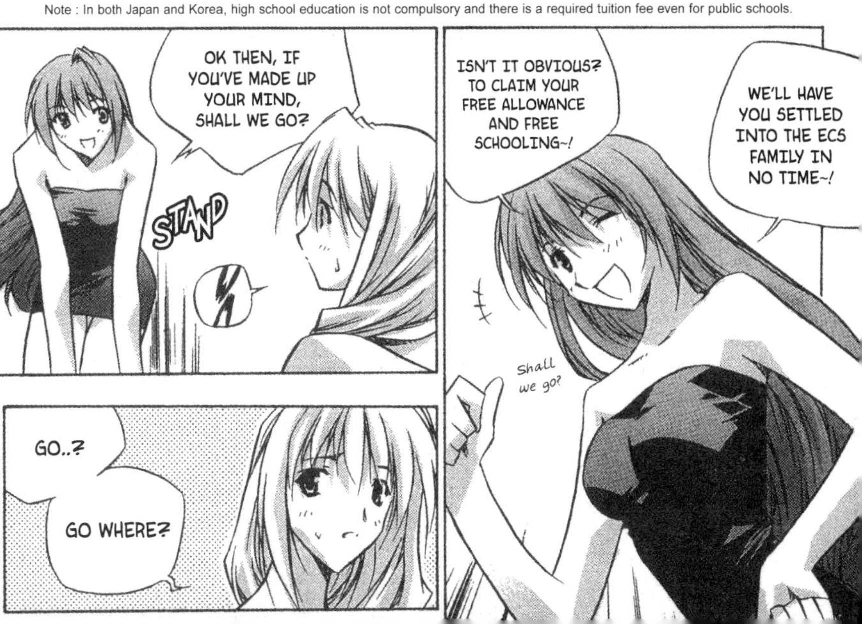
OK THEN, IF YOU'VE MADE UP YOUR MIND, SHALL WE GO?
STAND
GO..?
GO WHERE?
ISN'T IT OBVIOUS? TO CLAIM YOUR FREE ALLOWANCE AND FREE SCHOOLING~!
WE'LL HAVE YOU SETTLED INTO THE ECS FAMILY IN NO TIME~!
Shall we go?

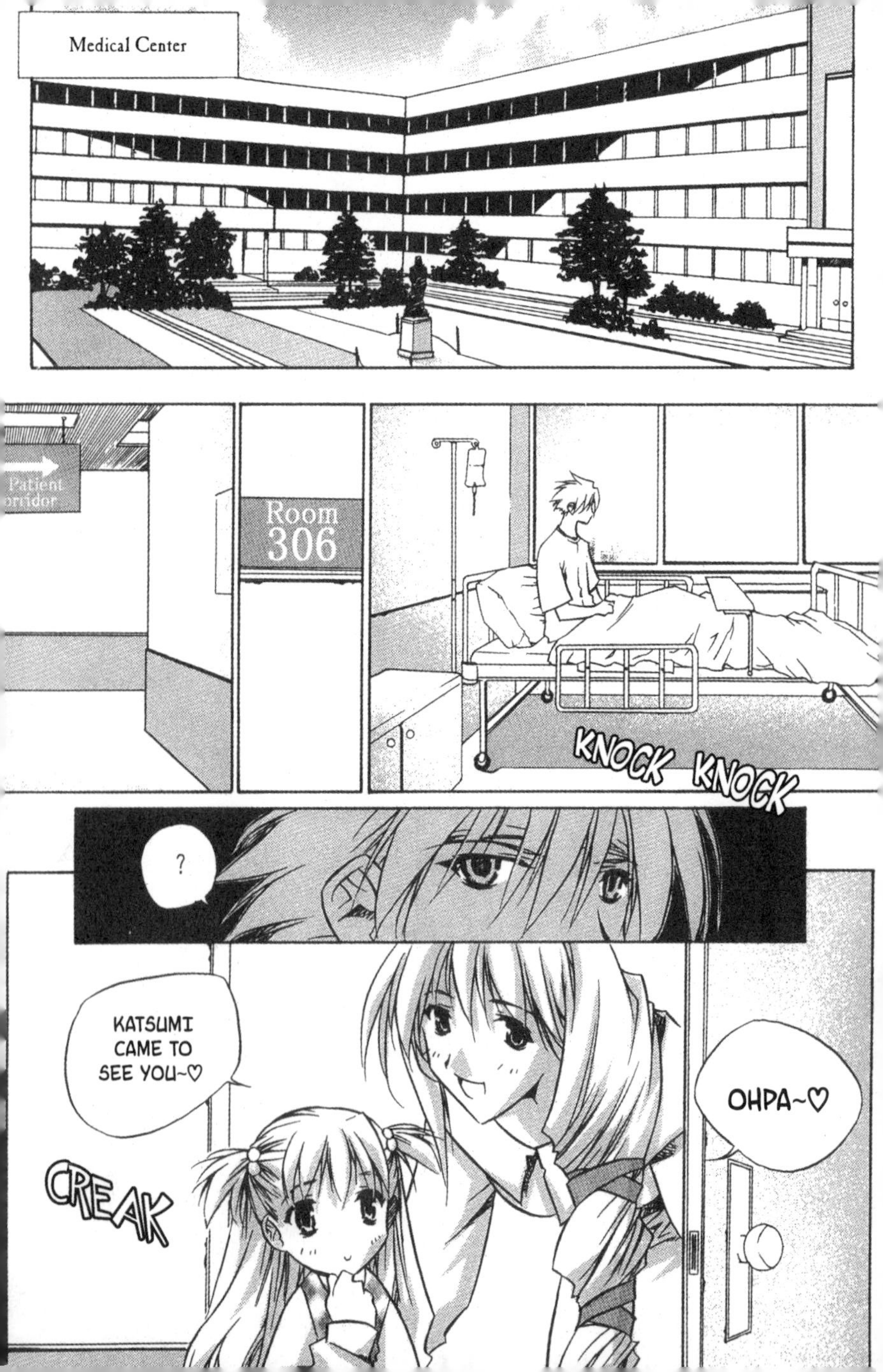
Medical Center
Patient
orridor
Room
306
KNOCK KNOCK
?
KATSUMI CAME TO SEE YOU~♡
OHPA~♡
CREAK

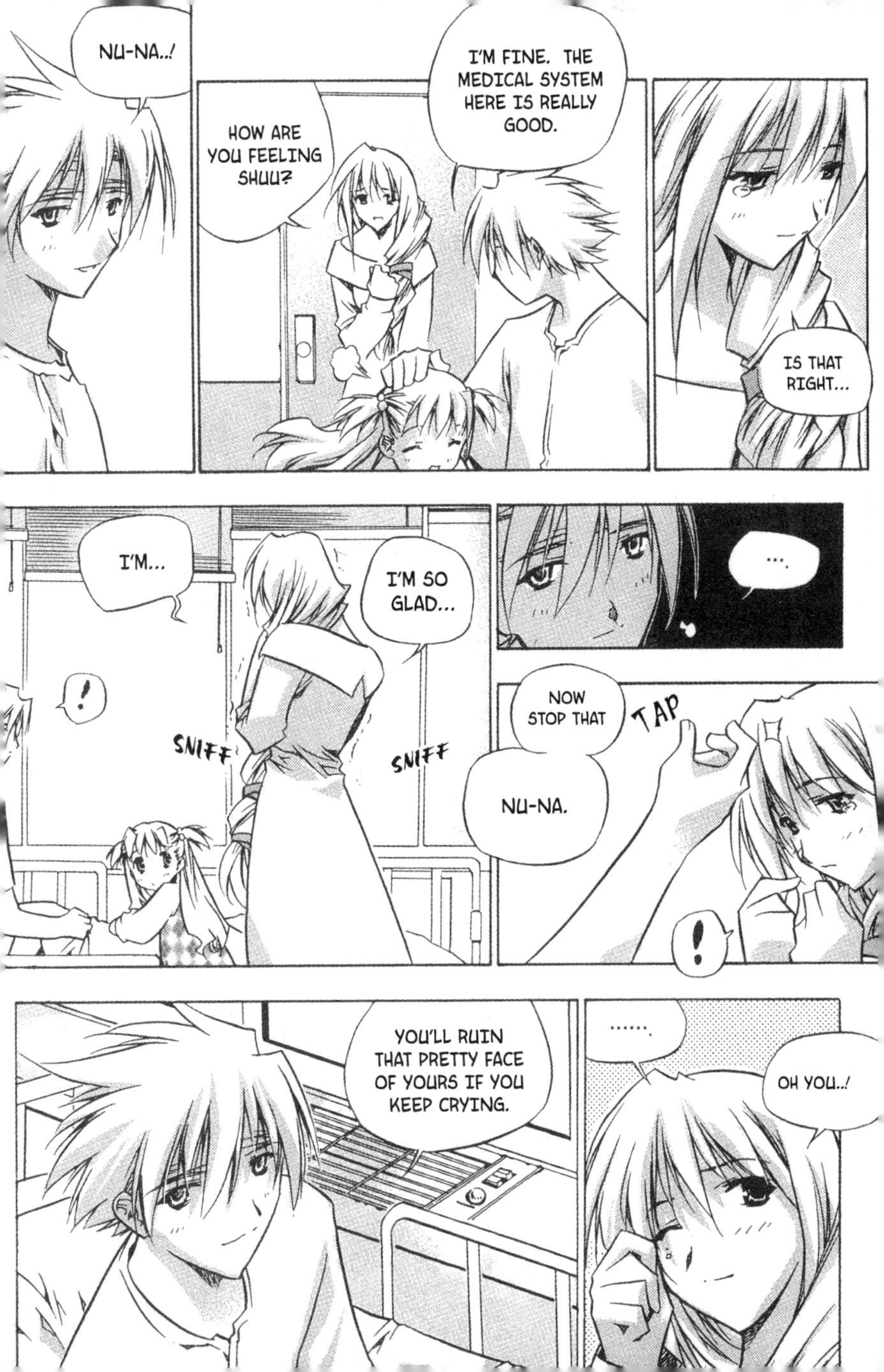
NU-NA..!
HOW ARE YOU FEELING SHUU?
I'M FINE. THE MEDICAL SYSTEM HERE IS REALLY GOOD.
IS THAT RIGHT...
I'M...
!
SNIFF
I'M SO GLAD...
SNIFF
...
NOW STOP THAT
TAP
NU-NA.
!
YOU'LL RUIN THAT PRETTY FACE OF YOURS IF YOU KEEP CRYING.
......
OH YOU..!

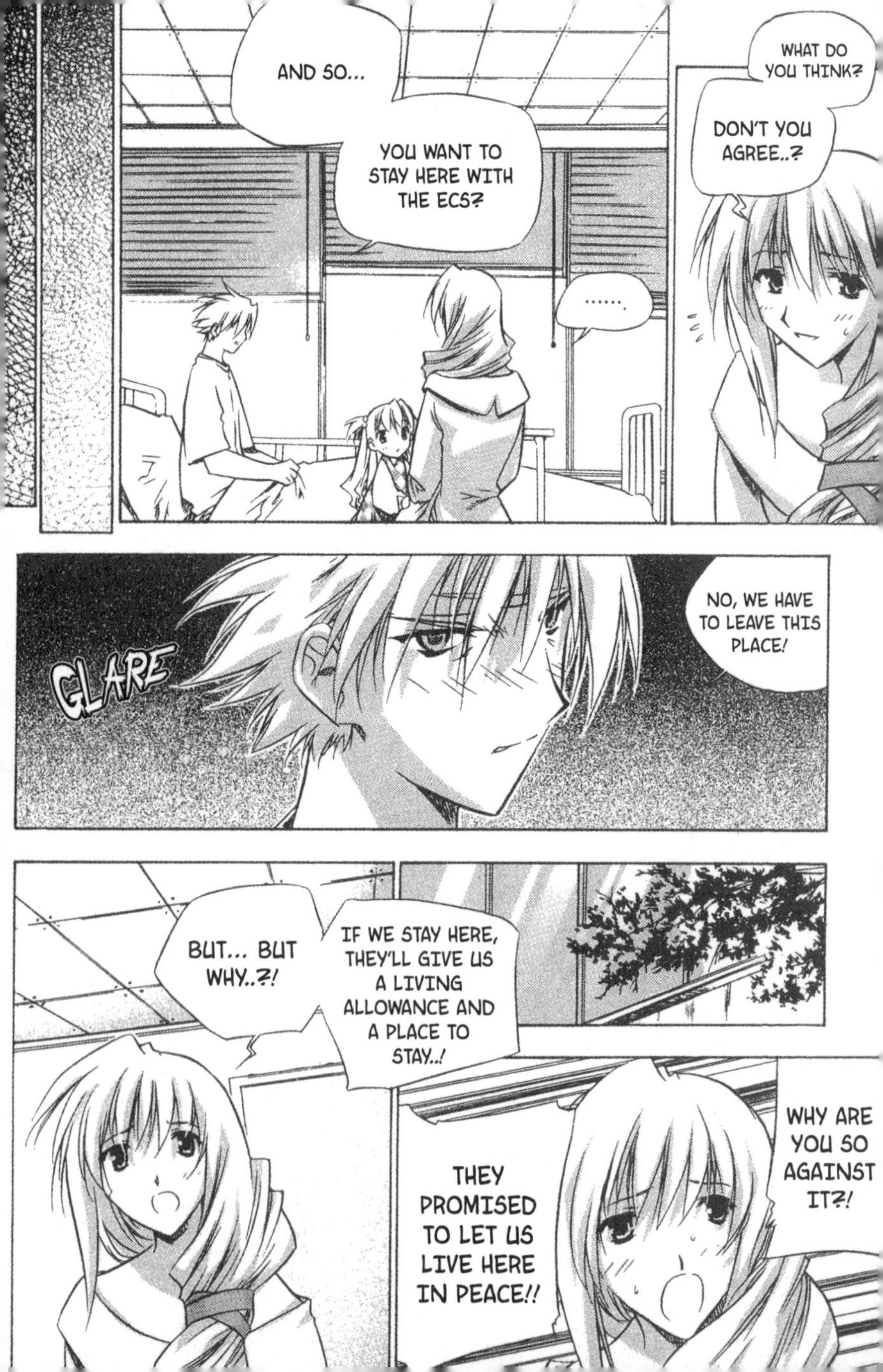
AND SO...
YOU WANT TO STAY HERE WITH THE ECS?
....
WHAT DO YOU THINK?
DON'T YOU AGREE..?
GLARE
NO, WE HAVE TO LEAVE THIS PLACE!
BUT... BUT WHY..?!
IF WE STAY HERE, THEY'LL GIVE US A LIVING ALLOWANCE AND A PLACE TO STAY..!
THEY PROMISED TO LET US LIVE HERE IN PEACE!!
WHY ARE YOU SO AGAINST IT?!

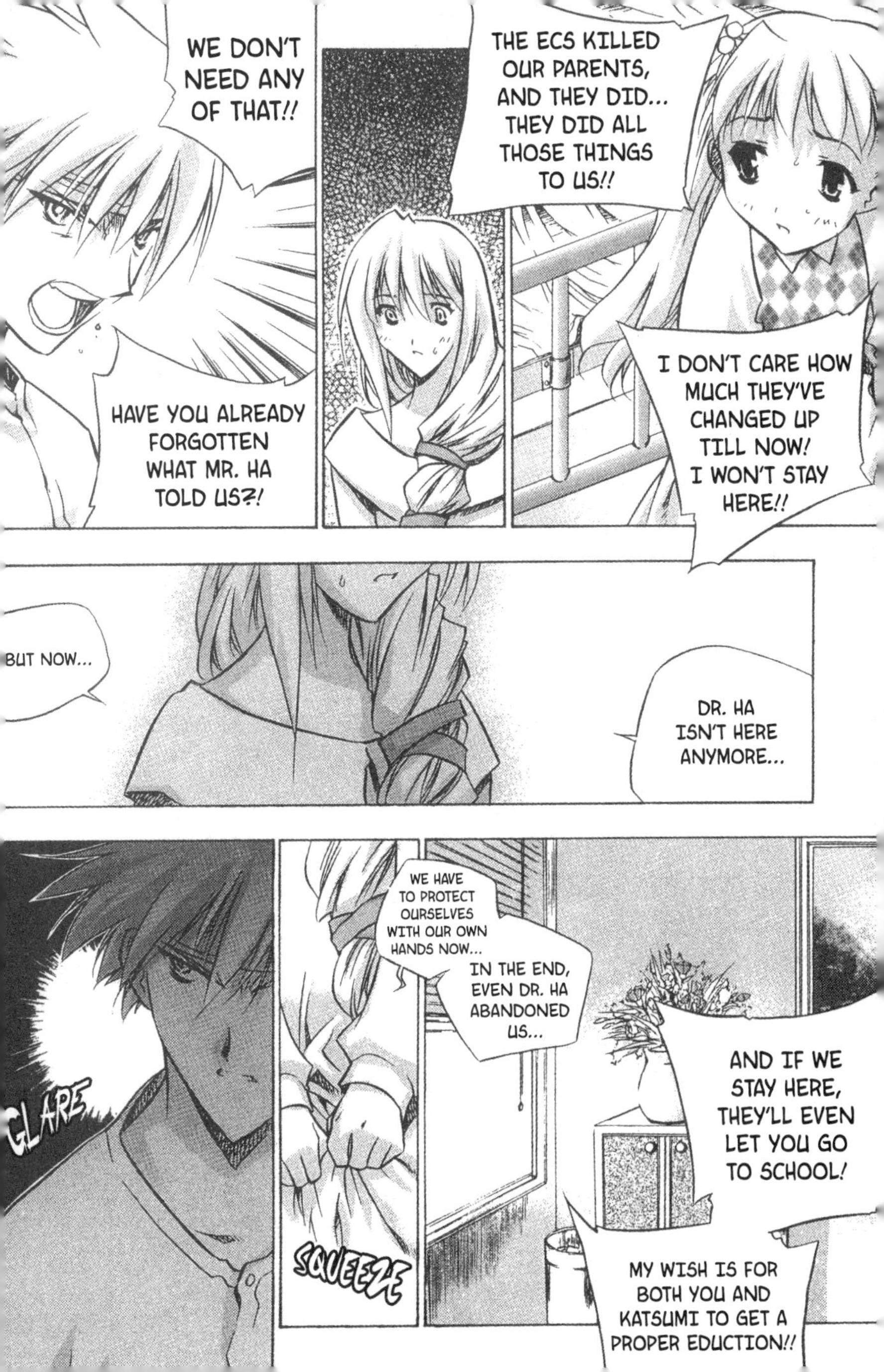
WE DON'T NEED ANY OF THAT!!
HAVE YOU ALREADY FORGOTTEN WHAT MR. HA TOLD US?!
THE ECS KILLED OUR PARENTS, AND THEY DID... THEY DID ALL THOSE THINGS TO US!!
I DON'T CARE HOW MUCH THEY'VE CHANGED UP TILL NOW! I WON'T STAY HERE!!
BUT NOW...
DR. HA ISN'T HERE ANYMORE...
GLARE
WE HAVE TO PROTECT OURSELVES WITH OUR OWN HANDS NOW...
IN THE END, EVEN DR. HA ABANDONED US...
SQUEEZE
AND IF WE STAY HERE, THEY'LL EVEN LET YOU GO TO SCHOOL!
MY WISH IS FOR BOTH YOU AND KATSUMI TO GET A PROPER EDUCTION!!

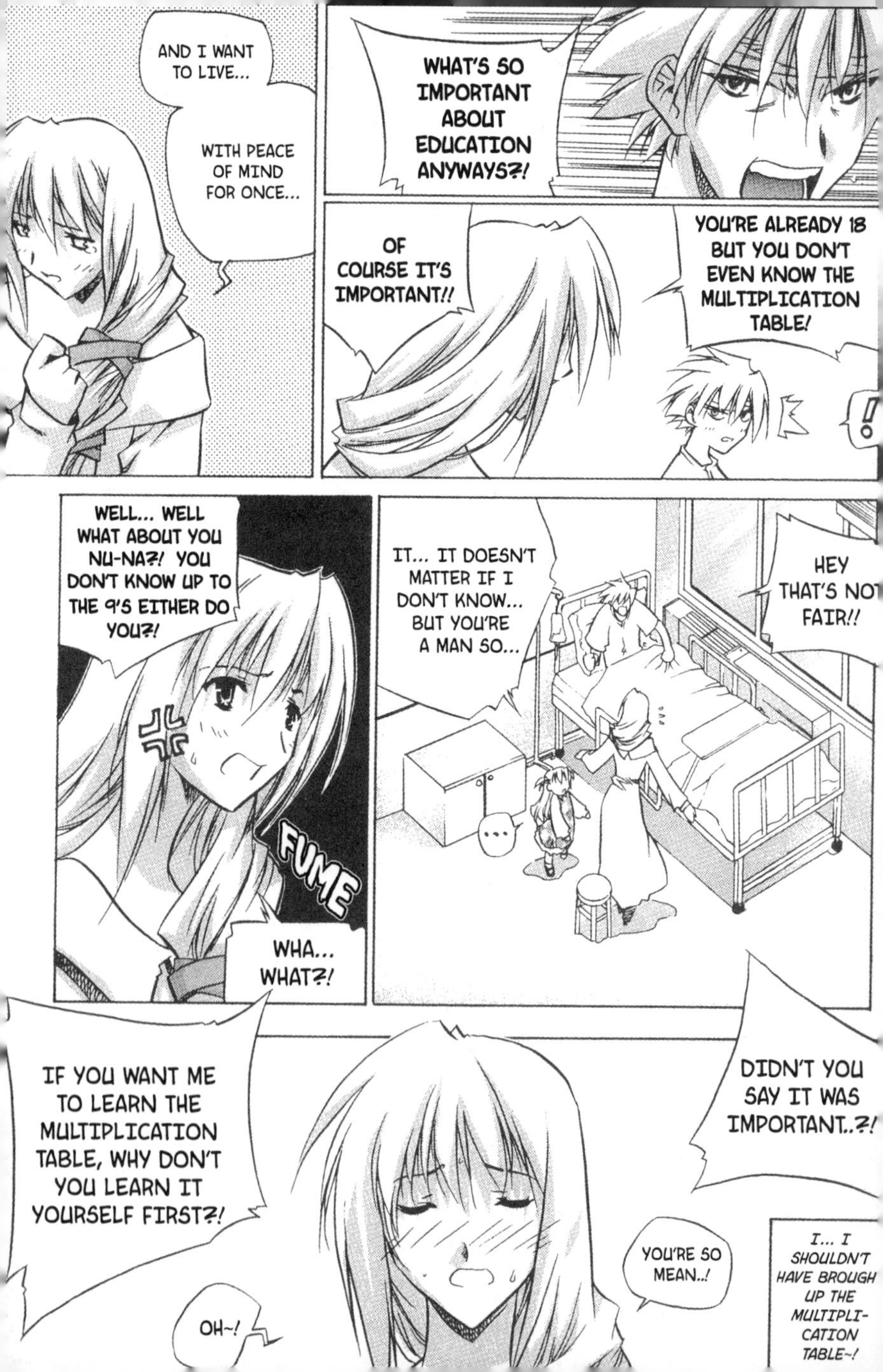
AND I WANT TO LIVE...
WITH PEACE OF MIND FOR ONCE...
WHAT'S SO IMPORTANT ABOUT EDUCATION ANYWAYS?!
OF COURSE IT'S IMPORTANT!!
YOU'RE ALREADY 18 BUT YOU DON'T EVEN KNOW THE MULTIPLICATION TABLE!
!
WELL... WELL WHAT ABOUT YOU NU-NA?! YOU DON'T KNOW UP TO THE 9'S EITHER DO YOU?!
FUME
WHA... WHAT?!
IT... IT DOESN'T MATTER IF I DON'T KNOW... BUT YOU'RE A MAN SO...
HEY THAT'S NOT FAIR!!
...
IF YOU WANT ME TO LEARN THE MULTIPLICATION TABLE, WHY DON'T YOU LEARN IT YOURSELF FIRST?!
DIDN'T YOU SAY IT WAS IMPORTANT..?!
YOU'RE SO MEAN..!
OH~!
I... I SHOULDN'T HAVE BROUGH UP THE MULTIPLICATION TABLE~!

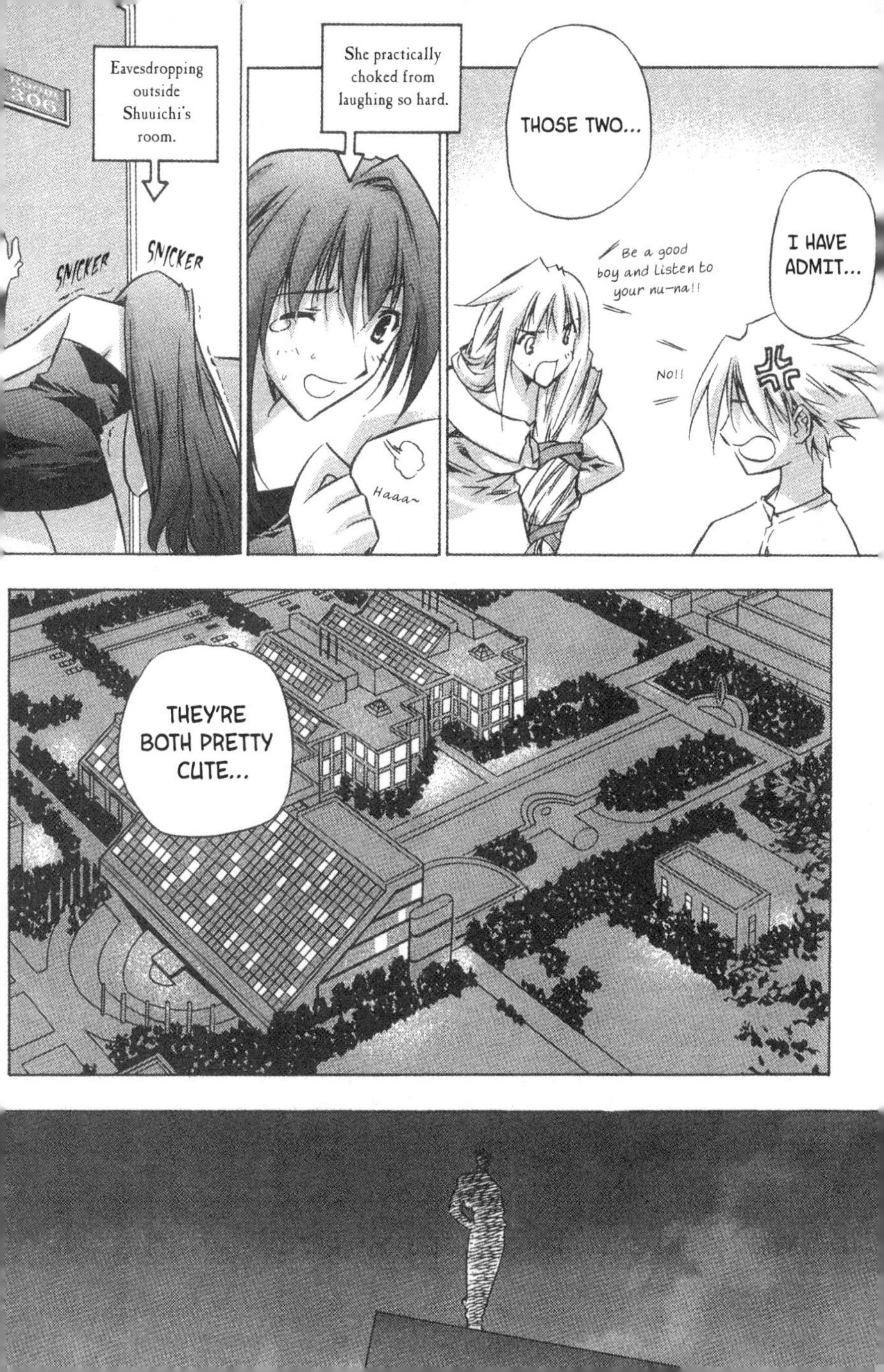
Eavesdropping outside Shuuichi's room.
SNICKER
SNICKER
She practically choked from laughing so hard.
Haaa~
THOSE TWO...
Be a good boy and listen to your nu-na!!
No!!
I HAVE ADMIT...
THEY'RE BOTH PRETTY CUTE...

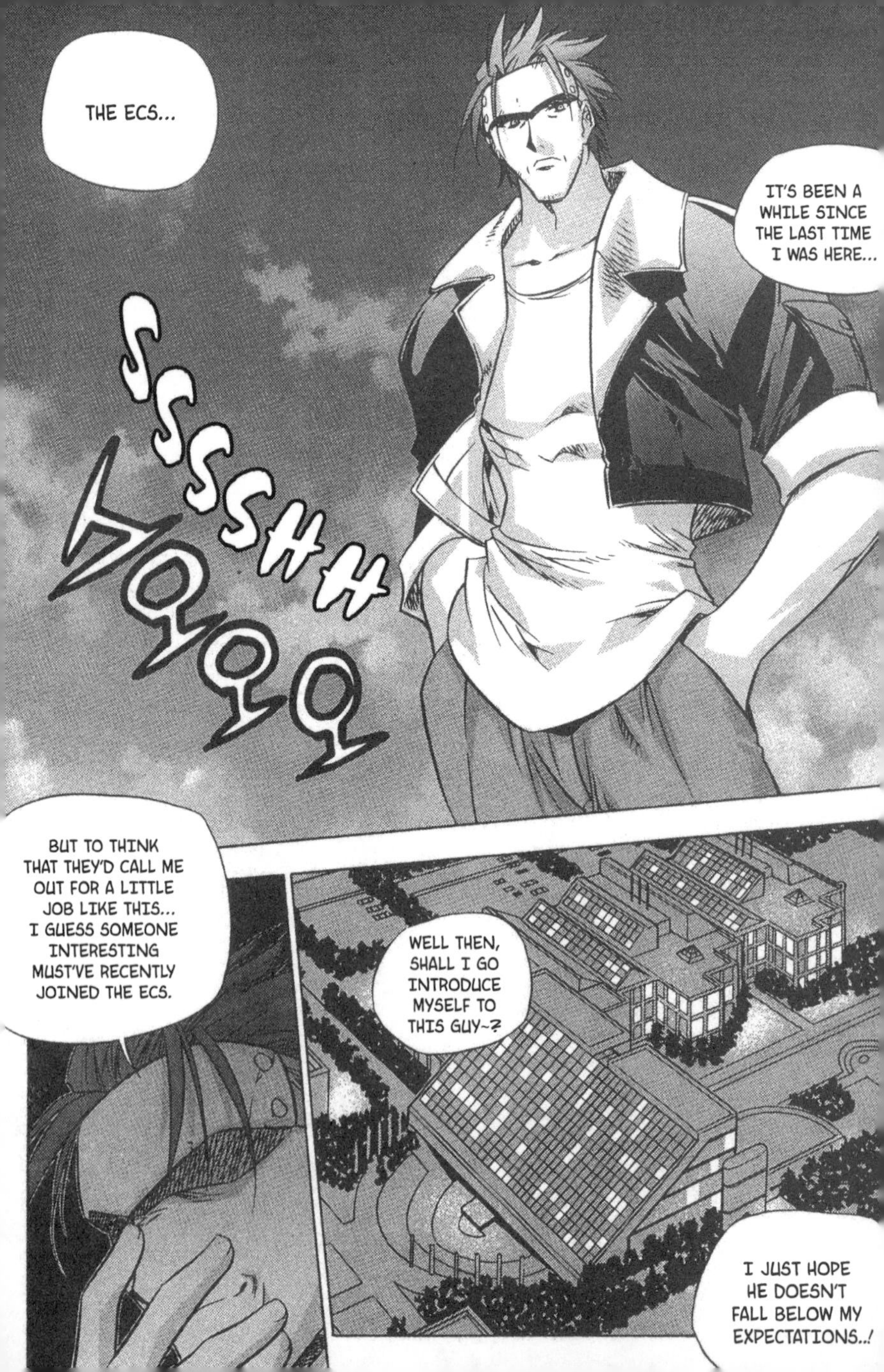
THE ECS...
IT'S BEEN A WHILE SINCE THE LAST TIME I WAS HERE...
SSSSHHOOOO
BUT TO THINK THAT THEY'D CALL ME OUT FOR A LITTLE JOB LIKE THIS... I GUESS SOMEONE INTERESTING MUST'VE RECENTLY JOINED THE ECS.
WELL THEN, SHALL I GO INTRODUCE MYSELF TO THIS GUY~?
I JUST HOPE HE DOESN'T FALL BELOW MY EXPECTATIONS..!

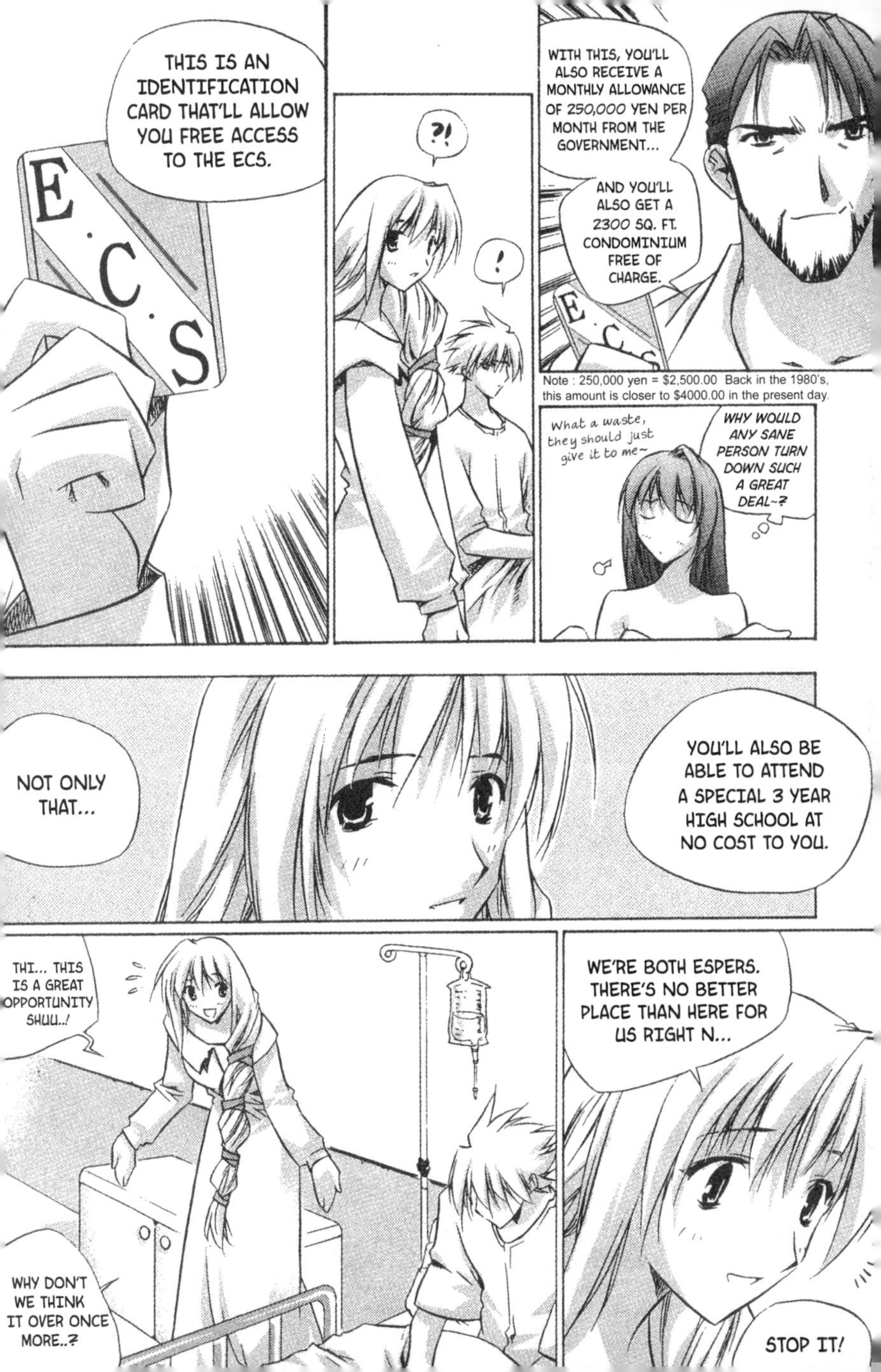
THIS IS AN IDENTIFICATION CARD THAT'LL ALLOW YOU FREE ACCESS TO THE ECS.
E.C.S
?!
!
WITH THIS, YOU'LL ALSO RECEIVE A MONTHLY ALLOWANCE OF 250,000 YEN PER MONTH FROM THE GOVERNMENT...
AND YOU'LL ALSO GET A 2300 SQ. FT. CONDOMINIUM FREE OF CHARGE.
E.C.S
Note : 250,000 yen = $2,500.00 Back in the 1980's, this amount is closer to $4000.00 in the present day.
What a waste, they should just give it to me~
WHY WOULD ANY SANE PERSON TURN DOWN SUCH A GREAT DEAL~?
NOT ONLY THAT...
YOU'LL ALSO BE ABLE TO ATTEND A SPECIAL 3 YEAR HIGH SCHOOL AT NO COST TO YOU.
THI... THIS IS A GREAT OPPORTUNITY SHUU..!
WHY DON'T WE THINK IT OVER ONCE MORE..?
WE'RE BOTH ESPERS. THERE'S NO BETTER PLACE THAN HERE FOR US RIGHT N...
STOP IT!

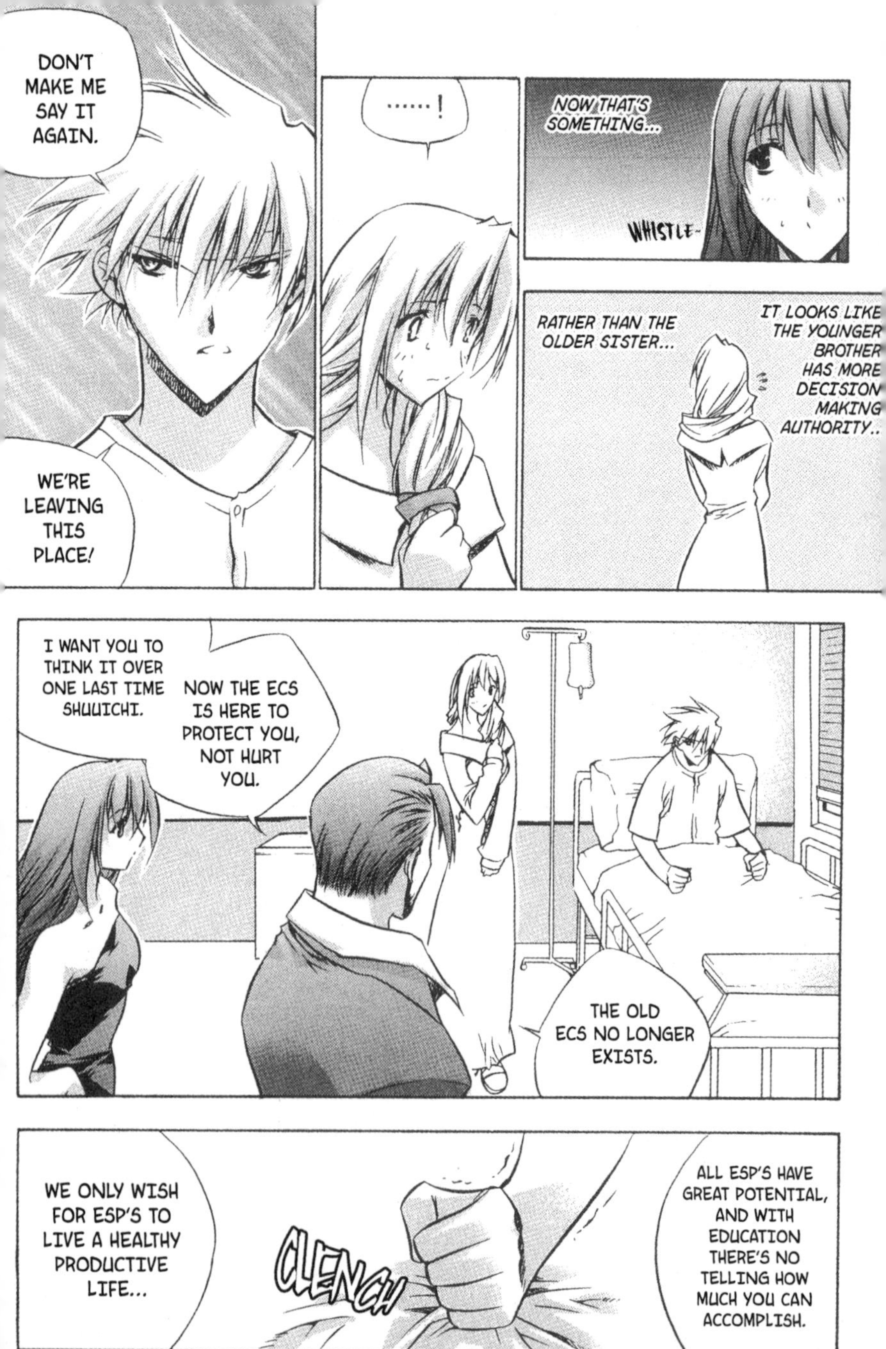
DON'T MAKE ME SAY IT AGAIN.
WE'RE LEAVING THIS PLACE!
......!
NOW THAT'S SOMETHING...
WHISTLE-
RATHER THAN THE OLDER SISTER...
IT LOOKS LIKE THE YOUNGER BROTHER HAS MORE DECISION MAKING AUTHORITY..
I WANT YOU TO THINK IT OVER ONE LAST TIME SHUUICHI.
NOW THE ECS IS HERE TO PROTECT YOU, NOT HURT YOU.
THE OLD ECS NO LONGER EXISTS.
WE ONLY WISH FOR ESP'S TO LIVE A HEALTHY PRODUCTIVE LIFE...
CLENCH
ALL ESP'S HAVE GREAT POTENTIAL, AND WITH EDUCATION THERE'S NO TELLING HOW MUCH YOU CAN ACCOMPLISH.

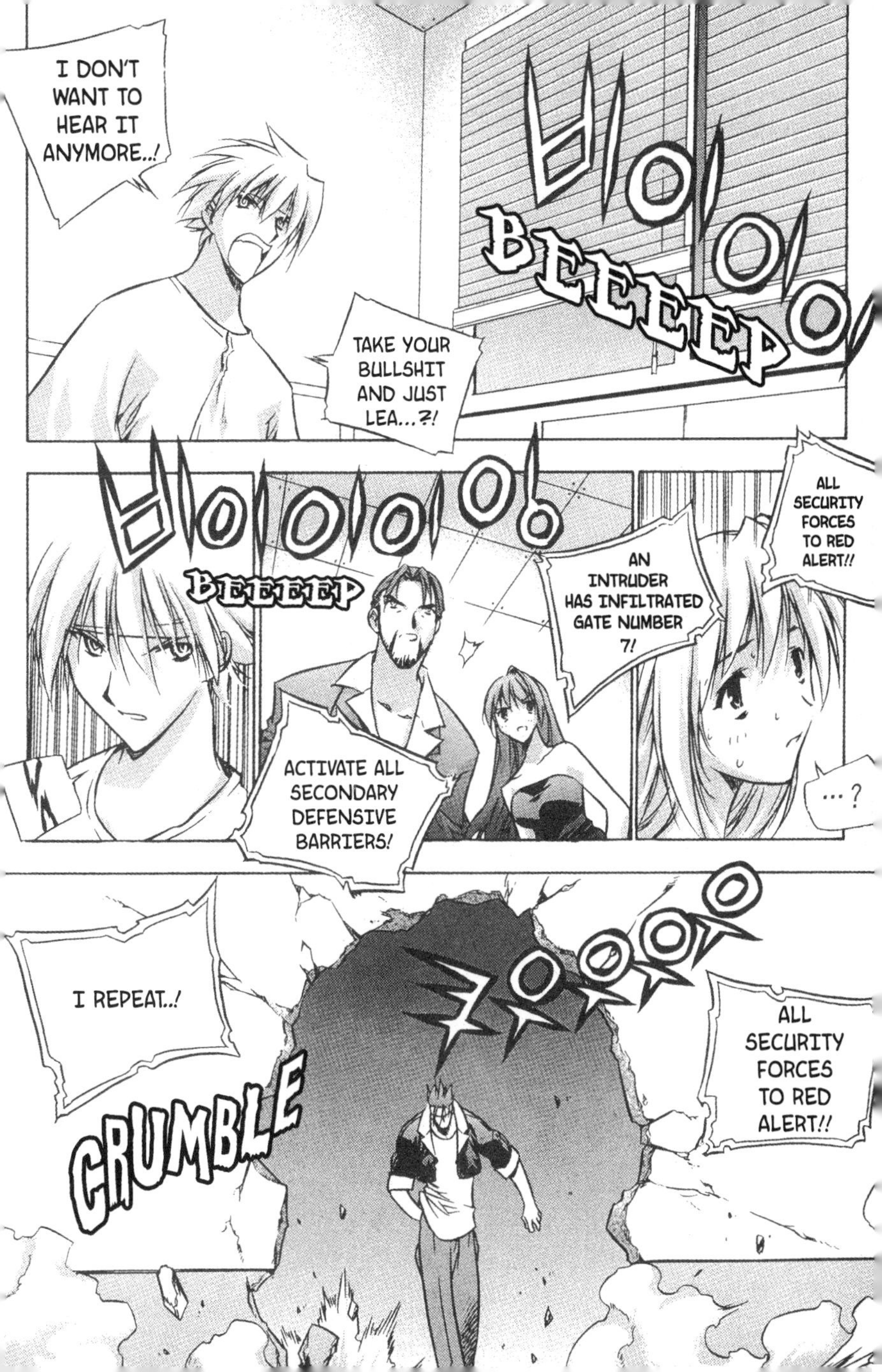
I DON'T WANT TO HEAR IT ANYMORE..!
TAKE YOUR BULLSHIT AND JUST LEA...?!
BEEEEP
BEEEEP
ACTIVATE ALL SECONDARY DEFENSIVE BARRIERS!
AN INTRUDER HAS INFILTRATED GATE NUMBER 7!
ALL SECURITY FORCES TO RED ALERT!!
...?
I REPEAT..!
CRUMBLE
ALL SECURITY FORCES TO RED ALERT!!

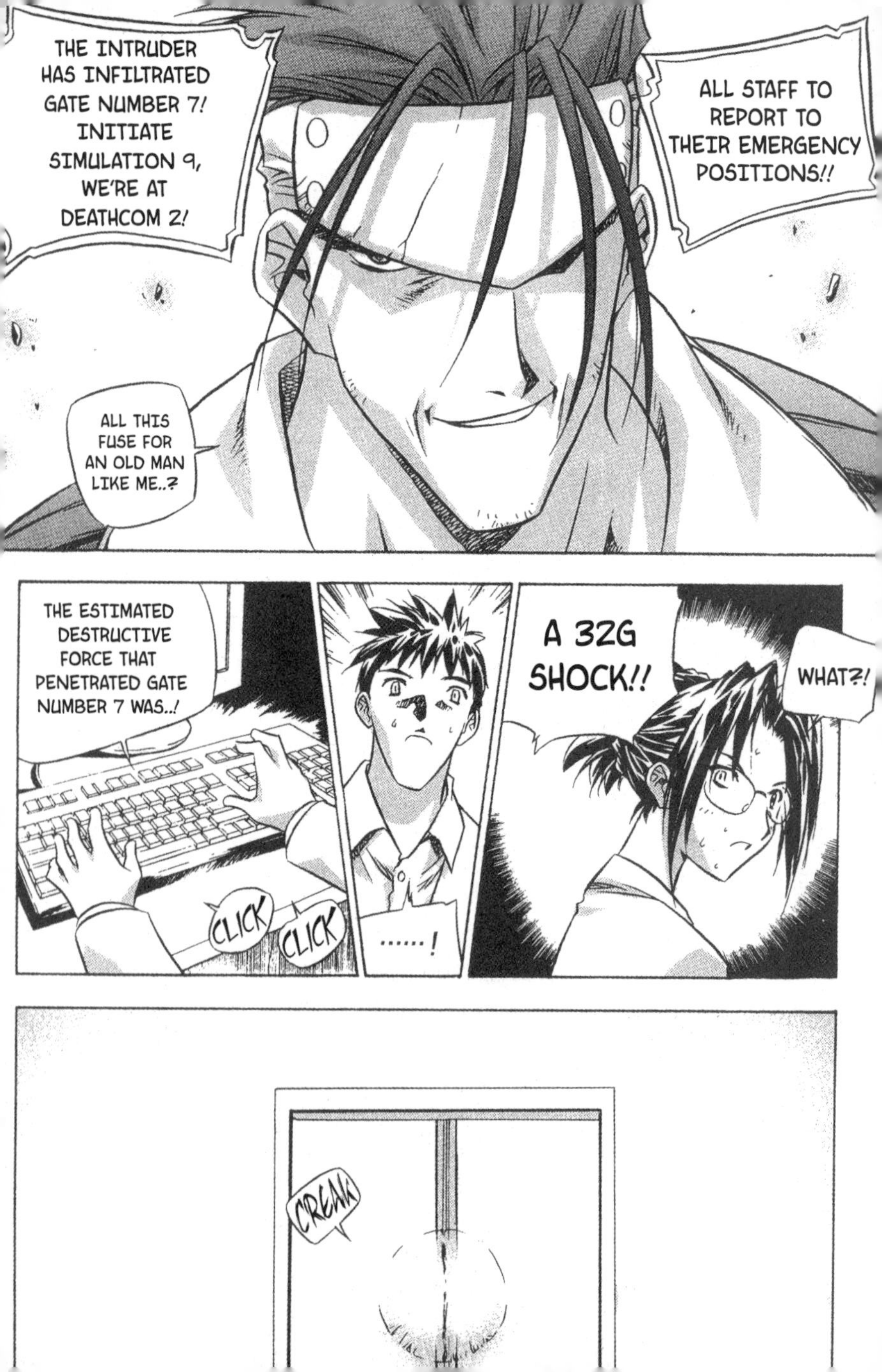
THE INTRUDER HAS INFILTRATED GATE NUMBER 7! INITIATE SIMULATION 9, WE'RE AT DEATHCOM 2!
ALL STAFF TO REPORT TO THEIR EMERGENCY POSITIONS!!
ALL THIS FUSE FOR AN OLD MAN LIKE ME..?
THE ESTIMATED DESTRUCTIVE FORCE THAT PENETRATED GATE NUMBER 7 WAS..!
CLICK
CLICK
......!
A 32G SHOCK!!
WHAT?!
CREAK

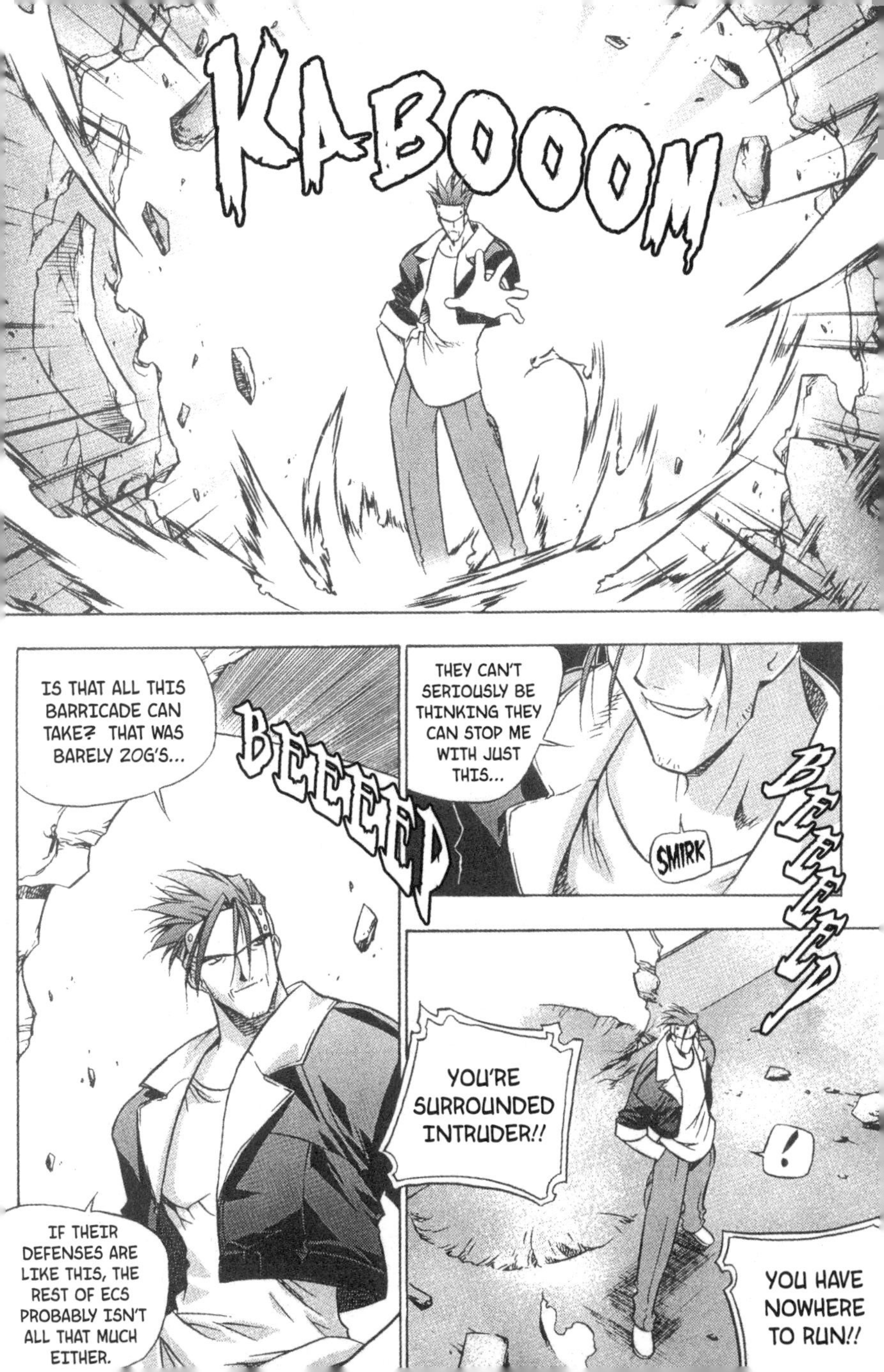
KABOOOM
IS THAT ALL THIS BARRICADE CAN TAKE? THAT WAS BARELY ZOG'S...
BEEEEP
IF THEIR DEFENSES ARE LIKE THIS, THE REST OF ECS PROBABLY ISN'T ALL THAT MUCH EITHER.
THEY CAN'T SERIOUSLY BE THINKING THEY CAN STOP ME WITH JUST THIS...
SMIRK
BEEEEP
YOU'RE SURROUNDED INTRUDER!!
!
YOU HAVE NOWHERE TO RUN!!

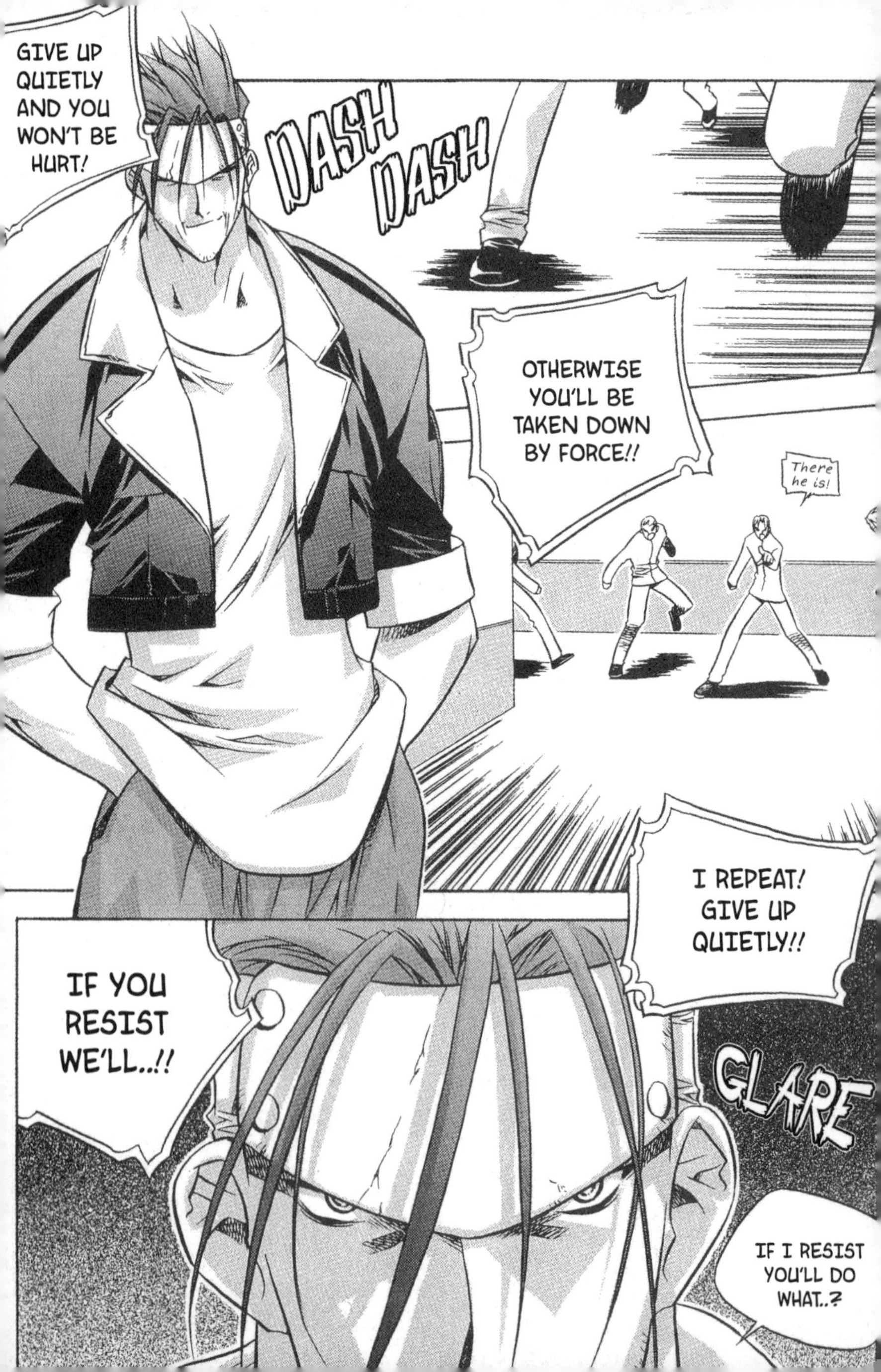
GIVE UP QUIETLY AND YOU WON'T BE HURT!
DASH DASH
OTHERWISE YOU'LL BE TAKEN DOWN BY FORCE!!
There he is!
I REPEAT! GIVE UP QUIETLY!!
IF YOU RESIST WE'LL..!!
GLARE
IF I RESIST YOU'LL DO WHAT..?

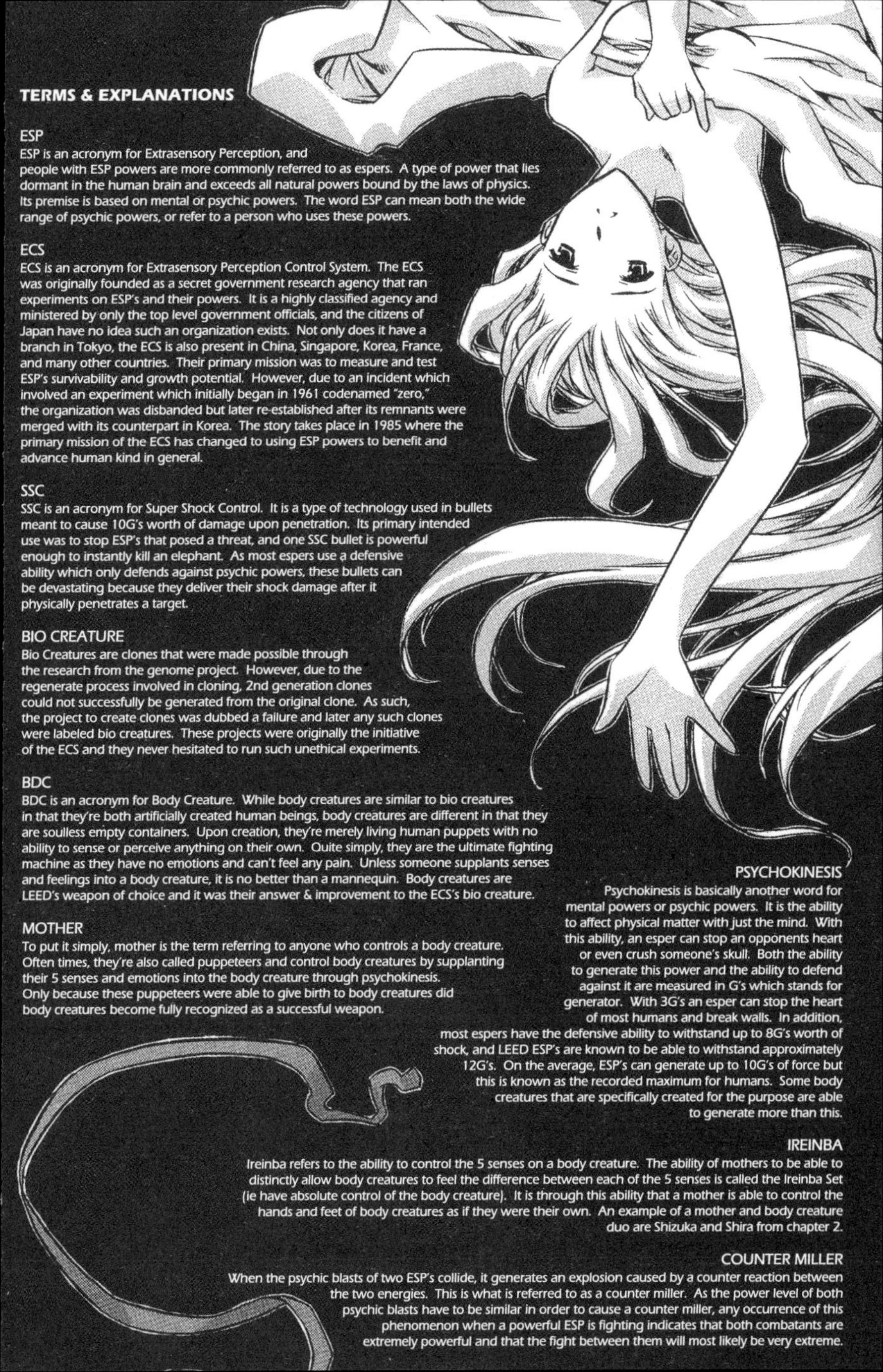

TERMS & EXPLANATIONS

ESP

ESP is an acronym for Extrasensory Perception, and people with ESP powers are more commonly referred to as espers. A type of power that lies dormant in the human brain and exceeds all natural powers bound by the laws of physics. Its premise is based on mental or psychic powers. The word ESP can mean both the wide range of psychic powers, or refer to a person who uses these powers.

ECS

ECS is an acronym for Extrasensory Perception Control System. The ECS was originally founded as a secret government research agency that ran experiments on ESP's and their powers. It is a highly classified agency and ministered by only the top level government officials, and the citizens of Japan have no idea such an organization exists. Not only does it have a branch in Tokyo, the ECS is also present in China, Singapore, Korea, France, and many other countries. Their primary mission was to measure and test ESP's survivability and growth potential. However, due to an incident which involved an experiment which initially began in 1961 codenamed "zero," the organization was disbanded but later re-established after its remnants were merged with its counterpart in Korea. The story takes place in 1985 where the primary mission of the ECS has changed to using ESP powers to benefit and advance human kind in general.

SSC

SSC is an acronym for Super Shock Control. It is a type of technology used in bullets meant to cause 10G's worth of damage upon penetration. Its primary intended use was to stop ESP's that posed a threat, and one SSC bullet is powerful enough to instantly kill an elephant. As most espers use a defensive ability which only defends against psychic powers, these bullets can be devastating because they deliver their shock damage after it physically penetrates a target.

BIO CREATURE

Bio Creatures are clones that were made possible through the research from the genome project. However, due to the regenerate process involved in cloning, 2nd generation clones could not successfully be generated from the original clone. As such, the project to create clones was dubbed a failure and later any such clones were labeled bio creatures. These projects were originally the initiative of the ECS and they never hesitated to run such unethical experiments.

BDC

BDC is an acronym for Body Creature. While body creatures are similar to bio creatures in that they're both artificially created human beings, body creatures are different in that they are soulless empty containers. Upon creation, they're merely living human puppets with no ability to sense or perceive anything on their own. Quite simply, they are the ultimate fighting machine as they have no emotions and can't feel any pain. Unless someone supplants senses and feelings into a body creature, it is no better than a mannequin. Body creatures are LEED's weapon of choice and it was their answer & improvement to the ECS's bio creature.

MOTHER

To put it simply, mother is the term referring to anyone who controls a body creature. Often times, they're also called puppeteers and control body creatures by supplanting their 5 senses and emotions into the body creature through psychokinesis. Only because these puppeteers were able to give birth to body creatures did body creatures become fully recognized as a successful weapon.

PSYCHOKINESIS

Psychokinesis is basically another word for mental powers or psychic powers. It is the ability to affect physical matter with just the mind. With this ability, an esper can stop an opponents heart or even crush someone's skull. Both the ability to generate this power and the ability to defend against it are measured in G's which stands for generator. With 3G's an esper can stop the heart of most humans and break walls. In addition, most espers have the defensive ability to withstand up to 8G's worth of shock, and LEED ESP's are known to be able to withstand approximately 12G's. On the average, ESP's can generate up to 10G's of force but this is known as the recorded maximum for humans. Some body creatures that are specifically created for the purpose are able to generate more than this.

IREINBA

Ireinba refers to the ability to control the 5 senses on a body creature. The ability of mothers to be able to distinctly allow body creatures to feel the difference between each of the 5 senses is called the Ireinba Set (ie have absolute control of the body creature). It is through this ability that a mother is able to control the hands and feet of body creatures as if they were their own. An example of a mother and body creature duo are Shizuka and Shira from chapter 2.

COUNTER MILLER

When the psychic blasts of two ESP's collide, it generates an explosion caused by a counter reaction between the two energies. This is what is referred to as a counter miller. As the power level of both psychic blasts have to be similar in order to cause a counter miller, any occurrence of this phenomenon when a powerful ESP is fighting indicates that both combatants are extremely powerful and that the fight between them will most likely be very extreme.

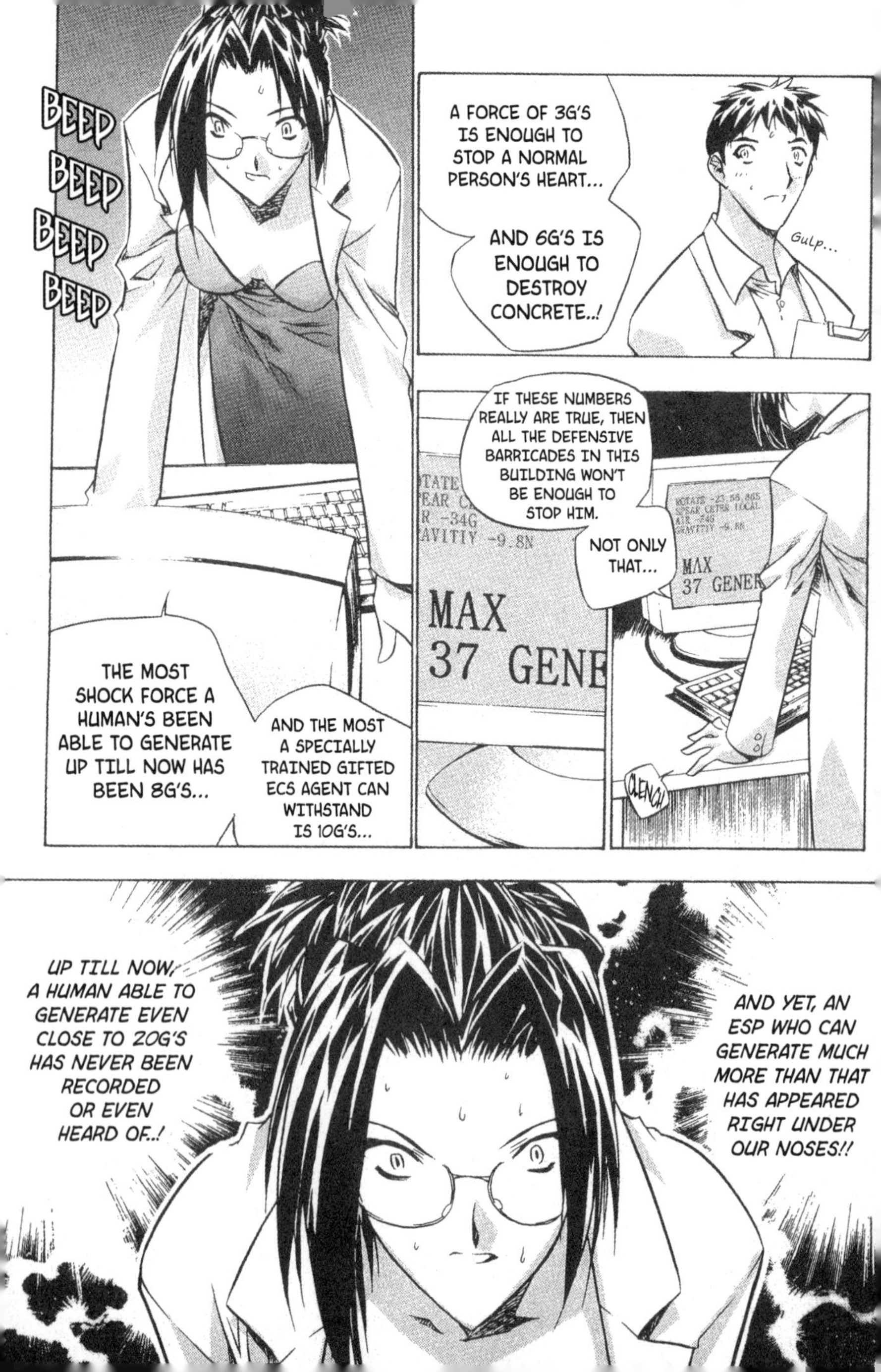
BEEP
BEEP
BEEP
BEEP
THE MOST SHOCK FORCE A HUMAN'S BEEN ABLE TO GENERATE UP TILL NOW HAS BEEN 8G'S...
AND THE MOST A SPECIALLY TRAINED GIFTED ECS AGENT CAN WITHSTAND IS 10G'S...
A FORCE OF 3G'S IS ENOUGH TO STOP A NORMAL PERSON'S HEART...
AND 6G'S IS ENOUGH TO DESTROY CONCRETE..!
Gulp...
IF THESE NUMBERS REALLY ARE TRUE, THEN ALL THE DEFENSIVE BARRICADES IN THIS BUILDING WON'T BE ENOUGH TO STOP HIM.
MAX
37 GENE
NOT ONLY THAT...
CLENCH
UP TILL NOW, A HUMAN ABLE TO GENERATE EVEN CLOSE TO 20G'S HAS NEVER BEEN RECORDED OR EVEN HEARD OF..!
AND YET, AN ESP WHO CAN GENERATE MUCH MORE THAN THAT HAS APPEARED RIGHT UNDER OUR NOSES!!

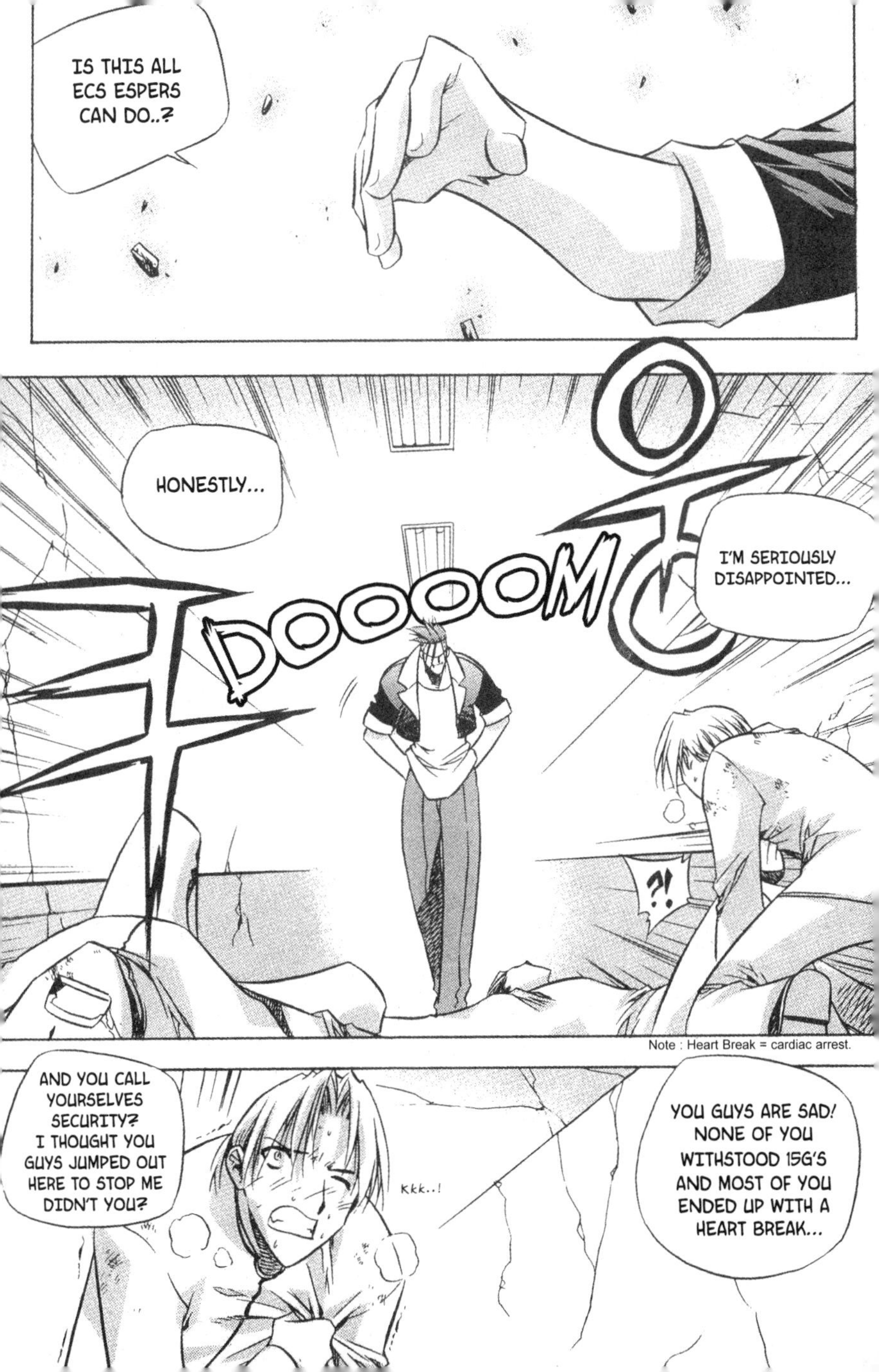
IS THIS ALL ECS ESPERS CAN DO..?
HONESTLY...
DOOOOOM
I'M SERIOUSLY DISAPPOINTED...
?!
AND YOU CALL YOURSELVES SECURITY? I THOUGHT YOU GUYS JUMPED OUT HERE TO STOP ME DIDN'T YOU?
Kkk..!
YOU GUYS ARE SAD! NONE OF YOU WITHSTOOD 15G'S AND MOST OF YOU ENDED UP WITH A HEART BREAK...
Note : Heart Break = cardiac arrest.

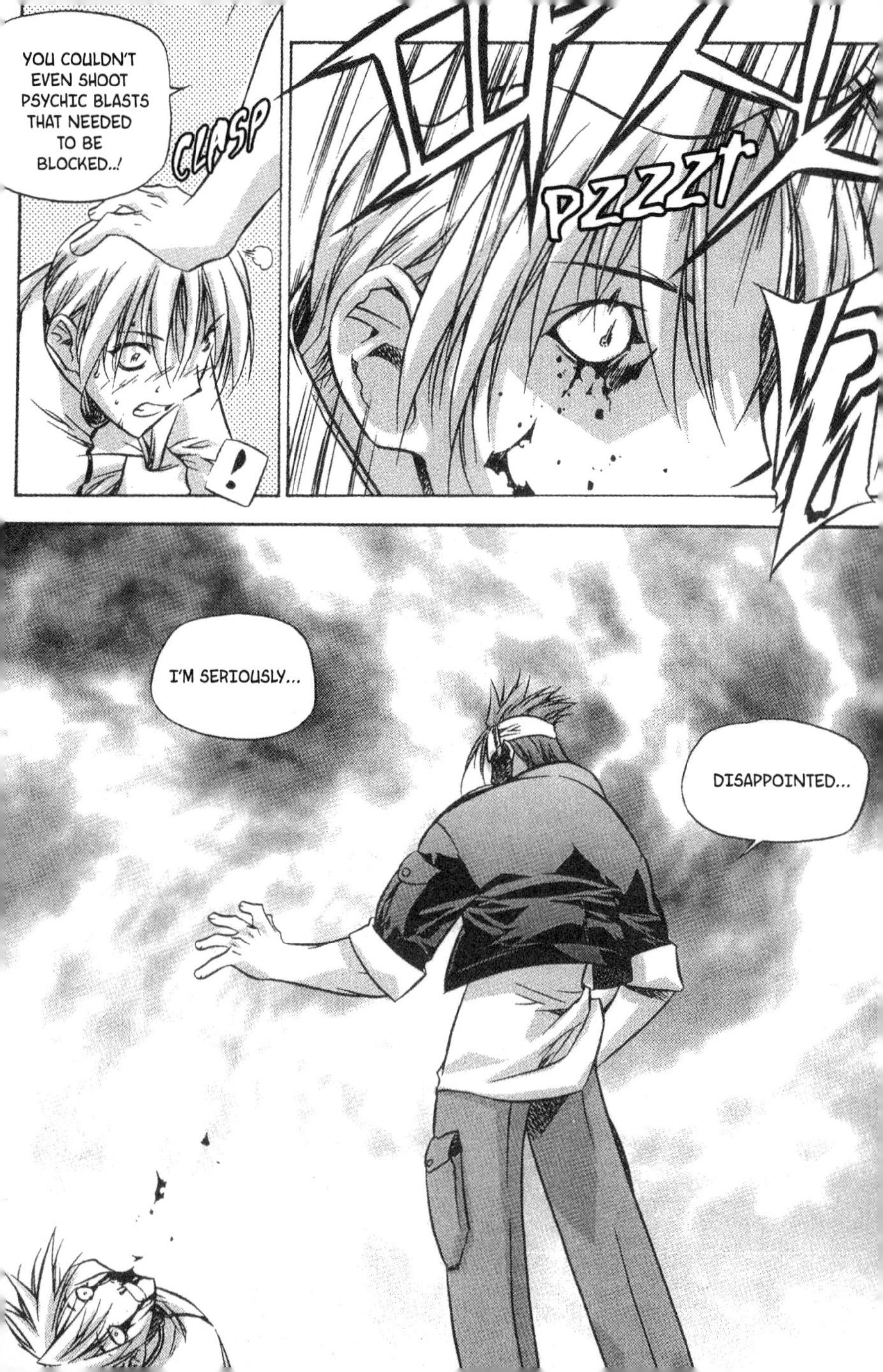
YOU COULDN'T EVEN SHOOT PSYCHIC BLASTS THAT NEEDED TO BE BLOCKED..!
CLASP
!
PZZZT
I'M SERIOUSLY...
DISAPPOINTED...

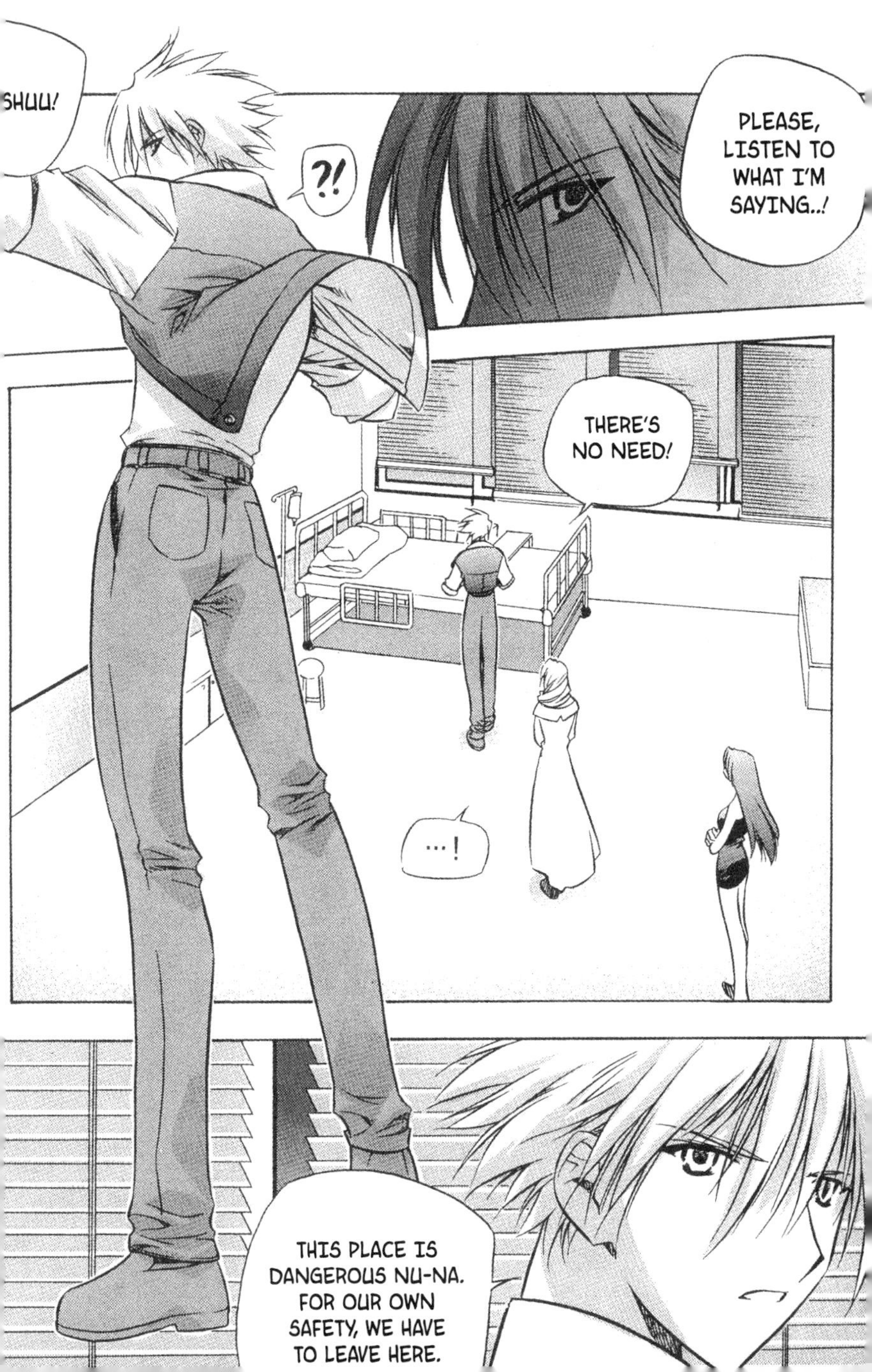
SHUU!
?!
PLEASE, LISTEN TO WHAT I'M SAYING..!
THERE'S NO NEED!
...!
THIS PLACE IS DANGEROUS NU-NA. FOR OUR OWN SAFETY, WE HAVE TO LEAVE HERE.

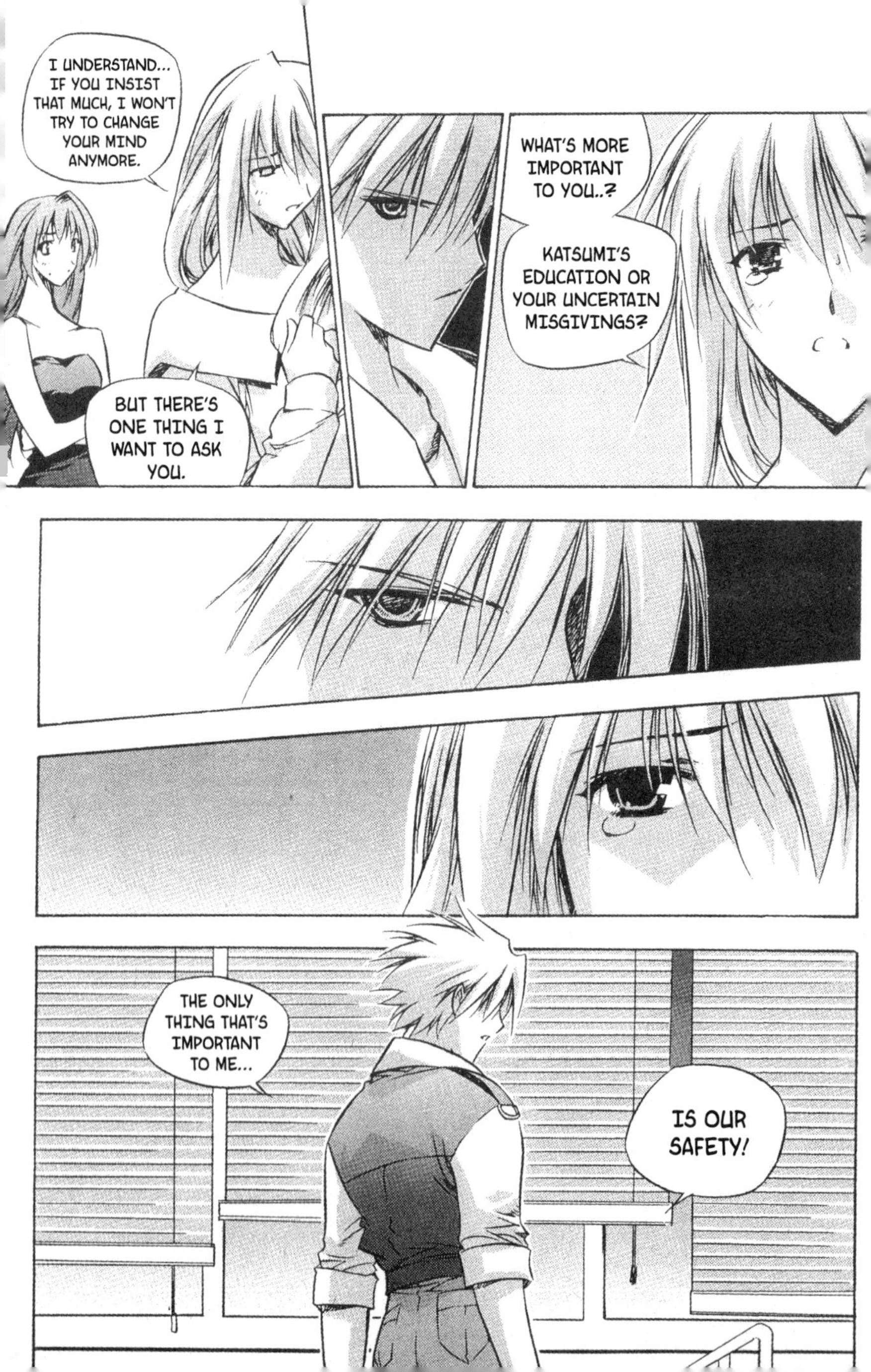
I UNDERSTAND... IF YOU INSIST THAT MUCH, I WON'T TRY TO CHANGE YOUR MIND ANYMORE.
BUT THERE'S ONE THING I WANT TO ASK YOU.
WHAT'S MORE IMPORTANT TO YOU..?
KATSUMI'S EDUCATION OR YOUR UNCERTAIN MISGIVINGS?
THE ONLY THING THAT'S IMPORTANT TO ME...
IS OUR SAFETY!

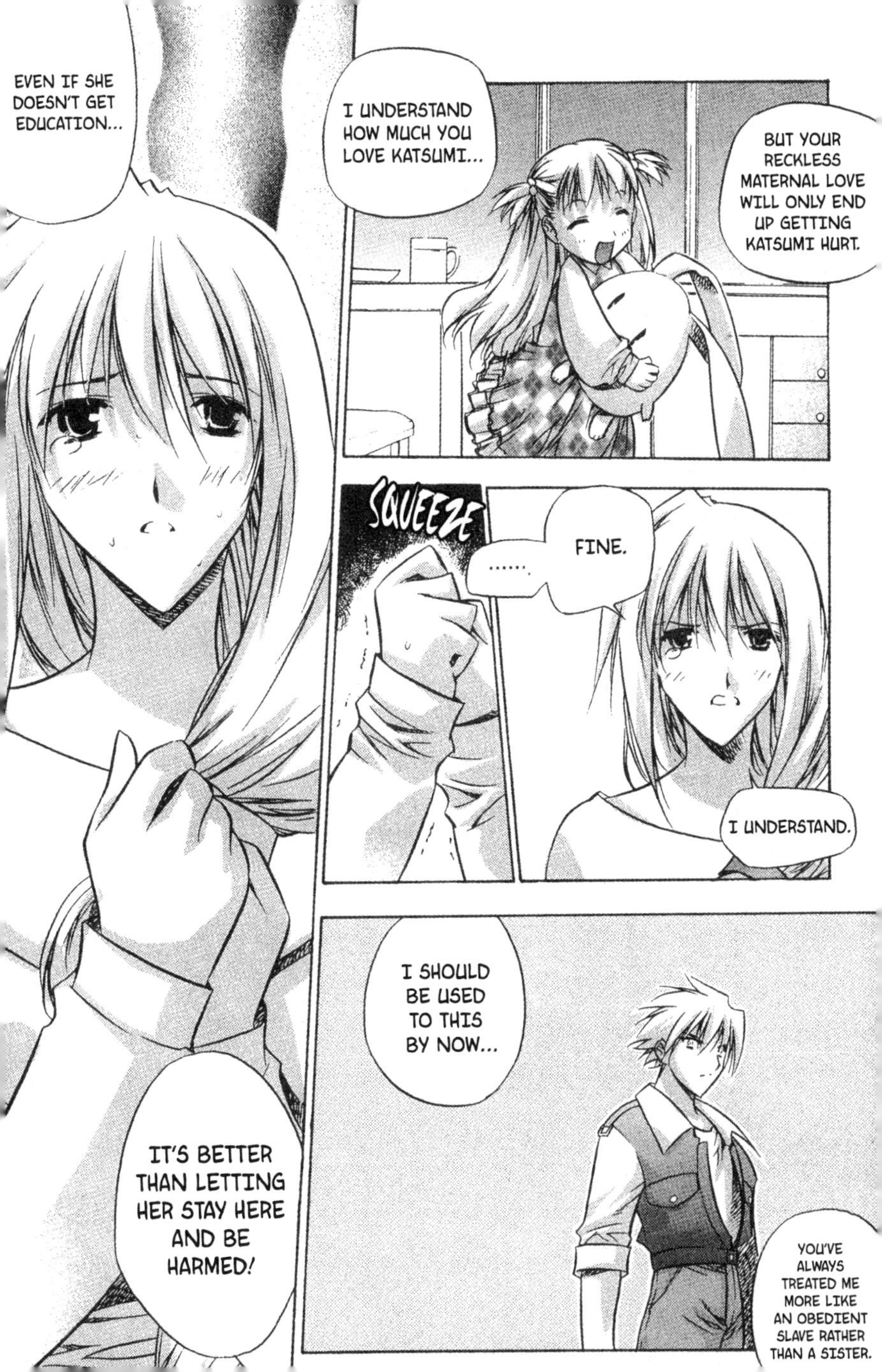
EVEN IF SHE DOESN'T GET EDUCATION...
IT'S BETTER THAN LETTING HER STAY HERE AND BE HARMED!
I UNDERSTAND HOW MUCH YOU LOVE KATSUMI...
BUT YOUR RECKLESS MATERNAL LOVE WILL ONLY END UP GETTING KATSUMI HURT.
SQUEEZE
....
FINE.
I UNDERSTAND.
I SHOULD BE USED TO THIS BY NOW...
YOU'VE ALWAYS TREATED ME MORE LIKE AN OBEDIENT SLAVE RATHER THAN A SISTER.

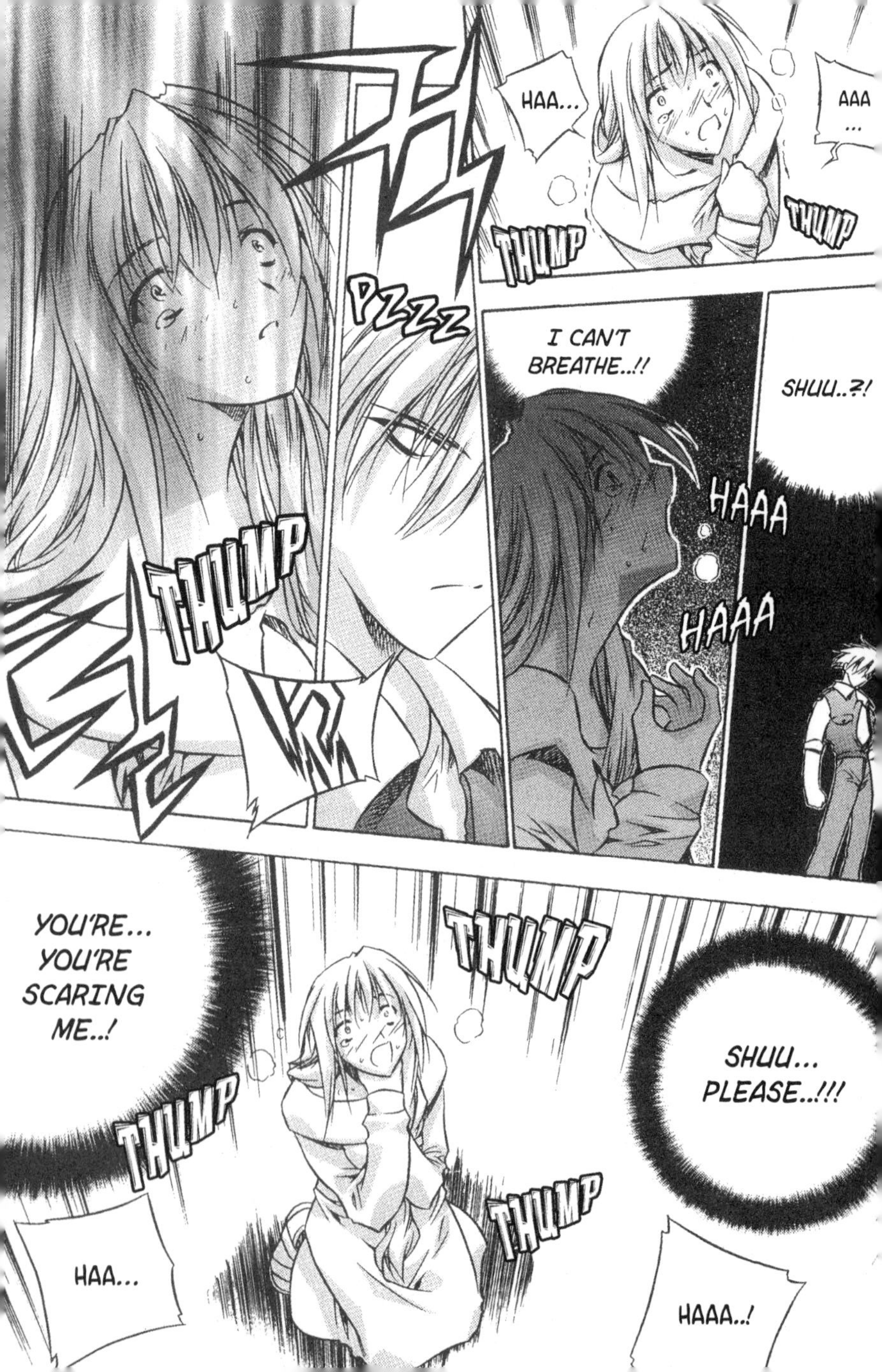
THUMP
PZZZ
HAA...
THUMP
AAA...
THUMP
I CAN'T BREATHE..!!
HAAA
HAAA
SHUU..?!
YOU'RE... YOU'RE SCARING ME..!
THUMP
HAA...
THUMP
THUMP
SHUU... PLEASE..!!!
HAAA..!

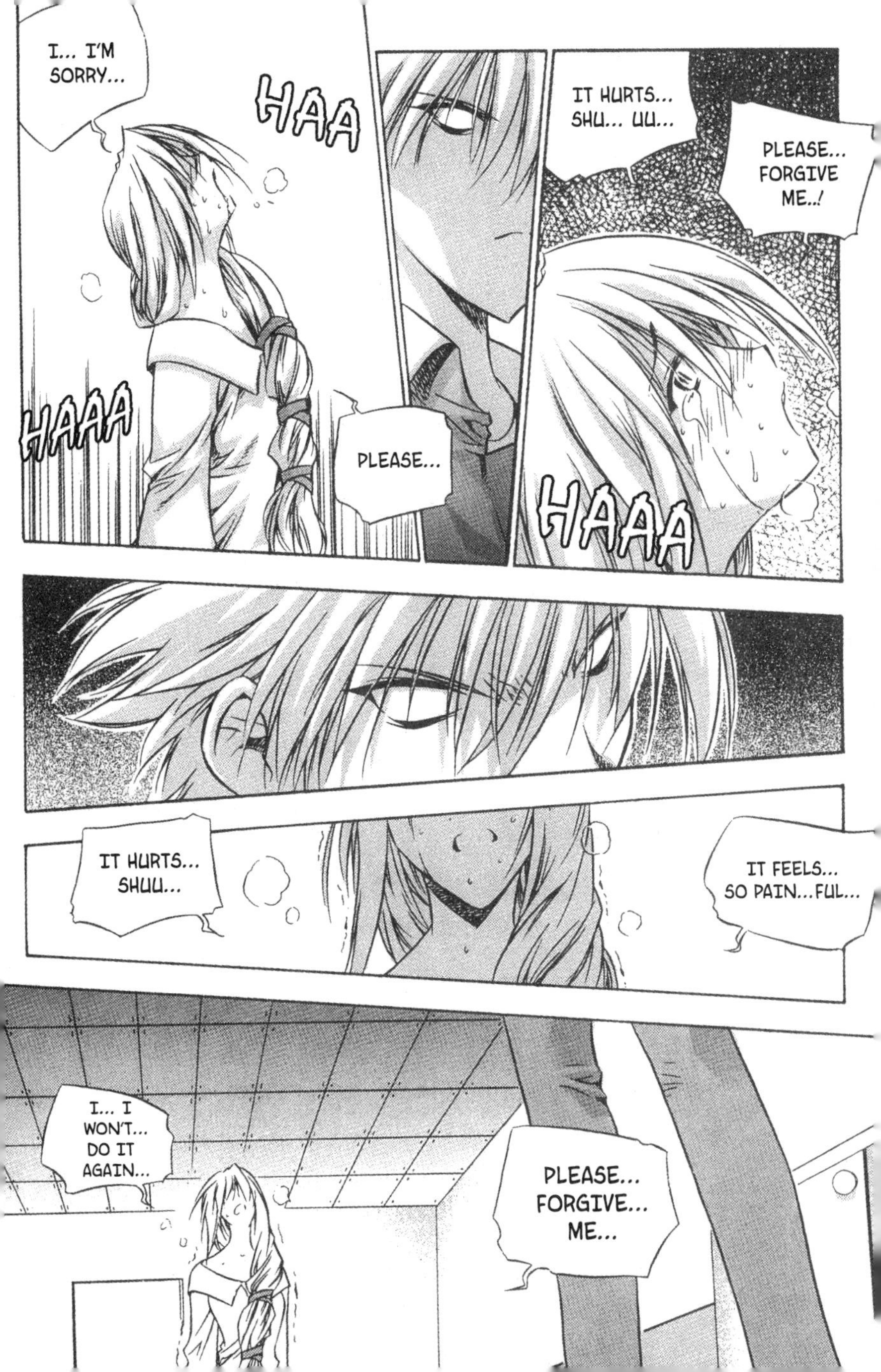
I... I'M SORRY...
HAA
HAAA
PLEASE...
IT HURTS... SHU... UU...
PLEASE... FORGIVE ME..!
HAAA
IT HURTS... SHUU...
IT FEELS... SO PAIN...FUL...
I... I WON'T... DO IT AGAIN...
PLEASE... FORGIVE... ME...

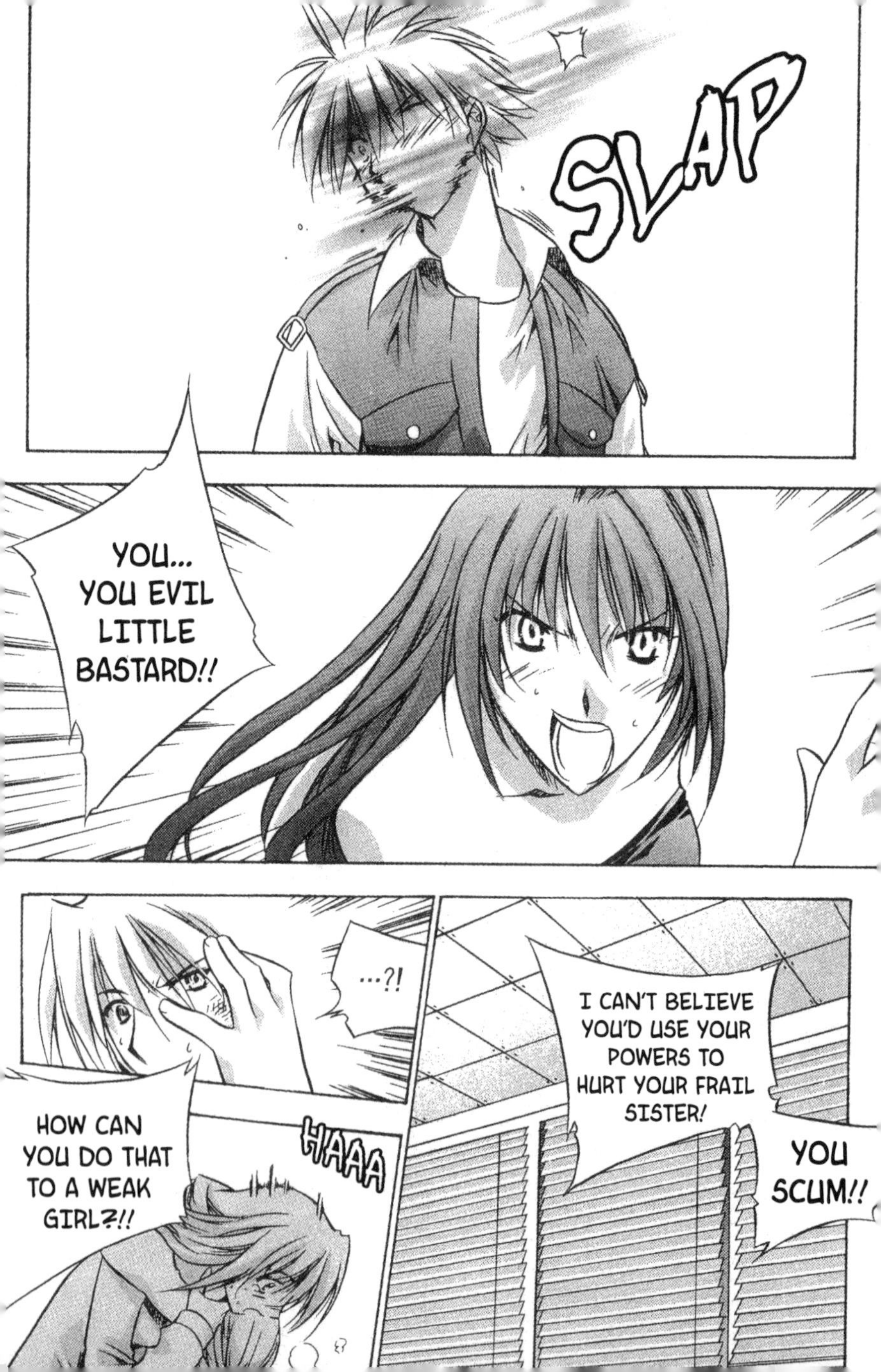
SLAP
YOU... YOU EVIL LITTLE BASTARD!!
...?!
HOW CAN YOU DO THAT TO A WEAK GIRL?!!
HAAA
I CAN'T BELIEVE YOU'D USE YOUR POWERS TO HURT YOUR FRAIL SISTER!
YOU SCUM!!

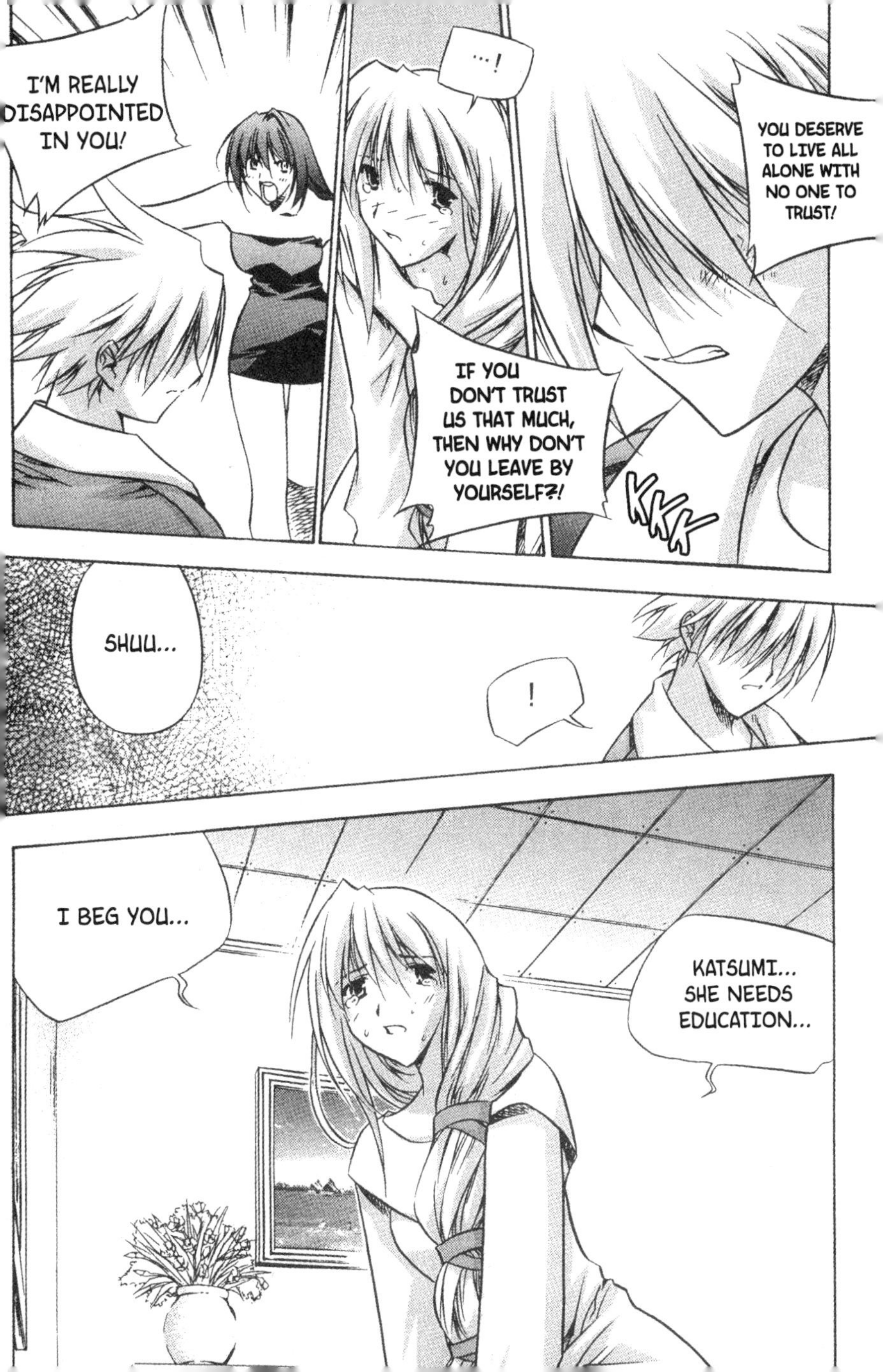
I'M REALLY DISAPPOINTED IN YOU!
...!
IF YOU DON'T TRUST US THAT MUCH, THEN WHY DON'T YOU LEAVE BY YOURSELF?!
YOU DESERVE TO LIVE ALL ALONE WITH NO ONE TO TRUST!
KKK
SHUU...
!
I BEG YOU...
KATSUMI... SHE NEEDS EDUCATION...

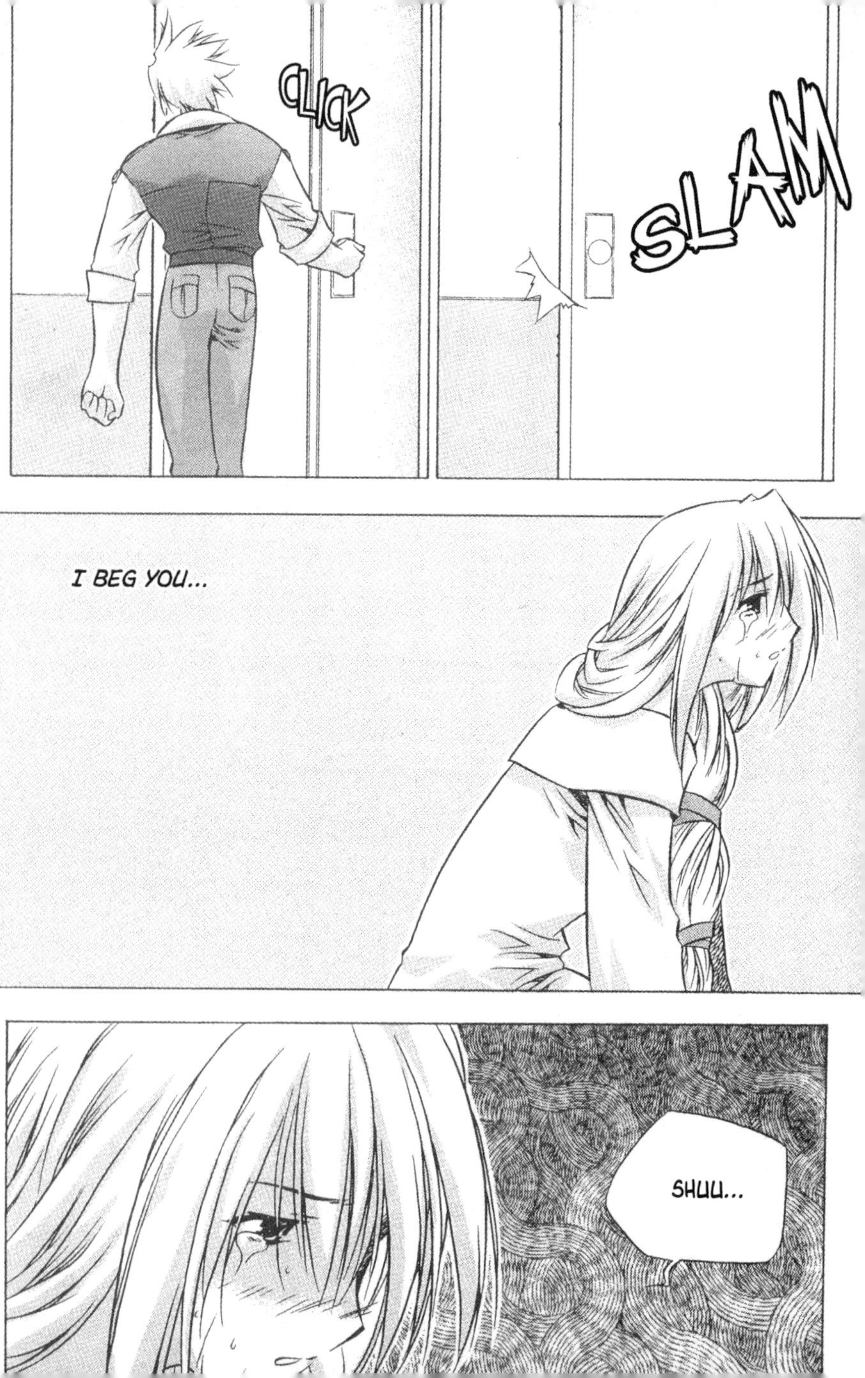
CLICK
SLAM
I BEG YOU...
SHUU...

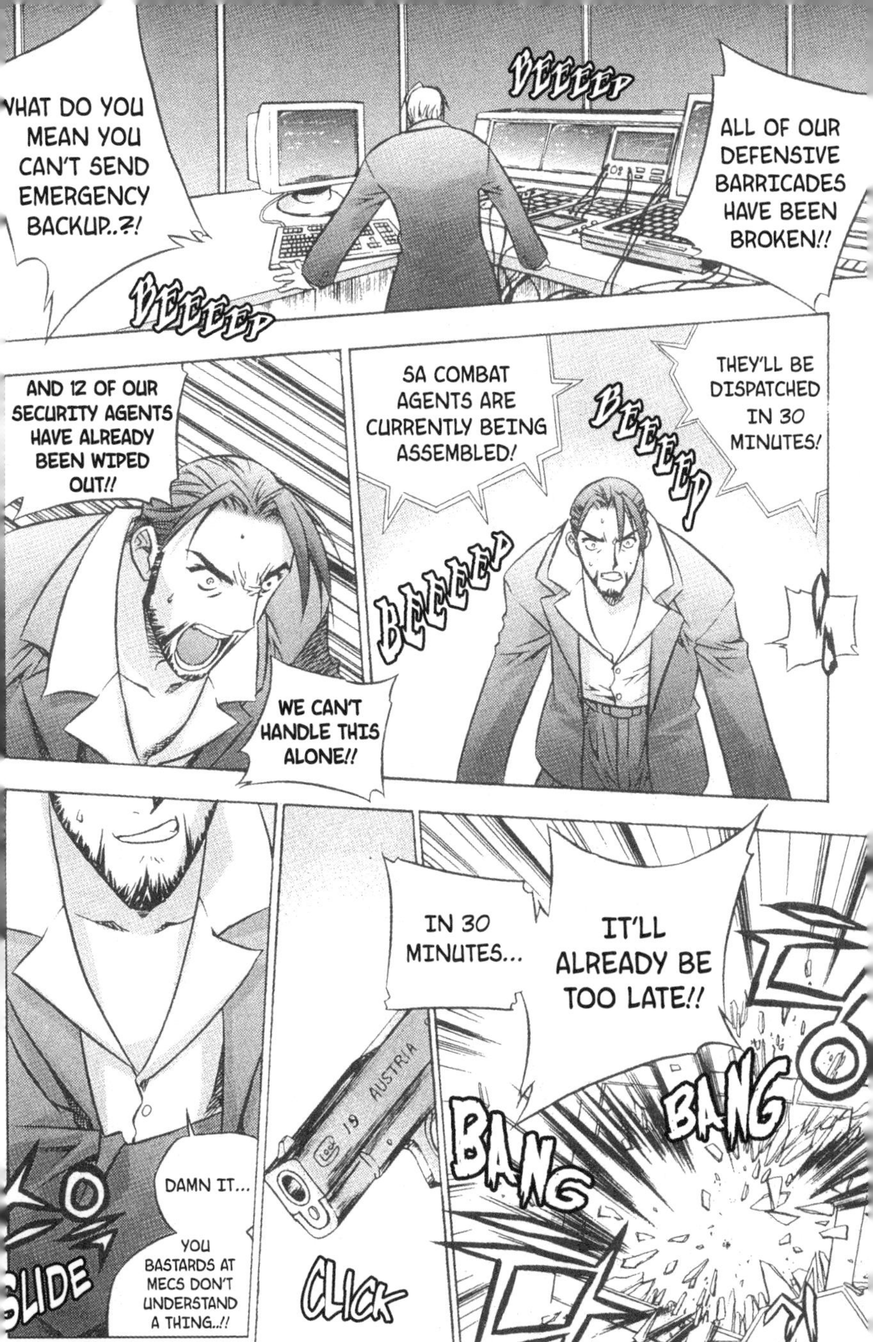
VHAT DO YOU MEAN YOU CAN'T SEND EMERGENCY BACKUP..?!
BEEEEP
ALL OF OUR DEFENSIVE BARRICADES HAVE BEEN BROKEN!!
BEEEEP
AND 12 OF OUR SECURITY AGENTS HAVE ALREADY BEEN WIPED OUT!!
WE CAN'T HANDLE THIS ALONE!!
SA COMBAT AGENTS ARE CURRENTLY BEING ASSEMBLED!
BEEEEP
THEY'LL BE DISPATCHED IN 30 MINUTES!
BEEEEP
DAMN IT...
YOU BASTARDS AT MECS DON'T UNDERSTAND A THING..!!
SLIDE
AUSTRIA
CLICK
IN 30 MINUTES...
IT'LL ALREADY BE TOO LATE!!
BANG
BANG

Note : MECS = Main Branch ECS
(ie headquarters)

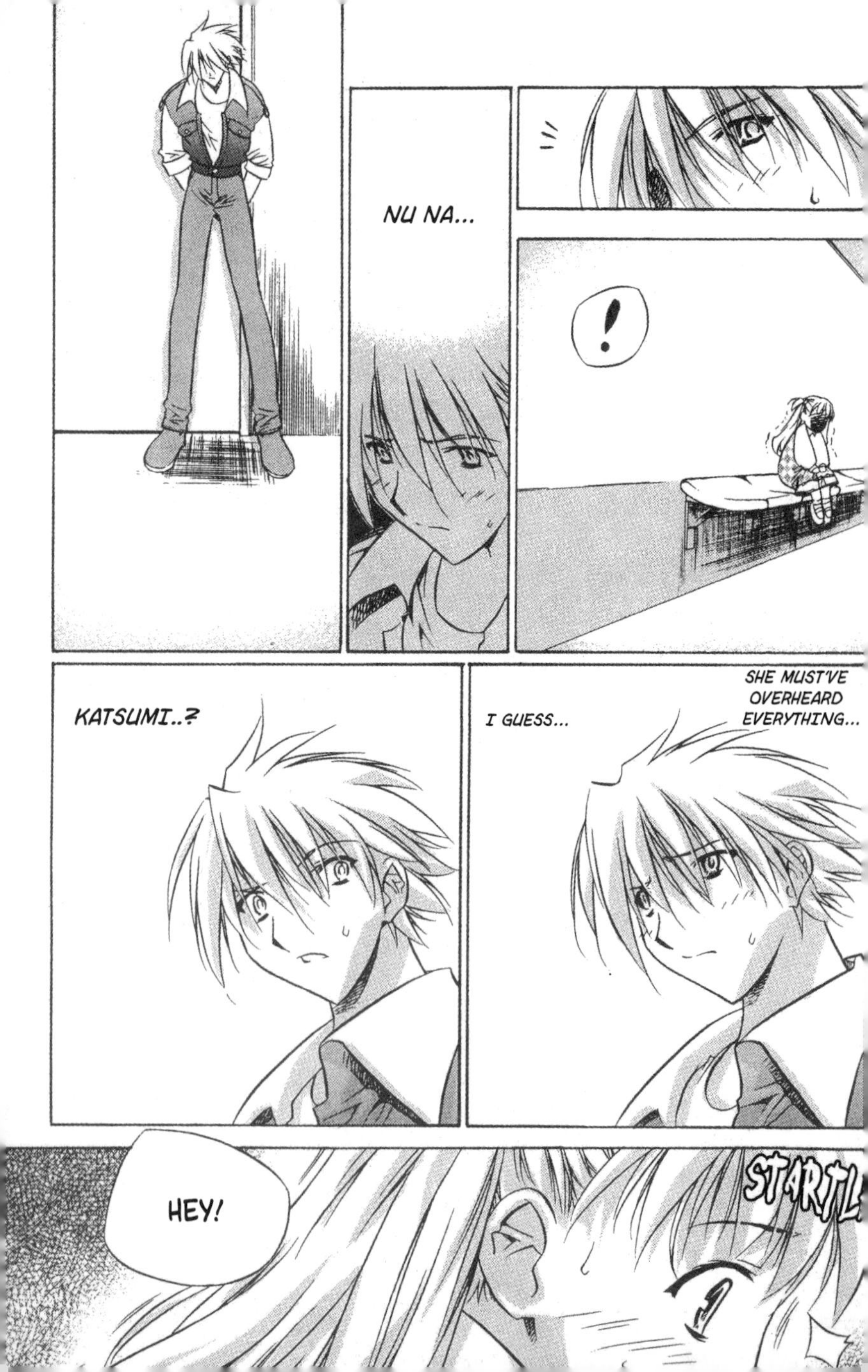
NU NA...
!
KATSUMI..?
I GUESS...
SHE MUST'VE OVERHEARD EVERYTHING...
HEY!
STARTL

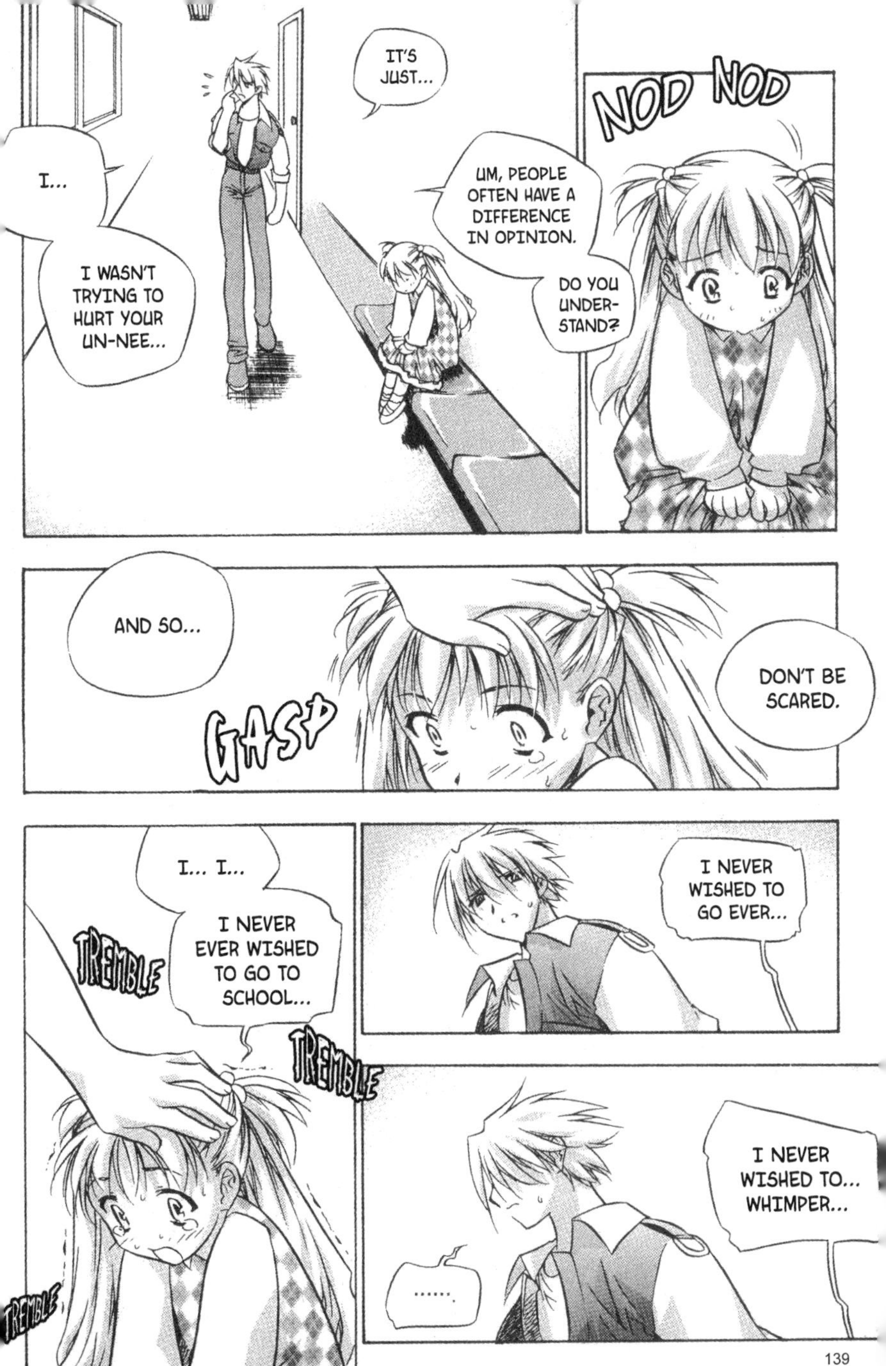
I...
I WASN'T TRYING TO HURT YOUR UN-NEE...
IT'S JUST...
UM, PEOPLE OFTEN HAVE A DIFFERENCE IN OPINION.
DO YOU UNDERSTAND?
NOD NOD
AND SO...
GASP
DON'T BE SCARED.
I... I...
I NEVER EVER WISHED TO GO TO SCHOOL...
TREMBLE
TREMBLE
TREMBLE
I NEVER WISHED TO GO EVER...
....
I NEVER WISHED TO... WHIMPER...

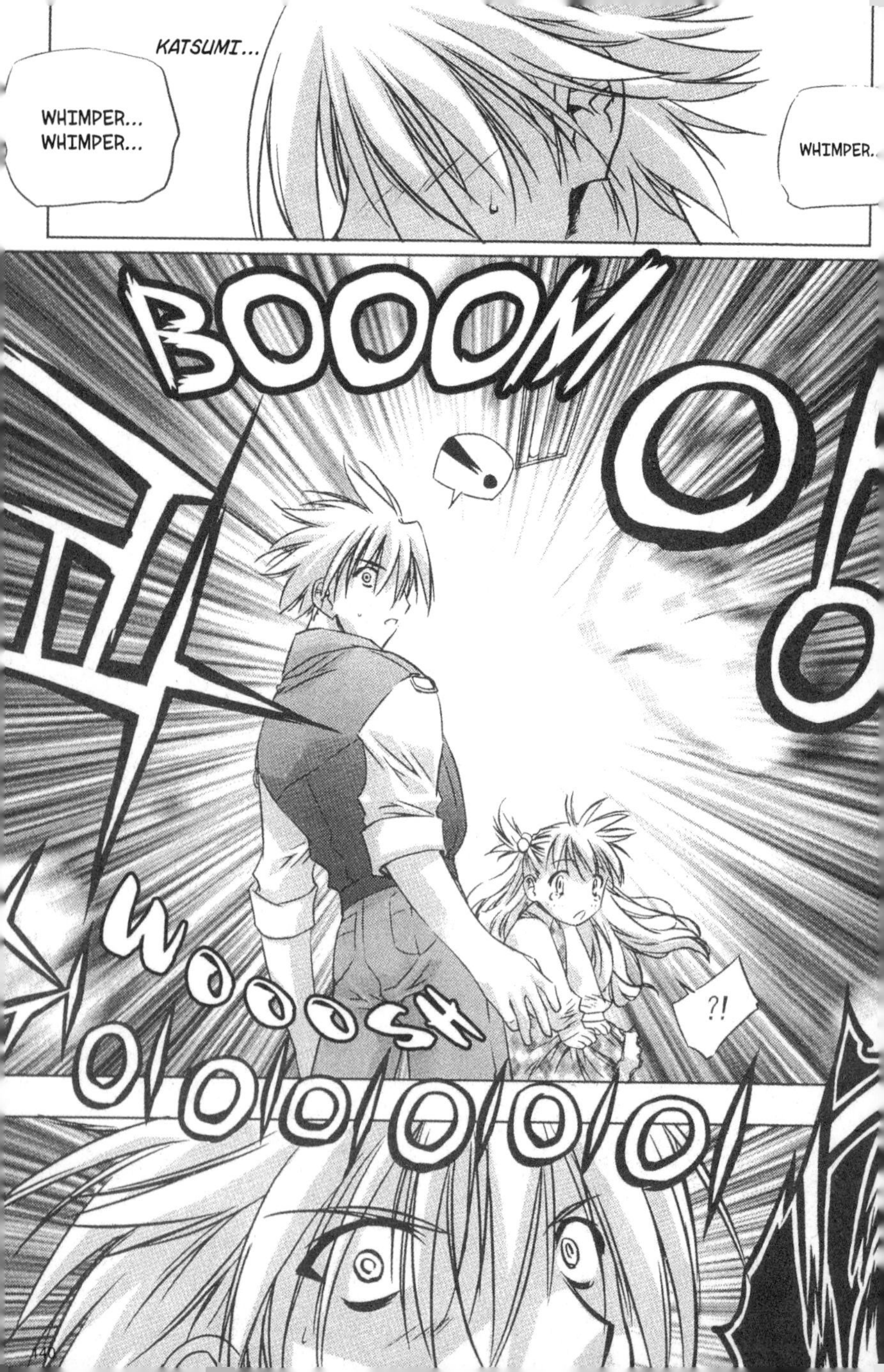
WHIMPER...
WHIMPER...
KATSUMI...
WHIMPER..
BOOOM
?!

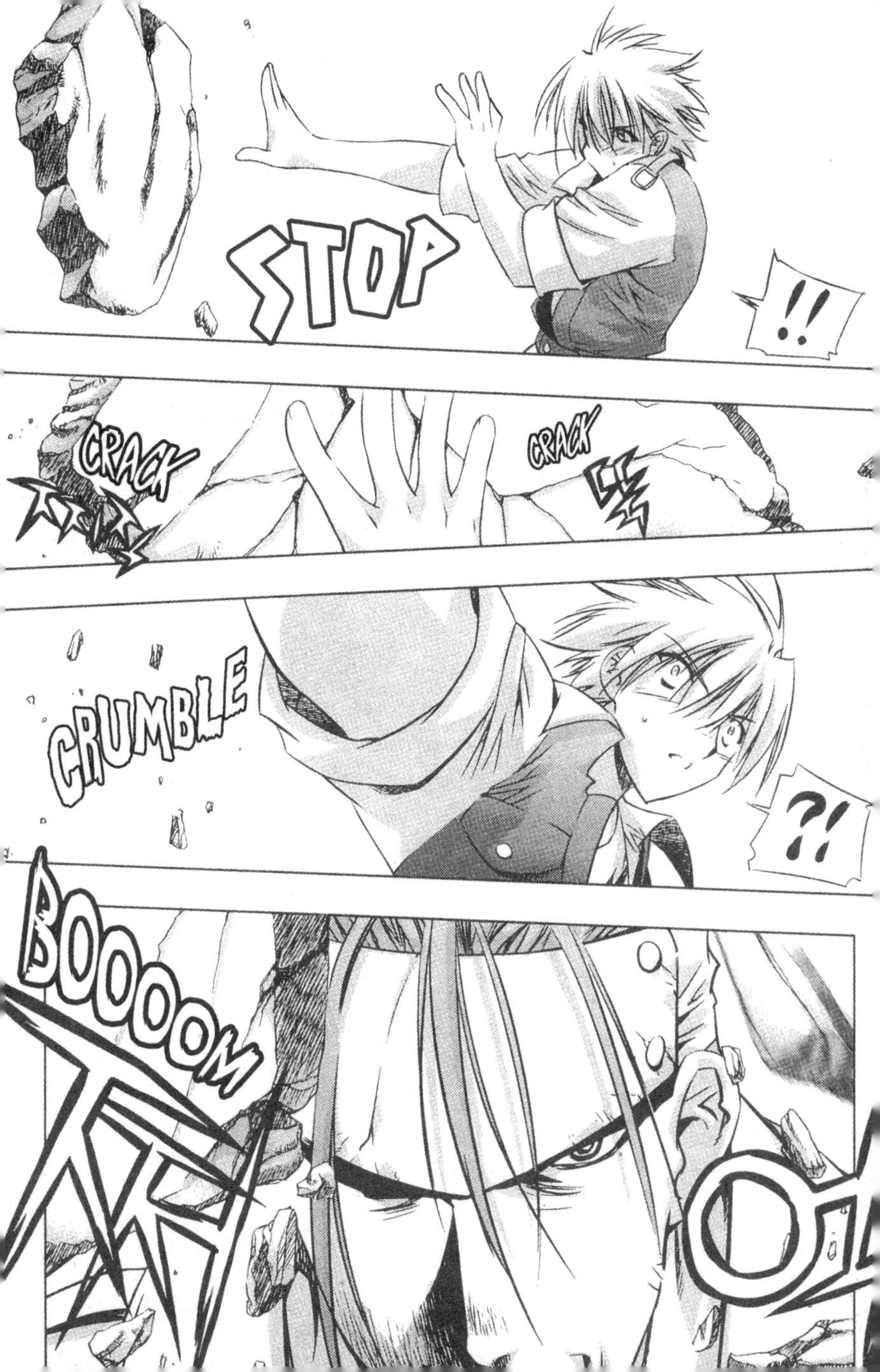
STOP
!!
CRACK
CRACK
CRUMBLE
?!
BOOOOOM

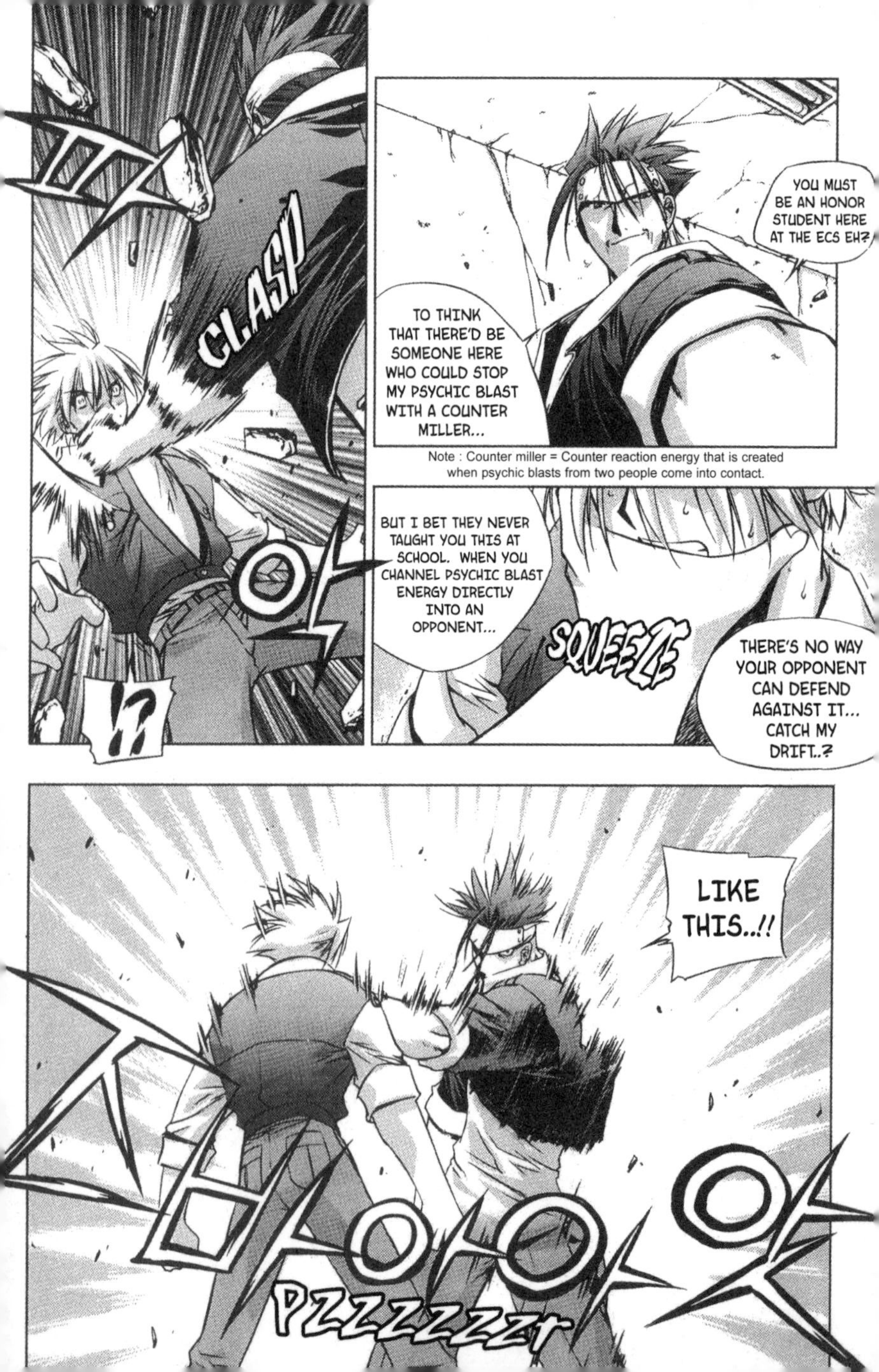
CLASP
!?
YOU MUST BE AN HONOR STUDENT HERE AT THE ECS EH?
TO THINK THAT THERE'D BE SOMEONE HERE WHO COULD STOP MY PSYCHIC BLAST WITH A COUNTER MILLER...
Note : Counter miller = Counter reaction energy that is created when psychic blasts from two people come into contact.
BUT I BET THEY NEVER TAUGHT YOU THIS AT SCHOOL. WHEN YOU CHANNEL PSYCHIC BLAST ENERGY DIRECTLY INTO AN OPPONENT...
SQUEEZE
THERE'S NO WAY YOUR OPPONENT CAN DEFEND AGAINST IT... CATCH MY DRIFT..?
LIKE THIS..!!
PZZZZZZZr

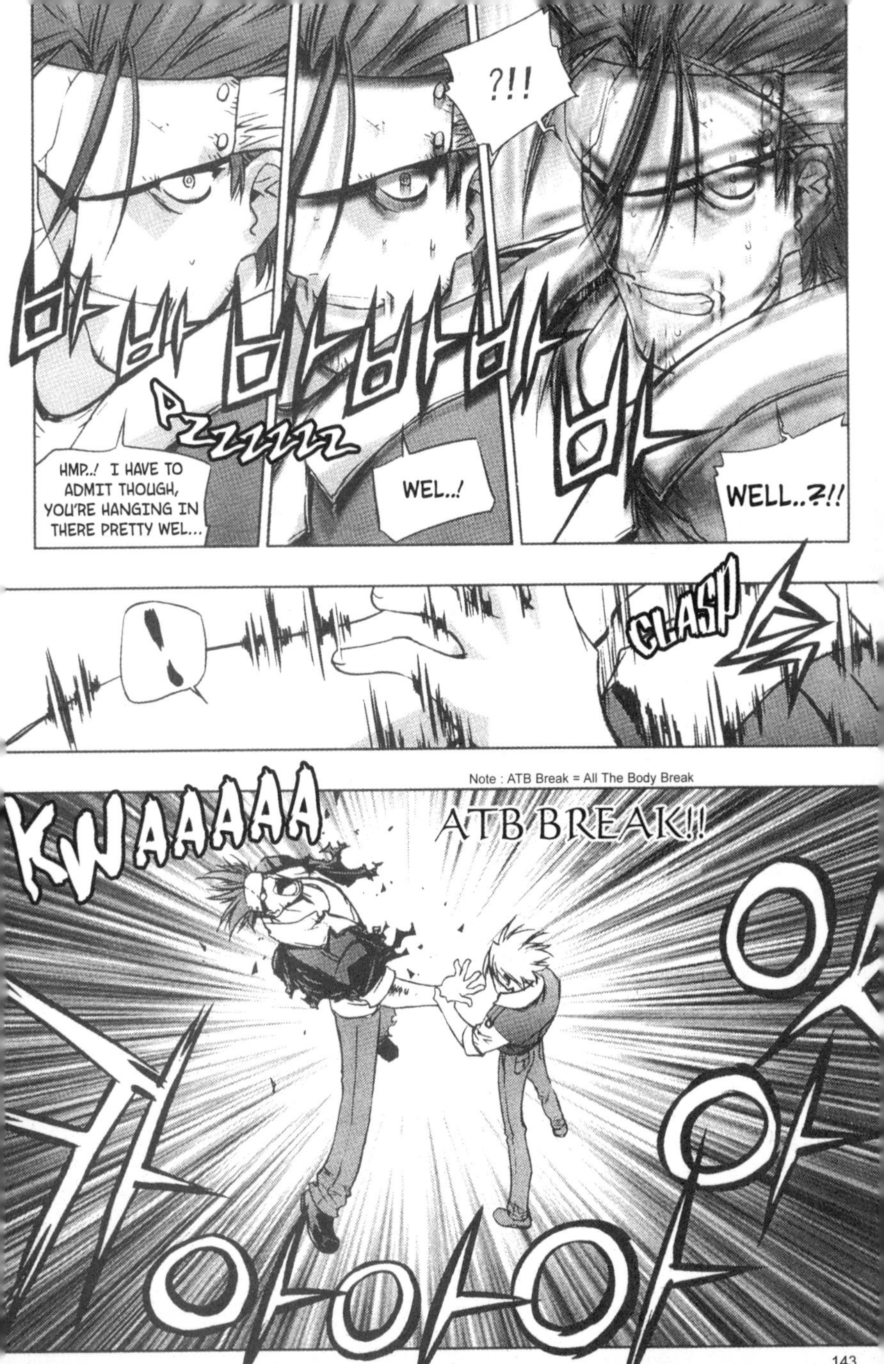
HMP..! I HAVE TO ADMIT THOUGH, YOU'RE HANGING IN THERE PRETTY WEL...
PZZZZZZ
WEL..!
?!!
WELL..?!!
!
CLASP
Note : ATB Break = All The Body Break
KWAAAAAA
ATB BREAK!!

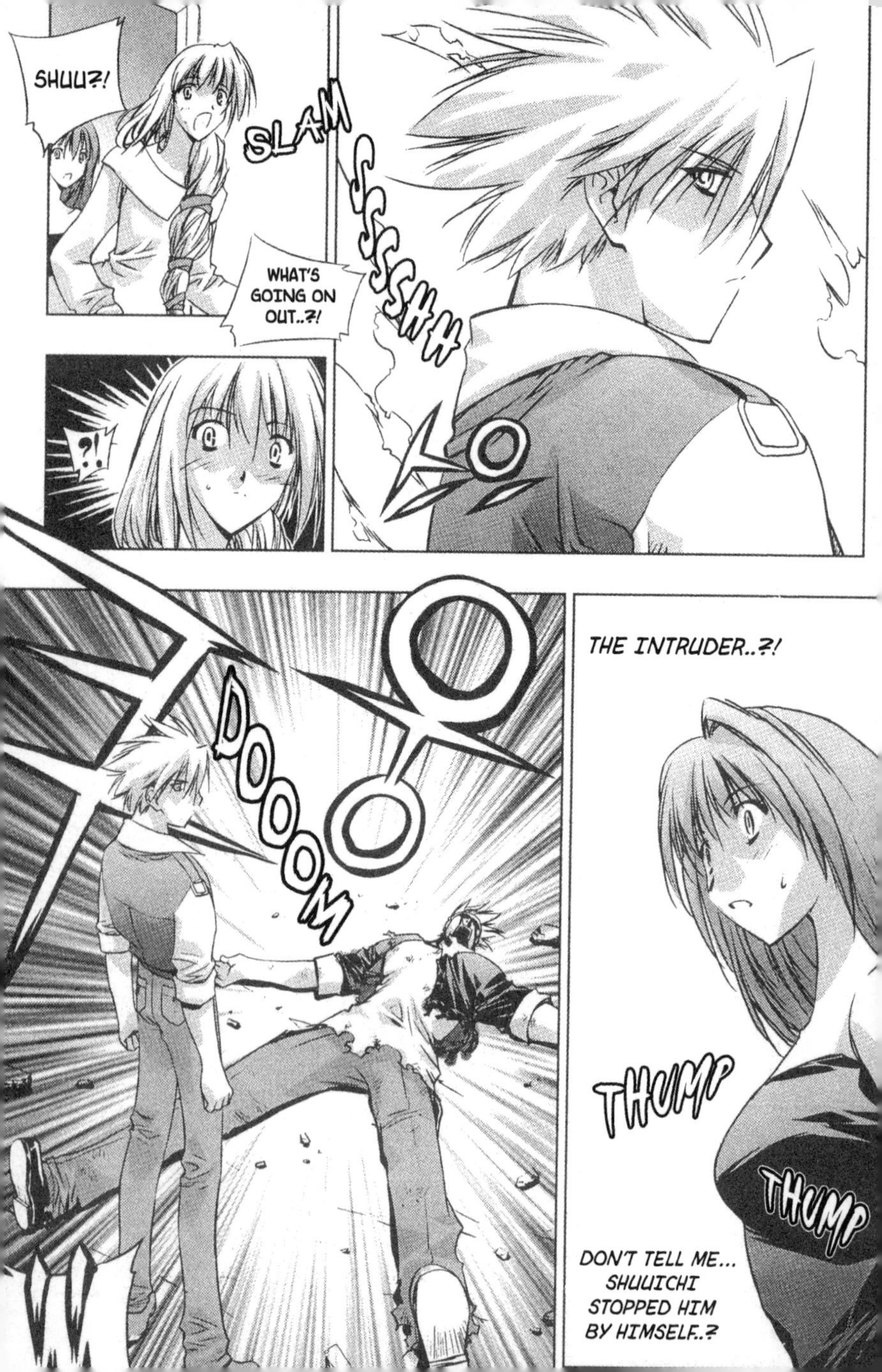
SHUU?!
WHAT'S GOING ON OUT..?!
?!
SLAM
SSSSHH
DOOOOM
THE INTRUDER..?!
THUMP
THUMP
DON'T TELL ME... SHUUICHI STOPPED HIM BY HIMSELF..?

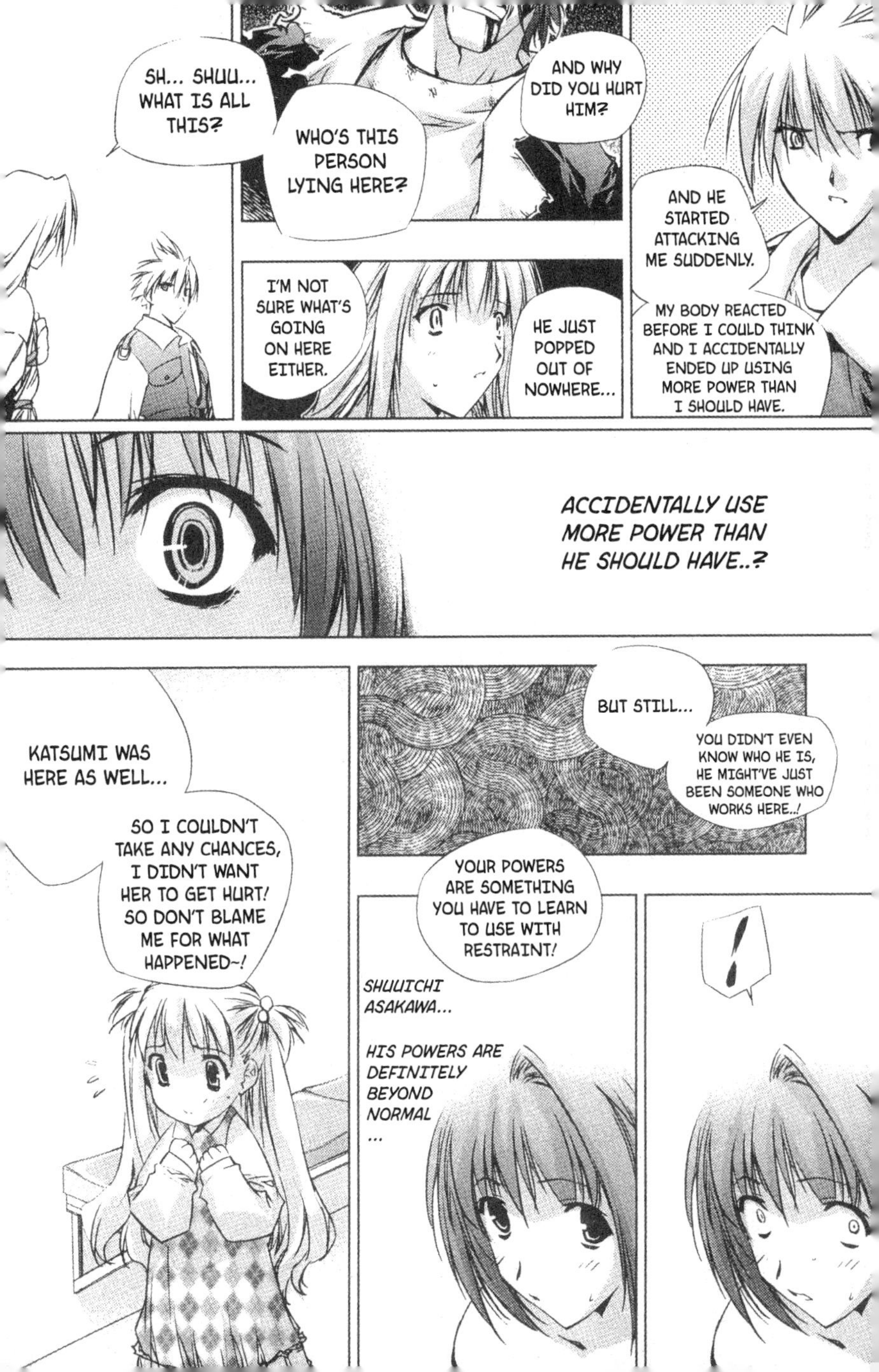
SH... SHUU... WHAT IS ALL THIS?
WHO'S THIS PERSON LYING HERE?
AND WHY DID YOU HURT HIM?
I'M NOT SURE WHAT'S GOING ON HERE EITHER.
HE JUST POPPED OUT OF NOWHERE...
AND HE STARTED ATTACKING ME SUDDENLY.
MY BODY REACTED BEFORE I COULD THINK AND I ACCIDENTALLY ENDED UP USING MORE POWER THAN I SHOULD HAVE.
ACCIDENTALLY USE MORE POWER THAN HE SHOULD HAVE..?
KATSUMI WAS HERE AS WELL...
SO I COULDN'T TAKE ANY CHANCES, I DIDN'T WANT HER TO GET HURT! SO DON'T BLAME ME FOR WHAT HAPPENED~!
BUT STILL...
YOU DIDN'T EVEN KNOW WHO HE IS, HE MIGHT'VE JUST BEEN SOMEONE WHO WORKS HERE..!
YOUR POWERS ARE SOMETHING YOU HAVE TO LEARN TO USE WITH RESTRAINT!
SHUUICHI ASAKAWA...
HIS POWERS ARE DEFINITELY BEYOND NORMAL ...
!

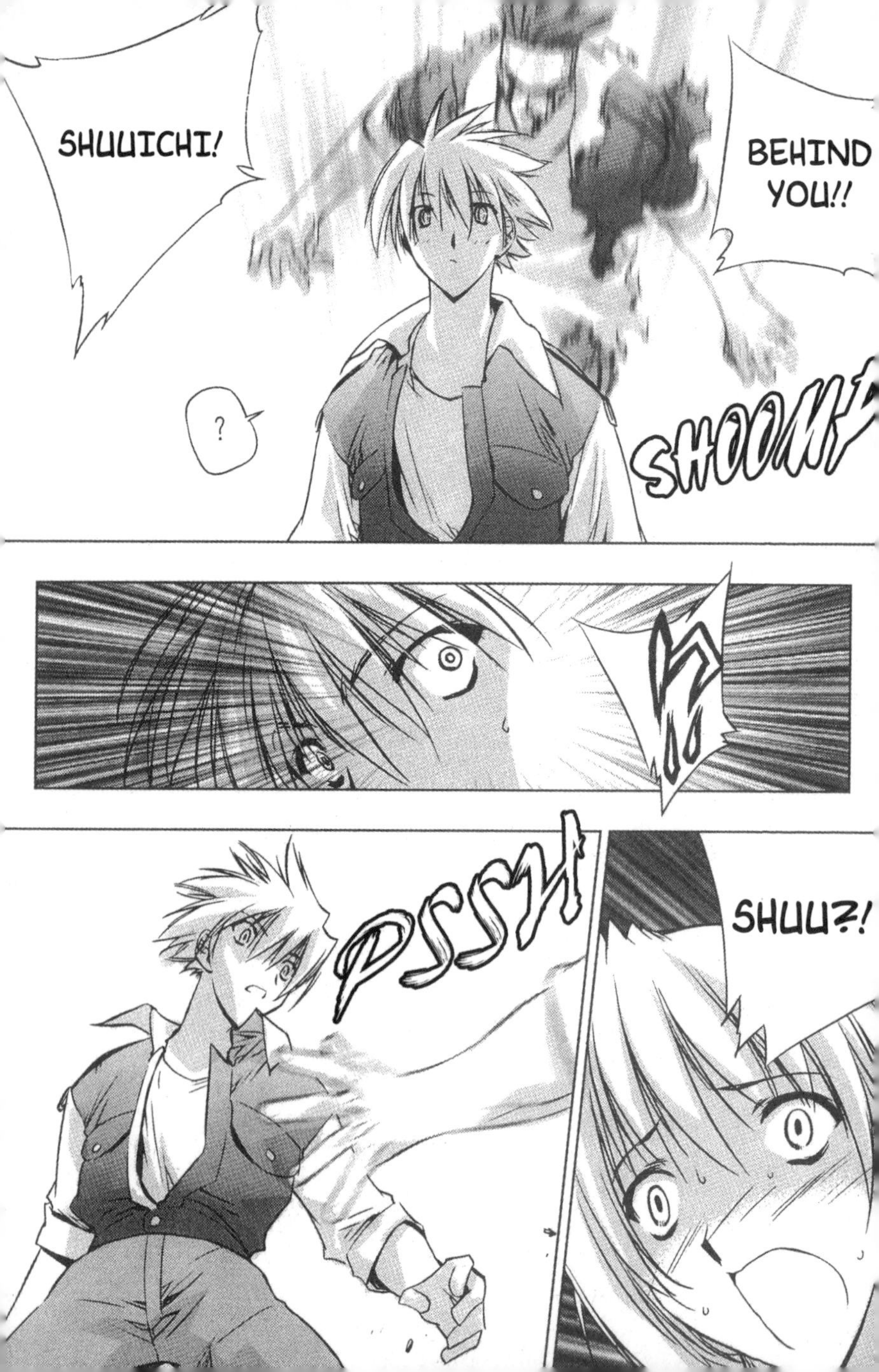
SHUUICHI!
BEHIND YOU!!
?
SHOOM!
PSSH
SHUU?!

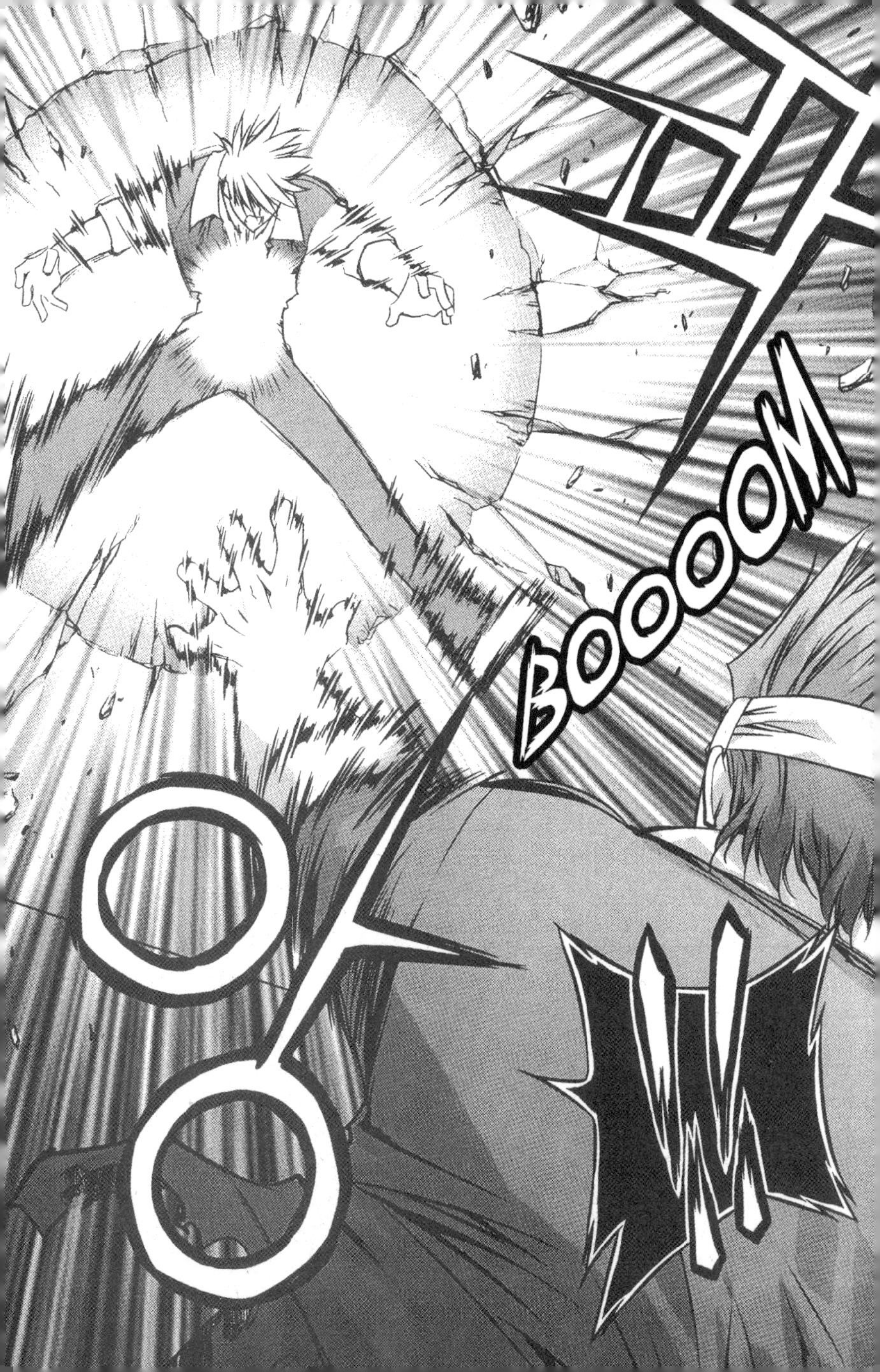
BOOOOOM

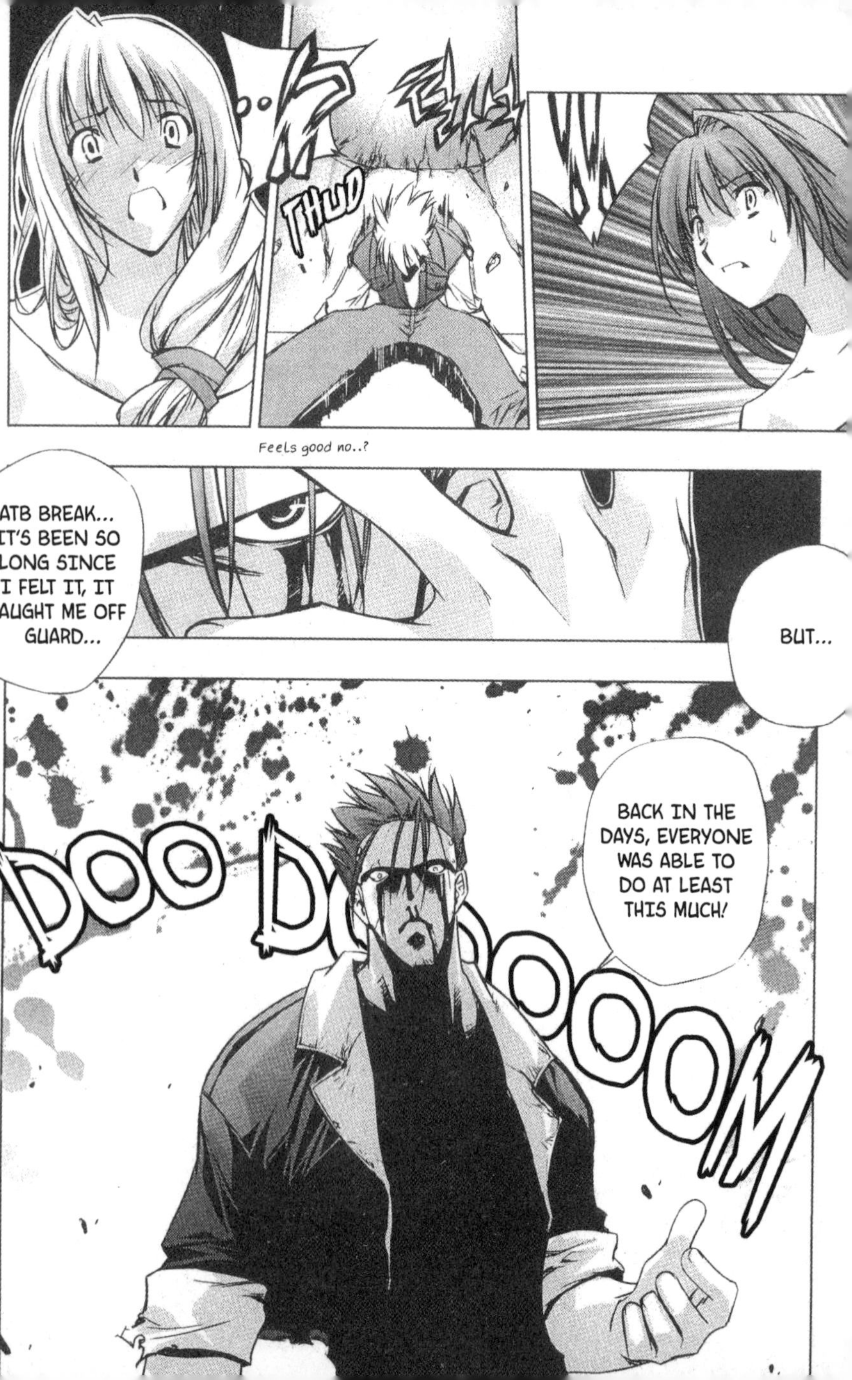

THUD
Feels good no..?
ATB BREAK... IT'S BEEN SO LONG SINCE I FELT IT, IT CAUGHT ME OFF GUARD...
BUT...
DOO DOOOOOOM
BACK IN THE DAYS, EVERYONE WAS ABLE TO DO AT LEAST THIS MUCH!

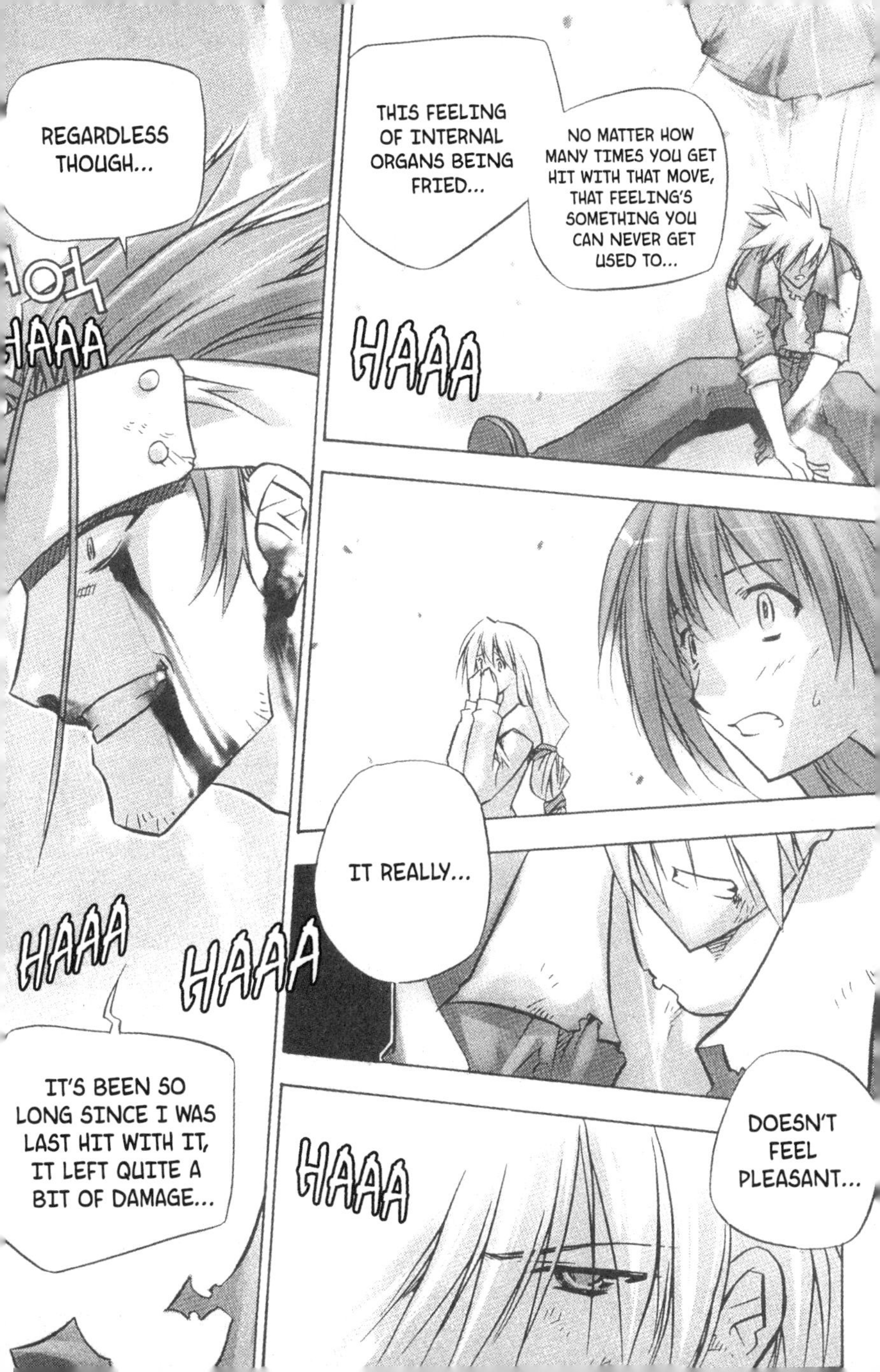
REGARDLESS THOUGH...
HAAA
HAAA
HAAA
IT'S BEEN SO LONG SINCE I WAS LAST HIT WITH IT, IT LEFT QUITE A BIT OF DAMAGE...
THIS FEELING OF INTERNAL ORGANS BEING FRIED...
NO MATTER HOW MANY TIMES YOU GET HIT WITH THAT MOVE, THAT FEELING'S SOMETHING YOU CAN NEVER GET USED TO...
HAAA
IT REALLY...
HAAA
DOESN'T FEEL PLEASANT...

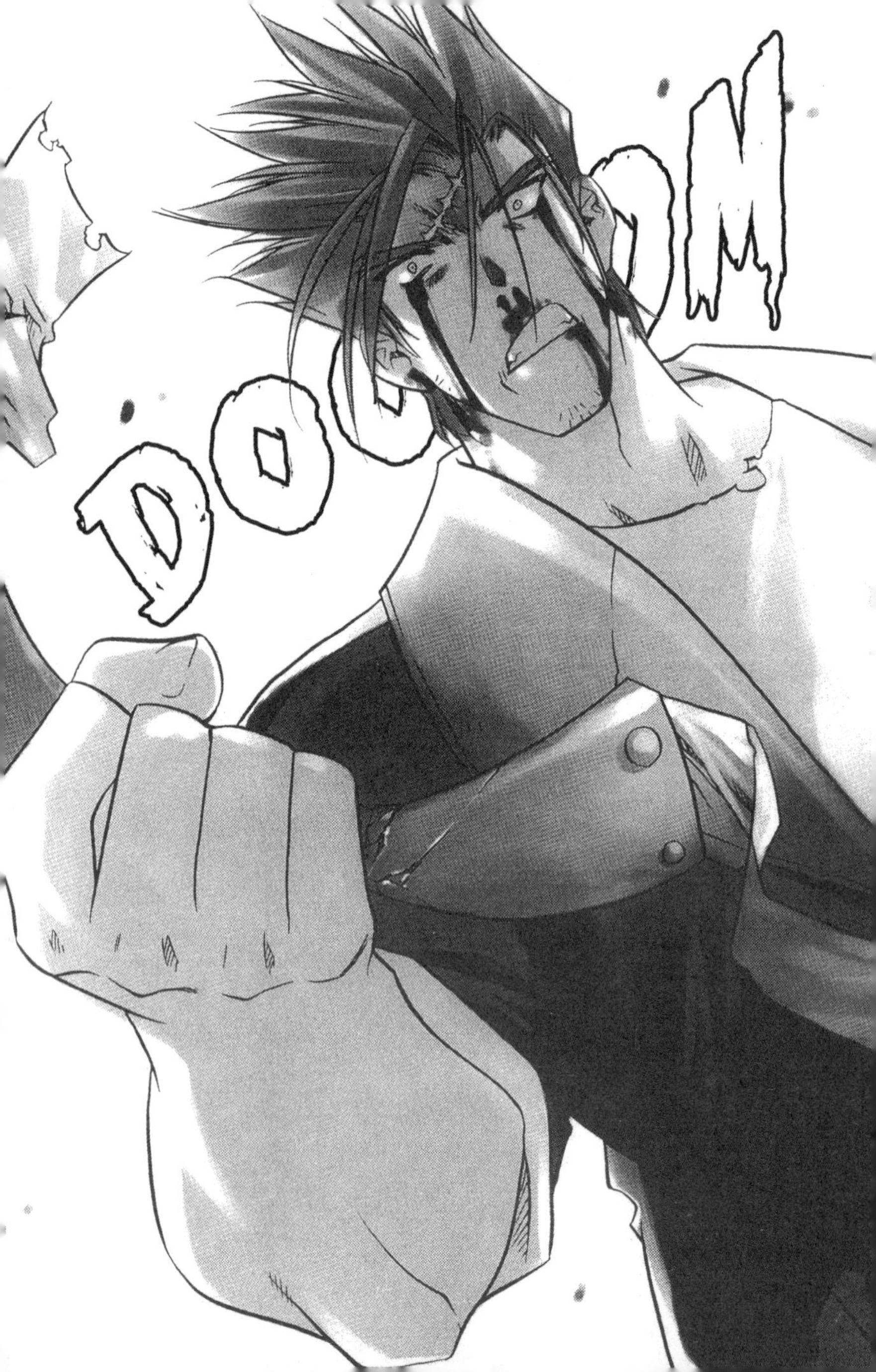
DOOOM

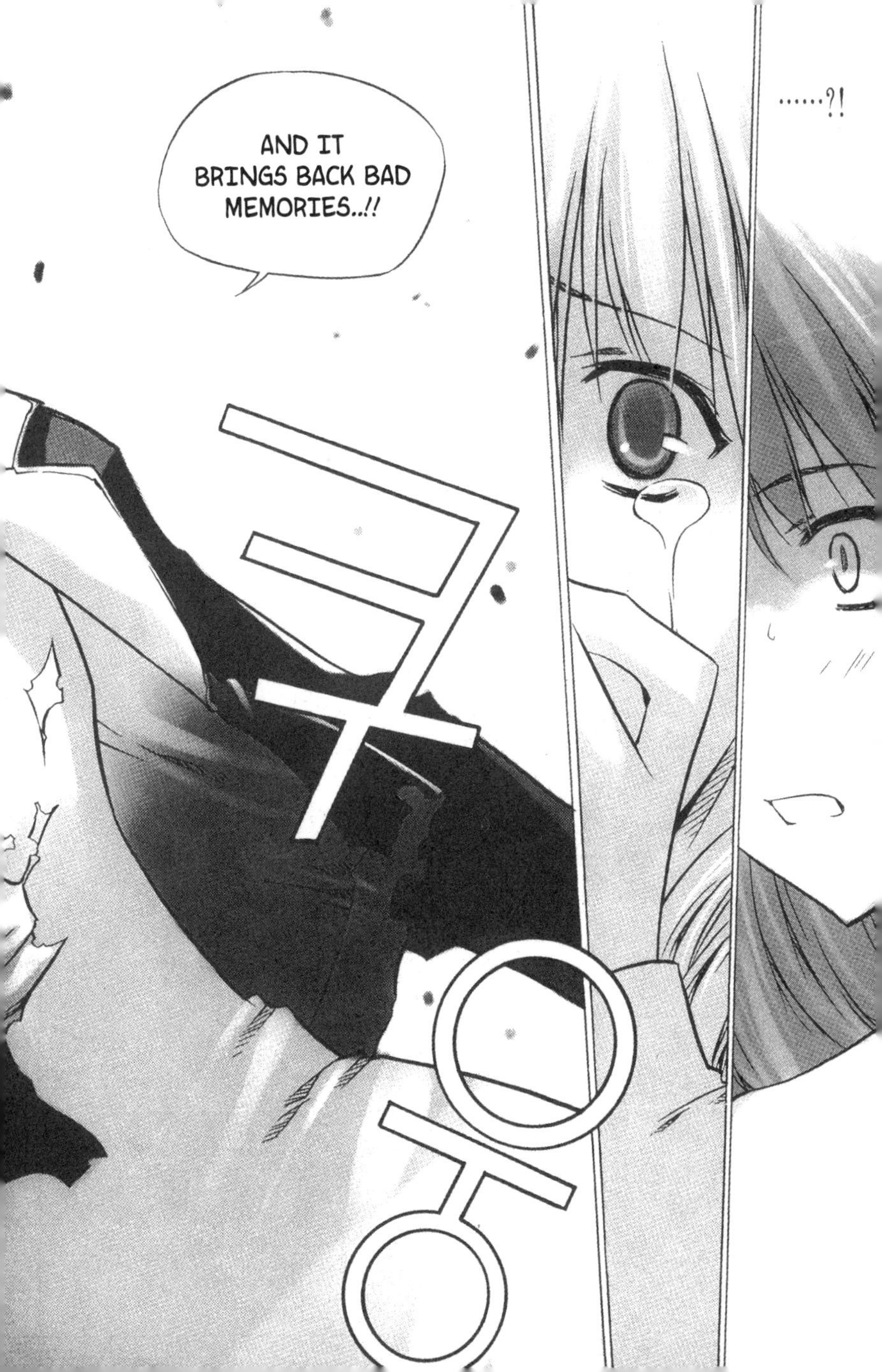
AND IT BRINGS BACK BAD MEMORIES..!!
......?!

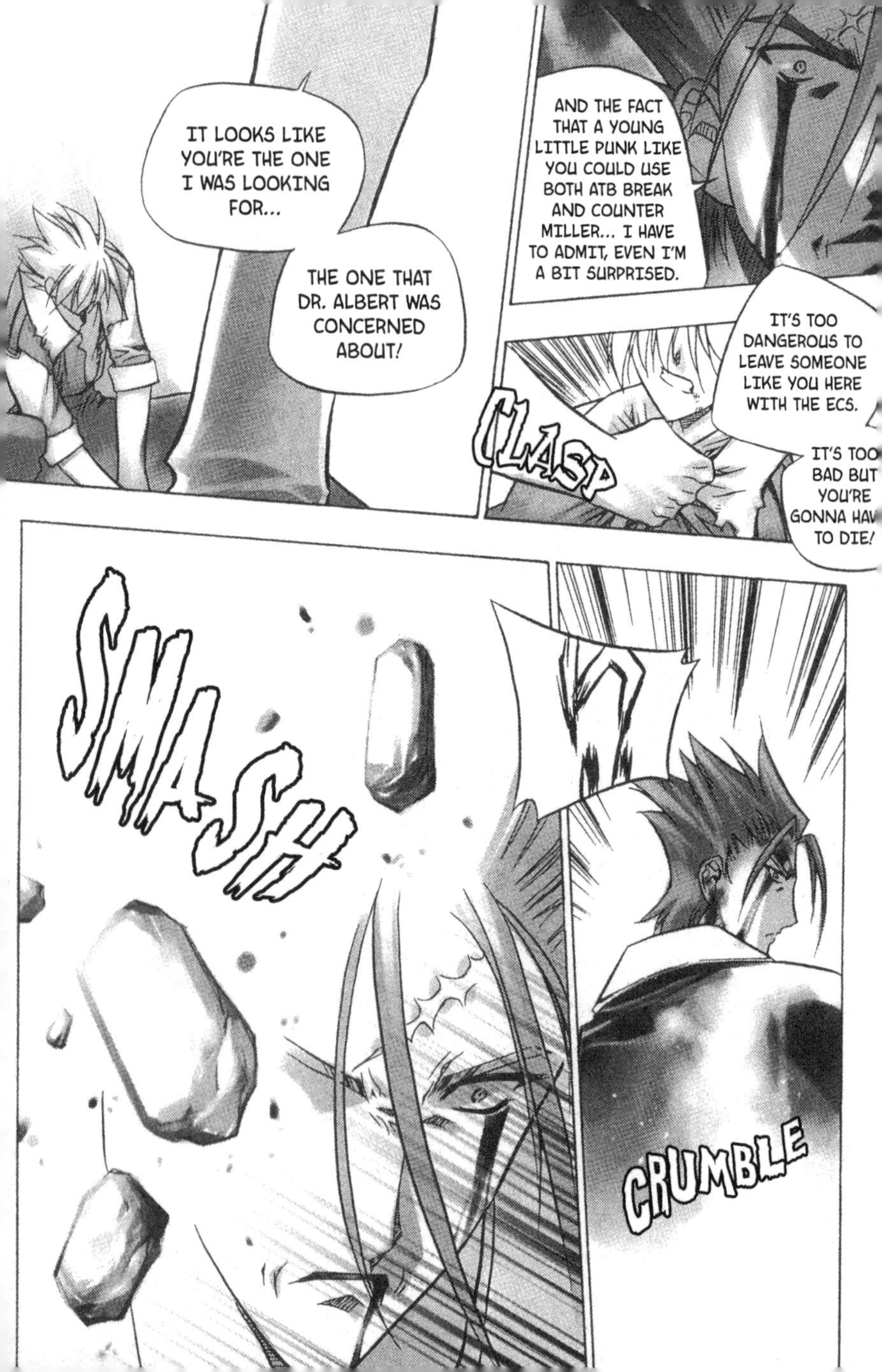
IT LOOKS LIKE YOU'RE THE ONE I WAS LOOKING FOR...
THE ONE THAT DR. ALBERT WAS CONCERNED ABOUT!
AND THE FACT THAT A YOUNG LITTLE PUNK LIKE YOU COULD USE BOTH ATB BREAK AND COUNTER MILLER... I HAVE TO ADMIT, EVEN I'M A BIT SURPRISED.
CLASP
IT'S TOO DANGEROUS TO LEAVE SOMEONE LIKE YOU HERE WITH THE ECS.
IT'S TOO BAD BUT YOU'RE GONNA HAV TO DIE!
SMASH
CRUMBLE

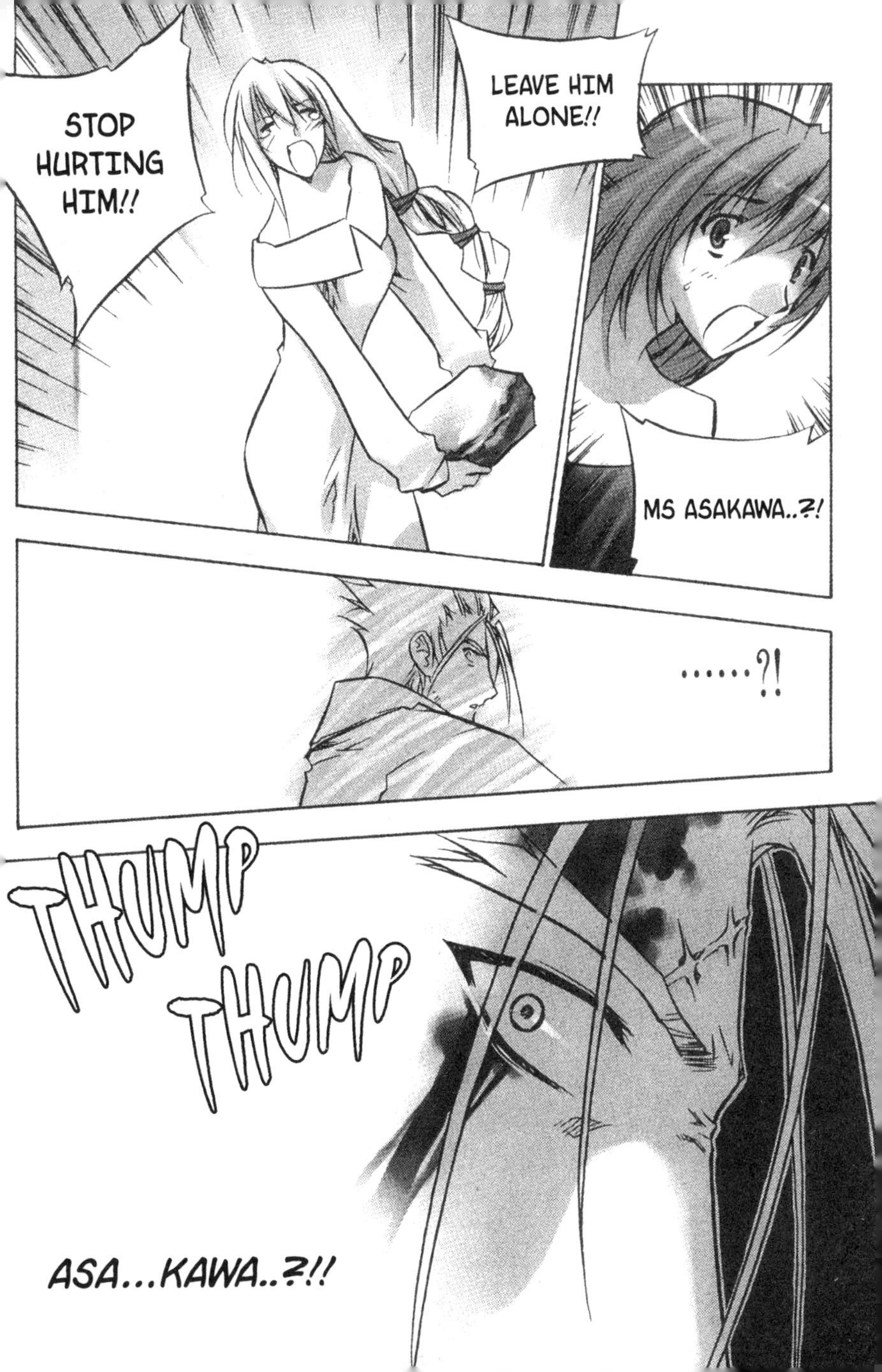
STOP HURTING HIM!!
LEAVE HIM ALONE!!
MS ASAKAWA..?!
......?!
THUMP THUMP
ASA...KAWA..?!!

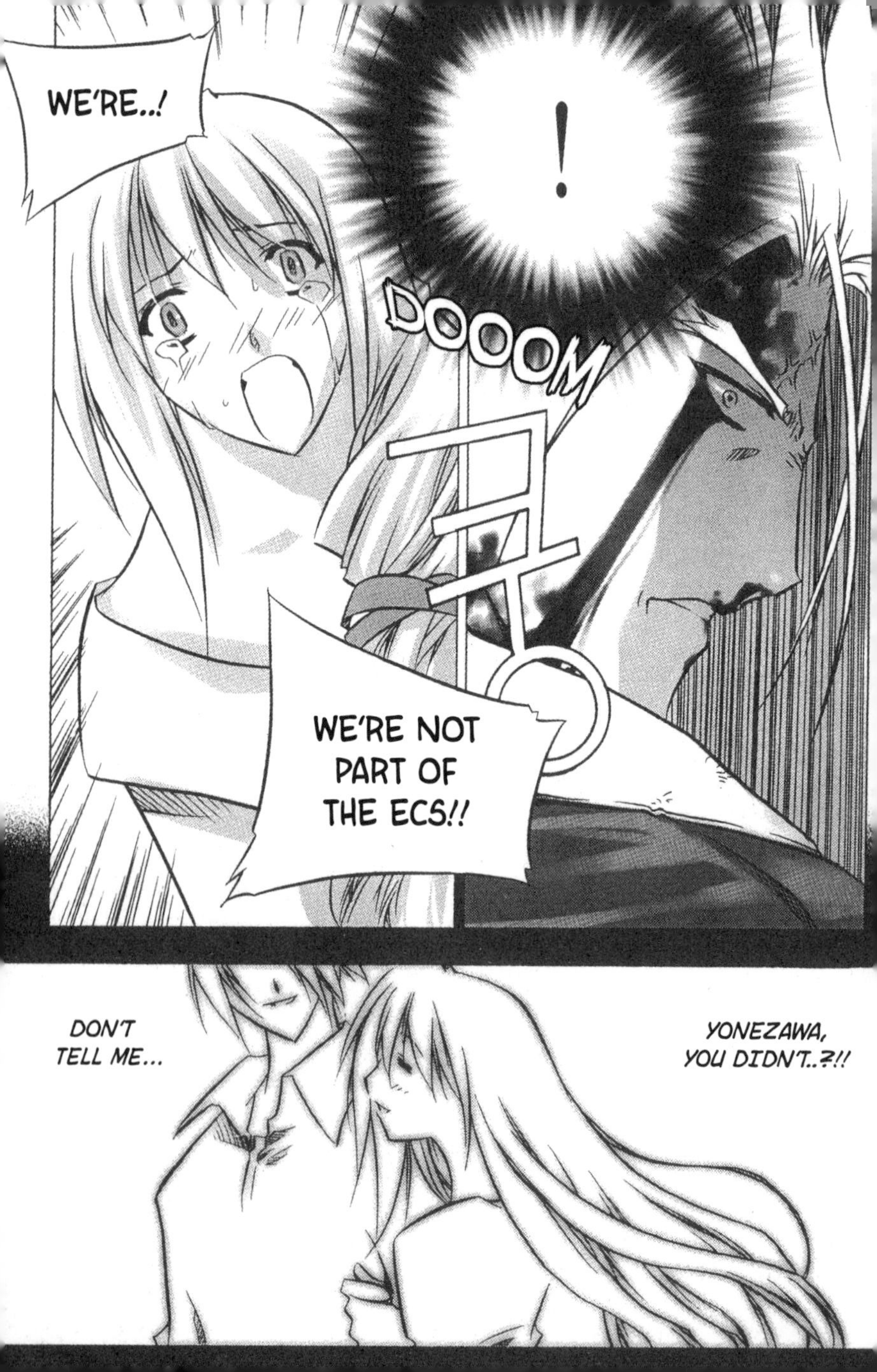
WE'RE..!
!
DOOOM
WE'RE NOT PART OF THE ECS!!
DON'T TELL ME...
YONEZAWA, YOU DIDN'T..?!!

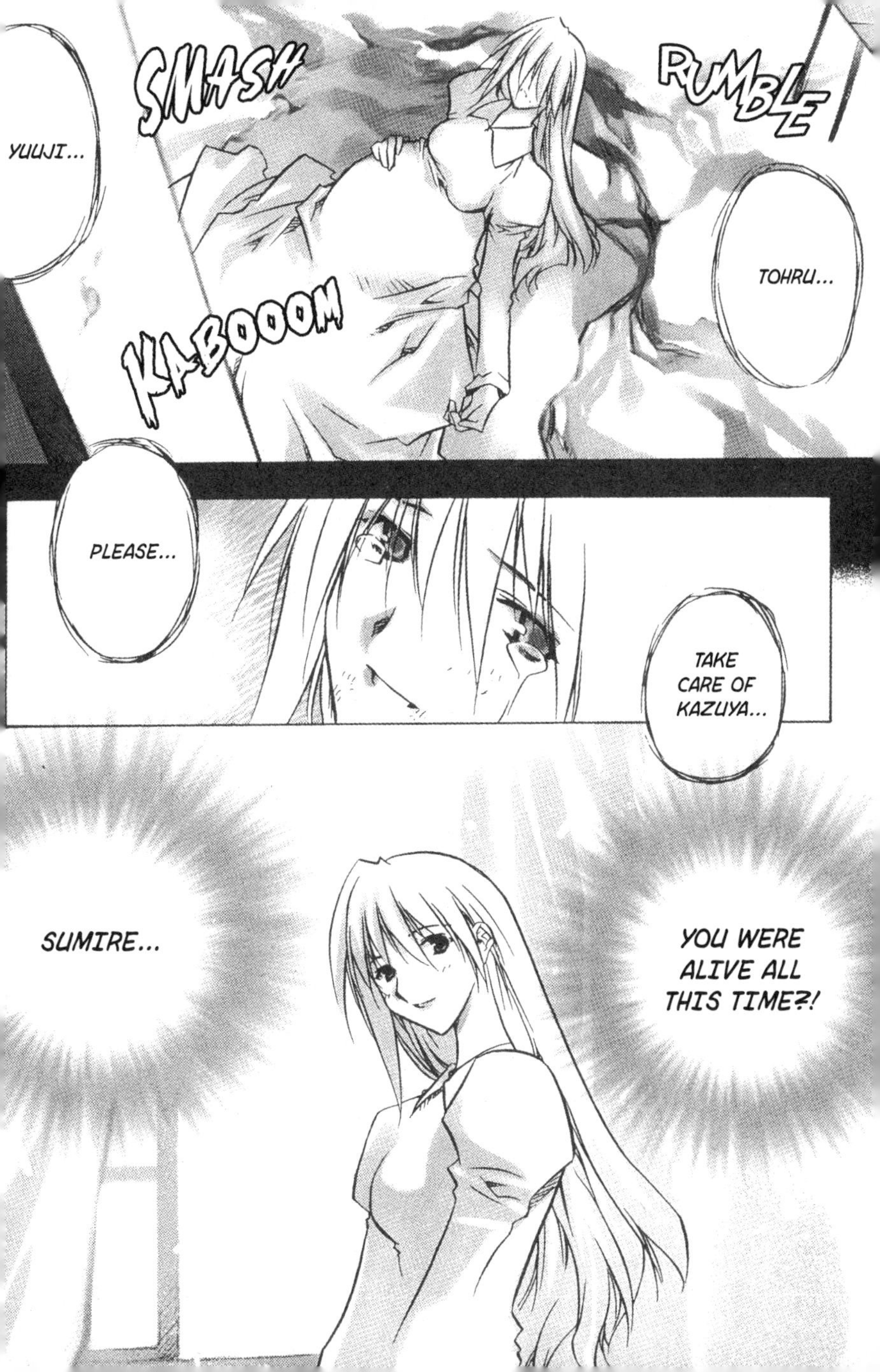
YUUJI...
SMASH
RUMBLE
TOHRU...
KABOOOM
PLEASE...
TAKE CARE OF KAZUYA...
SUMIRE...
YOU WERE ALIVE ALL THIS TIME?!

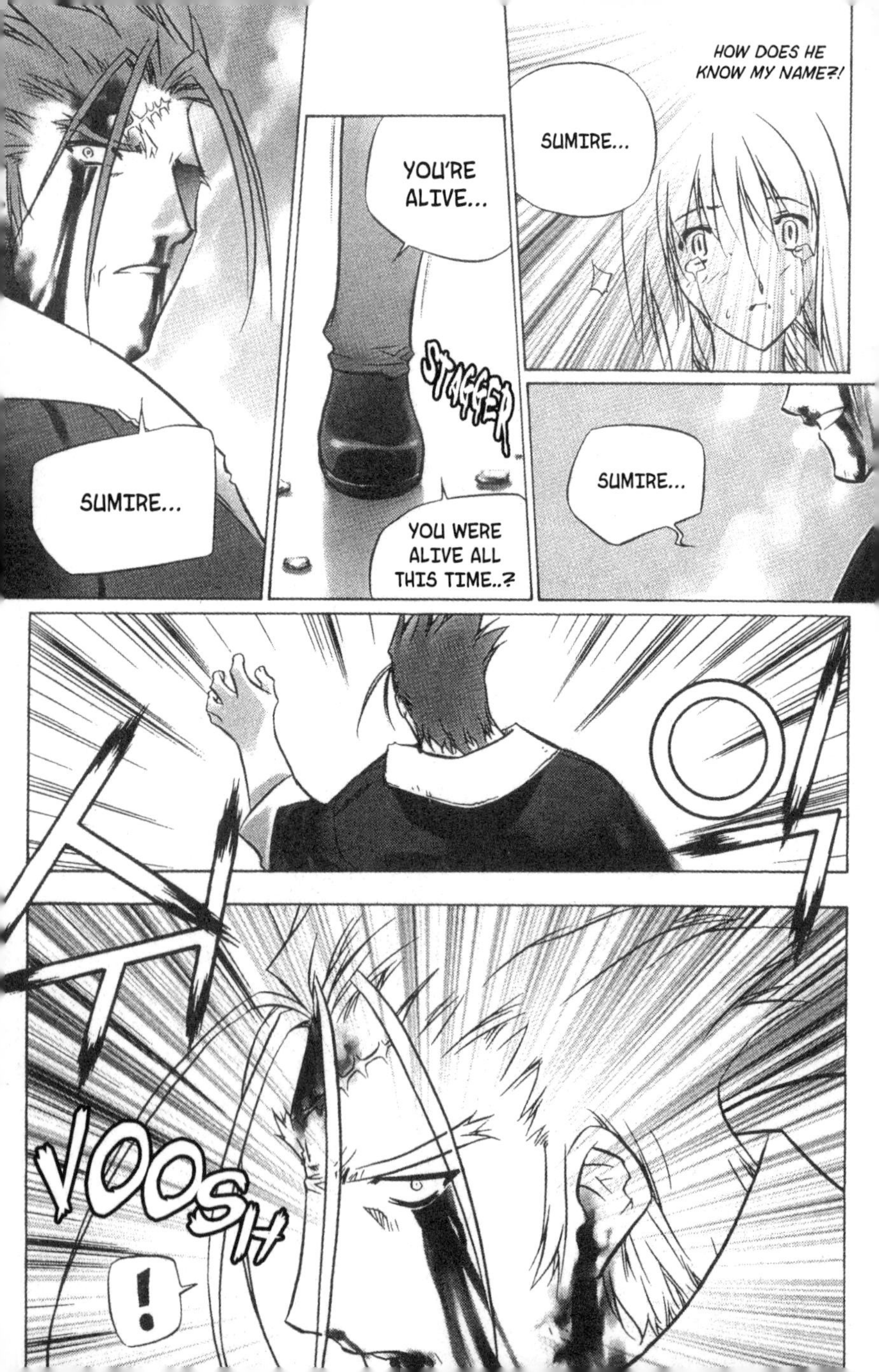
HOW DOES HE KNOW MY NAME?!
SUMIRE...
SUMIRE...
YOU'RE ALIVE...
STAGGER
YOU WERE ALIVE ALL THIS TIME..?
SUMIRE...
VOOSH
!

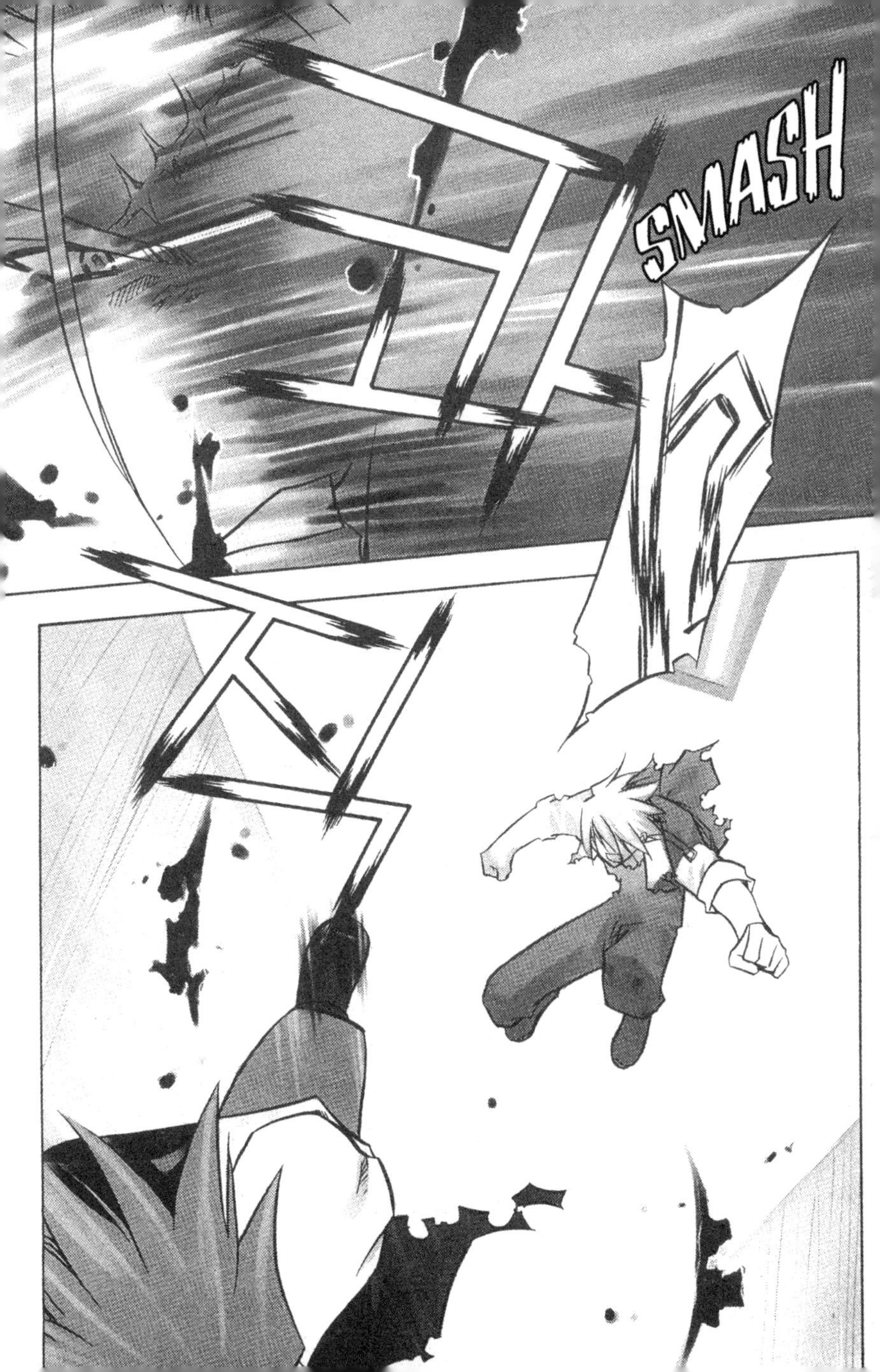
SMASH

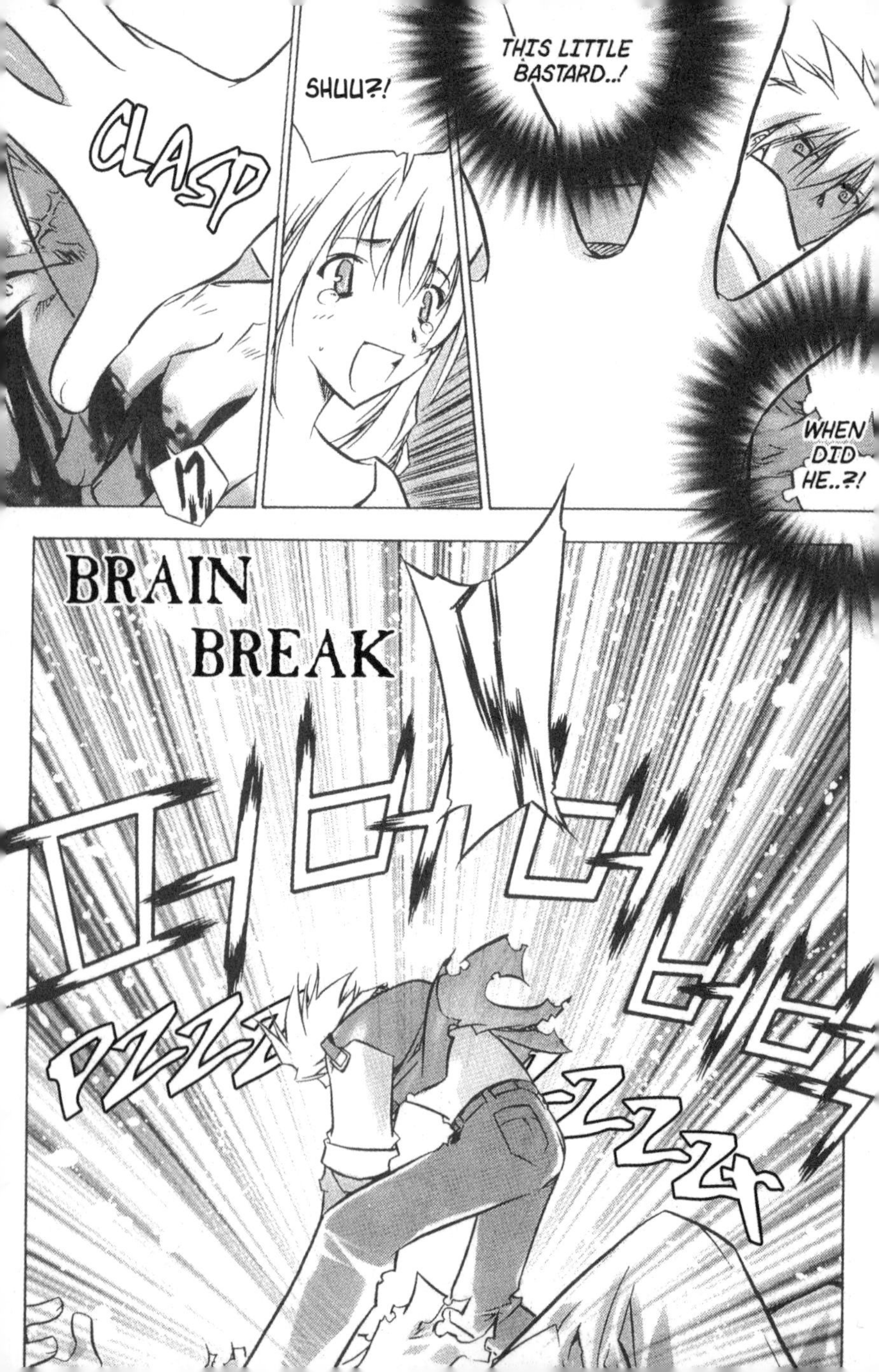
CLASP
SHUU?!
THIS LITTLE BASTARD..!
WHEN DID HE..?!
BRAIN BREAK

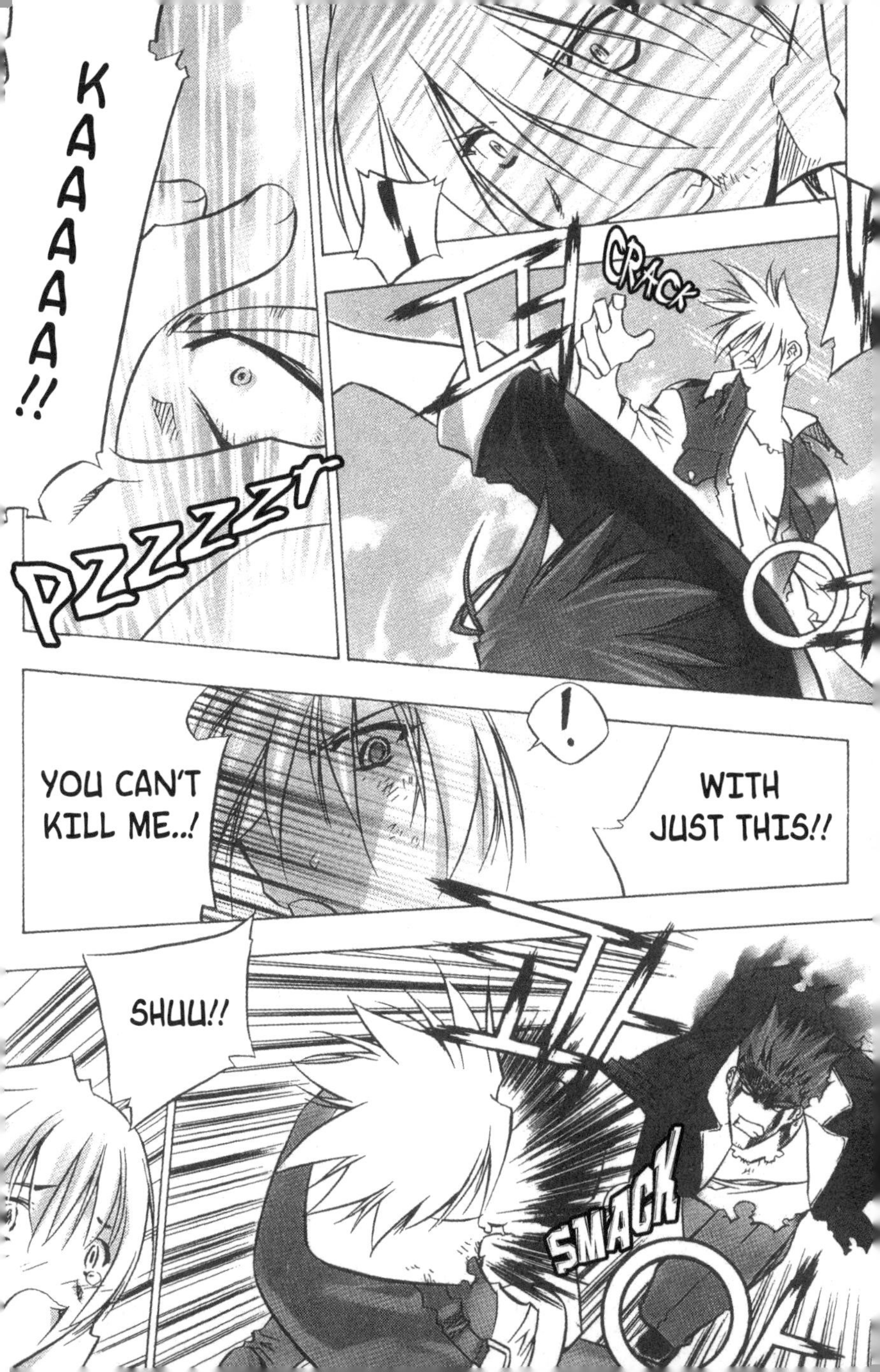
KAAAAA!!
PZZZZr
CRACK
!
YOU CAN'T KILL ME..!
WITH JUST THIS!!
SHUU!!
SMACK

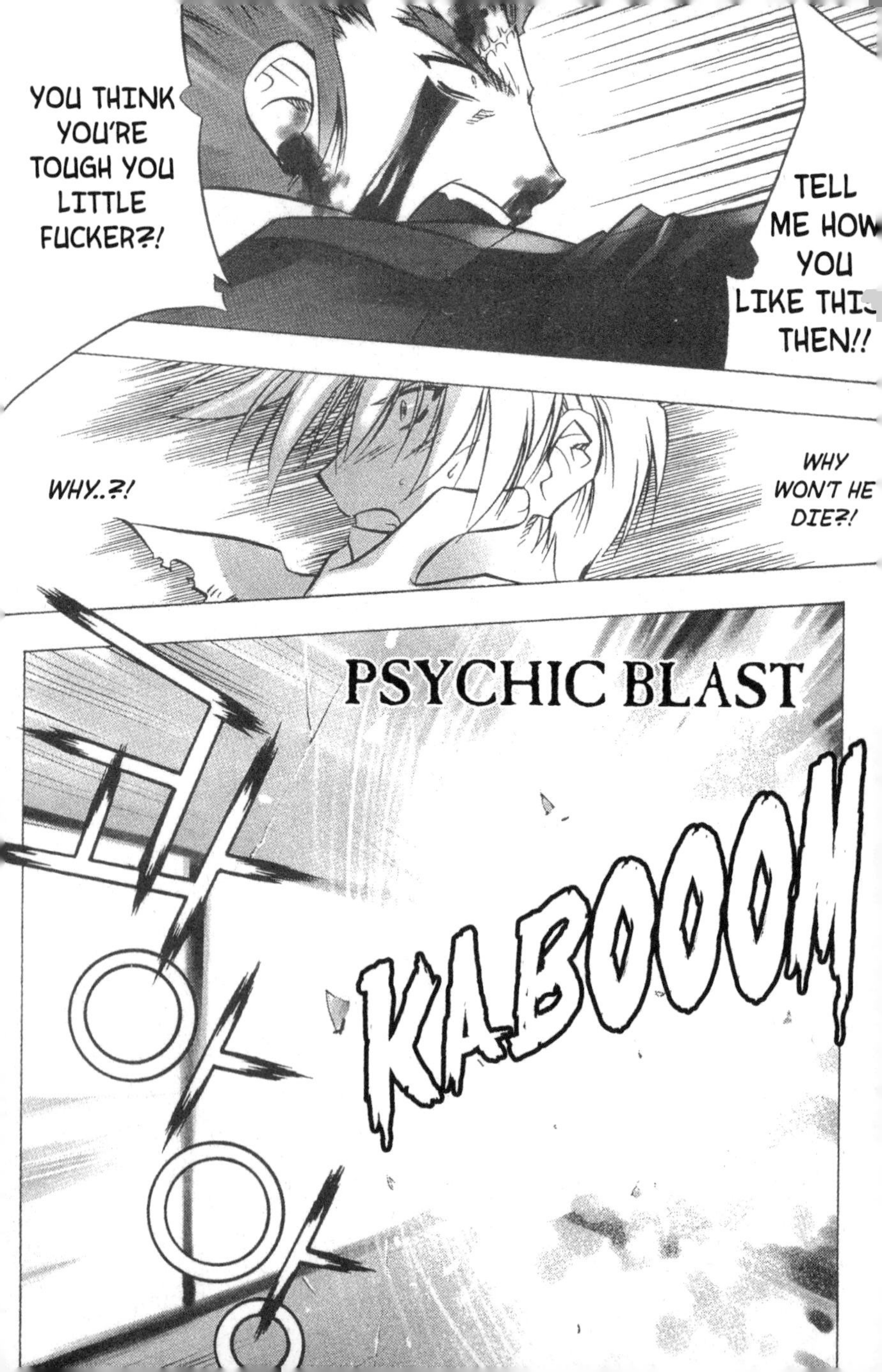
YOU THINK YOU'RE TOUGH YOU LITTLE FUCKER?!
TELL ME HOW YOU LIKE THIS THEN!!
WHY..?!
WHY WON'T HE DIE?!
PSYCHIC BLAST
KABOOOM

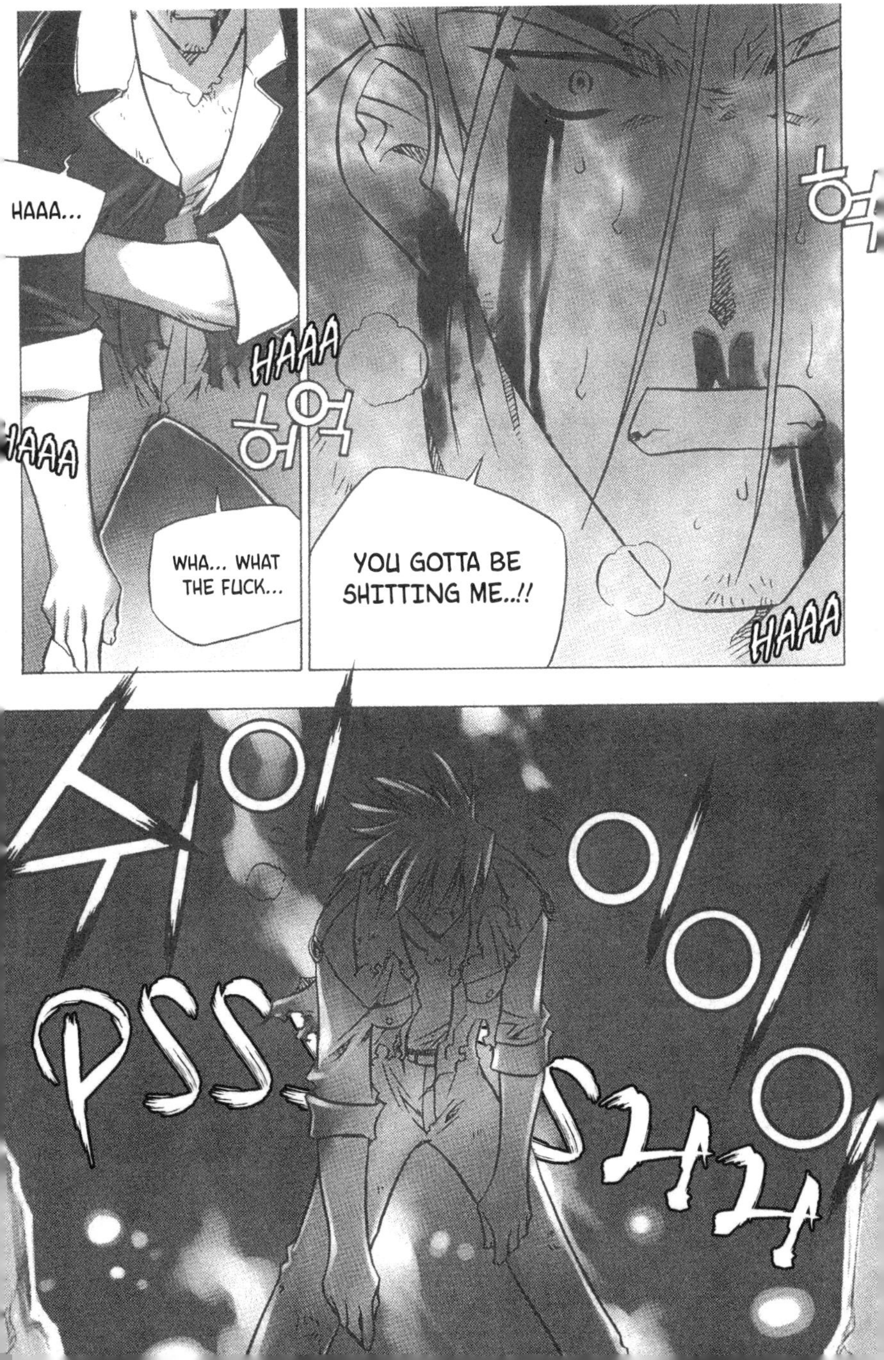
HAAA...
HAAA
HAAA
WHA... WHAT THE FUCK...
YOU GOTTA BE SHITTING ME..!!
HAAA
PSSS
SHAAA

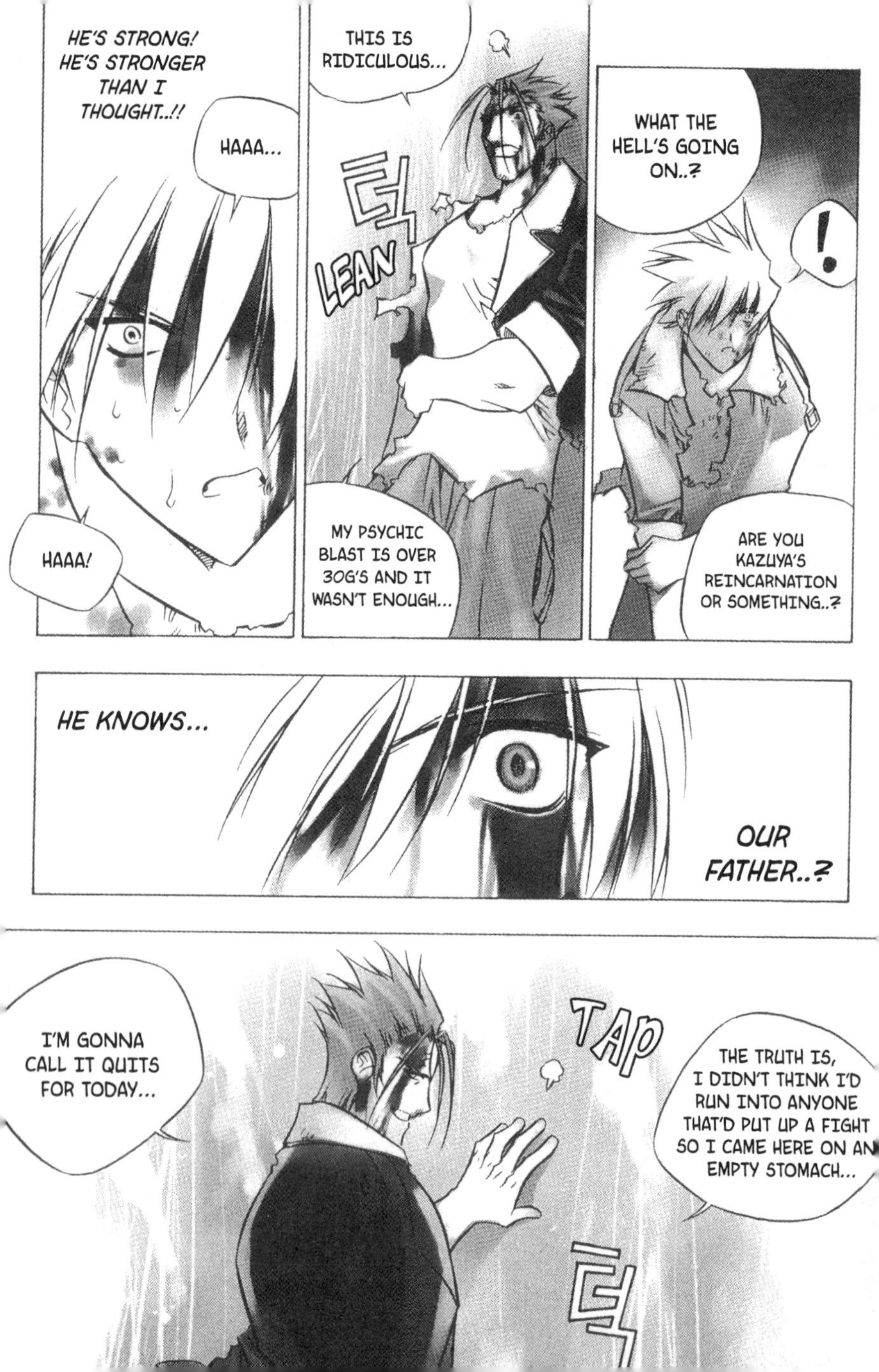
HE'S STRONG! HE'S STRONGER THAN I THOUGHT..!!
HAAA...
HAAA!
THIS IS RIDICULOUS...
LEAN
MY PSYCHIC BLAST IS OVER 30G'S AND IT WASN'T ENOUGH...
WHAT THE HELL'S GOING ON..?
!
ARE YOU KAZUYA'S REINCARNATION OR SOMETHING..?
HE KNOWS...
OUR FATHER..?
I'M GONNA CALL IT QUITS FOR TODAY...
TAP
THE TRUTH IS, I DIDN'T THINK I'D RUN INTO ANYONE THAT'D PUT UP A FIGHT SO I CAME HERE ON AN EMPTY STOMACH...

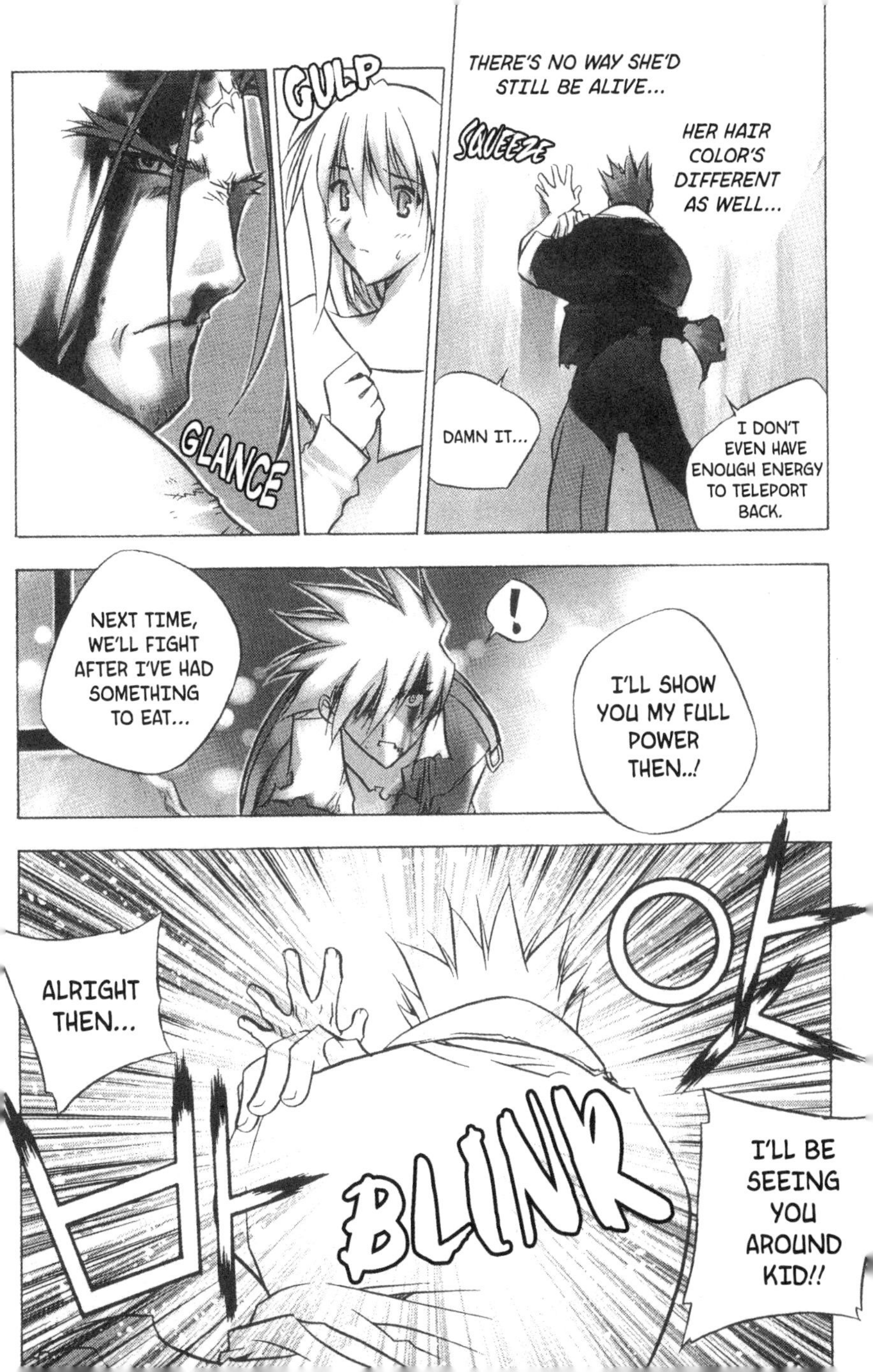
GULP
GLANCE
THERE'S NO WAY SHE'D STILL BE ALIVE...
SQUEEZE
HER HAIR COLOR'S DIFFERENT AS WELL...
DAMN IT...
I DON'T EVEN HAVE ENOUGH ENERGY TO TELEPORT BACK.
NEXT TIME, WE'LL FIGHT AFTER I'VE HAD SOMETHING TO EAT...
!
I'LL SHOW YOU MY FULL POWER THEN..!
ALRIGHT THEN...
BLINK
I'LL BE SEEING YOU AROUND KID!!

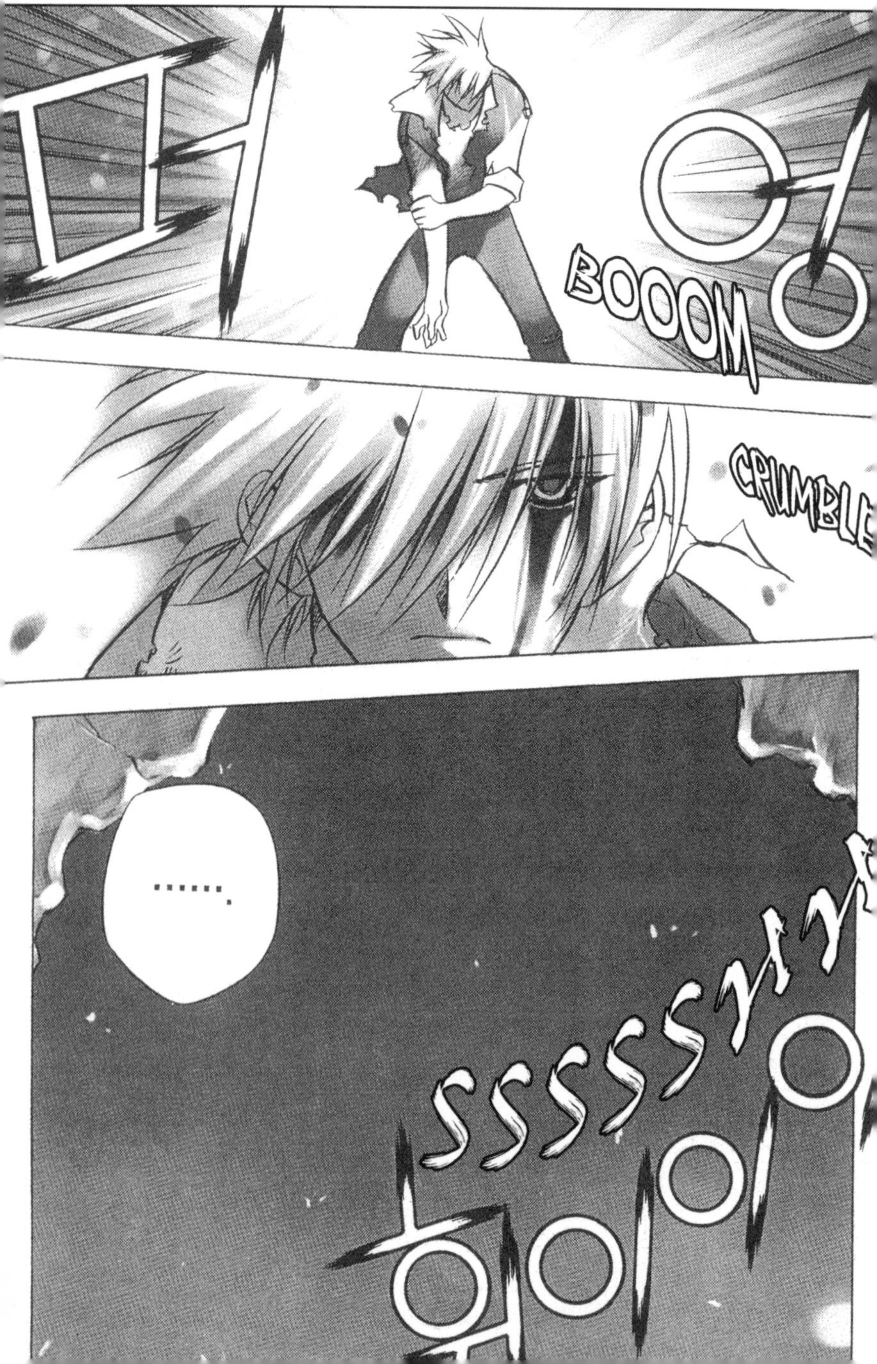
BOOOM
CRUMBLE
......

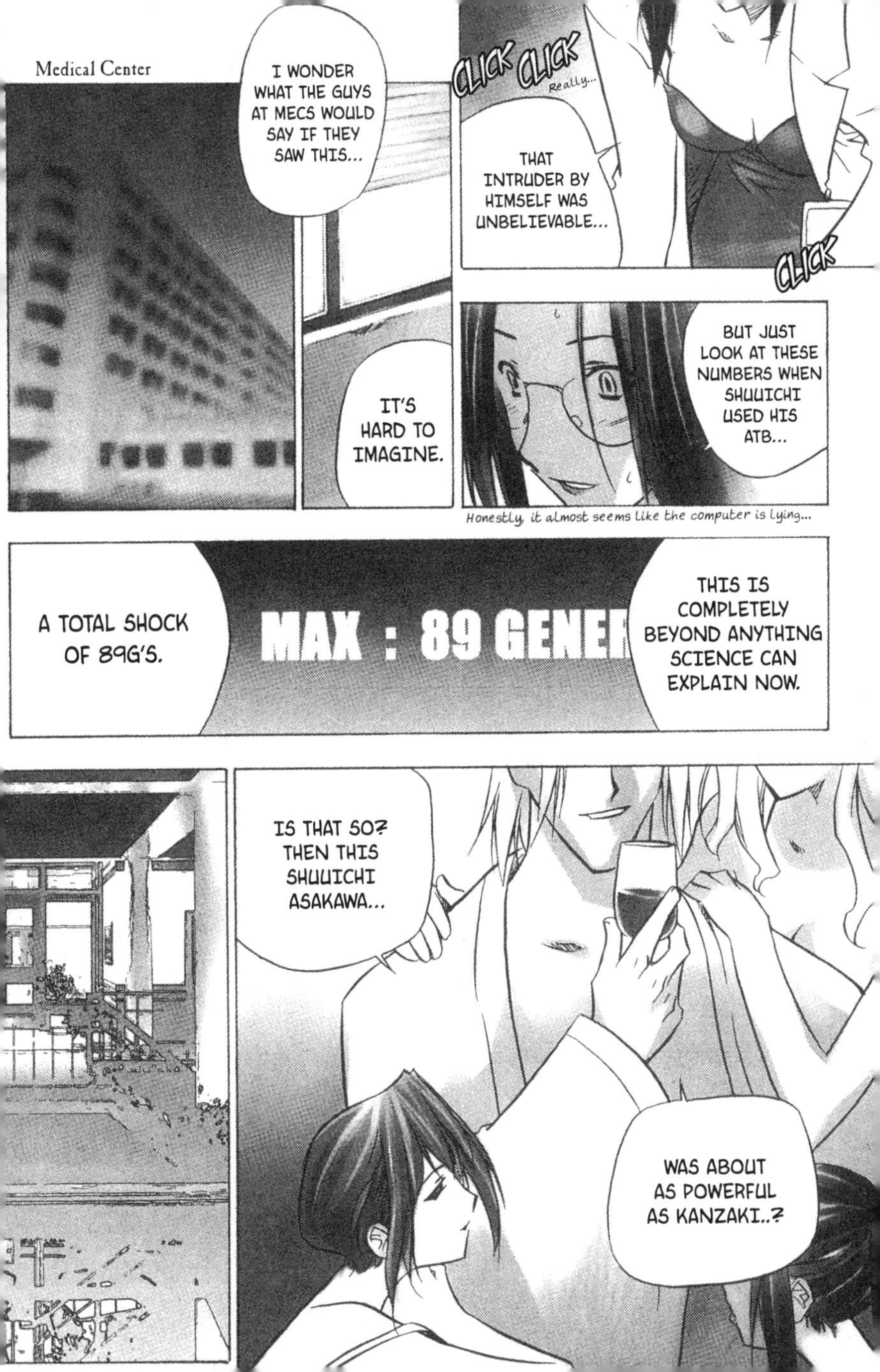
Medical Center
I WONDER WHAT THE GUYS AT MECS WOULD SAY IF THEY SAW THIS...
IT'S HARD TO IMAGINE.
CLICK CLICK
Really...
THAT INTRUDER BY HIMSELF WAS UNBELIEVABLE...
CLICK
BUT JUST LOOK AT THESE NUMBERS WHEN SHUUICHI USED HIS ATB...
Honestly, it almost seems like the computer is lying...
A TOTAL SHOCK OF 89G'S.
MAX : 89 GENER
THIS IS COMPLETELY BEYOND ANYTHING SCIENCE CAN EXPLAIN NOW.
IS THAT SO? THEN THIS SHUUICHI ASAKAWA...
WAS ABOUT AS POWERFUL AS KANZAKI..?

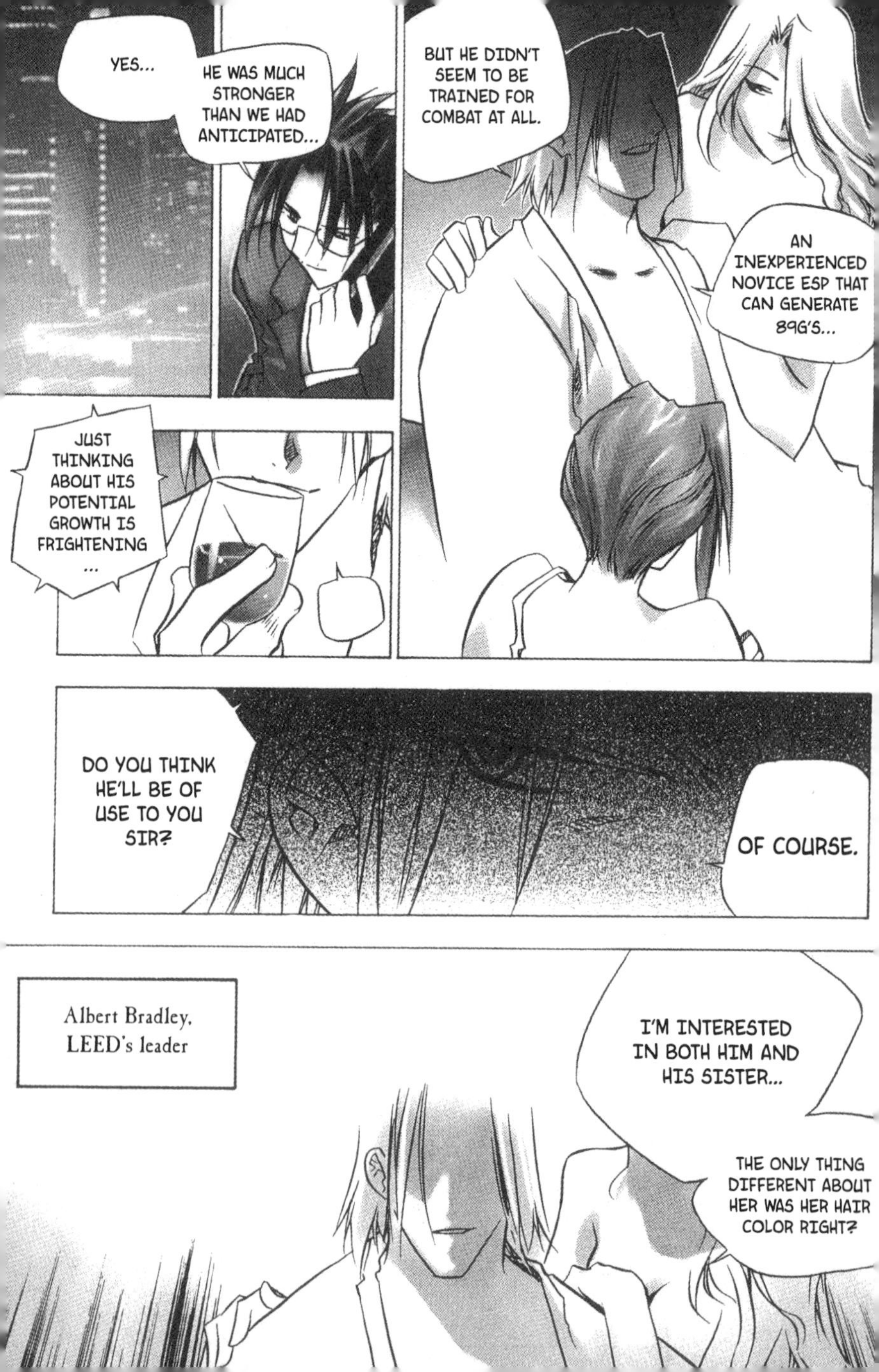
YES...
HE WAS MUCH STRONGER THAN WE HAD ANTICIPATED...
BUT HE DIDN'T SEEM TO BE TRAINED FOR COMBAT AT ALL.
AN INEXPERIENCED NOVICE ESP THAT CAN GENERATE 89G'S...
JUST THINKING ABOUT HIS POTENTIAL GROWTH IS FRIGHTENING ...
DO YOU THINK HE'LL BE OF USE TO YOU SIR?
OF COURSE.
Albert Bradley, LEED's leader
I'M INTERESTED IN BOTH HIM AND HIS SISTER...
THE ONLY THING DIFFERENT ABOUT HER WAS HER HAIR COLOR RIGHT?

IF POSSIBLE...

I WANT TO MAKE BOTH OF THEM MINE.

I WOULDN'T BE SURPRISED IF THE ECS BROUGHT HER BACK ON PURPOSE.

...

DO YOU REALLY THINK IT'S HER SIR?

HMP

THERE'S NO DOUBT ABOUT IT.

THE WAY THE ECS THINKS IS TOO SIMPLE, THEY'VE ALWAYS BEEN THAT WAY.

BUT UNTIL YOU'VE CONFIRMED EVERYTHING, MAKE SURE TO KEEP YOUR EYE ON THEM.

I UNDERSTAND SIR...

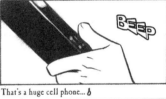

BEEP

That's a huge cell phone... ♪

...

SUMIRE...

ASAKAWA...

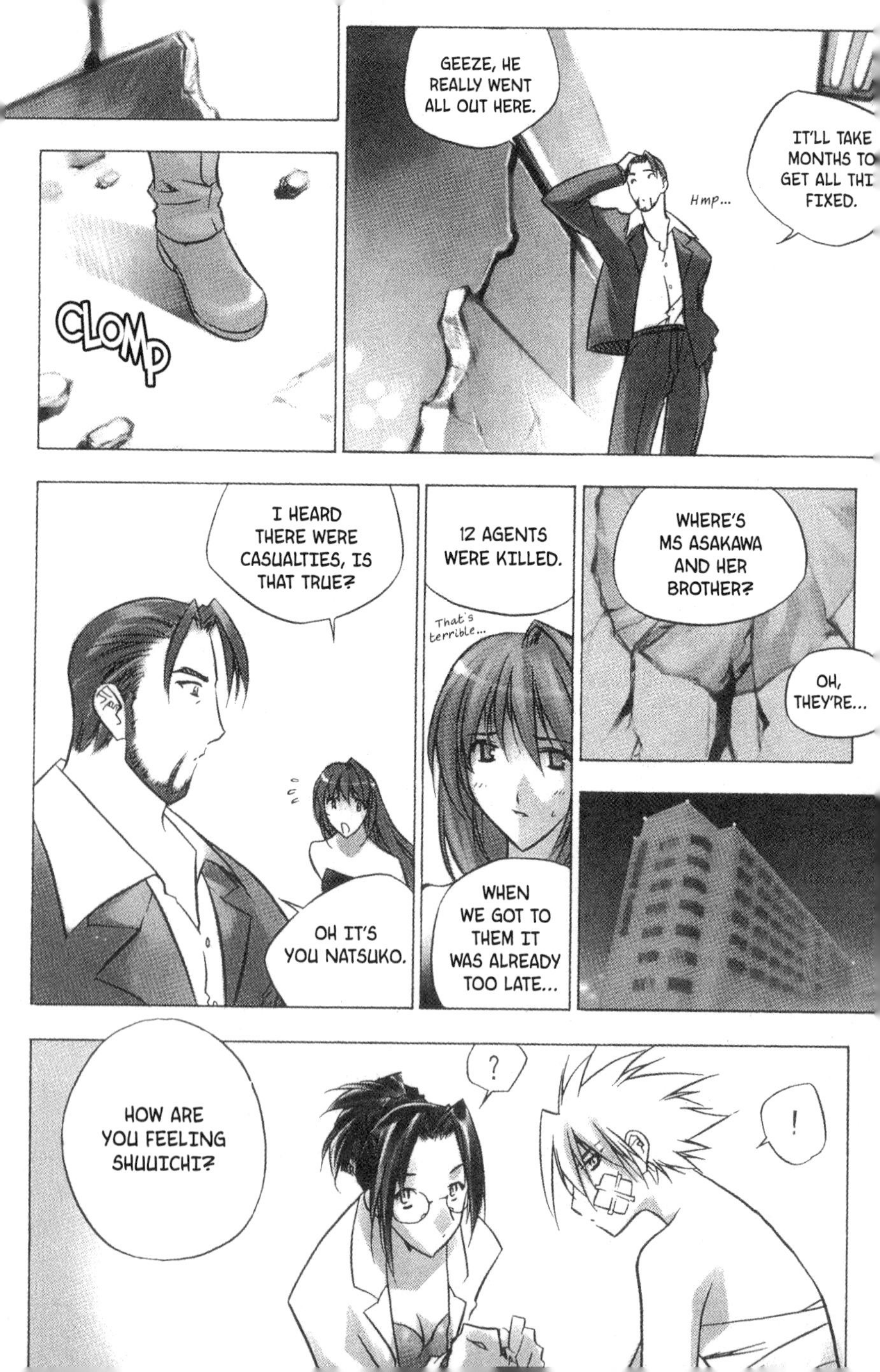
CLOMP
GEEZE, HE REALLY WENT ALL OUT HERE.
Hmp...
IT'LL TAKE MONTHS TO GET ALL THI FIXED.
I HEARD THERE WERE CASUALTIES, IS THAT TRUE?
OH IT'S YOU NATSUKO.
12 AGENTS WERE KILLED.
That's terrible...
WHEN WE GOT TO THEM IT WAS ALREADY TOO LATE...
WHERE'S MS ASAKAWA AND HER BROTHER?
OH, THEY'RE...
HOW ARE YOU FEELING SHUUICHI?
?
!

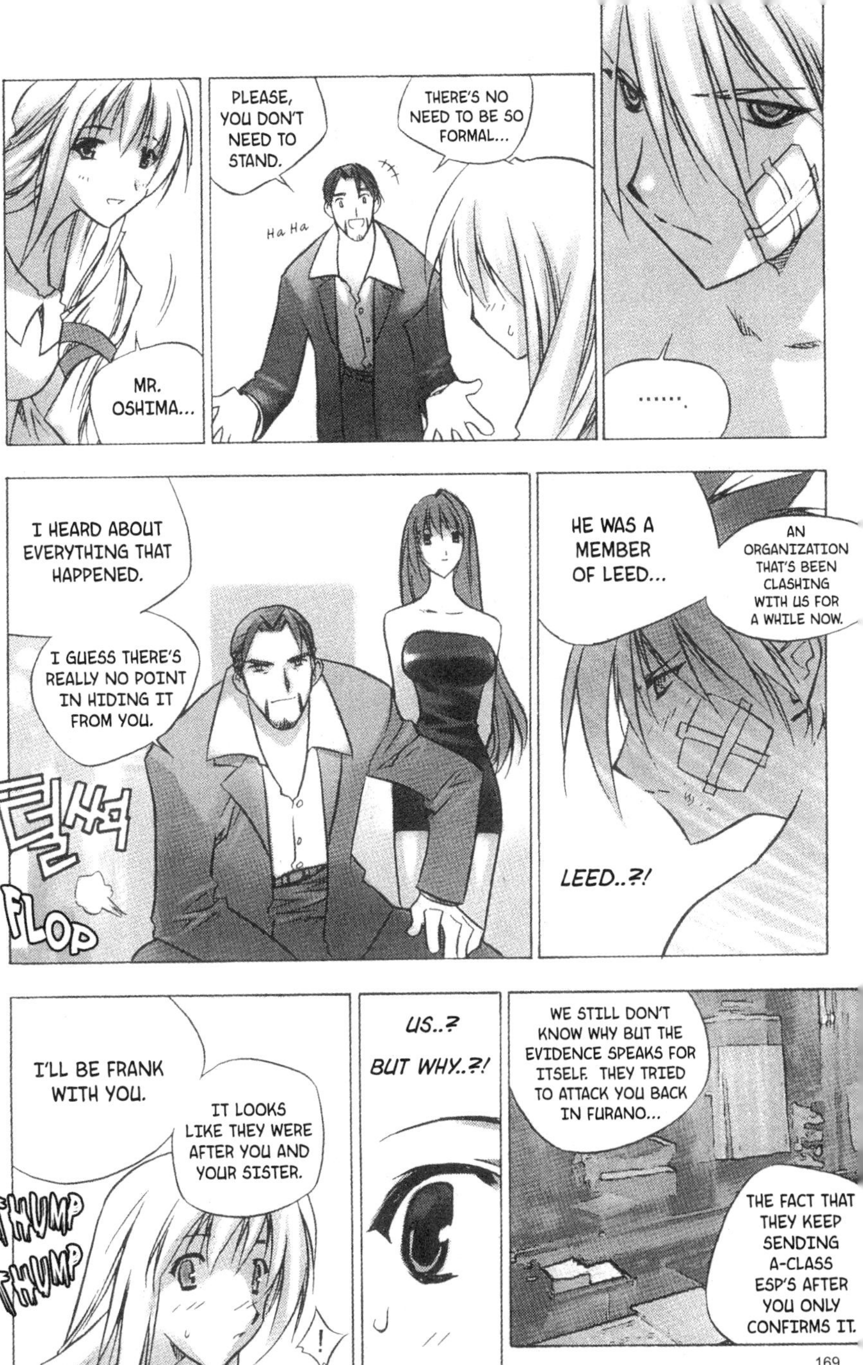
MR. OSHIMA...
PLEASE, YOU DON'T NEED TO STAND.
Ha Ha
THERE'S NO NEED TO BE SO FORMAL...
....
I HEARD ABOUT EVERYTHING THAT HAPPENED.
I GUESS THERE'S REALLY NO POINT IN HIDING IT FROM YOU.
FLOP
HE WAS A MEMBER OF LEED...
AN ORGANIZATION THAT'S BEEN CLASHING WITH US FOR A WHILE NOW.
LEED..?!
I'LL BE FRANK WITH YOU.
IT LOOKS LIKE THEY WERE AFTER YOU AND YOUR SISTER.
THUMP THUMP
!
US..?
BUT WHY..?!
WE STILL DON'T KNOW WHY BUT THE EVIDENCE SPEAKS FOR ITSELF. THEY TRIED TO ATTACK YOU BACK IN FURANO...
THE FACT THAT THEY KEEP SENDING A-CLASS ESP'S AFTER YOU ONLY CONFIRMS IT.

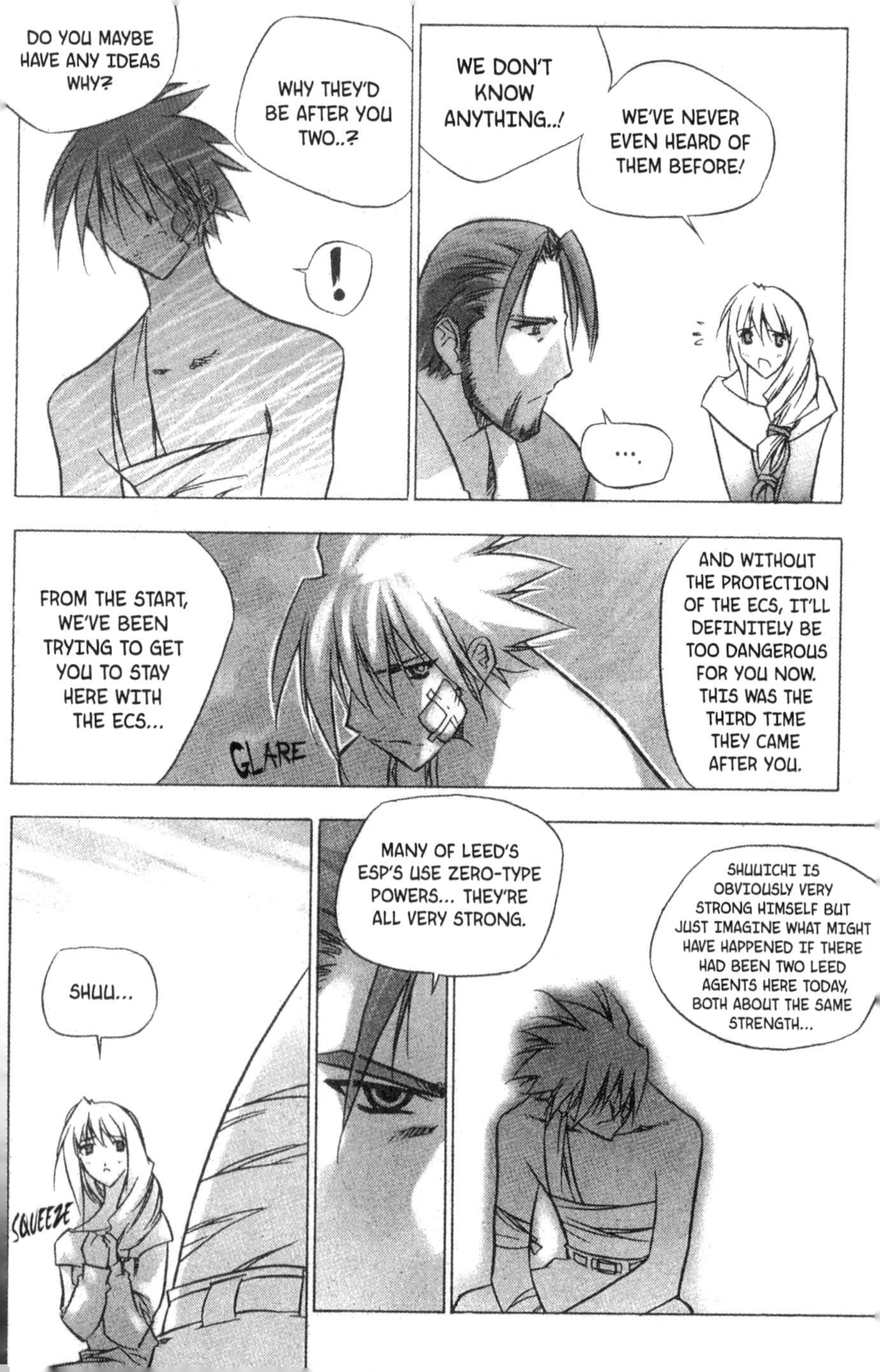
DO YOU MAYBE HAVE ANY IDEAS WHY?
WHY THEY'D BE AFTER YOU TWO..?
!
WE DON'T KNOW ANYTHING..!
WE'VE NEVER EVEN HEARD OF THEM BEFORE!
...
FROM THE START, WE'VE BEEN TRYING TO GET YOU TO STAY HERE WITH THE ECS...
GLARE
AND WITHOUT THE PROTECTION OF THE ECS, IT'LL DEFINITELY BE TOO DANGEROUS FOR YOU NOW. THIS WAS THE THIRD TIME THEY CAME AFTER YOU.
SHUU...
SQUEEZE
MANY OF LEED'S ESP'S USE ZERO-TYPE POWERS... THEY'RE ALL VERY STRONG.
SHUUICHI IS OBVIOUSLY VERY STRONG HIMSELF BUT JUST IMAGINE WHAT MIGHT HAVE HAPPENED IF THERE HAD BEEN TWO LEED AGENTS HERE TODAY, BOTH ABOUT THE SAME STRENGTH...

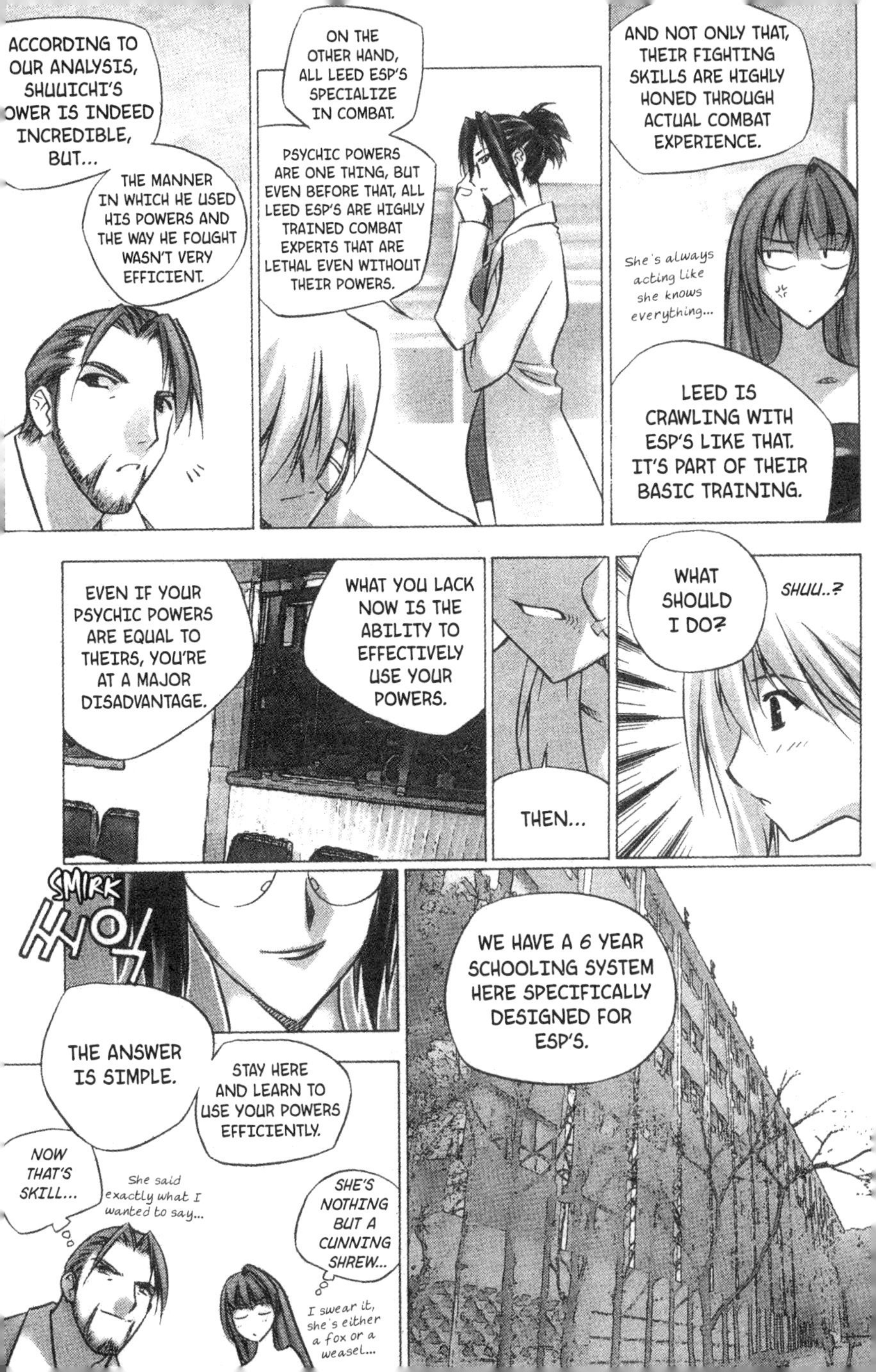
ACCORDING TO OUR ANALYSIS, SHUUICHI'S OWER IS INDEED INCREDIBLE, BUT...
THE MANNER IN WHICH HE USED HIS POWERS AND THE WAY HE FOUGHT WASN'T VERY EFFICIENT.
ON THE OTHER HAND, ALL LEED ESP'S SPECIALIZE IN COMBAT.
PSYCHIC POWERS ARE ONE THING, BUT EVEN BEFORE THAT, ALL LEED ESP'S ARE HIGHLY TRAINED COMBAT EXPERTS THAT ARE LETHAL EVEN WITHOUT THEIR POWERS.
AND NOT ONLY THAT, THEIR FIGHTING SKILLS ARE HIGHLY HONED THROUGH ACTUAL COMBAT EXPERIENCE.
She's always acting like she knows everything...
LEED IS CRAWLING WITH ESP'S LIKE THAT. IT'S PART OF THEIR BASIC TRAINING.
EVEN IF YOUR PSYCHIC POWERS ARE EQUAL TO THEIRS, YOU'RE AT A MAJOR DISADVANTAGE.
WHAT YOU LACK NOW IS THE ABILITY TO EFFECTIVELY USE YOUR POWERS.
THEN...
WHAT SHOULD I DO?
SHUU..?
SMIRK
THE ANSWER IS SIMPLE.
STAY HERE AND LEARN TO USE YOUR POWERS EFFICIENTLY.
NOW THAT'S SKILL...
She said exactly what I wanted to say...
SHE'S NOTHING BUT A CUNNING SHREW...
I swear it, she's either a fox or a weasel...
WE HAVE A 6 YEAR SCHOOLING SYSTEM HERE SPECIFICALLY DESIGNED FOR ESP'S.

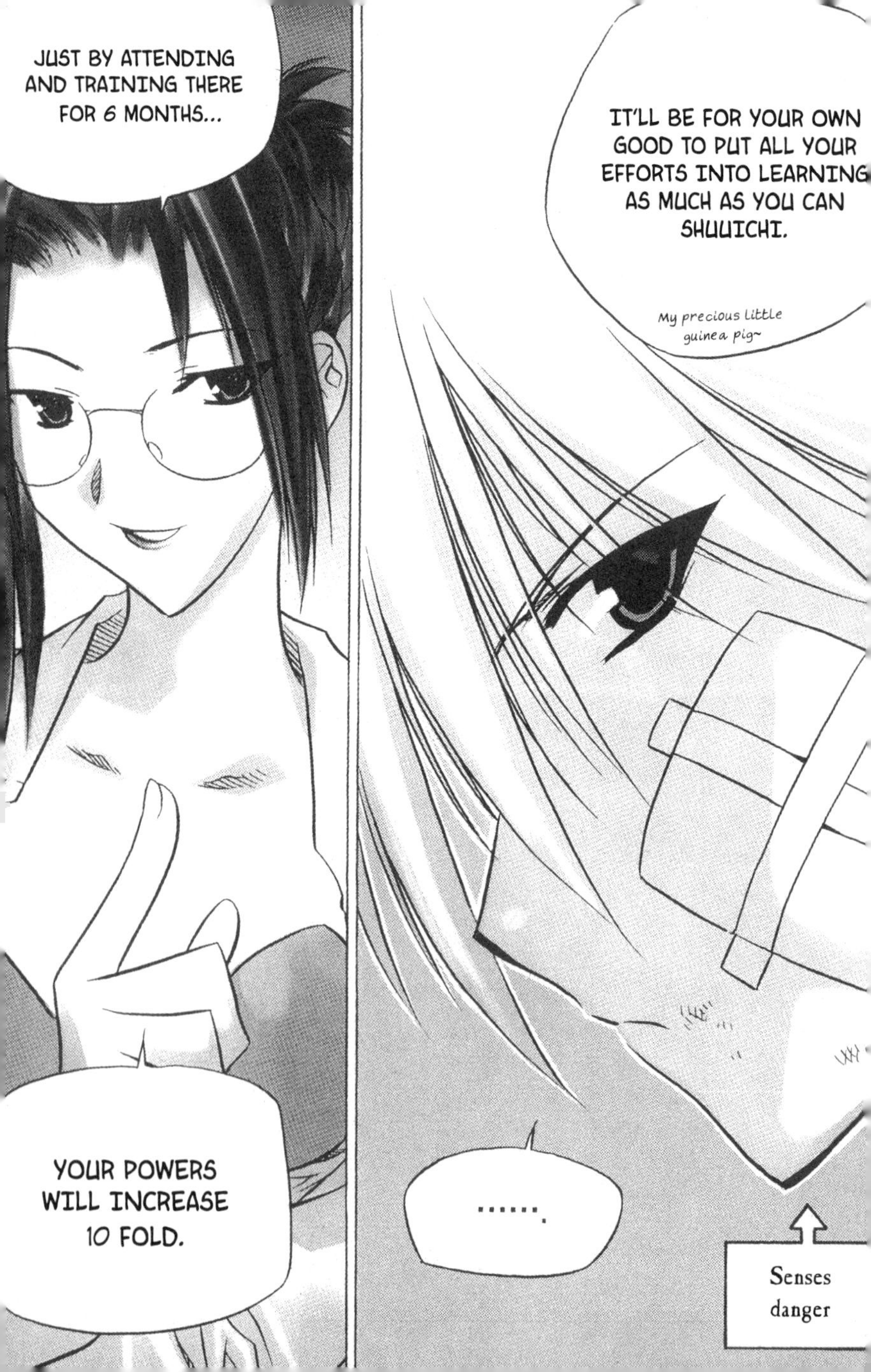
JUST BY ATTENDING AND TRAINING THERE FOR 6 MONTHS...
YOUR POWERS WILL INCREASE 10 FOLD.
IT'LL BE FOR YOUR OWN GOOD TO PUT ALL YOUR EFFORTS INTO LEARNING AS MUCH AS YOU CAN SHUUICHI.
My precious little guinea pig~
....
Senses danger

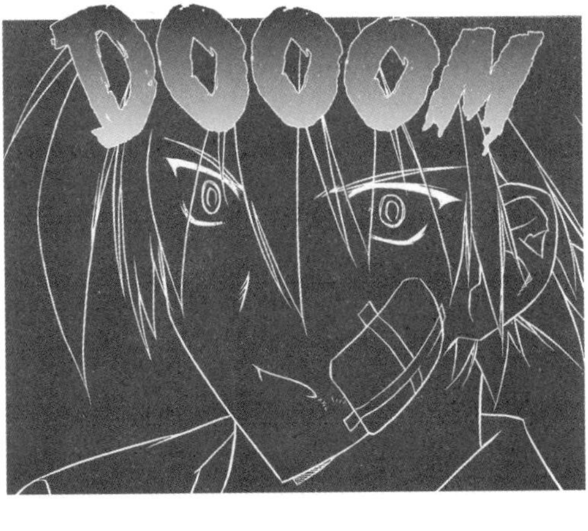
DOOOM

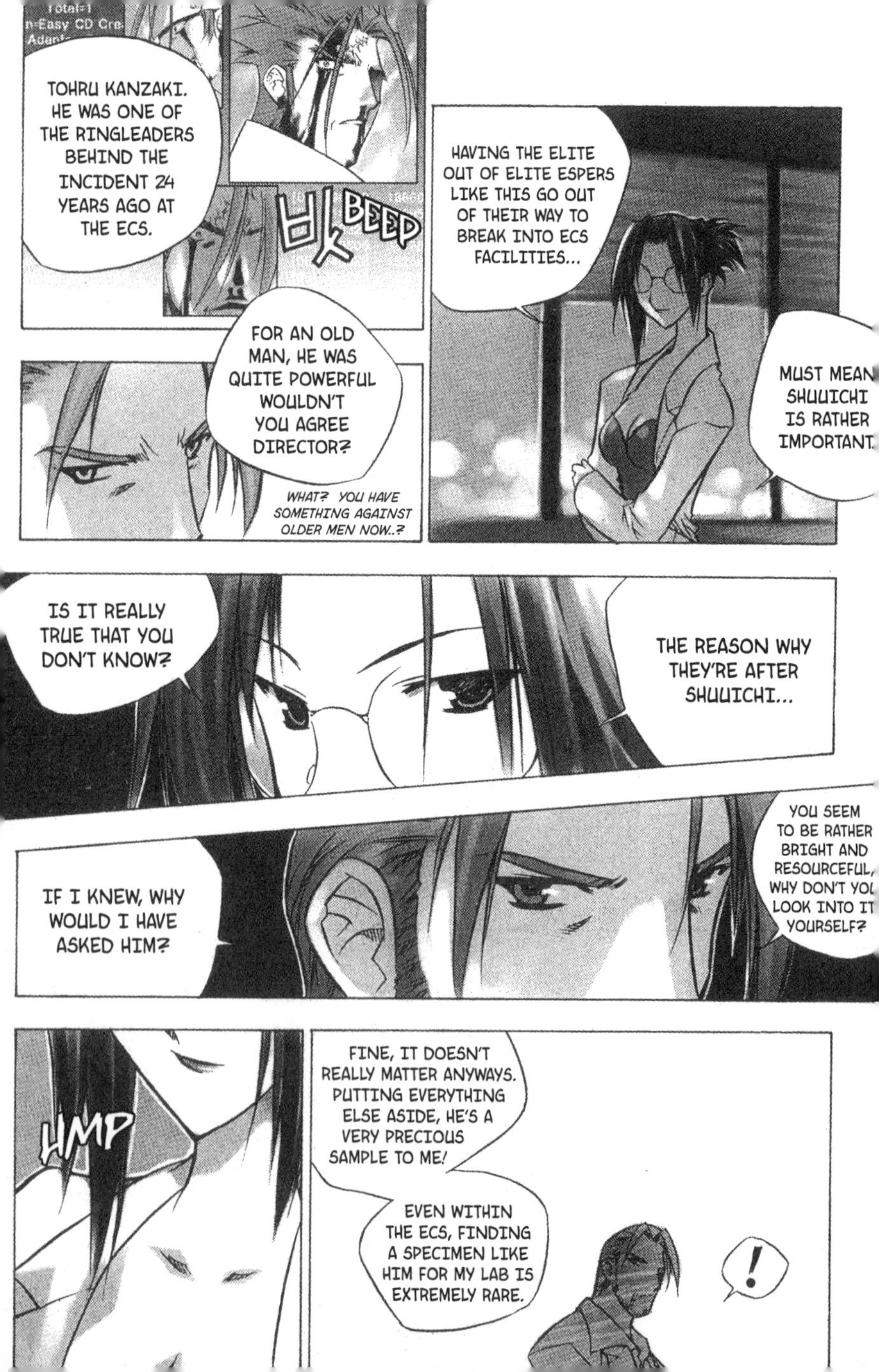
TOHRU KANZAKI. HE WAS ONE OF THE RINGLEADERS BEHIND THE INCIDENT 24 YEARS AGO AT THE ECS.
BEEP
FOR AN OLD MAN, HE WAS QUITE POWERFUL WOULDN'T YOU AGREE DIRECTOR?
WHAT? YOU HAVE SOMETHING AGAINST OLDER MEN NOW..?
HAVING THE ELITE OUT OF ELITE ESPERS LIKE THIS GO OUT OF THEIR WAY TO BREAK INTO ECS FACILITIES...
MUST MEAN SHUUICHI IS RATHER IMPORTANT.
IS IT REALLY TRUE THAT YOU DON'T KNOW?
THE REASON WHY THEY'RE AFTER SHUUICHI...
IF I KNEW, WHY WOULD I HAVE ASKED HIM?
YOU SEEM TO BE RATHER BRIGHT AND RESOURCEFUL, WHY DON'T YOU LOOK INTO IT YOURSELF?
HMP
FINE, IT DOESN'T REALLY MATTER ANYWAYS. PUTTING EVERYTHING ELSE ASIDE, HE'S A VERY PRECIOUS SAMPLE TO ME!
EVEN WITHIN THE ECS, FINDING A SPECIMEN LIKE HIM FOR MY LAB IS EXTREMELY RARE.
!

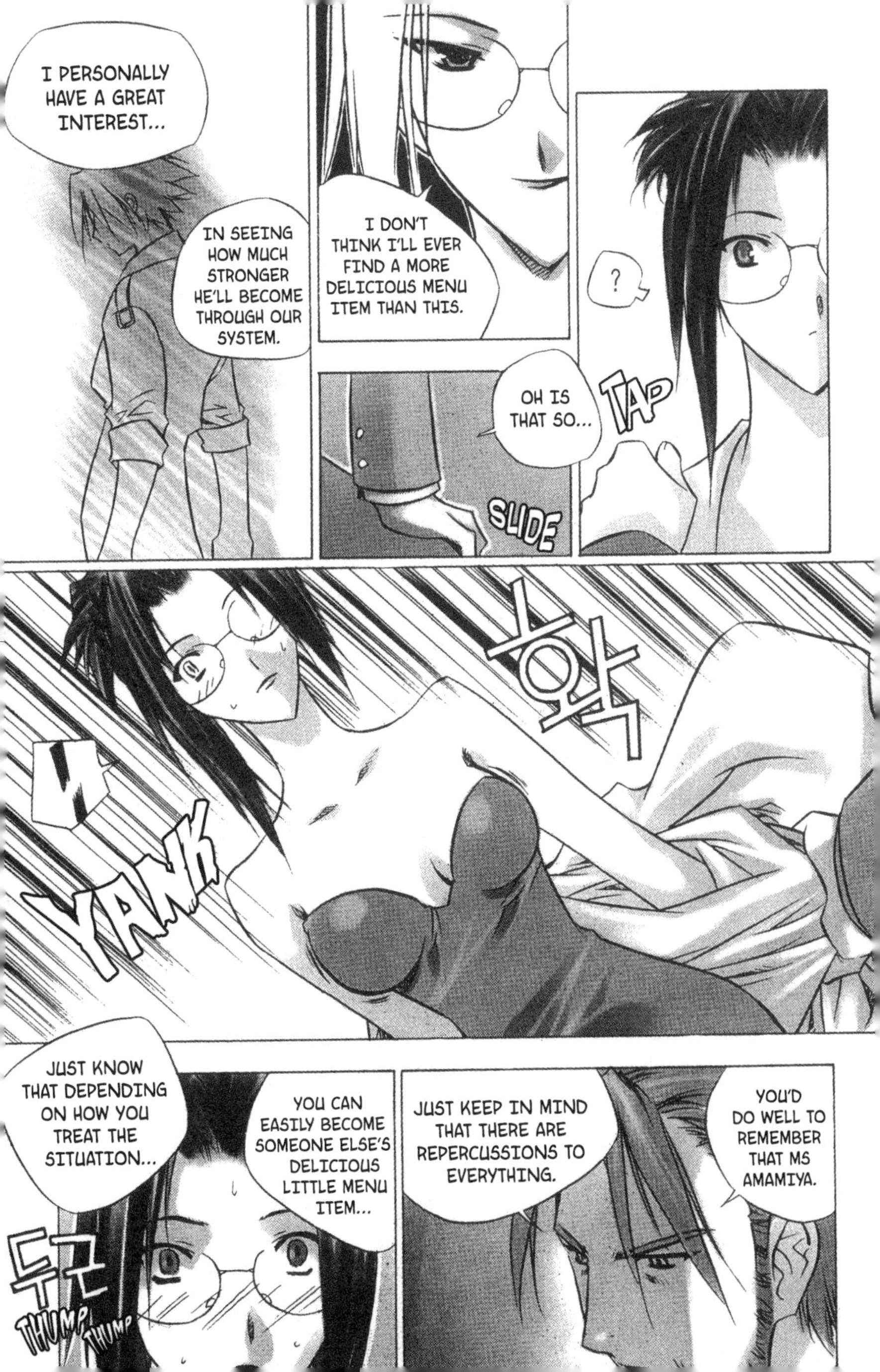
I PERSONALLY HAVE A GREAT INTEREST...
IN SEEING HOW MUCH STRONGER HE'LL BECOME THROUGH OUR SYSTEM.
I DON'T THINK I'LL EVER FIND A MORE DELICIOUS MENU ITEM THAN THIS.
OH IS THAT SO...
SLIDE
?
TAP
YANK
JUST KNOW THAT DEPENDING ON HOW YOU TREAT THE SITUATION...
YOU CAN EASILY BECOME SOMEONE ELSE'S DELICIOUS LITTLE MENU ITEM...
두근
THUMP THUMP
JUST KEEP IN MIND THAT THERE ARE REPERCUSSIONS TO EVERYTHING.
YOU'D DO WELL TO REMEMBER THAT MS AMAMIYA.

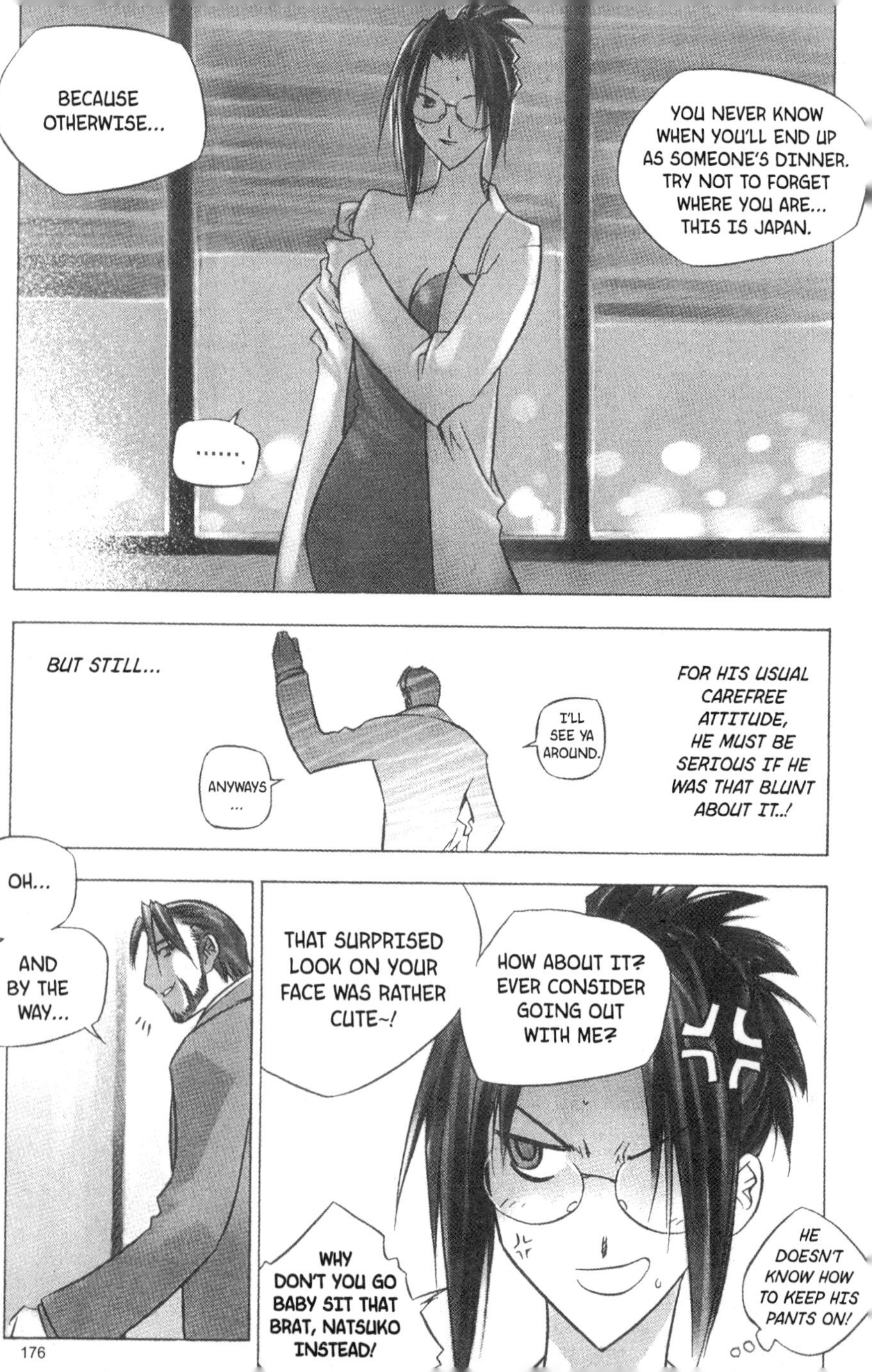
BECAUSE OTHERWISE...
YOU NEVER KNOW WHEN YOU'LL END UP AS SOMEONE'S DINNER. TRY NOT TO FORGET WHERE YOU ARE... THIS IS JAPAN.
....
BUT STILL...
ANYWAYS ...
I'LL SEE YA AROUND.
FOR HIS USUAL CAREFREE ATTITUDE, HE MUST BE SERIOUS IF HE WAS THAT BLUNT ABOUT IT..!
OH...
AND BY THE WAY...
THAT SURPRISED LOOK ON YOUR FACE WAS RATHER CUTE~!
HOW ABOUT IT? EVER CONSIDER GOING OUT WITH ME?
WHY DON'T YOU GO BABY SIT THAT BRAT, NATSUKO INSTEAD!
HE DOESN'T KNOW HOW TO KEEP HIS PANTS ON!

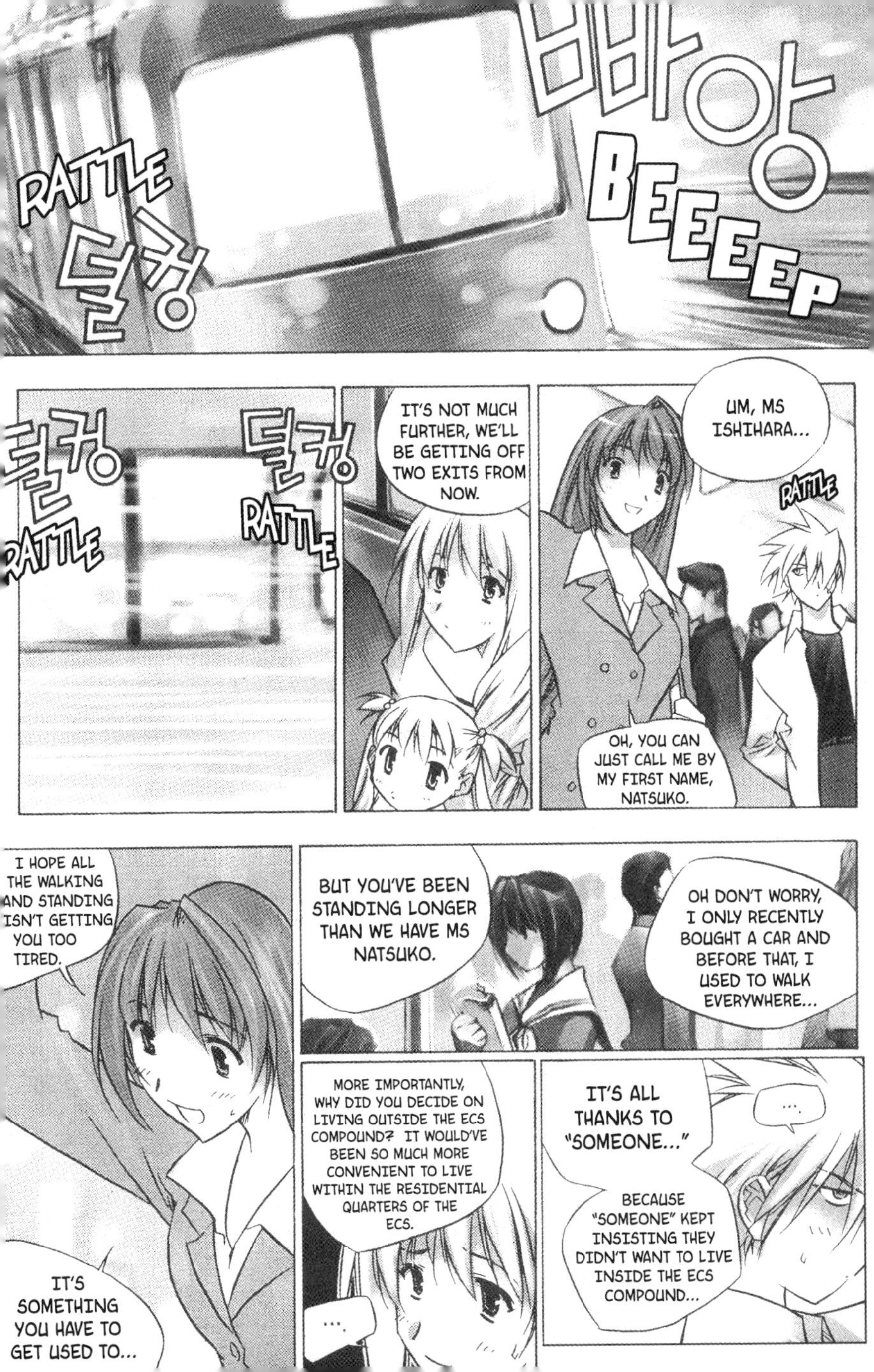
RATTLE
덜컹
빠앙
BEEEEEP
덜컹
RATTLE
덜컹
RATTLE
IT'S NOT MUCH FURTHER, WE'LL BE GETTING OFF TWO EXITS FROM NOW.
UM, MS ISHIHARA...
RATTLE
OH, YOU CAN JUST CALL ME BY MY FIRST NAME, NATSUKO.
I HOPE ALL THE WALKING AND STANDING ISN'T GETTING YOU TOO TIRED.
IT'S SOMETHING YOU HAVE TO GET USED TO...
BUT YOU'VE BEEN STANDING LONGER THAN WE HAVE MS NATSUKO.
OH DON'T WORRY, I ONLY RECENTLY BOUGHT A CAR AND BEFORE THAT, I USED TO WALK EVERYWHERE...
MORE IMPORTANTLY, WHY DID YOU DECIDE ON LIVING OUTSIDE THE ECS COMPOUND? IT WOULD'VE BEEN SO MUCH MORE CONVENIENT TO LIVE WITHIN THE RESIDENTIAL QUARTERS OF THE ECS.
....
IT'S ALL THANKS TO "SOMEONE..."
....
BECAUSE "SOMEONE" KEPT INSISTING THEY DIDN'T WANT TO LIVE INSIDE THE ECS COMPOUND...

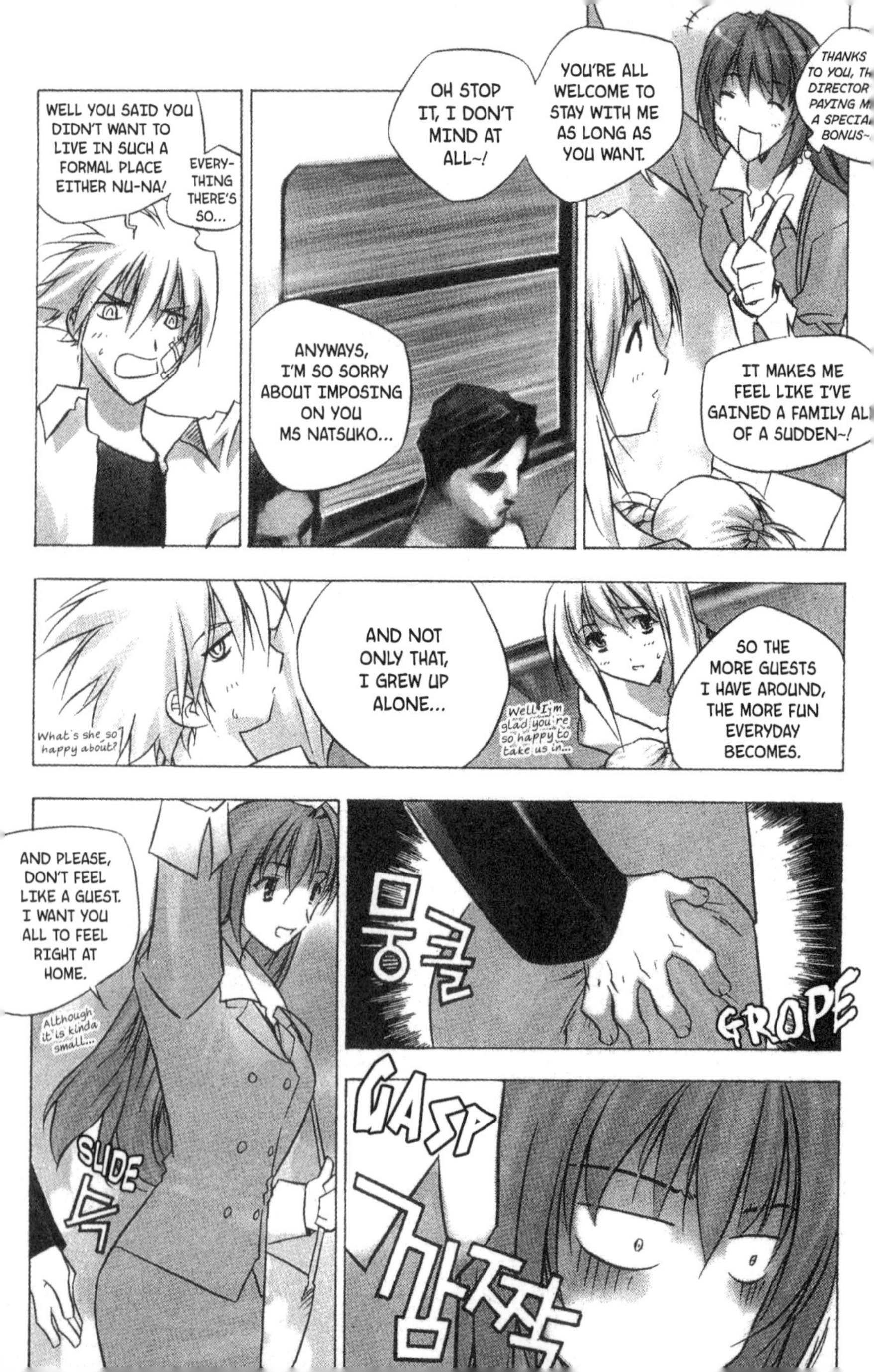

WELL YOU SAID YOU DIDN'T WANT TO LIVE IN SUCH A FORMAL PLACE EITHER NU-NA!
EVERY-THING THERE'S SO...
ANYWAYS, I'M SO SORRY ABOUT IMPOSING ON YOU MS NATSUKO...
OH STOP IT, I DON'T MIND AT ALL~!
YOU'RE ALL WELCOME TO STAY WITH ME AS LONG AS YOU WANT.
THANKS TO YOU, TH DIRECTOR PAYING M A SPECIA BONUS~
IT MAKES ME FEEL LIKE I'VE GAINED A FAMILY AL OF A SUDDEN~!
What's she so happy about?
AND NOT ONLY THAT, I GREW UP ALONE...
Well I'm glad you're so happy to take us in...
SO THE MORE GUESTS I HAVE AROUND, THE MORE FUN EVERYDAY BECOMES.
AND PLEASE, DON'T FEEL LIKE A GUEST. I WANT YOU ALL TO FEEL RIGHT AT HOME.
Although it is kinda small...
SLIDE
GROPE
GASP

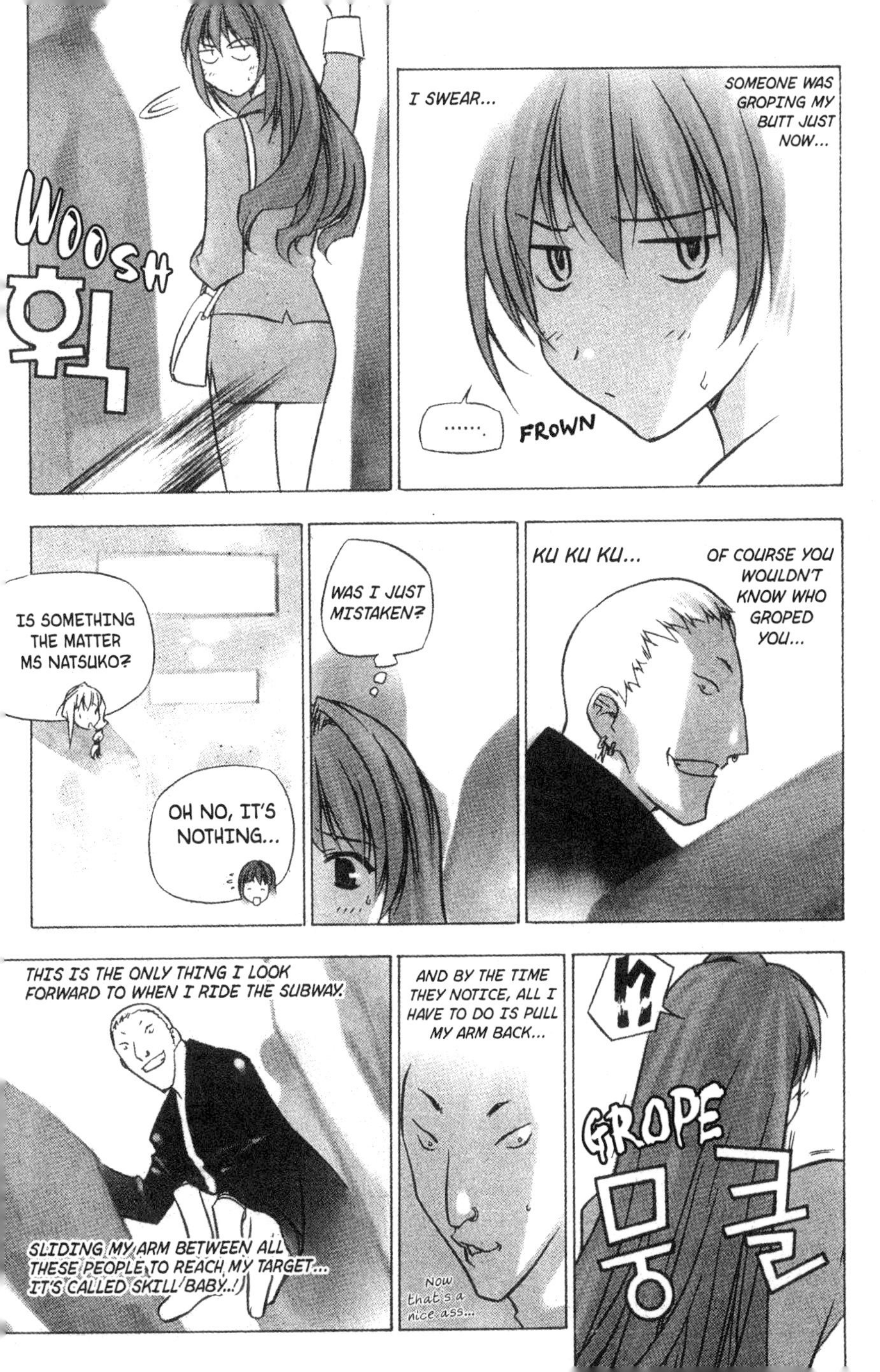
WOOSH
휙
I SWEAR...
SOMEONE WAS GROPING MY BUTT JUST NOW...
....
FROWN
IS SOMETHING THE MATTER MS NATSUKO?
OH NO, IT'S NOTHING...
WAS I JUST MISTAKEN?
KU KU KU...
OF COURSE YOU WOULDN'T KNOW WHO GROPED YOU...
THIS IS THE ONLY THING I LOOK FORWARD TO WHEN I RIDE THE SUBWAY.
SLIDING MY ARM BETWEEN ALL THESE PEOPLE TO REACH MY TARGET... IT'S CALLED SKILL BABY..!
AND BY THE TIME THEY NOTICE, ALL I HAVE TO DO IS PULL MY ARM BACK...
Now that's a nice ass...
GROPE
뭉클

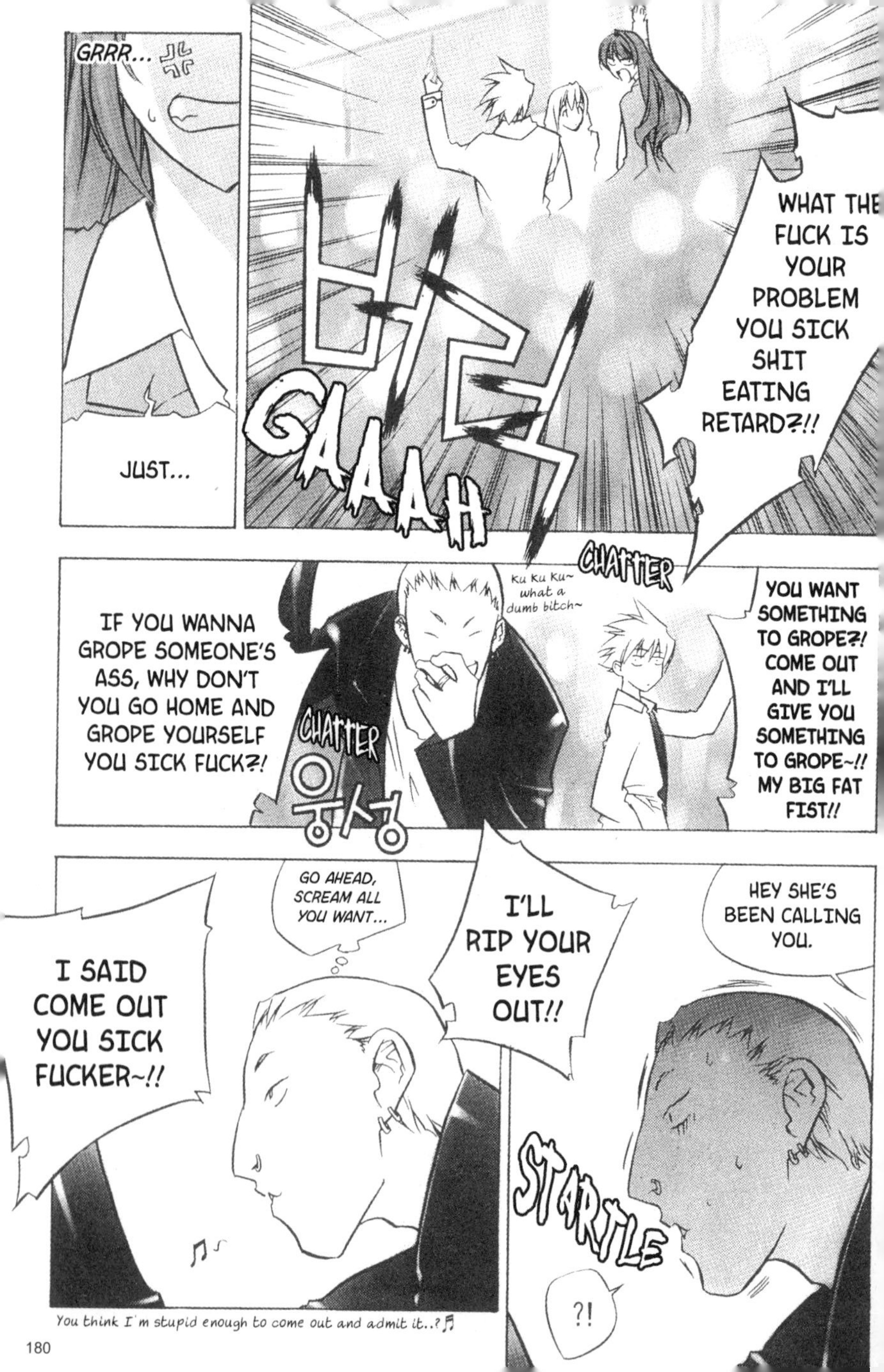
GRRR...
JUST...
버럭
GAAAH
WHAT THE FUCK IS YOUR PROBLEM YOU SICK SHIT EATING RETARD?!!
IF YOU WANNA GROPE SOMEONE'S ASS, WHY DON'T YOU GO HOME AND GROPE YOURSELF YOU SICK FUCK?!
CHATTER
Ku Ku Ku~ what a dumb bitch~
CHATTER
웅성
YOU WANT SOMETHING TO GROPE?! COME OUT AND I'LL GIVE YOU SOMETHING TO GROPE~!! MY BIG FAT FIST!!
I SAID COME OUT YOU SICK FUCKER~!!
GO AHEAD, SCREAM ALL YOU WANT...
I'LL RIP YOUR EYES OUT!!
You think I'm stupid enough to come out and admit it..?
HEY SHE'S BEEN CALLING YOU.
STARTLE
?!

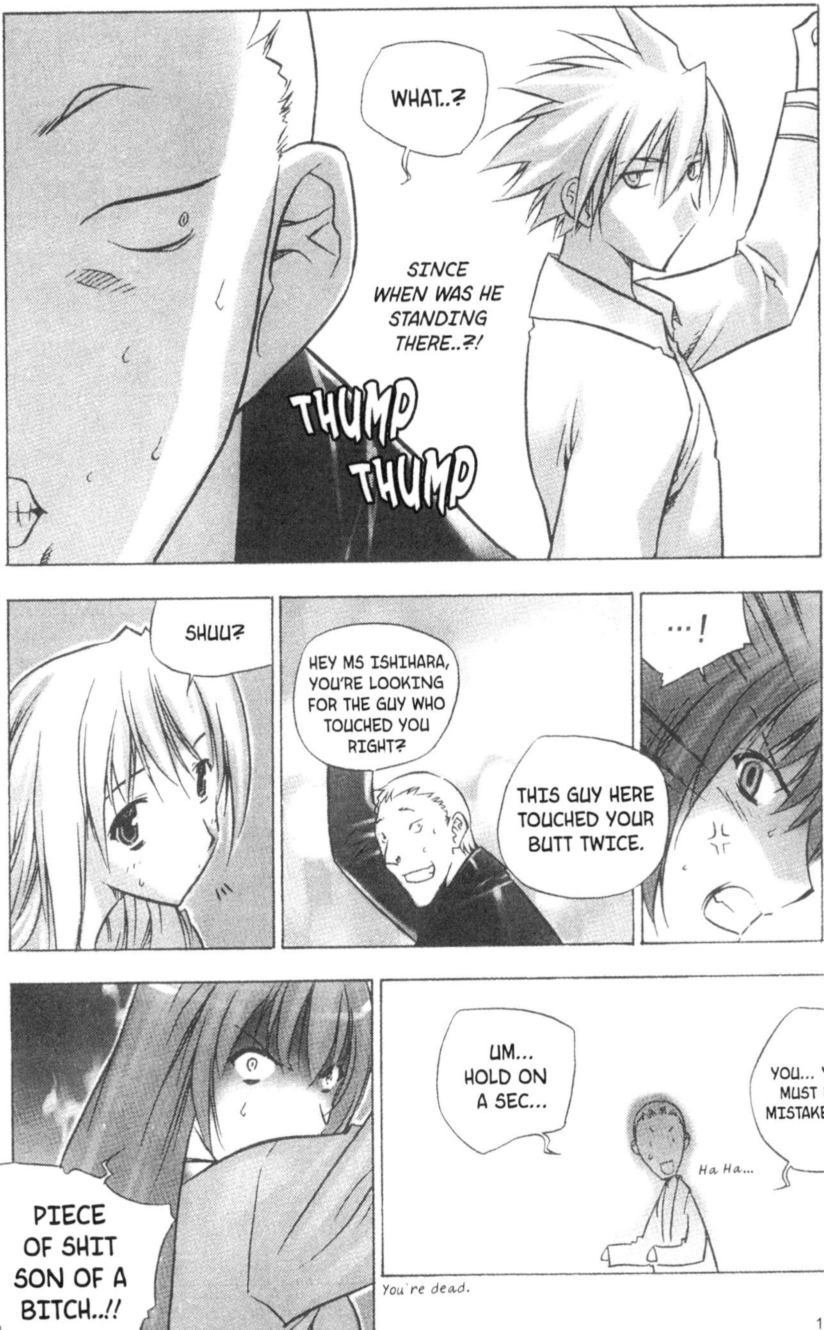
WHAT..?
SINCE WHEN WAS HE STANDING THERE..?!
THUMP THUMP
SHUU?
HEY MS ISHIHARA, YOU'RE LOOKING FOR THE GUY WHO TOUCHED YOU RIGHT?
THIS GUY HERE TOUCHED YOUR BUTT TWICE.
...!
PIECE OF SHIT SON OF A BITCH..!!
UM... HOLD ON A SEC...
YOU... YOU MUST BE MISTAKEN...
Ha Ha...
You're dead.

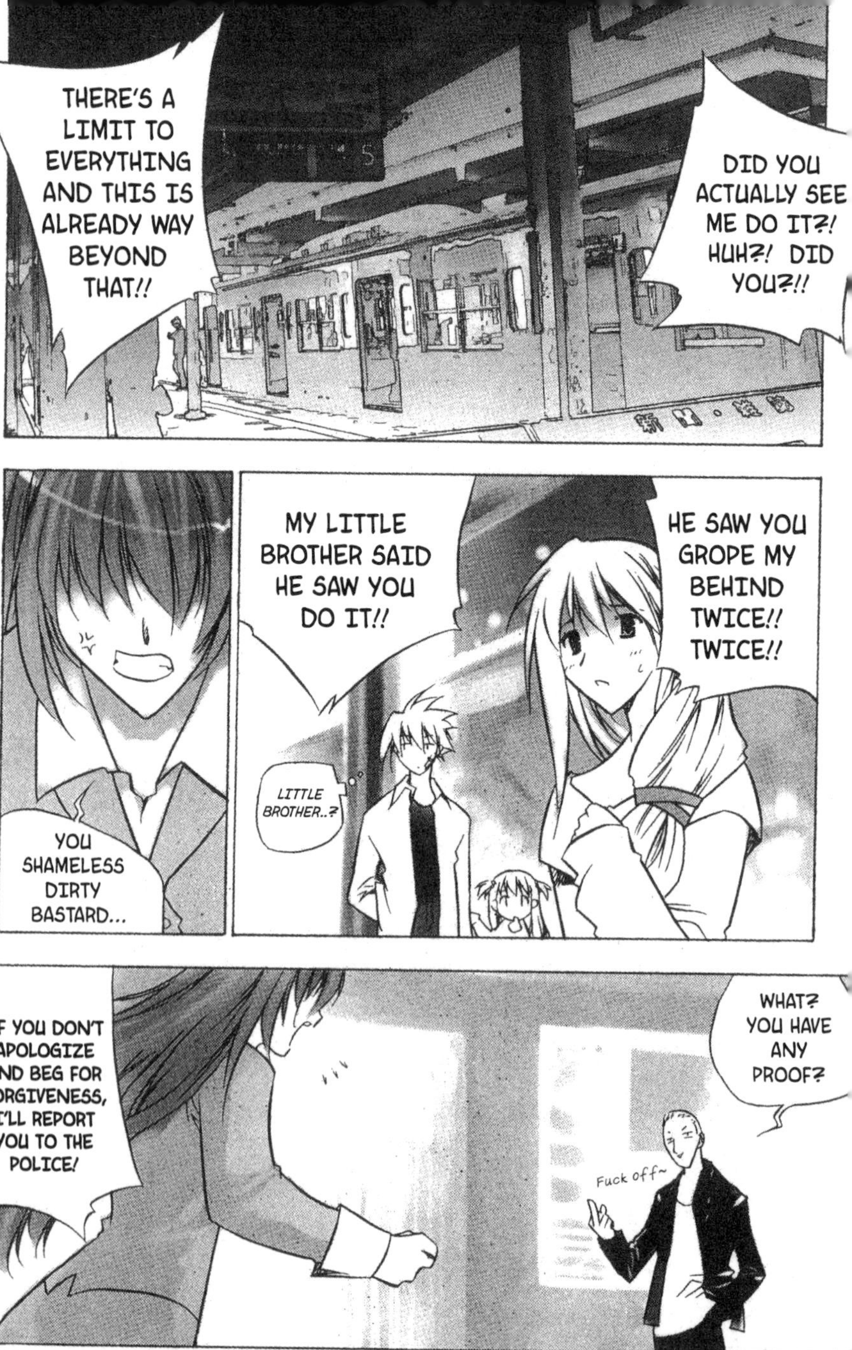
THERE'S A LIMIT TO EVERYTHING AND THIS IS ALREADY WAY BEYOND THAT!!
DID YOU ACTUALLY SEE ME DO IT?! HUH?! DID YOU?!!
YOU SHAMELESS DIRTY BASTARD...
MY LITTLE BROTHER SAID HE SAW YOU DO IT!!
HE SAW YOU GROPE MY BEHIND TWICE!! TWICE!!
LITTLE BROTHER..?
IF YOU DON'T APOLOGIZE AND BEG FOR FORGIVENESS, I'LL REPORT YOU TO THE POLICE!
WHAT? YOU HAVE ANY PROOF?
Fuck off~

THAT PISS OFF ATTITUDE OF YOURS IS PROOF ENOUGH!

GROPING WOMEN ON THE SUBWAY... YOU'RE NOTHING BUT A 3RD RATE SCUM PIECE OF SHIT!!

GET ON YOUR KNEES NOW AND START APOLOGIZING!!

DON'T MAKE ME LAUGH, YOU'RE PROBABLY JUST ANOTHER WHORE ANYWAYS.

SMACK

MS... MS NATSUKO..?!

My goodness...

...

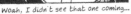

Woah, I didn't see that one coming...

HOW CAN YOU SAY THAT ABOUT A PURE (lie) INNOCENT (more lies) YOUNG LADY (...)?!

DOO DOOM

AND WHY DO I HAVE TO HEAR THIS KIND OF CRAP FROM A SEWER SCUM LIKE YOU?!

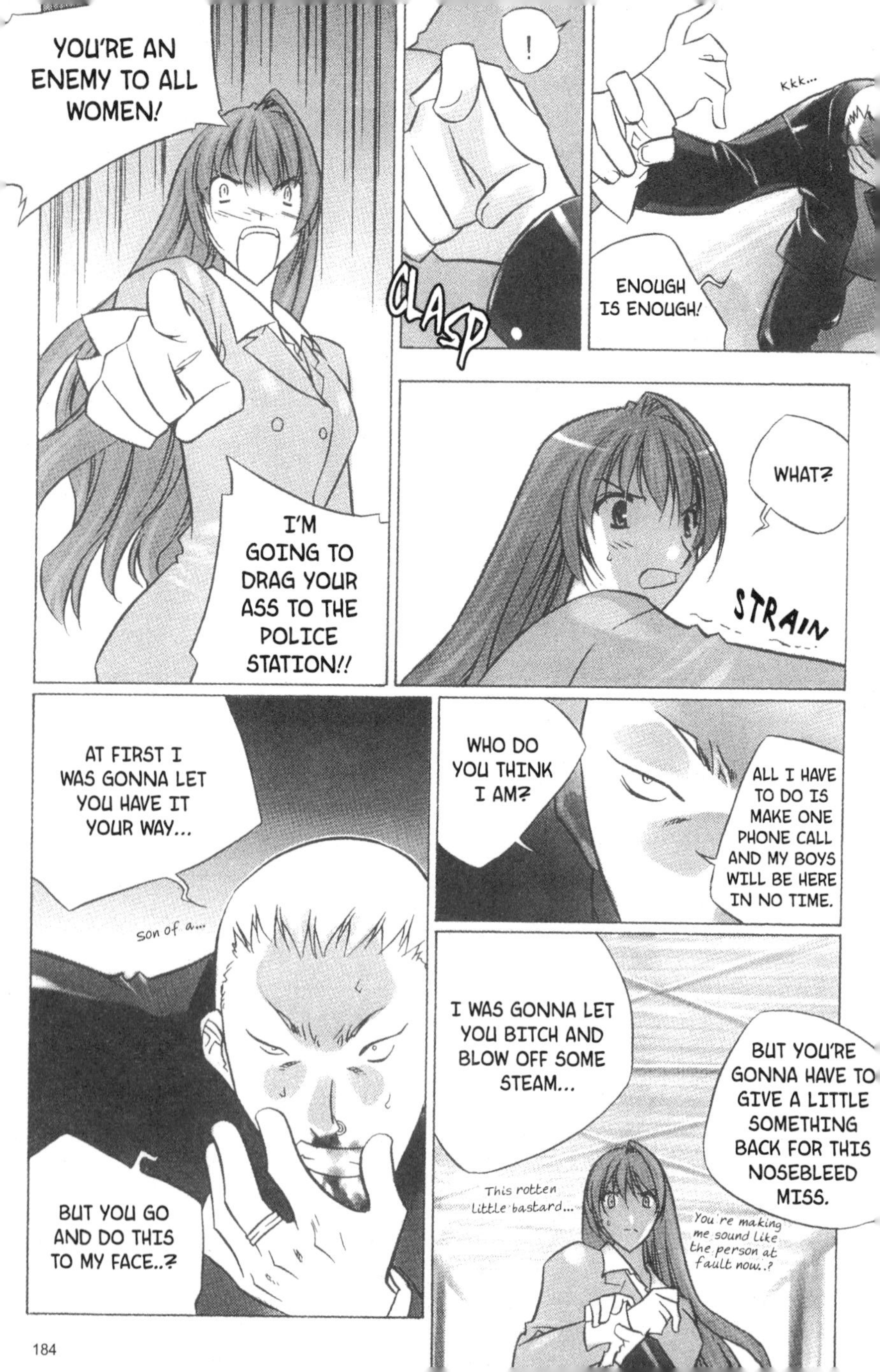
YOU'RE AN ENEMY TO ALL WOMEN!
I'M GOING TO DRAG YOUR ASS TO THE POLICE STATION!!
!
CLASP
Kkk...
ENOUGH IS ENOUGH!
WHAT?
STRAIN
AT FIRST I WAS GONNA LET YOU HAVE IT YOUR WAY...
son of a...
BUT YOU GO AND DO THIS TO MY FACE..?
WHO DO YOU THINK I AM?
ALL I HAVE TO DO IS MAKE ONE PHONE CALL AND MY BOYS WILL BE HERE IN NO TIME.
I WAS GONNA LET YOU BITCH AND BLOW OFF SOME STEAM...
BUT YOU'RE GONNA HAVE TO GIVE A LITTLE SOMETHING BACK FOR THIS NOSEBLEED MISS.
This rotten little bastard...
You're making me sound like the person at fault now..?

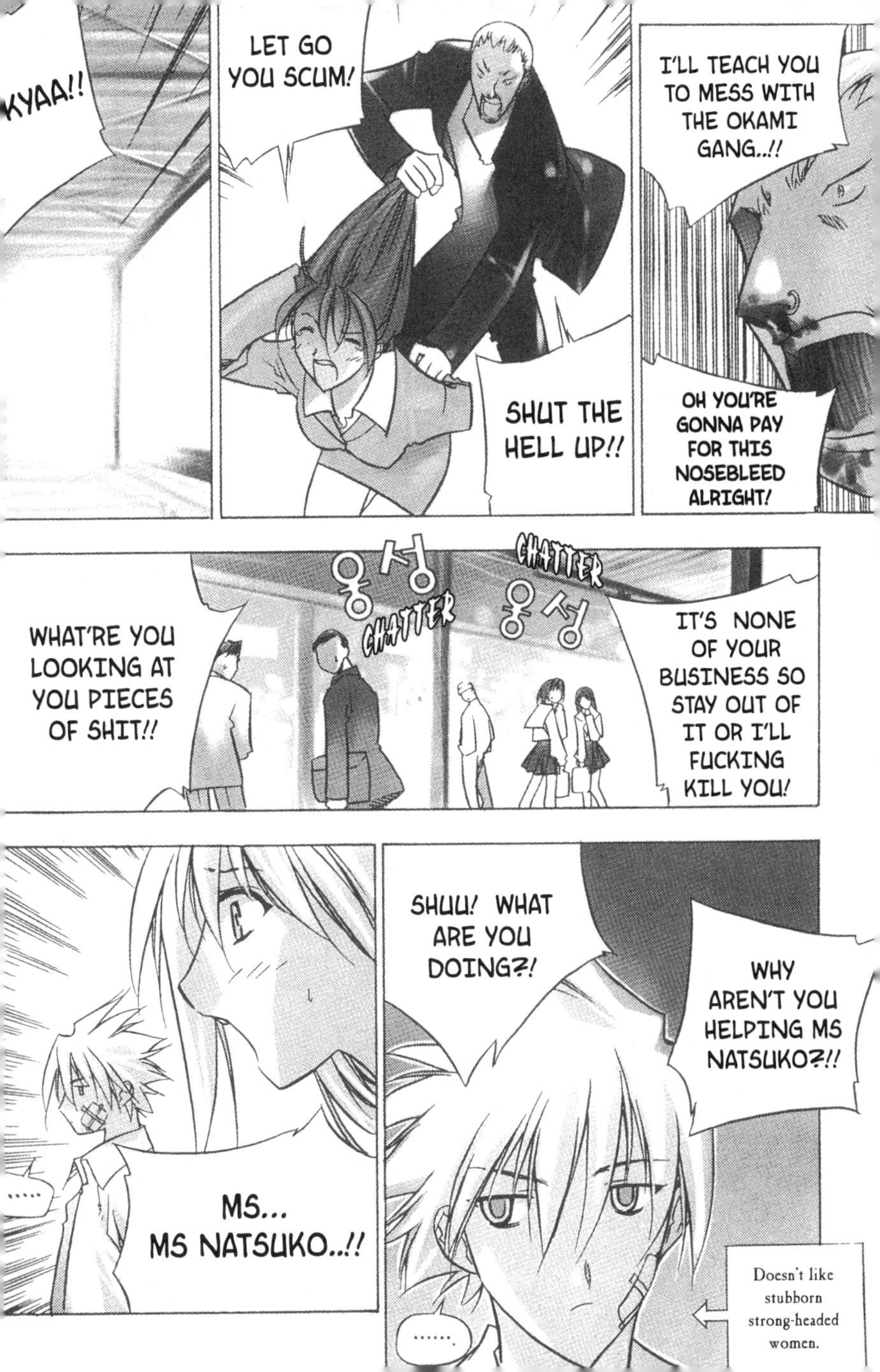
KYAA!!
LET GO YOU SCUM!
SHUT THE HELL UP!!
I'LL TEACH YOU TO MESS WITH THE OKAMI GANG..!!
OH YOU'RE GONNA PAY FOR THIS NOSEBLEED ALRIGHT!
WHAT'RE YOU LOOKING AT YOU PIECES OF SHIT!!
웅성
CHATTER
CHATTER
웅성
IT'S NONE OF YOUR BUSINESS SO STAY OUT OF IT OR I'LL FUCKING KILL YOU!
.....
MS... MS NATSUKO..!!
SHUU! WHAT ARE YOU DOING?!
WHY AREN'T YOU HELPING MS NATSUKO?!!
....
Doesn't like stubborn strong-headed women.

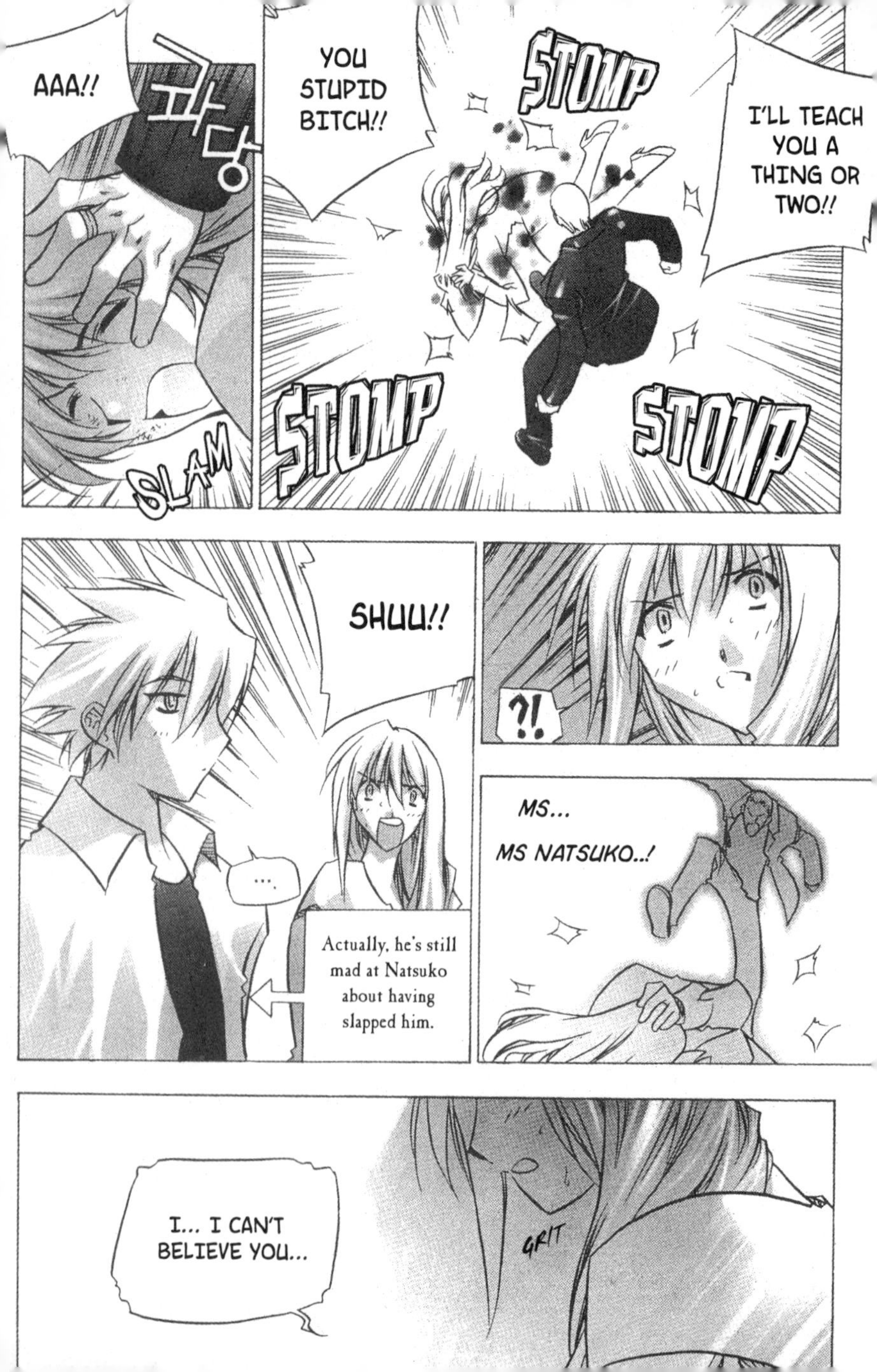
AAA!!
콰당
SLAM
YOU STUPID BITCH!!
STOMP
I'LL TEACH YOU A THING OR TWO!!
STOMP
STOMP
SHUU!!
....
Actually, he's still mad at Natsuko about having slapped him.
?!
MS...
MS NATSUKO..!
I... I CAN'T BELIEVE YOU...
GRIT

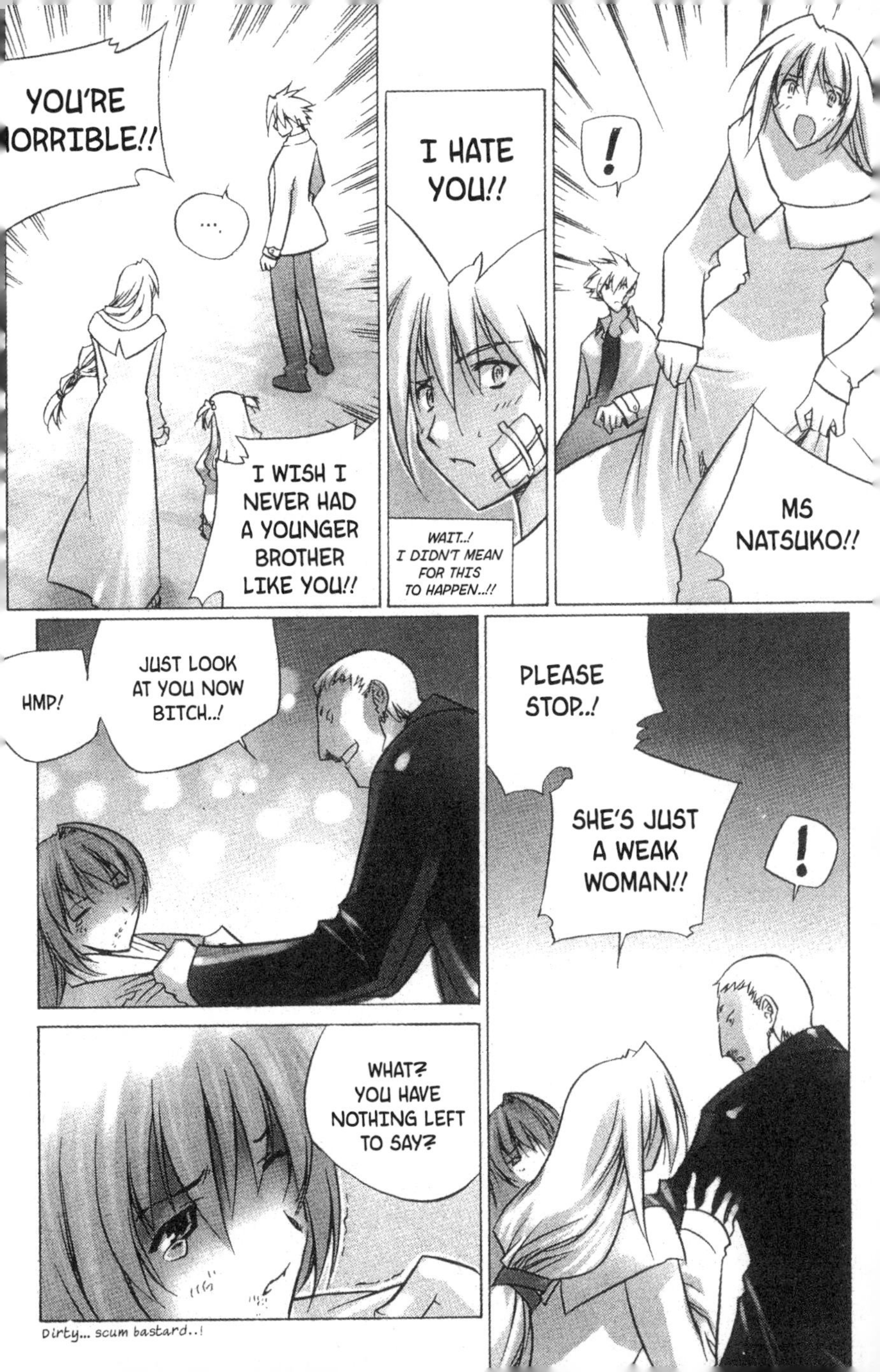
YOU'RE ORRIBLE!!
...
I WISH I NEVER HAD A YOUNGER BROTHER LIKE YOU!!
I HATE YOU!!
WAIT..! I DIDN'T MEAN FOR THIS TO HAPPEN..!!
!
MS NATSUKO!!
HMP!
JUST LOOK AT YOU NOW BITCH..!
WHAT? YOU HAVE NOTHING LEFT TO SAY?
Dirty... scum bastard..!
PLEASE STOP..!
SHE'S JUST A WEAK WOMAN!!
!

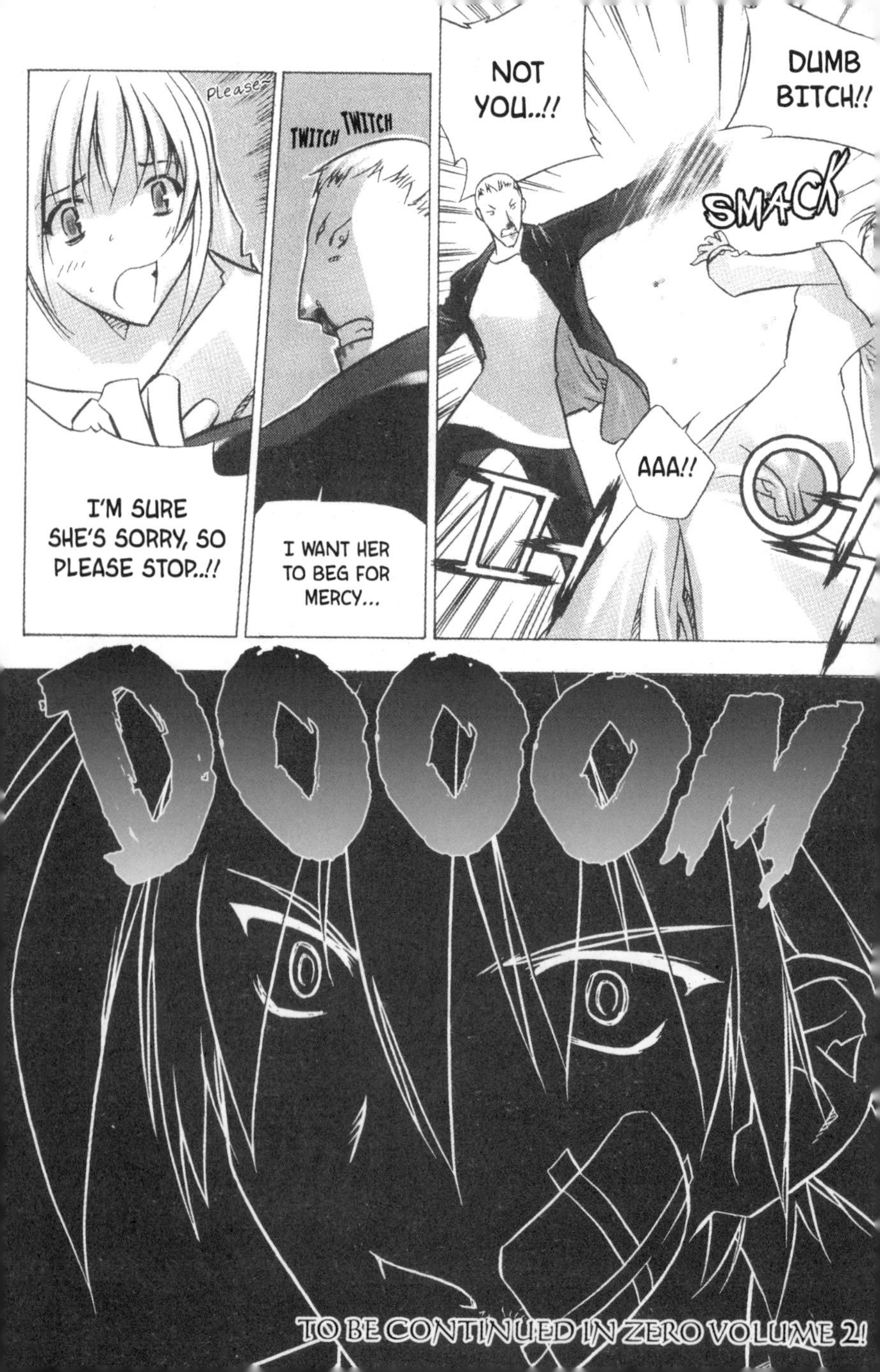
Please~
I'M SURE SHE'S SORRY, SO PLEASE STOP..!!
TWITCH TWITCH
I WANT HER TO BEG FOR MERCY...
NOT YOU..!!
DUMB BITCH!!
SMACK
AAA!!
DOOOM
TO BE CONTINUED IN ZERO VOLUME 2!

Z ERO
THE BEGINNING
OF THE COFFIN

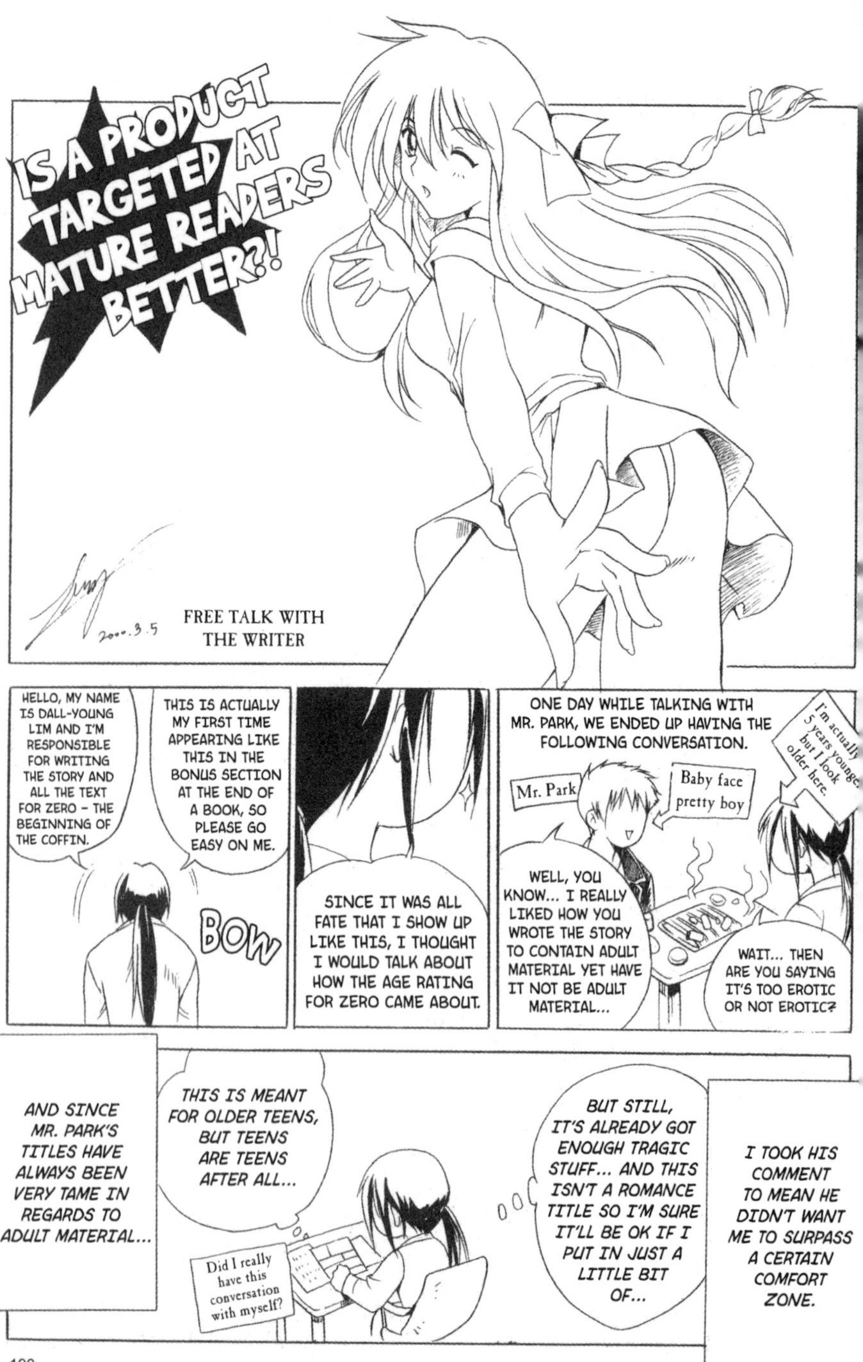
IS A PRODUCT TARGETED AT MATURE READERS BETTER?!
2000.3.5
FREE TALK WITH THE WRITER
HELLO, MY NAME IS DALL-YOUNG LIM AND I'M RESPONSIBLE FOR WRITING THE STORY AND ALL THE TEXT FOR ZERO - THE BEGINNING OF THE COFFIN.
THIS IS ACTUALLY MY FIRST TIME APPEARING LIKE THIS IN THE BONUS SECTION AT THE END OF A BOOK, SO PLEASE GO EASY ON ME.
BOW
SINCE IT WAS ALL FATE THAT I SHOW UP LIKE THIS, I THOUGHT I WOULD TALK ABOUT HOW THE AGE RATING FOR ZERO CAME ABOUT.
ONE DAY WHILE TALKING WITH MR. PARK, WE ENDED UP HAVING THE FOLLOWING CONVERSATION.
I'm actually 5 years younge but I look older here.
Mr. Park
Baby face pretty boy
WELL, YOU KNOW... I REALLY LIKED HOW YOU WROTE THE STORY TO CONTAIN ADULT MATERIAL YET HAVE IT NOT BE ADULT MATERIAL...
WAIT... THEN ARE YOU SAYING IT'S TOO EROTIC OR NOT EROTIC?
AND SINCE MR. PARK'S TITLES HAVE ALWAYS BEEN VERY TAME IN REGARDS TO ADULT MATERIAL...
THIS IS MEANT FOR OLDER TEENS, BUT TEENS ARE TEENS AFTER ALL...
Did I really have this conversation with myself?
BUT STILL, IT'S ALREADY GOT ENOUGH TRAGIC STUFF... AND THIS ISN'T A ROMANCE TITLE SO I'M SURE IT'LL BE OK IF I PUT IN JUST A LITTLE BIT OF...
I TOOK HIS COMMENT TO MEAN HE DIDN'T WANT ME TO SURPASS A CERTAIN COMFORT ZONE.

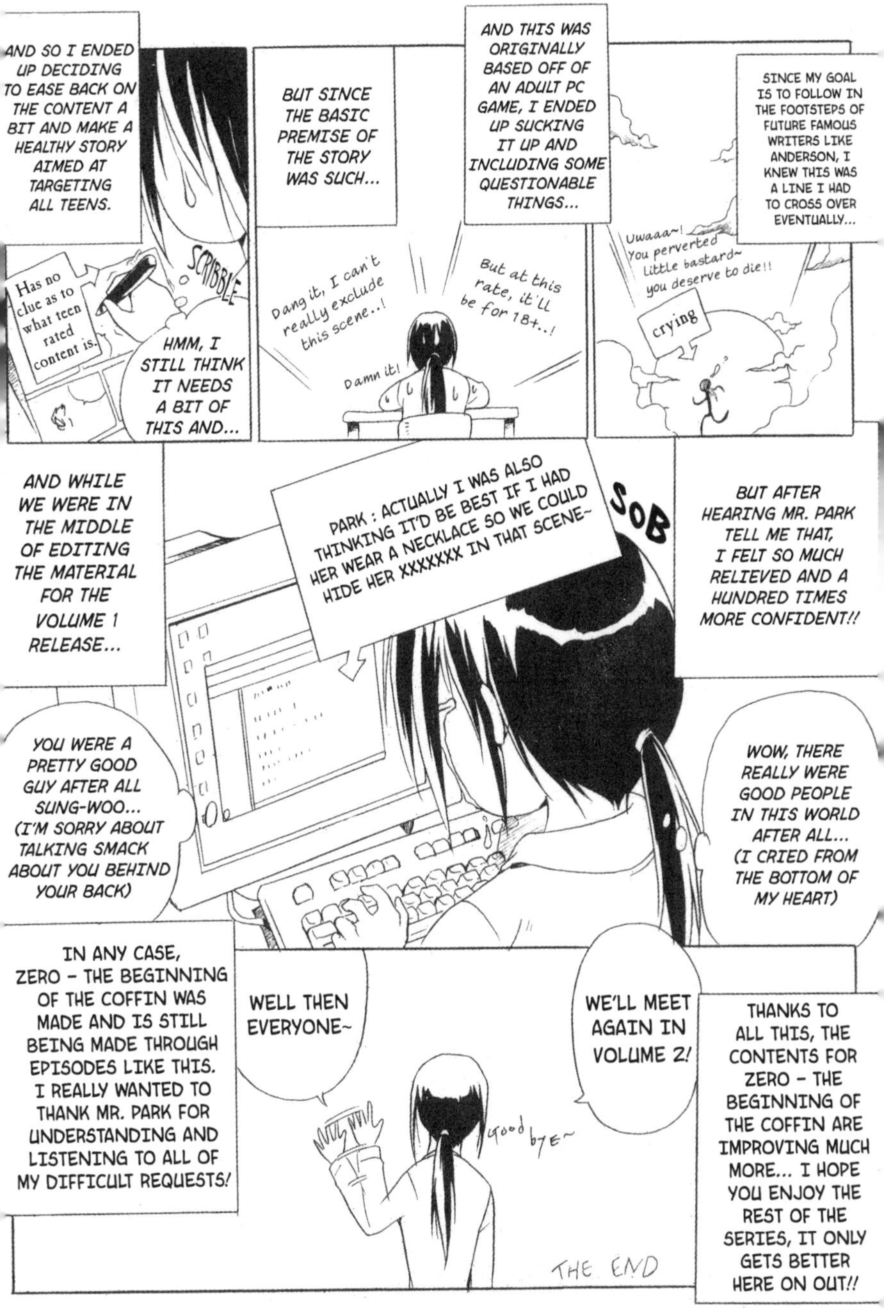
AND SO I ENDED UP DECIDING TO EASE BACK ON THE CONTENT A BIT AND MAKE A HEALTHY STORY AIMED AT TARGETING ALL TEENS.
Has no clue as to what teen rated content is.
SCRIBBLE
HMM, I STILL THINK IT NEEDS A BIT OF THIS AND...
BUT SINCE THE BASIC PREMISE OF THE STORY WAS SUCH...
AND THIS WAS ORIGINALLY BASED OFF OF AN ADULT PC GAME, I ENDED UP SUCKING IT UP AND INCLUDING SOME QUESTIONABLE THINGS...
Dang it, I can't really exclude this scene..!
Damn it!
But at this rate, it'll be for 18+..!
SINCE MY GOAL IS TO FOLLOW IN THE FOOTSTEPS OF FUTURE FAMOUS WRITERS LIKE ANDERSON, I KNEW THIS WAS A LINE I HAD TO CROSS OVER EVENTUALLY...
Uwaaa~! You perverted little bastard~ you deserve to die!!
crying
AND WHILE WE WERE IN THE MIDDLE OF EDITING THE MATERIAL FOR THE VOLUME 1 RELEASE...
PARK : ACTUALLY I WAS ALSO THINKING IT'D BE BEST IF I HAD HER WEAR A NECKLACE SO WE COULD HIDE HER XXXXXXX IN THAT SCENE~
SOB
BUT AFTER HEARING MR. PARK TELL ME THAT, I FELT SO MUCH RELIEVED AND A HUNDRED TIMES MORE CONFIDENT!!
YOU WERE A PRETTY GOOD GUY AFTER ALL SUNG-WOO... (I'M SORRY ABOUT TALKING SMACK ABOUT YOU BEHIND YOUR BACK)
WOW, THERE REALLY WERE GOOD PEOPLE IN THIS WORLD AFTER ALL... (I CRIED FROM THE BOTTOM OF MY HEART)
IN ANY CASE, ZERO - THE BEGINNING OF THE COFFIN WAS MADE AND IS STILL BEING MADE THROUGH EPISODES LIKE THIS. I REALLY WANTED TO THANK MR. PARK FOR UNDERSTANDING AND LISTENING TO ALL OF MY DIFFICULT REQUESTS!
WELL THEN EVERYONE~
Good byE~
WE'LL MEET AGAIN IN VOLUME 2!
THANKS TO ALL THIS, THE CONTENTS FOR ZERO - THE BEGINNING OF THE COFFIN ARE IMPROVING MUCH MORE... I HOPE YOU ENJOY THE REST OF THE SERIES, IT ONLY GETS BETTER HERE ON OUT!!
THE END

ZERO
THE BEGINNING OF THE COFFIN

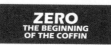

THE FOLLOWING ARE DESIGNS AND CHARACTER INFORMATION FROM THE ORIGINAL GAME CREATOR.

Original Character Designer : ANICD (Artlim Media Staff)

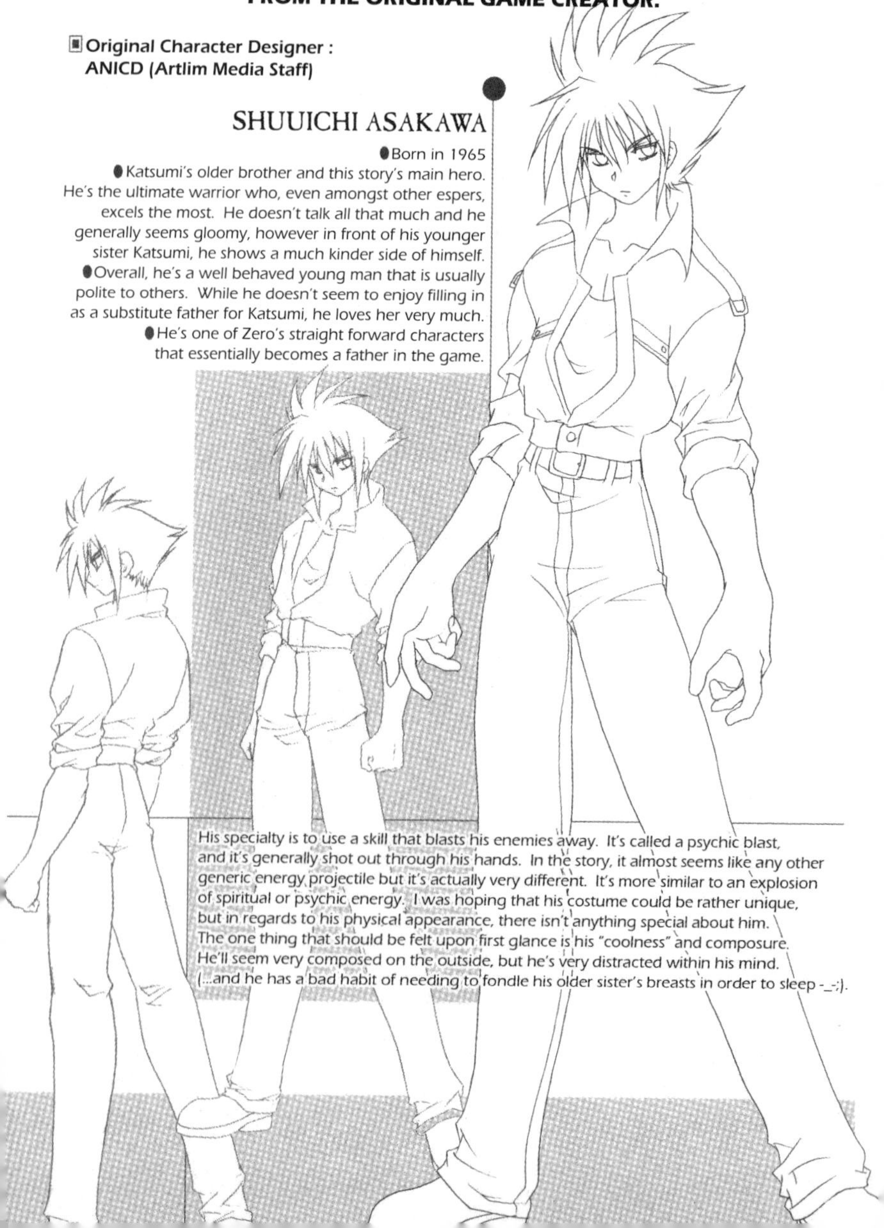

SHUUICHI ASAKAWA

● Born in 1965

● Katsumi's older brother and this story's main hero. He's the ultimate warrior who, even amongst other espers, excels the most. He doesn't talk all that much and he generally seems gloomy, however in front of his younger sister Katsumi, he shows a much kinder side of himself.

● Overall, he's a well behaved young man that is usually polite to others. While he doesn't seem to enjoy filling in as a substitute father for Katsumi, he loves her very much.

● He's one of Zero's straight forward characters that essentially becomes a father in the game.

His specialty is to use a skill that blasts his enemies away. It's called a psychic blast, and it's generally shot out through his hands. In the story, it almost seems like any other generic energy projectile but it's actually very different. It's more similar to an explosion of spiritual or psychic energy. I was hoping that his costume could be rather unique, but in regards to his physical appearance, there isn't anything special about him. The one thing that should be felt upon first glance is his "coolness" and composure. He'll seem very composed on the outside, but he's very distracted within his mind. (...and he has a bad habit of needing to fondle his older sister's breasts in order to sleep -_-;).

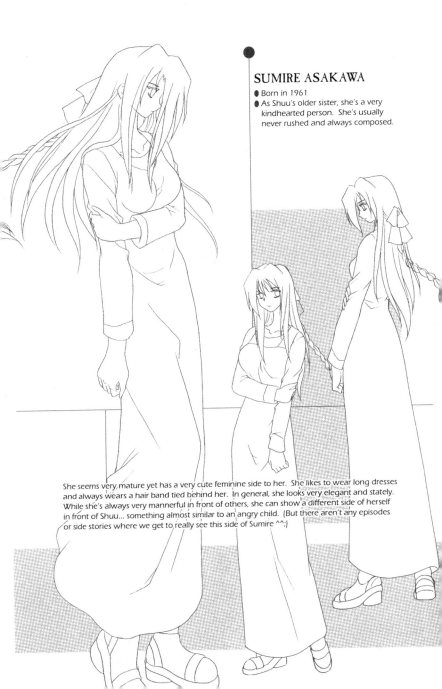

SUMIRE ASAKAWA

- Born in 1961
- As Shuu's older sister, she's a very kindhearted person. She's usually never rushed and always composed.

She seems very mature yet has a very cute feminine side to her. She likes to wear long dresses and always wears a hair band tied behind her. In general, she looks very elegant and stately. While she's always very mannerful in front of others, she can show a different side of herself in front of Shuu... something almost similar to an angry child. (But there aren't any episodes or side stories where we get to really see this side of Sumire ^^;)

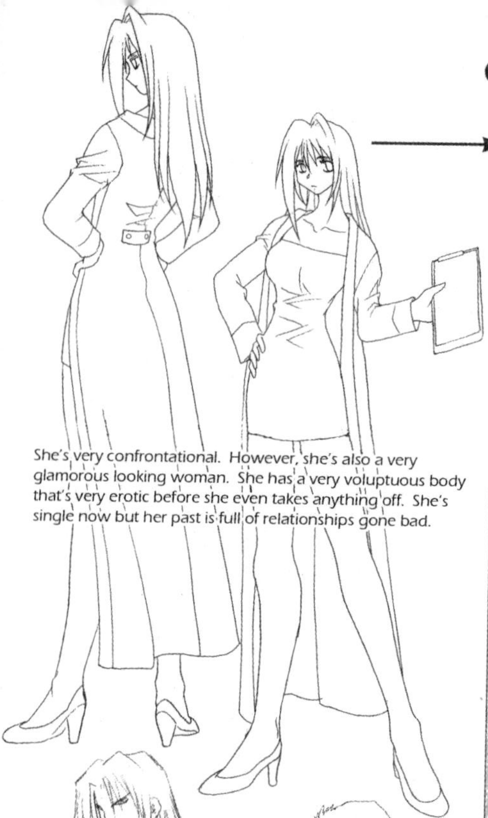

NATSUKO ISHIHARA

- Born in 1958
- Tokyo ECS Division, Senior Research Agent
  She's currently having a secret love relationship with Mr. Oshima, the branch director. She likes both older men and younger men, but not men of her age.
- She's the type that very much respects a man who can properly raise children.
- She's very energetic and always shows spirit.
- She can never tell a lie and she's weak against children.

She's very confrontational. However, she's also a very glamorous looking woman. She has a very voluptuous body that's very erotic before she even takes anything off. She's single now but her past is full of relationships gone bad.

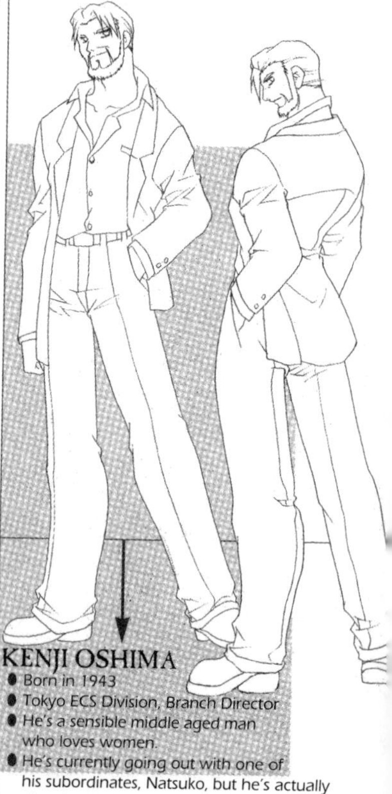

KENJI OSHIMA

- Born in 1943
- Tokyo ECS Division, Branch Director
- He's a sensible middle aged man who loves women.
- He's currently going out with one of his subordinates, Natsuko, but he's actually already married with 2 kids (Good God~!)

He's supposed to be an expert marksman, he's probably the one character who won't get an opportunity to really shine... His general appearance becomes younger when he shaves off his beard, and he was originally just the average nice guy. If he had any more powers than he already does, he'd end up becoming too much of a player... (but since this is rated for teens, we've always gotta be careful about characters like him!!)

VOLUME 1 EXTRAS

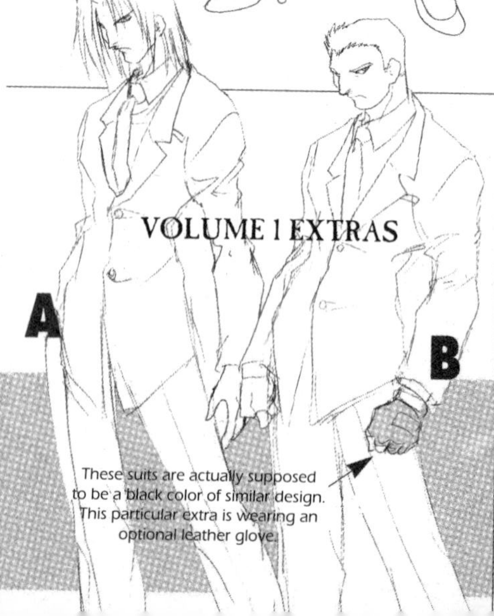
A
B

These suits are actually supposed to be a black color of similar design. This particular extra is wearing an optional leather glove.

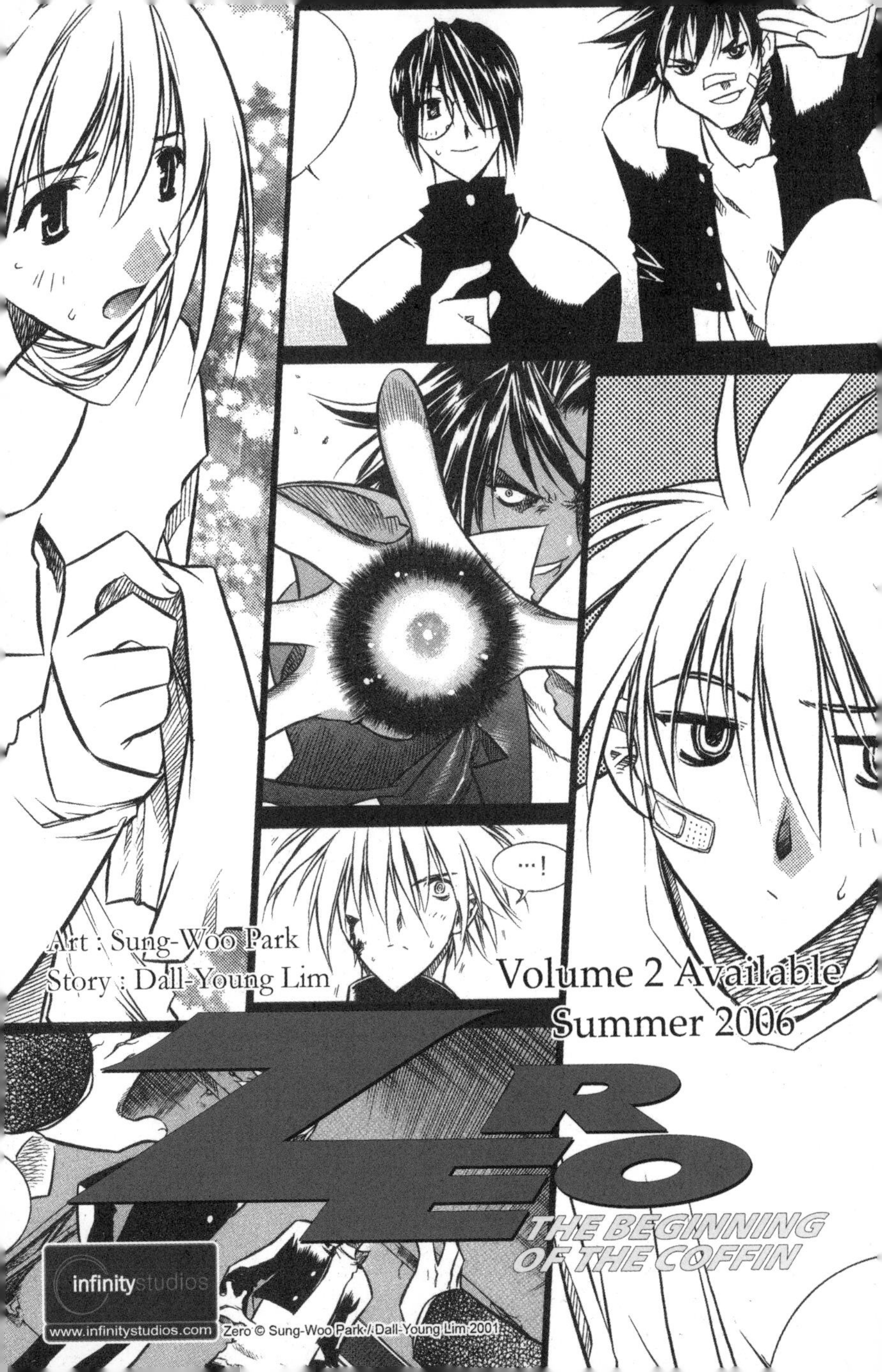

…!
Art : Sung-Woo Park
Story : Dall-Young Lim
Volume 2 Available
Summer 2006
ZERO
THE BEGINNING OF THE COFFIN
infinitystudios
www.infinitystudios.com
Zero © Sung-Woo Park / Dall-Young Lim 2001

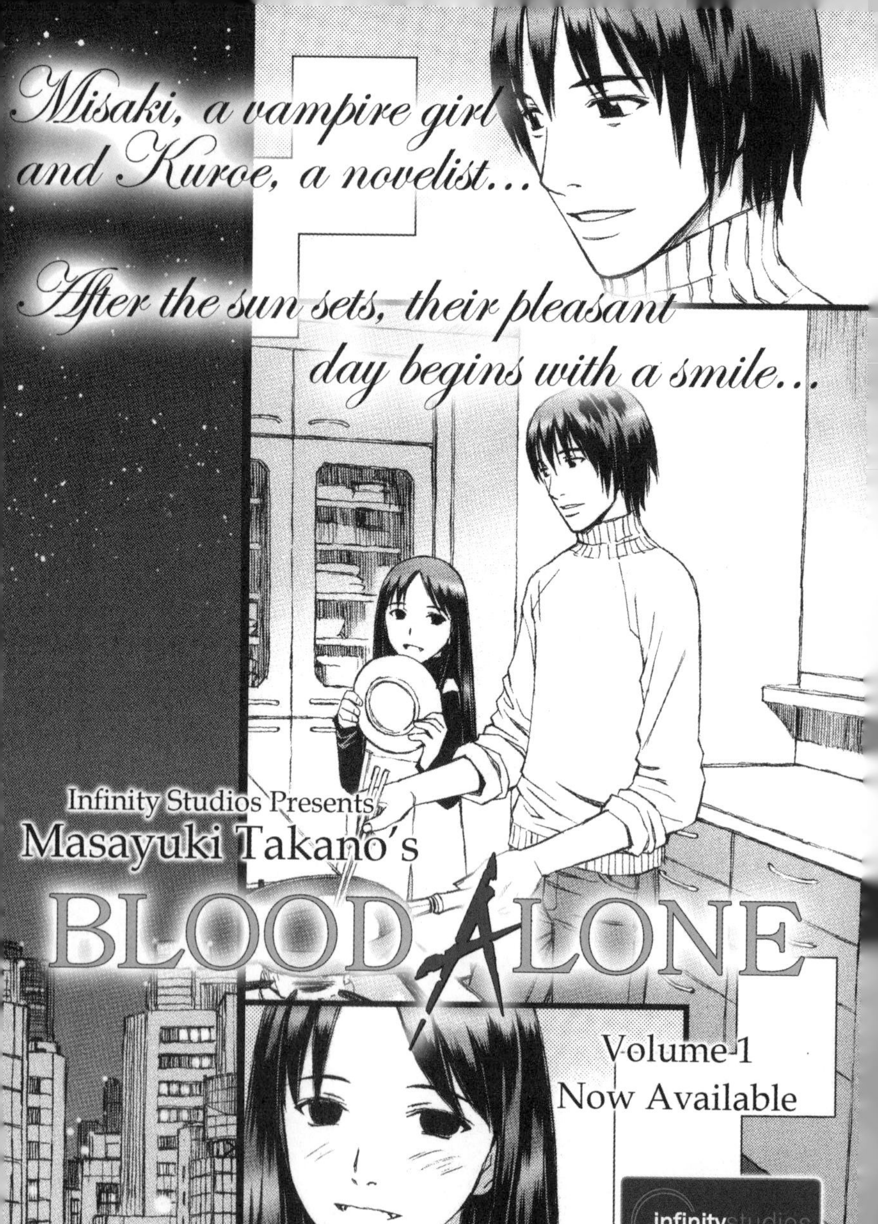
Misaki, a vampire girl
and Kuroe, a novelist...
After the sun sets, their pleasant
day begins with a smile...
Infinity Studios Presents
Masayuki Takano's
BLOOD ALONE
Volume 1
Now Available
infinitystudios
www.infinitystudios.com

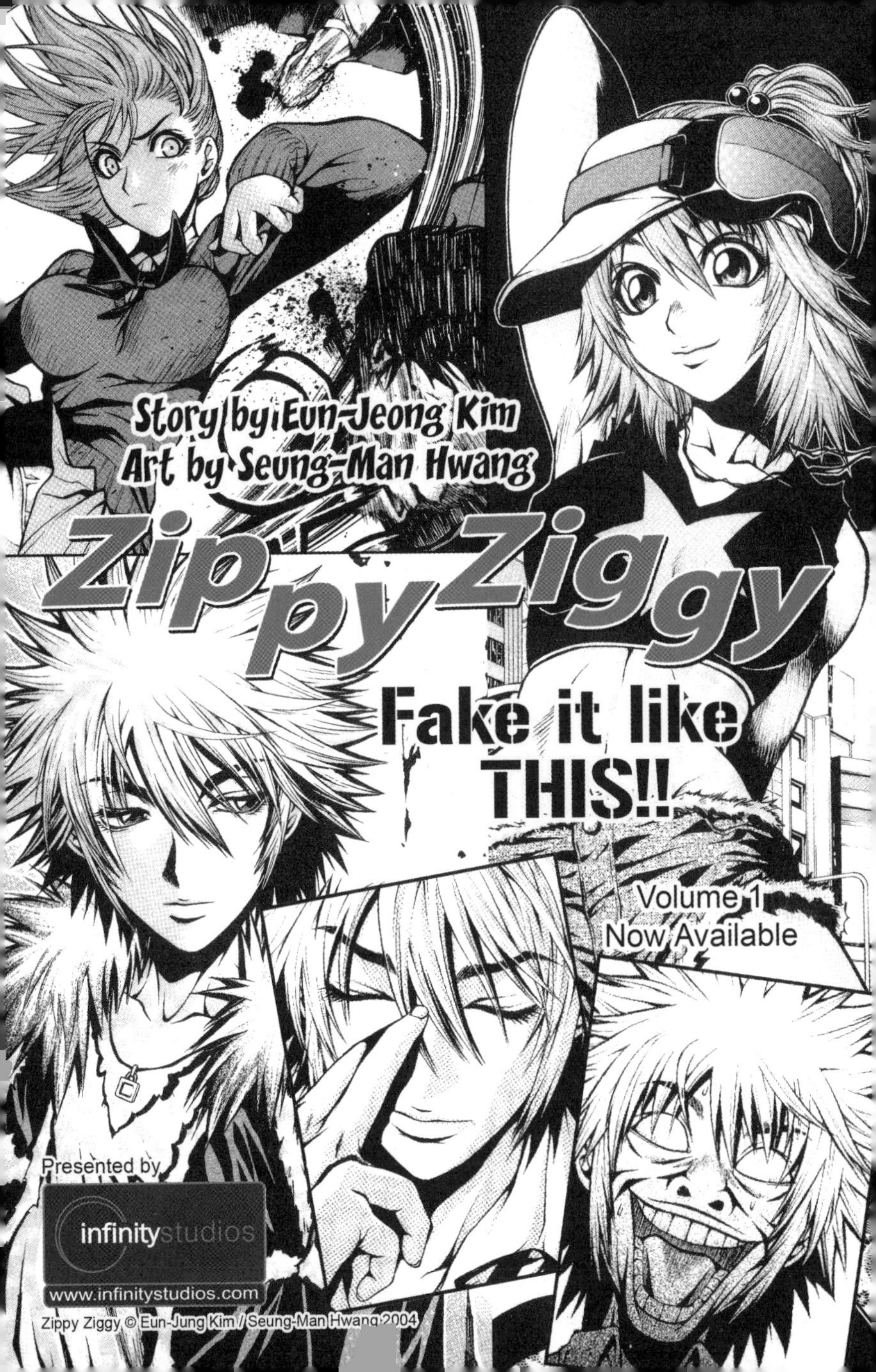
Story by Eun-Jeong Kim
Art by Seung-Man Hwang
Zippy Ziggy
Fake it like THIS!!
Volume 1
Now Available
Presented by
infinitystudios
www.infinitystudios.com
Zippy Ziggy © Eun-Jung Kim / Seung-Man Hwang 2004

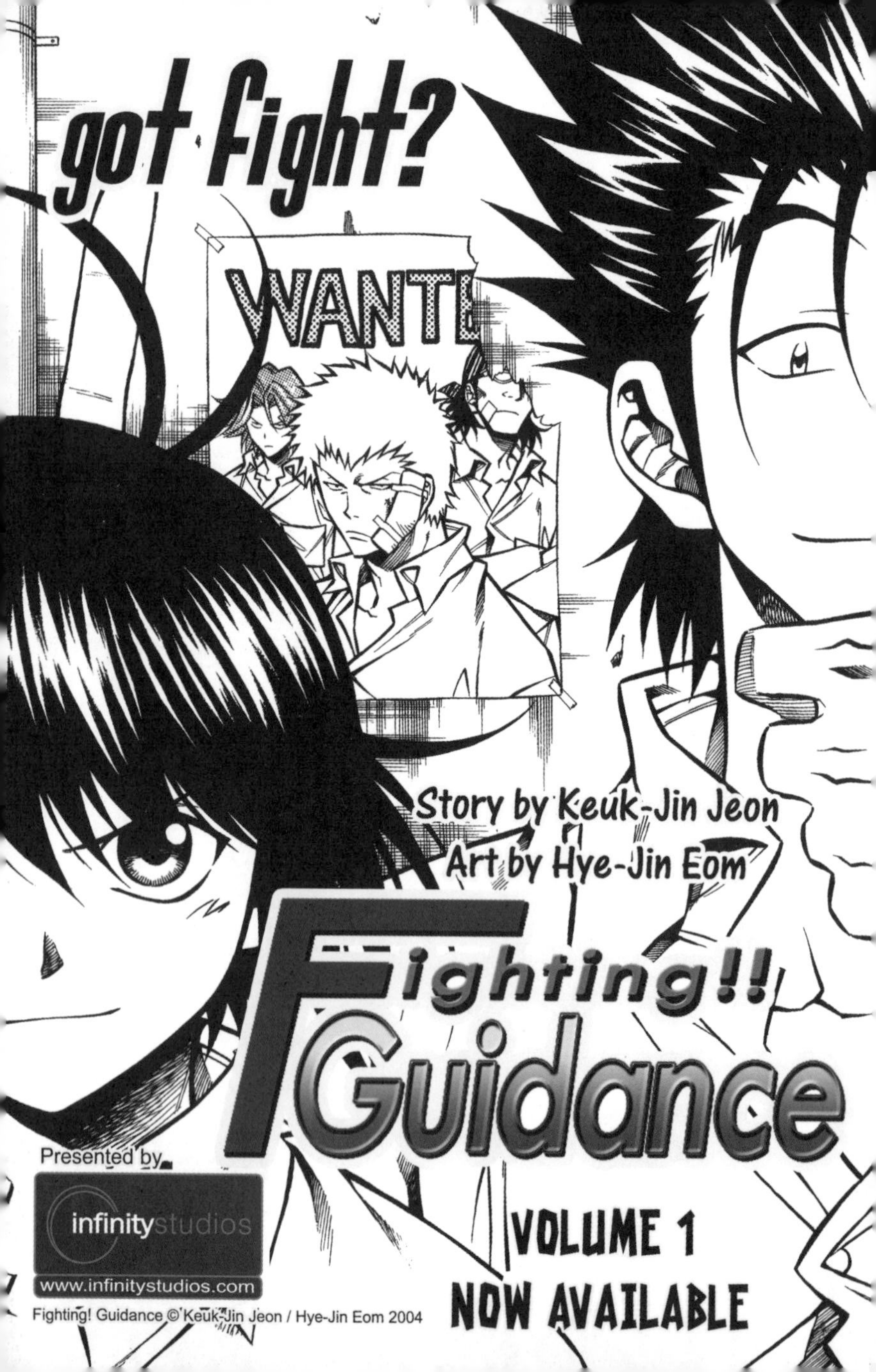

got fight?
WANTE
Story by Keuk-Jin Jeon
Art by Hye-Jin Eom
Fighting!! Guidance
Presented by
infinitystudios
www.infinitystudios.com
Fighting! Guidance © Keuk-Jin Jeon / Hye-Jin Eom 2004
VOLUME 1
NOW AVAILABLE

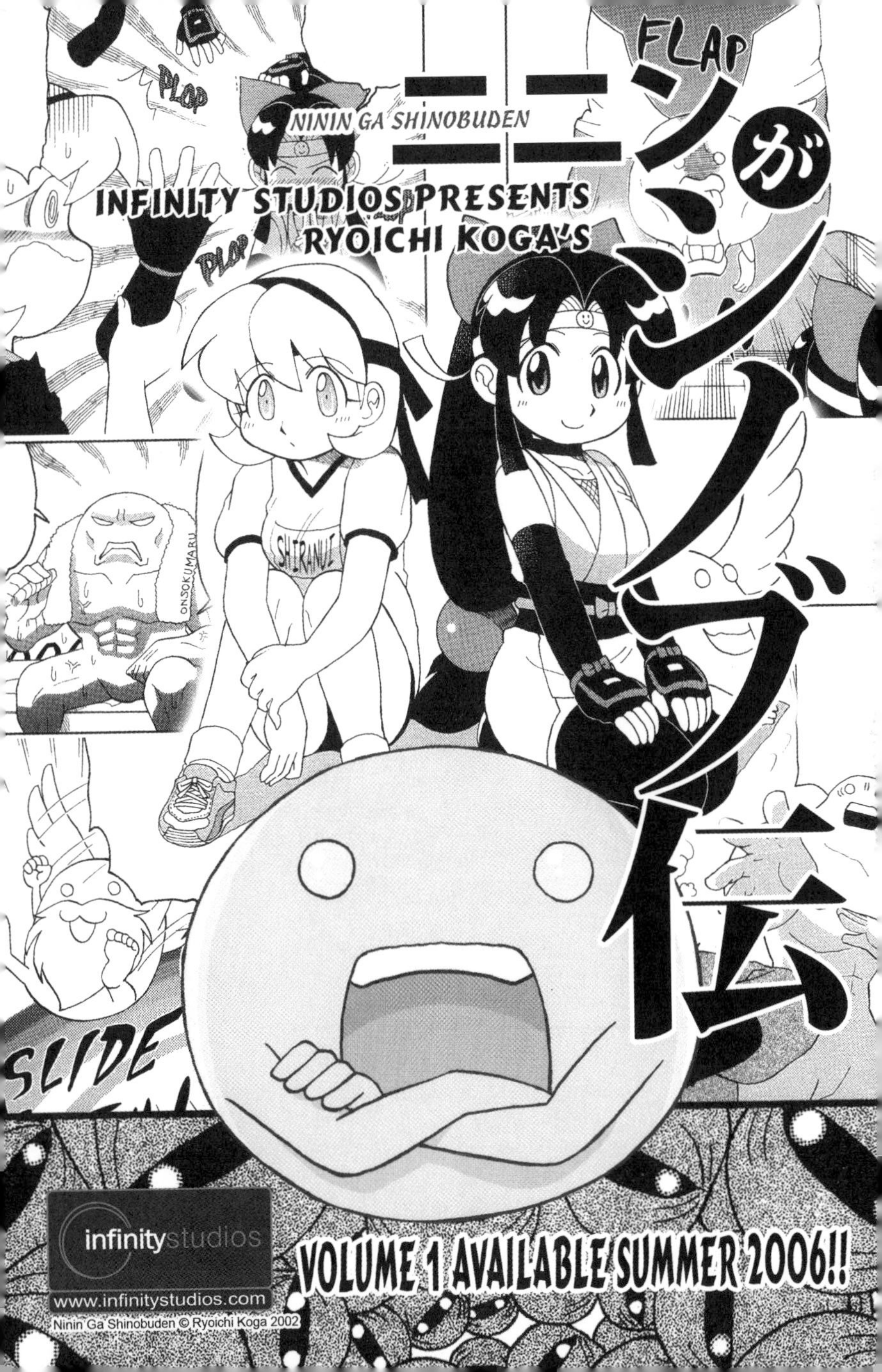FLAP
PLOP
NININ GA SHINOBUDEN
ニニンがシノブ伝
INFINITY STUDIOS PRESENTS
RYOICHI KOGA'S
PLOP
SHIRANUI
ONSOKUMARU
SLIDE
infinitystudios
www.infinitystudios.com
VOLUME 1 AVAILABLE SUMMER 2006!!
Ninin Ga Shinobuden © Ryoichi Koga 2002

Infinity Studios Presents

Show=TAROU HARADA's

NANANANA

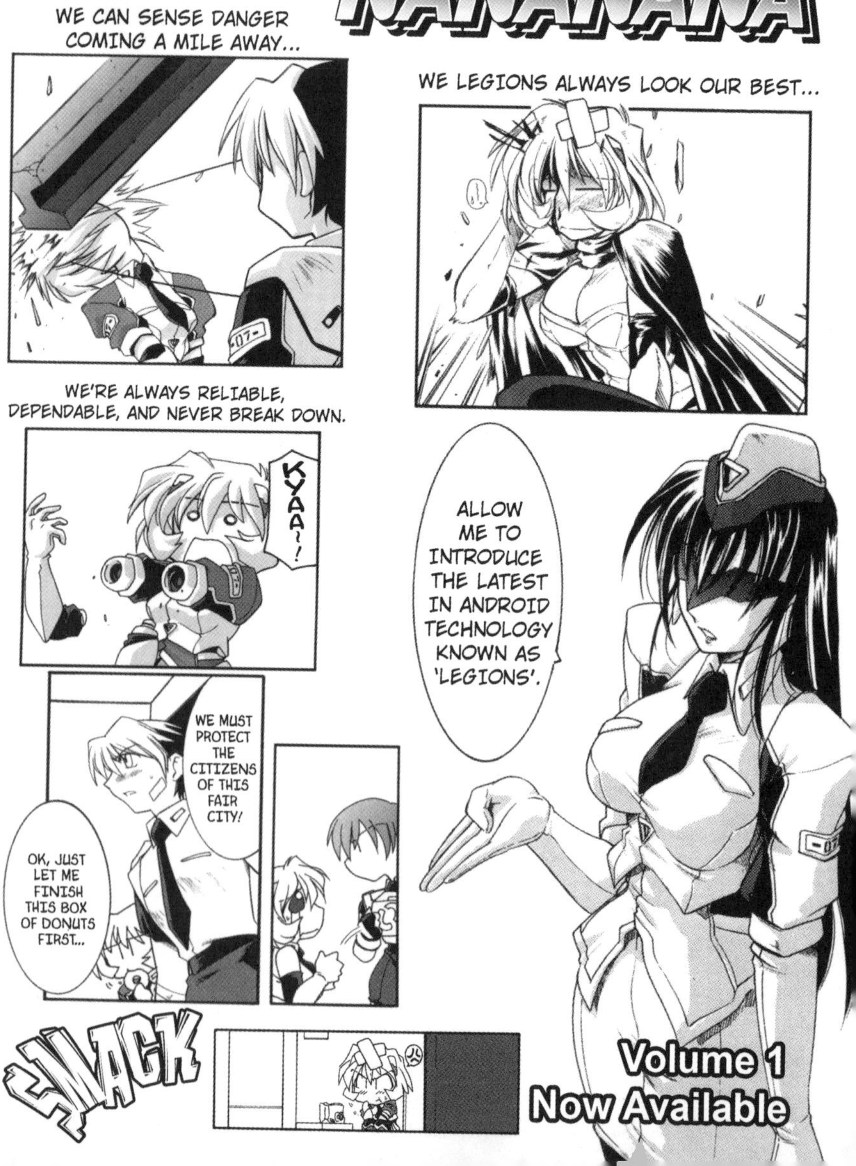
WE CAN SENSE DANGER COMING A MILE AWAY...
WE LEGIONS ALWAYS LOOK OUR BEST...
WE'RE ALWAYS RELIABLE, DEPENDABLE, AND NEVER BREAK DOWN.
KYAA~!
ALLOW ME TO INTRODUCE THE LATEST IN ANDROID TECHNOLOGY KNOWN AS 'LEGIONS'.
WE MUST PROTECT THE CITIZENS OF THIS FAIR CITY!
OK, JUST LET ME FINISH THIS BOX OF DONUTS FIRST...
SMACK
Volume 1
Now Available

Infinity Studios Presents
Masakazu Iwasaki's

POPO CAN

Super Trouble Heroine?

Volume 1 Now Available

Popo Can © Masakazu Iwasaki 2003

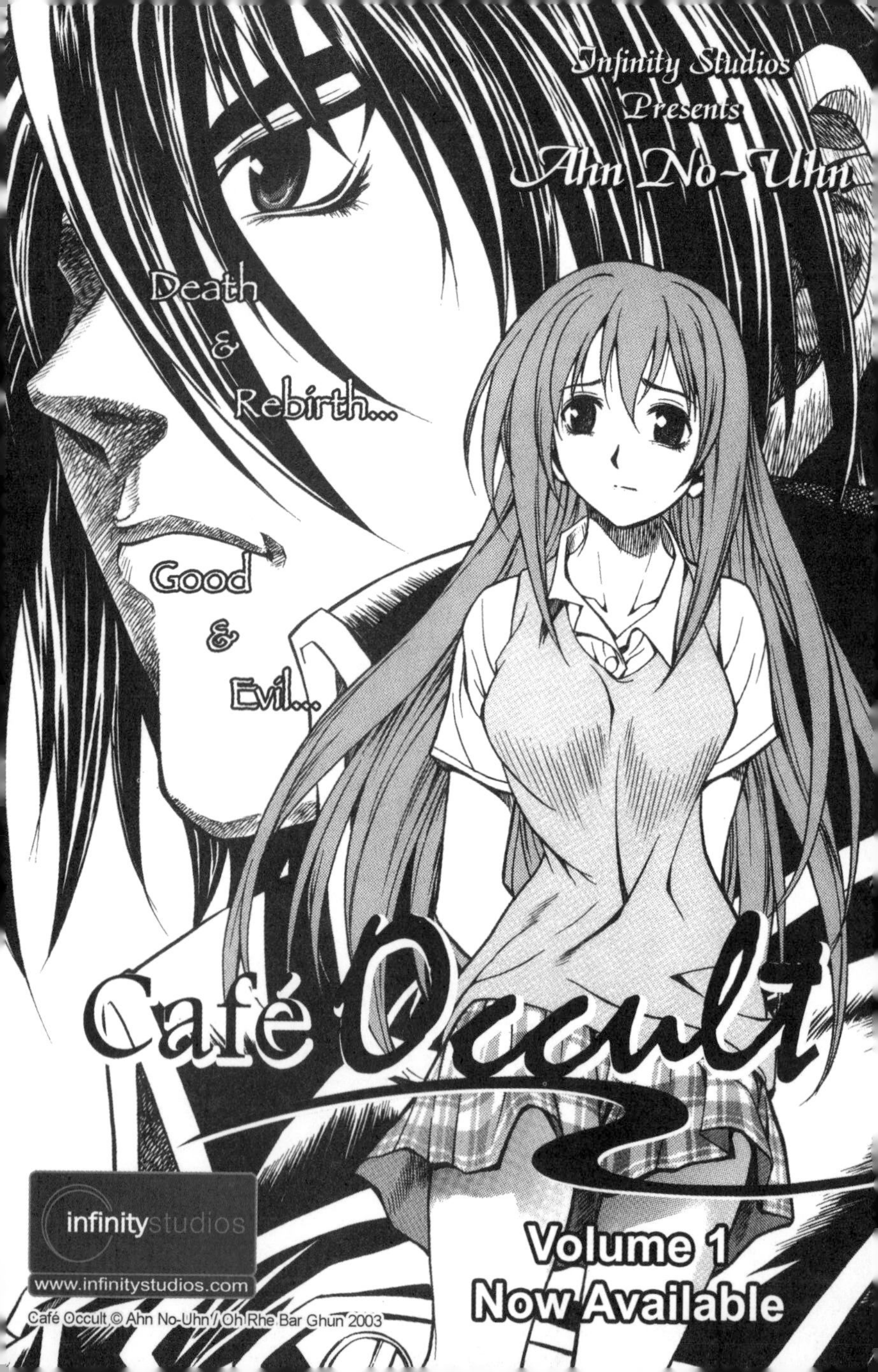
Infinity Studios
Presents
Ahn No-Uhn
Death
&
Rebirth...
Good
&
Evil...
Café Occult
infinitystudios
www.infinitystudios.com
Volume 1
Now Available
Café Occult © Ahn No-Uhn / Oh Rhe Bar Ghun 2003

The Missing White Dragon

Infinity Studios Presents

STORY COLLECTIONS
by
PARK YOUNG HA

Volume 1
Now Available

Infinity Studios Presents

Witch Class

Story & Art By ✿ Lee Ru

Name : Dorothy
Occupation : Student
Goal : ""I want to become a witch to live out the romantic dream every girl wishes for... you know, like turning the world into a dark hellish cauldron, making everyone bow to me, and summoning cute zombies, tee hee hee~!

Volume 1 Now Available